A
CHANGELESS
LAND

Continuity and Change in
Philippine Politics

T0326022

A CHANGELESS LAND

Continuity and Change in
Philippine Politics

DAVID G. TIMBERMAN

Routledge
Taylor & Francis Group

LONDON AND NEW YORK

First published 1991 by M.E. Sharpe

Published 2015 by Routledge
2 Park Square, Milton Park, Abingdon, Oxon OX14 4RN
711 Third Avenue, New York, NY 10017, USA

Routledge is an imprint of the Taylor & Francis Group, an informa business

Library of Congress Cataloging-in-Publication Data

Timberman. David G.
    A changeless land: continuity and change in Philippine politics/
by David G. Timberman.
        p.   cm.
    ISBN 1-56324-011-4
    ISBN 1-56324-012-2 (pbk.)
    1. Philippines—Politics and government—1988. 2. Political
culture—Philippines. 3. Philippines—Economic conditions—1986.
I. Title.
JO1416.T56 1991
959.904—dc20   91-24055
                                                           CIP

ISBN 981-3035-86-2 (soft cover, ISEAS, Singapore)
ISBN 981-3035-87-0 (hard cover, ISEAS, Singapore)

*The responsibility for facts and opinions expressed in this publication rests
exclusively with the author and his interpretations do not necessarily
reflect the views or the policy of the Institute or its supporters.*

Typeset by The Fototype Business

ISBN 13: 9781563240119 (hbk)

*This book is dedicated to
the friends and family members
who helped me see it
through to completion.*

Contents

Acknowledgements

This book is the product of the intellectual, emotional, and financial support generously given by many people over the course of more than three years. Without this assistance and encouragement this book simply would not have become a reality.

First, I am in debt to the many people in the Philippines I met and came to regard as friends during the three-year period I lived in or regularly visited the Philippines. I am particularly indebted to Professors Cayetano Paderanga, Alex Magno, and Carolina Hernandez, all of the University of the Philippines, for their interest and assistance. My thanks also go to Governors Daniel Lacson and Luis Villafuerte, Senator Heherson Alvarez, Congressman Bonifacio Gillego, and Mayor Richard Gordon. I also owe a great deal to Elena Lichauco Small, Bien Tan III, Agnes Caballa, and through his writing, Frankie Jose, for introducing me to many wonderful and fascinating aspects of life in the Philippines. Special thanks are also due to Susan Lampadio, who taught me more about the Philippines than I could ever have learned from reading any number of books. I am also grateful to a number of American friends who assisted me in ways large and small: Mary Carlin-Yates, James Callahan, and Bryant George, all from the U.S. Embassy; Marjorie and Albert Ravenholt at the Ramon Magsaysay Foundation; Steve Golub of the Asia Foundation; and journalist-cum-historian Gregg Jones.

Secondly, it is with deep appreciation that I acknowledge the encouragement provided by Professor K.S. Sandhu, Director of the Institute of Southeast Asian Studies (ISEAS) in Singapore, and the generous research fellowship and financial support provided by ISEAS. I am also grateful to Chandran Jeshurun for his valuable support and encouragement as well as to the staff of the Institute's Publications Unit for their patience and excellent editorial assistance.

Thirdly, I wish to acknowledge the valuable assistance provided by a number of colleagues and friends in the United States. David J. Steinberg of Long Island University and John Bresnan of Columbia University gave generously of their time and advice. Marshall Bouton of The Asia Society, Terry George of the Ford Foundation, Christopher Sigur of the Carnegie Council on Ethics and International Affairs, Russell Phillips of the Rockefeller Brothers Fund, and Donald Klein of Tufts University all gave much appreciated support and encouragement. Thanks also go to my friends, James Weaver and Percy and Ken Langstaff, for their hospitality during the hot summer of 1988. Lastly, this manuscript might never have been completed without the encouragement of Teri Dieu-Huong Vo and the editorial advice of my father, E.L. Timberman, Jr.

While all of these people, individually and collectively, deserve a large share of the credit for this book, I alone am responsible for all of its contents and shortcomings. For this reason, nothing in it should be construed as representing the views of any of the organizations with which I have been or presently am affiliated.

Continuity and Change in a "Changeless Land"

> Looking fretfully at the land around him, he realized that in all the years he had been in Manila nothing in the countryside had changed, not the thatched houses, not the ragged vegetation, not the stolid people.
>
> Changeless land, burning sun — the words turned in his mind and he decided that they would someday make the opening lines for a poem.
>
> Changeless land?
>
> — F. Sionil Jose,
> *My Brother, My Executioner*

This book examines the elements of continuity and change in Philippine politics and government over the last quarter century. The period covered, from the early 1960s through 1988, encompasses three distinct phases: the decline of "traditional" élite democracy, the imposition of martial law and "constitutional authoritarianism" under Ferdinand Marcos, and, most recently, the restoration of democracy under Corazon Aquino. By examining the elements of continuity and change during this period, this study attempts to provide a context for understanding current and future political developments in the Philippines.

Is the Philippines, to borrow Philippine novelist F. Sionil Jose's phrase, a "changeless land"? Looked at one way, the events of the last twenty-five years suggest that there have been important changes in Philippine politics and society. The declaration of martial law by Ferdinand Marcos in 1972 was a dramatic break with the post-war democratic tradition. Moreover, Marcos claimed his authoritarian regime was carrying out a "revolution from the center" in order to create a "new society". The toppling of Marcos in February 1986 has come to be known as a "people power revolution". The resulting restoration of democracy by Corazon Aquino, though not revolutionary, was a significant (and welcomed) change after almost fourteen years of dictatorship. More recently, the nearly successful military coup attempts in August 1987 and December 1989 were the bloody indicators of another important change, namely, the increased role of the military in politics.

Accompanying and perhaps underlying these changes, however, is considerable "changelessness". There is a sad constancy to the poverty, inequity, and injustice that characterize Philippine society, particularly in the countryside. There is a long history of society, politics and economic affairs being dominated by a relatively small and surprisingly durable group of conservative families. Consequently, there is also a history of successive governments — both democratic and authoritarian — being unwilling or unable to enact much needed socio-economic reforms such as land reform. There is a timelessness to the highly personalistic nature of politics as well as to the rituals and rhetoric of political discourse. There is a predictable repetitiveness to the charges of election fraud, corruption, nepotism, and incompetence. And there are recurring debates over what it means to be a Filipino, the appropriate role of the government in the economy, and the Philippines' complex "love–hate" relationship with the United States.

This mixture of continuity and change raises several important questions. First, how could a nation that has gone through so many changes actually have changed so little? Second, why has the long-standing poverty and injustice of Philippine society not caused more change, and more radical or violent change? Third, is the Philippines' apparent resistance to change a source of political stability or instability? And finally, does a mechanism exist to enable peaceful and positive change in the future?

These questions are of more than just intellectual interest for at least two reasons. First, the issue of change in Philippine society is an important, enduring, and very real concern to many Filipinos. For many members of the traditional élite, change is viewed as inherently threatening, and therefore it is something to be minimized and controlled. But for many other Filipinos, the promise of sweeping – and perhaps violent – change has considerable appeal, as demonstrated by their willingness to follow leaders who have called for such change – leaders as diverse as Ferdinand Marcos, Jose Maria Sison, founder of the Communist Party, and Gregorio "Gringo" Honasan, the leader of several military coup attempts.

For still other Filipinos, however, the effects of change, and their attitudes about it, have been more mixed. Consider the peasants of Central Luzon, for example. A particular socio-economic change – the break-down of traditional patron–client relations under the pressure of the increasing commercialization of agriculture – prompted many peasants to join the Hukbalahap revolt in the late 1940s and early 1950s in an effort to restore the status quo. Twenty years later, however, some of these same peasants were transformed into staunch supporters of the Marcos government because of its land reform programme. As these examples show, Filipinos continue to debate how much change there has been, how much change is desirable, and how it should occur.

Secondly, the exploration of continuity and change in the Philippines is also of interest as a case study of the transition from an authoritarian government to a democratic one. The transition from authoritarianism to democracy was a dominant global trend during the later half of the 1980s, and was one that Filipinos can take pride in contributing to. The case of the Philippines, however, is different from many others because it is that of a society attempting to return to democracy. The Aquino government's programme of political and economic reform implicitly assumed that the restoration of the main features of pre-martial law democracy was both desirable and possible. A closer look at democracy as it was practised before martial law, however, raises worrisome questions about the effectiveness and equity of traditional élite democracy. And if traditional democracy was seriously flawed in 1970, then it is reasonable to question if its restoration in the latter half of the 1980s is in the best interests of the country as it faces the even larger challenges of the 1990s.

By examining the elements of continuity and change in the Philippines this book seeks to do four things that, to the best of my knowledge, have not been done elsewhere. First, it seeks to place both the Marcos era and the Aquino government in a broader cultural and historical context. Secondly, it attempts to present a comprehensive account of Philippine government and politics during the critical first years of the Aquino government. Thirdly, it offers an explanation of why the restoration of democracy under Aquino, with all its attendant shortcomings, occurred as it did. And finally, it attempts to go beyond the personality-oriented approach most journalists have used when describing contemporary Philippine politics, and instead looks at the policies and institutions.

I attempt to show that after almost fourteen years of authoritarianism, a predominantly "traditional" style of democratic government and politics has re-emerged since 1986. At the same time, however, no society is static, and there have been a number of significant changes in the traditional pattern of government and politics. The re-emergence of traditional government and politics raises two important questions about the future. First, can traditional democracy successfully cope with the political, social, and economic challenges that the Philippines faces in the 1990s? And secondly, is this type of democracy enduring, or is it so flawed that it cannot survive? The future is, of course, impossible to predict, but the evidence gives little cause for optimism.

My assessment of democracy under Aquino focuses on the first two and a half crisis-filled years of the Aquino government (February 1986 to July 1988). Only passing reference is given to subsequent developments, such as the December 1989 coup attempt. This may seem too limited or dated to some readers. However, I believe that it was precisely during this earlier period that the major contours and dynamics of Philippine politics in the post-Marcos era emerged and solidified. The Aquino government made fundamental choices about its ideology, politics, and policies. A new pattern of civilian–military relations was established. A new constitution was promulgated and congressional and local elections were held. The national legislature and local governments became operative, and political parties began to realign. The economy began to recover from the worst abuses of the Marcos era and important economic policy decisions were made.

What has happened since mid-1988 is largely just a continuation of these earlier developments.

It will quickly become obvious to the reader that this book is a highly synthetic work. I sift through and borrow from the observations and analysis of many people. The cement that holds it together and gives it value, I hope, is my effort to trace the elements of continuity and change from the pre-Marcos period to the present. I make no pretenses of offering a new, tidy, or all-encompassing model of Philippine politics. Instead, I have tried to identify important influences and recurring patterns of behaviour, as well as present and weigh the varied interpretations of Philippine affairs that I find most plausible. The result is, I hope, a composite framework that can serve as a helpful guide to understanding contemporary Philippine affairs.

In Part I of this book (Chapters 1–3) I sketch the key characteristics of traditional pre-martial law government and politics and identify the political and socio-economic changes that were under way prior to the imposition of martial law in 1972. I conclude that traditional élite democracy was seriously, but not necessarily fatally, flawed. Its failure, I believe, was due primarily to Marcos's personal political ambition, but also to the absence of a strong commitment to democracy within the traditional political and economic leadership.

In Part II (Chapters 4 and 5) I trace the initial successes and subsequent failures of the Marcos dictatorship. I show that while Marcos was responsible for many significant changes in the nature of government and politics, he also succumbed to or chose to reinforce a number of "traditional" patterns of government and politics. I discuss the sad legacy of the Marcos era in considerable detail because of its important influence on politics and the economy during the first years of the Aquino government.

In Part III (Chapters 6–11), the major part of the book, I describe the return to democratic government and politics under President Corazon Aquino. I show how a combination of factors caused Aquino to restore a political system similar in many respects to pre-martial law élite democracy. At the same time I identify the ways in which the post-Marcos political landscape is different from the pre-martial law period, including the increased influence of the military and entrenchment of the communist movement. I also examine the Aquino government's major economic policy decisions with a view towards determining the government's commitment to improving the distribution of economic opportunities and benefits. Particular attention is paid to the process resulting in the passage of the 1988 Comprehensive Agrarian Reform Law (CARL), which, I believe, reveals an extremely limited commitment to genuine socio-economic change on the part of the political leadership. Finally, I conclude by suggesting a number of major challenges that the democratic system will face in the 1990s, and identifying some of the factors likely to determine the system's success in meeting these challenges.

The division of this book into three parts reflects the three major periods of Philippine politics since the 1960s: élite democracy, authoritarianism, and restored democracy. The divisions, however, also serve a second purpose, relating to the reader's level of expertise. The first part is intended to provide the non-specialist reader with the historical and cultural context I believe is necessary to understand contemporary Philippine politics. It is a distillation and interpretation of many earlier works familiar to specialists on the Philippines. The second part is a review and assessment of Marcos's authoritarianism, considerably more detailed than Part I. Its value to the specialist reader, I hope, will be in its fairly comprehensive analysis of the effects of Marcos's policies on government, politics, and the economy. Part III, which covers the restoration of democracy under Aquino, will be of interest to the specialist and non-specialist alike.

There is at least one important topic *not* covered in great depth in this book: the role the United States plays in Philippine politics. An extended treatment of this complex and controversial topic is omitted in part because of the limitations of time and space, and in part because I believe that the U.S. role in domestic Philippine affairs is often over-stated. This is not to say that the role of the United States in Philippine affairs is insignificant. American popular culture continues to pervade the Philippines. The United States still has a significant, though much reduced influence on the Philippine economy. The Philippine-U.S. relationship, and particularly the presence of the U.S. military bases, continues to be an important issue in domestic Philippine politics. Moreover, the United States has played a very important role at certain critical points in Philippine history, such as when the U.S. Government quietly accepted Marcos's imposition of martial law in 1972; when the United States pressured Marcos to hold a free and fair election in 1986; or most recently, when the U.S. air force intervened to help quell the December 1989 coup attempt. On the whole, however, I do not believe that the U.S. Government has a sustained or decisive influence on most of the political and governmental processes described in this book. Put another way, I believe Filipinos – and not Americans – are the ultimate determiners of their nation's political destiny.

Finally, this book is a personal effort to understand and explain a sometimes frustrating, often paradoxical, and always fascinating country. Like many other foreigners who have lived there, I have been simultaneously impressed and distressed by Philippine society. I have been impressed by the hospitality and generosity, the patience and perseverance, and the intelligence and humour of Filipinos. But at the same time, I have been distressed by the predominance of self-interest, the inequity and injustice, and the lack of unity and consensus in Philippine society. This book, therefore, is my own effort to understand, and where possible reconcile, some of these apparent contradictions.

Over the years, more than a few American observers of Philippine affairs have been guilty of judging the Philippines by American standards. I have tried to avoid perpetuating this tradition by drawing extensively on Filipino commentary and analysis. Moreover, when criticizing certain shortcomings and failures of Philippine politics, I have tried to use the standards and criteria I have heard Filipinos use. And when assessing the challenges facing the Philippines, I have tried to view these in the context of the national goals and aspirations articulated by many Filipinos. But in the final analysis, I am what I am – an American commenting on another culture and society. I hope the Filipinos who read this will accept that my observations are based on a genuine interest in and concern for their country.

San Francisco   David G. Timberman
August 1990

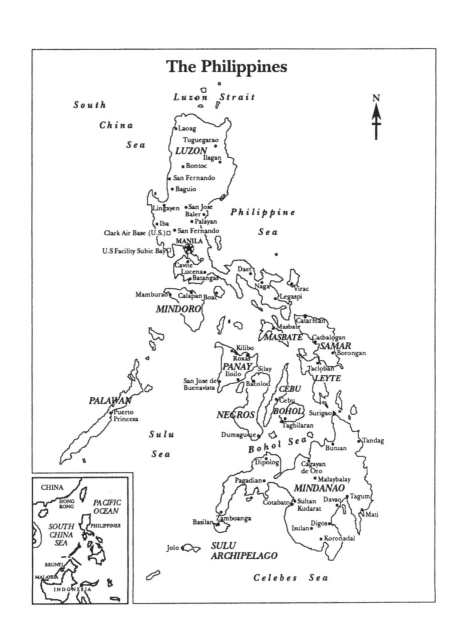

The Philippines

PART ONE

Traditional Philippine Politics

chapter 1

Philippine Society and Political Culture

> The Philippines is in a strategic position — it is both East and West,
> right and left, rich and poor. . . We are neither here nor there.
>
> — Imelda Marcos, 1982[1]

Where is the Philippines? An island nation lying off the Asian mainland, the Philippines is easy enough to locate on a map. But to those who have visited the country it often seems closer to Latin America or Southern California than to Asia. So where is it located culturally? Is it Asian, Latin, or American? Is it a unique amalgam of "East and West" or is it simply "neither here nor there"?

Where is the Philippines in terms of its political development? Where has it come from and what is the lasting legacy of that journey? We know, of course, that in February 1986 the Filipino people overthrew Ferdinand Marcos to end almost fourteen years of dictatorship and begin a new era of democracy under Corazon Aquino. Those who have followed developments in the Philippines since 1986 know that the Aquino government has restored many of the features of government and politics that existed before Marcos declared martial law in 1972. So which is the real Philippines: the authoritarian Philippines personified by Marcos or the democratic Philippines personified by Aquino? And where is the Philippines headed: back to the 1960s or into the twenty-first century? To begin to answer these questions it is first necessary to understand the major influences shaping Philippine society and the dominant political values of most Filipinos.

The Philippines' Diversity and Complexity

The Philippines is a large country. With more than 58 million people in 1988, it is the twelfth or thirteenth largest nation in the world in terms of population, roughly the same as that of France, West Germany, and Great Britain. The Philippines is, in many respects, also particularly diverse and complex. It is diverse geographically, linguistically, ethnically, culturally, and socio-economically. And it is complex in large part because its historical experience has created a culture and society with multiple layers of sometimes contradictory characteristics.

The Philippines is an archipelago consisting of more than 7,100 islands stretching over 1,100 miles from north to south. Only about 1,000 of the Philippines' islands are inhabited, with the largest populations being on the islands of Luzon, Mindanao, Cebu, Leyte, Negros, and Mindoro. Because of their volcanic origin, many islands have hilly or mountainous centres with arable areas limited to narrow strips of coastal plain or central valleys. The major exception to this is the Central Luzon plain, north of Metro Manila, which is the nation's premier rice-growing area.

The archipelagic nature of the Philippines has caused considerable fragmentation, but the relative ease of water transportation has facilitated inter-island commerce and migration, particularly within the central Visayan region. In contrast, the mountainous nature of much of the Philippines has tended to make intra-island interaction more difficult, especially among communities on the large southern island of Mindanao.

Geography and linguistics overlap to divide the Philippines into three regions, represented by the three stars on the Philippine flag. Progressing from north to south these are Luzon island, the Visayan islands, and Mindanao island. About 55 per cent of all Filipinos live on Luzon, with the rest equally divided between the Visayas and Mindanao.

There are some eighty languages spoken throughout the country (not including English), with nine of them used by about 90 per cent of the population. The official national language, Pilipino, which is derived mainly from Tagalog, the language of Central and Southern Luzon, is spoken by about 55 per cent of the population. English, which is spoken by about 40 per cent of the population, remains more of a lingua franca than Pilipino. Most Filipinos speak some English whereas Pilipino is not spoken by many groups outside the traditional Tagalog-speaking areas. In recent years many Filipinos have increasingly mixed Tagalog with English to create an informal and evolving spoken language called "Taglish". This has caused some Filipino educators and linguists to become concerned that current and future generations of Filipinos, accustomed to speaking "Taglish", will never learn to master either Pilipino or English.

Adding further to the nation's diversity is its ethnic mix, which includes Malay, Chinese, and numerous indigenous "tribal" groups. Superimposed on most of these (in varying degrees) are Muslim, Spanish, and American influences. The potential divisiveness of these ethnic differences has been mitigated, however, by a widespread acceptance of mixed marriages in the Philippines — in contrast to most other Southeast Asian societies. Historically, intermarriage occurred between the sizeable population of Chinese merchants and traders and the native Malays, as well as between the smaller community of Spaniards and the Malays (called "Indios" by the Spaniards). During the Spanish era, being a Spanish-Filipino mestizo was the next best thing to being pure Spanish. But over time it was the predominantly Chinese-Filipino mestizos who came to dominate commerce and society. As historian David Steinberg has written, "One did not have to be mestizo to become a modern Filipino, but the mestizo determined the values of the modern Filipino".[2] Jose Rizal, for example, the Philippines' leading nationalist figure, was a fifth generation Chinese mestizo. Today, most of the leading families in the Philippines have Chinese blood (including Corazon Aquino's family, the Cojuangcos), and Chinese mestizo culture continues to dominate society.

Religion is another important influence on Philippine society. About 85 per cent of all Filipinos are Roman Catholics, making them one of the largest Catholic populations in the world. When Filipinos talk about "the Church", there is no confusion over which church they mean; and as will be pointed out in later chapters, the Catholic Church's influence on Philippine society is pervasive, though uneven. There are also sizeable groups of Muslims (perhaps 3 to 4 million people, concentrated in Southwestern Mindanao), Protestants (who claim to have 5 million followers), followers of the Iglesia ni Kristo (Church of Christ), and of the Aglipayan, or Philippine Independent Church. Perhaps because of the dominance of Catholicism, these religious minorities tend to be tightly-knit and protective of their positions in Philippine society.

A final important source of diversity is the considerable difference between urban and rural life. Today, about 45 per cent of all Filipinos live in urban areas, including towns. Metro Manila, with a population of about 8 million, is home to more than 13 per cent of all Filipinos. The two next largest cities, Davao City in Mindanao and Cebu City on the island of Cebu, have populations of about 800,000 and 600,000 respectively. City dwellers, on average, earn more income, are healthier and better educated, and are more exposed to Western values than people living in the countryside. The large majority of newspaper sales are in urban areas, and most television sets are owned by city dwellers. The upper and middle classes are concentrated almost completely in the cities. Consequently, rural Filipinos tend to be more traditional, more conservative, and less politically active than city dwellers.

Metro Manila casts a particularly long and influential shadow over the nation. In addition to having more than a tenth of the nation's total population, it is the home of the government, the mass media, most major universities, and much of the country's industry. The élite, regardless of where they actually reside in the Philippines, tend to have residences in Metro Manila, which often seems to be a world unto itself, far removed from the realities of the countryside.

An Ambiguous Historical Legacy

A nation's historical experience shapes, to varying degrees, its contemporary social, economic, and political structures. Equally important, history influences people's values, beliefs, and attitudes about themselves, their nation, and the world around them. A people's historical experience can be a source of national unity or disunity, stability or instability, confidence or insecurity.

Since the rise of Philippine nationalism in the 1880s to the present day, Filipinos have been sifting through their history in search of institutions and values that are truly and indigenously "Filipino" – what has been called "the search for a usable past". This section will briefly describe the more important of these historical influences.

When the first Spanish *conquistadors* arrived in the Philippines in 1521 the non-Muslim Malay communities they found were relatively small in size, local, and independent from one another (compared to the extensive kingdoms and empires that existed in Java and Sumatra). There was little concerted opposition to the Spanish conquest, although there were hundreds of sporadic revolts throughout the Spanish era. Nor did these communities have religious and cultural traditions that were preserved in writing, art, and music. Consequently, there were few purely indigenous Filipino traditions, values, and institutions that were strong enough to counter, or survive untainted, more than 350 years of Spanish influence.

This is not to suggest, however, that the Spanish influence was all pervasive or penetrating, for in reality the impact of Spanish colonization was decidedly mixed. The Philippines was the farthest outpost of the Spanish empire, and the chain of colonial authority ran first from Madrid to Mexico City, and then across the Pacific to Manila. It was, as one historian has described it, the pre-twentieth century equivalent of being "at the end of the subway line". Relatively few Spanish officials and soldiers actually inhabited the Philippines – probably no more than several thousands lived there prior to the beginning of the Filipino revolt in 1896. The local government of the islands was, for all intents and purposes, in the hands of friars, the members of Spanish religious orders active in the Philippines.

As a result of distance and disinterest, many Spanish institutions and influences were never successfully or fully transplanted. The basic unit of Philippine society, the family, remained largely untouched. It continued to be based on bilateral kinship, which accorded the wife considerable, if not equal, prestige and responsibility within the family. Furthermore, because of racist restrictions on education and the friars' use of the vernacular, the Spanish language was taught to relatively few Filipinos. And despite the friars' considerable influence, Catholicism was as much adapted as it was adopted by the "Indios".[3]

For the first 250 years of Spanish rule, the economy of the islands languished. The vast majority of Filipinos in the countryside engaged in subsistence agriculture, while the residents of Manila survived largely on the galleon trade between Mexico and China. But by the early nineteenth century, following the demise of that trade, the Philippines began to produce sugar, abaca, and tobacco for the international market. By then, Spain was no longer a major world power, and British and American business interests had begun to dominate the colonial economy. The growth of agricultural exports in the nineteenth century created a dual economy in which a relatively modern, commerce-oriented sector grew alongside a traditional and technologically backward subsistence agricultural sector.[4]

The development of an agricultural export sector in the late nineteenth century had important social consequences. In the other colonies of Southeast Asia most export crops were grown on large plantations owned by foreign companies or members of the native aristocracy. But the increasing commercialization of Philippine agriculture gave rise to a new class of commercially-oriented land-owners, the *caciques*. The *cacique* class consisted predominantly of Chinese mestizos, who were quite independent from the Spanish ruling class. In the absence of an indigenous aristocracy or bureaucracy, the *caciques* became the Philippines' economic élite by the latter half of the nineteenth century. As a class, the *caciques* were scattered throughout the archipelago, creating a decentralized and dispersed power structure in the Philippines. According to political scientist Harold Crouch, this provided a favourable setting for the introduction of "proto-democratic institutions" during the American period.[5] However, it also put political and economic power in the hands of a group of wealthy and conservative land-owners.

The Philippine nationalist struggle began in the 1870s and exploded into open rebellion in 1896, becoming Asia's first "war of national liberation". It was a bold and path-breaking undertaking, but like every political movement since, it was weakened by ideological and regional differences, class divisions, and personal rivalries. These divisions make it far from certain that the revolt against Spain would have succeeded had not the United States declared war against Spain in 1898. The independence movement also boasted of being republican, but it is similarly unclear whether a Philippine republic, or for that matter, an independent Philippine nation, would have survived in the predatory international environment of the early twentieth century.

In any case, the controversial American decision in 1898 to colonize the Philippines was the beginning of the end of the armed struggle for independence. The Filipino revolutionaries, however, did not give up without first demonstrating the intensity of their desire for independence. They waged a fierce conventional-cum-guerrilla war (called an "insurrection" by the Americans) that lasted from 1899 until 1902 and took the lives of some 200,000 Filipinos. After using considerable force to pacify the Filipinos, the United States moved quickly to co-opt and gain the collaboration of the native élite through a policy of "benevolent assimilation". A legislative assembly was elected in 1907. By 1912 Filipinos were holding a majority of posts on the governing Philippine Commission, 60 per cent of insular offices, 90 per cent of provincial offices, and all municipal offices.[6] In 1916 a Senate was elected, and by 1920 there were less than 600 American officials in the Philippines.

The American colonial period was characterized by a devolution of power to the Filipino élite and a lively give and take between American colonial officials and Philippine leaders.[7] The native élite was happy to assume the political power and responsibility denied them by the Spanish. And in the absence of a well developed civil service (such as existed in India), the American colonial administrators had to rely on the educated landed élite. The colonial government was increasingly placed in the hands of the nationalistic, but conservative, élite. Given the beliefs about class and race that prevailed in the West at the time, as well as the existing circumstances in the Philippines, this approach was understandable, and perhaps even commendable.

But the American approach also had important and far-reaching consequences for Philippine government and politics. First, both the Americans and the Filipino leaders equated the Philippines' national interest (and American interests) with the élite's self-interest – a view that both have clung to. Secondly, the legitimacy of the Filipino political leadership came to be based almost exclusively on its ability to wrest political concessions from the Americans. Thus, the leadership developed very sophisticated political skills but had relatively limited interest in, or aptitude for socio-economic policy-making. Finally, according to political scientist Lucian Pye, "Almost from the beginning of American rule the Filipinos were taught that politics meant elections, not careers in the civil service. With this rule came the free-for-all spirit of grandiose promises, back-room deals, and patronage".[8]

The economic legacy of American colonization is also mixed. The Americans entered into a close economic relationship with the landed élite. Free trade between the United States and the Philippines — established, in spite of Filipino protests, by the Payne–Aldrich Tariff Act of 1909 — cemented a close trading relationship that continues to this day. But it was a classically colonial relationship, with the Philippines exporting a variety of raw materials (primarily Manila hemp, sugar, and coconut oil) in exchange for American manufactured goods. By 1930, 63 per cent of Philippine imports came from, and 79 per cent of its exports went to, the United States. At the same time, however, the American demand for Philippine raw materials was limited by various agricultural lobbies in the United States, which feared competition from the Philippines. Because of this pressure, the U.S. Congress limited the size of acquisitions of public land in the Philippines by American corporations to 2,500 acres, a limit low enough to successfully discourage large corporate agriculture.

Compared to the investments of other colonial powers in Southeast Asia, American investment in the Philippines prior to World War II was relatively small. In addition to the restriction on land ownership, the American business community was ambivalent about investing in a far away land that (by 1916) had been promised eventual independence. While this retarded the development of the colony's infrastructure, it also allowed for relatively more native participation in business, compared to the other countries of Southeast Asia. In 1916, for example, the government-owned Philippine National Bank (PNB) was founded. It quickly became the Filipino's "chief instrument for affecting the economy and maximizing their role in it".[9] Although Filipino investments outside agriculture were not extensive, by 1935 they provided 43 per cent of the capital for sugar centrals, owned one of the eight large coconut-oil plants, and controlled 40 per cent of the spindle capacity in the manufacture of Manila hemp.[10]

World War II had a profound influence on the Philippines that went far beyond the huge loss of life and property between 1942 and 1945. Filipinos took pride in the brave and effective fight many waged against the Japanese. And the Japanese occupation, brutal as it was, introduced many Filipinos to the rest of Asia for the first time. According to Steinberg: "The war broke the hermetically sealed isolation created by colonialism and gave Filipinos a real sense of their place in Asia."[11]

But the war and its immediate aftermath also generated a new ambivalence among some Filipinos about their ties with the United States. True, Americans fought and died alongside Filipinos, first to defend (unsuccessfully) the islands against the Japanese and then to vanquish them. And in 1946, as promised, Washington granted the Philippines independence (against the wishes of some Filipinos who thought the Philippines needed more time under American protection to recover from the war). Many Filipinos felt, however, that Washington failed to live up to its financial and moral obligations to the Philippines, first by not providing enough rehabilitation aid, and secondly, by making independence conditional on Philippine acceptance of several post-war economic and military agreements that effectively created a neo-colonial relationship.

Another far-reaching consequence of the war was the damaging controversy over whether members of the Philippine élite had willingly collaborated with the Japanese during the war. The collaboration issue divided the political élite as never before and diminished public respect for the political leadership.

The unsettled condition of Philippine society as it entered the post-war era has been succinctly described by Amando Doronila, a leading journalist and scholar. According to Doronila:

> By the time of the resumption of electoral politics after the war, the social environment in which the prewar elite tried to restore upper class rule had changed. Apart from the weakening of the alliance between rich and poor based on the paternalistic relationship, the legitimacy of the upper class' right to rule had been undermined by social divisions forced to the surface by the war. Elite hegemony had been sundered by the bitter issue over collaboration of a segment of the political oligarchy with the Japanese during the Occupation. New and younger leaders including Ferdinand Marcos and Ramon Magsaysay, mainly through their leadership in the resistance movement, had risen to important national and provincial offices outside the mediation

of prewar provincial families. With new social forces creating
a state of flux, Filipino society was now ready for new forms of
political mobilization.[12]

National Identity Crises

In the course of just fifty years – from 1896 to 1946 – the Filipino
people went from living as second-class citizens in a Spanish colonial
backwater, to being taught American-style civic values, to being caught
in the conflagration of World War II, to gaining independence. In
less than three generations, educated Filipinos went from speaking
Spanish to English to Pilipino. During this same half century, Philippine nationalists produced Asia's first independence movement, led
an effective revolt against the Spanish, unsuccessfully fought against
American imperialism, and then were co-opted by America's policy
of "benevolent assimilation". As a result, after gaining their independence in 1946 most Filipinos preferred to maintain close ties with
the United States, politically, economically, militarily, and culturally.
The closeness of the "special relationship" has led many Filipinos to
view the United States as the single most important determinant of
their country's destiny.

It is not surprising, therefore, that the history of the Philippines
has left many Filipinos uncertain of and dissatisfied with their national
identity. What is a Filipino? Is there an indigenous Filipino identity,
or is it something synthetic? Are Filipinos predominantly Asian or
Latin? One leading Filipino nationalist, the late Senator Claro Recto,
observed in 1955 that:

> We apologize for our western customs because we know we
> are orientals. But we are ashamed also of what characterizes
> us as orientals, fearing that such traits are old-fashioned and
> backward.[13]

Filipinos, uncomfortable with their multi-cultural heritage, search
Philippine history for indications of a pure "Filipino" culture and
society not tainted by Spanish or American influences. But to begin
to do this, they must go a long way back into their past, to the pre-
modern society that existed before the Spanish arrived, and then find
ways of making that relatively primitive society relevant to today's concerns. Moreover, as Steinberg has pointed out:

> There is no evocative era prior to the Spanish period to which the Filipinos can now turn with pride. Philippine history, at least what has survived in a written form, began with the foreigners — the Chinese, the Muslim Malays, the Arab traders, and the Spaniards. The ambiguity of Philippine history is compounded by the insidious consequences of Spanish and American colonial rule, which, among other things, have negated Philippine self-confidence.[14]

Today, the continuing close identification of many Filipinos with the United States and with American culture is perhaps the most striking example of the unsettled identity of most Filipinos. Many Filipinos sheepishly acknowledge the national infatuation with things American, what Claro Recto in 1960 called "the indiscriminant assimilation of the grossest aspects of foreign culture; the aimless Americanization of our ways, our customs and attitudes; the disregard, bordering on contempt, for all things native".[15] More than twenty-five years after Recto made this remark the "aimless Americanization" of the Philippines lives on. American-style shopping malls have sprung up in Metro Manila and other large cities. Consumer products with American brand-names are still preferred to most local brands, as are American music, television, and movies. The wealthy still vacation in the United States, send their children there to study, and invest their money there. Millions more Filipinos have relatives who have emigrated to America, or who work there.

Because the United States looms large in the thinking of so many Filipinos, they assume that Washington can and will try to intervene in the Philippines' domestic affairs whenever it wishes to. Moreover, in a tacit admission of either national incompetence or weakness, many Filipinos take it for granted that their government and leaders can be easily manipulated, threatened, enticed, or deceived to go along with whatever the United States wants. Indeed, American intervention is sometimes welcomed and encouraged. Many erstwhile "nationalists" who had railed at the United States for supporting Ferdinand Marcos turned around in late 1985 and called on Washington to intervene on behalf of Corazon Aquino.

Some Filipinos try to make a virtue out of their cultural and historical diversity by pointing to a unique "Filipino way" of doing things. The Filipino way has been used to explain everything from Marcos's brand of authoritarianism, to pervasive corruption and nepotism in the government, to the non-violence of the February 1986 "EDSA revolution". Others, like Imelda Marcos, have presented the Philippines as the bridge between East and West. But as economist Frank Golay has pointed out, "Filipinos would like to believe that they have a foot in both camps. . . [b]ut, in fact, they fall between two stools, and this is a source of deep frustration to the Philippine elites".[16] Or, as Imelda Marcos has admitted, many Filipinos feel they are "neither here nor there".

Many Filipinos, particularly those in urban areas, are also torn by the conflict between traditional and "modern" values and behaviour. Traditional values, as we will see, emphasize loyalty to the family, patron–client ties, and conservative land-based economic activity. Modern values put a greater emphasis on loyalty to non-family entities, less personalistic relationships, and greater entrepreneurship. It has been suggested that the conflict between traditional and modern values is exemplified by the contradictory tendency of Filipinos to pass laws and regulations against corruption and nepotism (in a desire to be "modern"), even though the norms of traditional society, which emphasize kinship ties, reciprocity, and personal loyalty, compel almost everyone to ignore or violate these laws.

Finally, there is also something of an identity crisis among the middle and upper classes in Metro Manila and other large cities. Many of these more affluent Filipinos seem disdainful of their own society and culture. These Filipinos are often American-educated or trained. Many have visited more foreign countries than the Philippine provinces and hold "green cards" – visas enabling them to travel to and reside in the United States. They are divorced from traditional rural life, frustrated by their country's problems, and envious of Western affluence and efficiency. They are, in a very real sense, strangers in their own land.

Traditional Political Culture

The previous sections have presented a brief sketch of the diversity, complexity and ambiguity that characterize Philippine society. Despite this diversity, there are important cultural norms and values that are common to most Filipinos. Some of these cultural factors have important, if sometimes difficult to quantify, influences on politics and economic affairs in the Philippines. Lucian Pye has written: "Culture is unquestionably significant, in some undetermined degree, in shaping the aspirations and fears, the preferences and prejudices, the priorities and expectations of a people as they confront the challenges of social and political change".[17] Therefore, to understand Philippine politics it is first necessary to identify and understand the key elements of Philippine political culture.

Political culture, according to Almond and Powell, "is the pattern of individual attitudes and orientations toward politics among the members of a political system. It is the subjective realm which underlies and gives meaning to political actions".[18] Identifying a nation's political culture and using it to help explain political behaviour is as controversial and as problematic as it is necessary. Societies and cultures constantly evolve. Different classes and ethnic groups within a society — or in different regions — have varied values and patterns of behaviour. Thus, for any one generalization about a society or culture there frequently are numerous exceptions. Moreover, one leading sociologist has cautioned: "notable differences in value systems are caused not so much by differences in the individual values as by the differences in ranking and emphasis".[19]

Given these difficulties, it is necessary to preface the following discussion of political culture with several qualifiers. First, the values and characteristics are noted not because they are necessarily *unique* to the Philippines — or shared by all Filipinos — but rather because they are *relatively* important in shaping the dominant political culture of the Philippines. Nor are they offered as an all-encompassing explanation of Philippine political behaviour, but only as a catalogue of forces influencing politics, to greater or lesser degrees at different times. Finally, as already noted, Philippine society is very diverse — divided into urban and rural areas and into different regions and ethnic groups — and always evolving. Therefore, the absolute and relative influence of the values and traits described below are subject to change.

While acknowledging the inevitability of some change in culture and values, it is important to recognize and understand the enduring aspects as well. In the Philippines, these include the primacy of kinship, the influence of particularism and personalism, the importance of reciprocity and patron–client relations, the emphasis on smooth interpersonal relations, and the effect of pervasive poverty on values and behaviour. The following section describes these important elements of the Philippines' culture and value system and suggests some of the ways that they affect national unity, government, and politics.

The Primacy of Kinship Ties

Any description of Philippine society and politics must begin with an explanation of the central role of the family. The extended family is the most important social and economic unit in the Philippines, as it is in other predominantly traditional agrarian societies. It is the primary vehicle for socialization of the young; the source of emotional and financial support for its members; and the chief claimant of loyalty. It also is the foundation of most political organizations and the building block for local and national politics. The primacy of the family is reinforced by custom, embedded in Catholic teachings, and proclaimed in the 1987 Constitution. The social and economic importance of having a large family is one reason why the Philippines' population growth rate continues to be one of the highest in Southeast Asia.

In the Philippines, kinship ties extend bilaterally to include the families of both spouses. They are further broadened by the frequent use of *compadrazgo* or ritual kinship, which is used to bond unrelated families of equal socio-economic status together. It is also a mechanism for creating bonds between poorer or less influential families and relatively wealthier or more influential ones. Less-well-off Filipinos regularly seek a wealthier or more powerful friend or acquaintance as *compadres* (godfathers) for their children. The practice extends to the highest levels of society. It is reported, for example, that Ferdinand Marcos was a *compadre* to some 20,000 people.[20]

Another important aspect of the Filipino family system is the role it accords to women, who traditionally have managed the family finances and have been treated as co-equals in most family matters. Over the years, with the influence of American education, the role of women in society has broadened so that they are accepted in almost all the professions. Inequality still exists, to be sure, and a "macho" style is still accepted and expected among men. But the opportunities open to women are greater in the Philippines than in almost every other Asian country. Corazon Aquino's ascendancy to the presidency is the most prominent example of this, but many other women hold senior and important positions in government, business, and academe. It is estimated that at least 20 per cent of the members of the Communist Party and New People's Army are women.

The powerful influence of the family shapes most social, political, and economic interactions. Inter-family relations can determine personal friendships and enmities, marriages, and political and economic alliances and rivalries. The strength of blood and ritual kinship ties discourages trust among non-family members to create a "we versus them" mentality. According to historian Theodore Friend: "By blood, by rite, by ritualized affinity, the Filipino knew his kin; they made up his 'we'; and those outside it were 'they' — enemies, neutrals and persons of no significance".[21] In 1987, journalist James Fallows noted, with only slight exaggeration, "when observing Filipino friendships I thought often of the Mafia families portrayed in The Godfather: total devotion to those within the circle, total war on those outside".[22]

The centrality of the family has a powerful influence on the Philippine economy. Most businesses and foundations are family-owned and managed. Most profits and wealth have remained within the family. Wealthy families have created their own banks to finance their own companies and acquire others. It has been estimated that, prior to martial law, the Philippines was controlled by about 400 families. By the late 1970s, at the high point of the Marcos regime, it is estimated that the economy was dominated by a total of only 60 families.

Frank Golay observed that the primacy of family loyalties has "handicapped the development of co-operative business organization". It has also resulted in conservatism in economic decision-making. According to Golay, the emphasis has been on preserving family wealth rather than parlaying it: "The preferred form of investment has been rural and urban real estate, which has historically tended to maintain its relative value and has endowed the family with status not to be derived from other forms of wealth".[23]

The importance of the family can also be seen in the conduct of politics and government. Local politics traditionally have been dominated by two or three land-owning families. These families' landholdings give them the wealth and political base — thanks to the tenants who work their land — to control local politics. The only real issue is which one of the families will be dominant. As we will see, these family-based rivalries have a profound effect on the entire political system. Moreover, as we will also see, the obligation to provide for family members (no matter how distant or disliked) and the ingrained distrust of non-family members have combined to make nepotism and favouritism norms in government as well as business.

Reciprocity and Patron–Client Relations

Much of Philippine society and politics is governed by relationships built on reciprocity and patron–client relations. Reciprocity, in its simplest form, is a belief that a favour or gift received should be returned in the future. In the Philippines, this belief is made very concrete by the notion of *utang na loob* (literally meaning "debt inside oneself"), which requires that a favour be repaid. Consequently, in a society where almost all transactions are considered personal transactions (and therefore can be considered favours), *utang na loob* is the cement that creates a complex web of social and political obligations.

Reciprocity dictates that a "favour" granted (which can be construed as almost any beneficial act or service) creates *utang*, or a "debt", on the part of the recipient that eventually must be repaid in some fashion (though rarely by monetary means). To ignore or downplay one's debt, or to inadequately repay it, is to risk being considered *walang hiya* (literally, "without face") or shameless – perhaps the worst approbrium in Philippine society. The great significance attached to *utang* creates networks of interdependency among individuals, which often expand to exist between entire families and to cross generations as well. These ties can exist between people of the same socio-economic status or between superiors and subordinates.

If the amount of the debtor's *utang* is perceived to be great, then the debtor may be bound to follow the bidding of the creditor. This has caused many poor voters over the years, and particularly heavily indebted tenant farmers, to use their votes in elections as a way of repaying their *utang* to land-owners and politicians. A person having unpaid *utang* is also expected to support and be loyal to the person to whom the debt is owed. The power of loyalty derived from *utang na loob* helps to explain why many Filipinos remained supporters of Marcos for so long. Those who were direct or indirect beneficiaries of Marcos's programmes and decrees – and there were many – felt "indebted" to Marcos, causing them to remain genuine "loyalists" to the bitter end.

The bonds created by reciprocity and *utang na loob* strengthen social ties among equals and can provide security to the poorer or weaker clients (such as tenant farmers) in a patron–client relationship. But in such relationships the ties are, by definition, asymmetrical and the obligations are often unclear or determined unilaterally by the patron. Often, the client's obligations to the patron are exploitative and never-ending, creating lasting dependency on the part of the client, rather than interdependency.

The prevalence of patron–client relationships has had important consequences for Philippine politics. Historically, the patron–client bonds that existed between land-owners and tenant farmers created ready-made political bases for families with large landholdings. The more land and tenants they had, the more votes they were guaranteed at election time. But as the population grew and became more urbanized, patron–client ties became less direct. Clients were expected to vote for a particular candidate as a way of repaying their *utang* for a service (real or contrived) that the candidate or someone associated with the candidate provided to the voter, a member of the voter's family, or the village.[24]

Pakikisama

Loosely translated, *pakikisama* means "to please the group". It is a behavioural norm that stresses the importance of smooth inter-personal relations or, in other words, "going along to get along". *Pakikisama* places value on being polite, respectful, accommodating, and non-confrontational. Someone who is rude, disrespectful or openly confrontational is considered to be *walang hiya*.

Values that discourage confrontation and encourage smooth social interaction are necessary in a heterogeneous society like the Philippines. But the effect of *pakikisama* can also be to emphasize "social process over social product". That is, the importance placed on maintaining smooth interpersonal relations can make it socially unacceptable to be straight-forward or to make controversial statements or decisions. Consequently, it can result in a tendency to paper over, rather than solve problems, and to resort to euphemisms and rhetoric rather than to directly address a sensitive issue. Most Filipinos are justifiably proud of their ability to compromise and they praise the virtues of their "creative ambiguity". But sometimes these compromises are fashioned in lieu of making tough decisions, and the creative ambiguity sometimes masks vague or inadequate thinking which leads to misunderstanding and confusion later on.

Pakikisama has also been blamed for contributing to a brand of politics that values style more than substance. Philippine politics has long been known for its "show biz" quality, its reliance on political rituals, and the indulgence of politicians in *palabas* (hyperbole and ostentatious show). Imelda Marcos once commented to an interviewer that "Ninoy [Aquino] was all sauce and no substance". In response to his wife's observation, Ferdinand Marcos replied: "Sweetheart, that is the essence of Filipino politics".[25]

Finally, although something of a contradiction, it should be noted that the superficial niceties of *pakikisama* are often ignored when the prerogatives of seniority, wealth, or power come into play. The older, more affluent, or more powerful members of society often exploit and mistreat subordinates. It is not uncommon to see this kind of uncaring treatment with household servants or in employer–employee relations. A study of Filipino–Japanese joint ventures in the mid-1970s found, for example, that the Japanese managers were "appalled" by the management style of the Filipinos which included highly authoritarian decision-making, irrational nepotism and "contemptuous attitudes towards their workers".[26]

A Culture of Poverty

Filipino historian Resil Mojares has suggested that Philippine political culture is a "culture of poverty". According to him, pervasive poverty causes a culture that occasions an immediate – instead of future – orientation, an interest in short-term gains and benefits for oneself, one's family or group, rather than one's class or nation.[27]

At first glance, the Philippines does not seem to be a country in need. The countryside appears lush, verdant, and idyllic, and parts of it are. But it also suffers from serious environmental degradation. It is battered by up to twenty typhoons per year, flooded by heavy rains and tidal waves, scorched by drought, and rocked by earthquakes and volcanoes. The trauma and uncertainty created by natural violence are compounded by man-made violence springing from the conflict between the government and communist and Muslim insurgencies and from the general lawlessness that prevails in many parts of the country.

And then there is the pervasive poverty. According to the National Census and Statistics Office (NCSO), in the latter half of 1985 some 7 million families, or 71 per cent of all Filipino families, had below average family incomes. Fifty-nine per cent of all Filipino families were living on or below the poverty line. In the poorest regions, such as Bicol and the Eastern Visayas, the incidence of poverty was as high as 73 per cent.

But these figures, disturbing as they are, do not fully convey the magnitude of the problem. For a better picture of the nation's poverty and hardship, consider the following: as of 1985 at least a quarter of the work-force was unemployed or underemployed; 3.5 million pre-schoolers were underweight, with a third suffering from second- or third-degree malnutrition; 5 million children were working, shelterless, or sexually exploited; and some 3.3 million women were classified as "marginalized or disadvantaged", meaning that they were engaged in involuntary prostitution, physically abused, or victims of illegal job recruitment.[28]

Poverty fosters a short-term, pragmatic, and often conservative approach to life. The poor must make a living any way they can, even if it means breaking laws or damaging the environment. They are also forced to seek land and shelter wherever they can find it, even if it means illegal farming or squatting. And finally, poverty also causes the poor to relinquish their one source of collective leverage – their votes – in exchange for small individual favours from politicians.

The Influence of Culture on Politics

The Philippines' culture and history have combined to influence contemporary politics in a number of ways. Culture and history have produced a society and a political culture characterized by personalism and particularism, ambiguous class affiliations, scepticism about the effectiveness of government and laws, ambivalence about democracy, and an uncertain concept of nationalism.

Personalism and Particularism

The exclusiveness of the Filipino family, the importance of patron–client ties, and the strength of regional and linguistic affinities cause Filipino politics and governance to be highly personalistic and particularistic.

A high level of personalism exists: routine political, bureaucratic, or business transactions considered in the West to be *im*personal (such as voting, applying for a permit or licence, or entering into a business contract) are instead considered to be *personal* interactions involving favours or other unspecified obligations. Most Filipinos believe that the decisions and events that shape their lives are determined more by particular individuals than by impersonal systems and institutions. Consequently, the maintenance of good personal relations with those in power is critical.

As a result of the personalization of public life there has been relatively little concern with institutions or ideologies on the part of leaders or the public. Indeed, over the last quarter century only two political figures have advocated and actually tried to implement reasonably well-defined ideologies: Jose Maria Sison, the founder of the Communist Party of the Philippines, and his arch enemy, Ferdinand Marcos. Conversely, the personalization of politics also encourages a naive belief that "better men. . .will do everything better".[29] Reflecting this, prior to the 1986 election, many Filipinos believed that most of the nation's problems were directly attributable to the corruption and venality of just two people – Ferdinand and Imelda Marcos. Consequently, they rallied behind Corazon Aquino, someone they thought would be an honest and moral leader.[30]

Personalization also blurs the distinction between public and private resources in the Philippines. Political scientist Carl Lande has observed: "Often the distinction between government funds and private funds is not very clear. When a congressman proudly 'gives' a town a new chapel or bridge, few may know or care whether the money came from his own pocket or from the government."[31] The effect, of course, is to make the people indebted to the particular congressman, not the government. As we will see, this highly personalized use of government resources shaped the conduct of the pre-martial law Congress, and was used by the Marcoses on a national scale, both before and after the declaration of martial law.

A high degree of particularism exists when political organization and decision-making is based on preserving or increasing benefits for a relatively small group of people (such as a family, a regional or linquistic group, or an interest group) to the exclusion of other groups and the nation as a whole. The power of particularism in the Philippines has made most politicians more concerned with securing funds for highly specific "pork barrel" projects and opportunities for patronage than with creating national or even regional socio-economic development programmes. In 1951 Claro Recto warned: "It is easier, perhaps to vote for a bridge, or a barrio road, or an artesian well, or a President's brother, than for a principle and for the ultimate good of the whole nation, but it is fatal to our primordial purpose of founding here a true democracy".[32] Today, forty years later, his warning has lost none of its relevance or resonance.

Particularism also reinforces the expectation of special or preferential treatment for a family member or friend. As a result, different rules apply for different people, undermining the concept of equality under the law. Finally, it also has impeded the establishment of a national consensus on most major issues and has retarded the development of a sense of national unity.

Ambiguous Class Identification

Two classes have traditionally existed in the rural areas in the Philippines — the wealthy upper class of landowners and the mass of poor *tao* (common people). The members of the upper class have owned large tracts of the best land, the mills which bought and processed the crops, and the ships or vehicles used to transport them. Their control of the land has given them control over the lives of the tenants who work their land. And their wealth has bought them political offices, influence, and favours. In contrast, the *tao* has had little or no land of their own; eked out a subsistence existence from farming or manual labour; has been dependent upon their landlords for loans for seeds, medical care and education; and has had little or no political power.

The political left has claimed that this sharply bifurcated class system is a feudal or semi-feudal one in which the poor majority of Filipinos has been exploited and oppressed by a small but powerful minority. The upper class has indeed controlled wealth and power in the Philippines, more often than not to the detriment of the poor majority. It is also true, however, that Philippine class relationships are considerably more complex and ambiguous than Marxist analysis suggests. This is because of the mutual obligations of traditional patron–client relationships, the bonds of ritual kinship, regional and linguistic ties, and (at least until recently) the "other worldliness" of the Church's teachings. As Carl Lande observed: "Filipinos see little need for collective action among members of their own class, especially if such action threatens to alienate dyadic partners. As a result, most Filipinos take little interest in class or interest group legislation."[33] In short, the personal and very tangible ties between a poor farmer and his landlord or between a poor worker and a government official who could provide him with a job have taken precedence over a sense of class solidarity.

There is some reason to believe, however, that the bonds of patron–client relationships are weakening. Benedict Kerkvliet has described how traditional patron–client relationships broke down in rural Central Luzon in the 1950s as a result of the modernization, monetarization, and mechanization of agriculture.[34] In the late 1960s the class consciousness of some Filipinos was raised when, in the wake of the Second Vatican Council of 1962–65, the Philippine Catholic Church devoted itself to exercising a "preferential option for the poor". This was coincident with both the growth of a fledgling middle-class in Metro Manila and the spread of Marxist analysis in intellectual circles. During the early 1970s Ferdinand Marcos used populist rhetoric to gain support for his regime and undermine the traditional "oligarchs".

To this list of new influences on class identification must be added the effect of more than a decade of communist proselytizing, education, and organizing. Fifteen years ago, most affluent residents of Manila were likely to dismiss the attraction and viability of communism in the Philippines. According to journalist William Chapman, "The Manila elite used to think there was something un-Filipino about the ideology of class struggle and a war on imperialism. These were foolish, alien concepts much too serious for the Filipino mentality, and the notion that peasants and fishermen might be induced to believe in them seemed absurd".[35] By the mid-1980s, however, many of these same families had sons or daughters in the communist underground.

Beyond making these general observations, it is difficult to determine the exact extent to which patron–client relations have weakened, class consciousness has grown, and class animosity has intensified. In considering this question in 1970, sociologist John Carroll doubted not that there would be social conflict in the Philippines, but rather, what form it would take. He wrote: "Does the fault line which will divide society in the 1970s run horizontally (between classes] rather than vertically [between traditional factions]? Will factional interests be replaced by class interests?"[36] The same question remains relevant – and still largely unanswered – in the 1990s.

Scepticism About Government, Law, and Justice

Public office in the Philippines has traditionally been viewed as a vehicle for preserving or increasing the office-holder's power and wealth; rewarding family-members and supporters with jobs, contracts or other benefits; and enlisting new supporters by offering similar rewards. There is, therefore, little confidence that the government is *inherently* fair, equitable, or just. Instead, it is widely understood that the benefits that one can expect to receive from the government are a function of one's relations with whomever is in office.

The use of public office for personal or highly particularistic purposes causes recurring cycles of scandal or alleged scandal at every level of government. The political "outs" charge the "ins" with corruption and abuse of power, only to have the same charges levelled at them if and when they take office. Indeed, it is a paradox of Philippine politics that corruption is assumed to be endemic to politics and government, but at the same time "exposing" corruption is a time-tested political tactic and guaranteed vote-getter. The prevalence of corruption is a serious problem, but perhaps even more serious is the widespread presumption that corruption is unavoidable. This perpetuates the problem, reduces the credibility of political leaders and, most importantly, undermines the legitimacy of political institutions.

The Philippines, somewhat paradoxically, is also a very legalistic society. As in the United States, the legal profession is the premier path to politics and power. Unfortunately, however, more emphasis has often been placed on the style rather than the substance of law and justice. The lawyers who have dominated Congress have, over the years, passed numerous laws claiming to promulgate land reform, establish minimum wages, and fight corruption. But most of these have been routinely ignored or circumvented. The integrity of law in the Philippines was further undermined by Marcos's insistence that even his most blatantly dictatorial and corrupt actions be clothed in constitutional legality.

The Democratic Tradition: Myth or Reality?

In 1898 the Philippines became the first Asian colony to promulgate an indigenous constitution and declare itself a republic. In 1935, after three decades of American "tutelage", the Philippines became a self-governing commonwealth – at a time when other Asian countries were still dreaming of, or fighting for, their independence. For the quarter of a century from 1946 to 1972, the country was one of a handful of developing countries to boast a democratic form of government. The Philippines' democratic tradition thus appeared to be deeply rooted. There was, however, little public uproar when Marcos brought democracy to an end in 1972, and for the next decade the proponents of democracy in the Philippines were weak and ineffective. How deeply rooted then is the democratic tradition?

According to political scientist Carolina Hernandez, there are numerous indications of the strength and persistence of the democratic ethic:

> The Propaganda Movement of the 19th century espoused the liberal democratic values its leaders imbibed in Europe. American tutelage contributed further to the development of this tradition. The 1973 constitution paid lip service to the values of liberal democracy and Marcos always claimed his actions were constitutional. In the 1980s there was a persistent clamor for a restoration of democratic institutions and participation in the elections of 1984 and 1986 indicate the commitment to electoral politics. Even many of those who boycotted did so because of their desire to see meaningful elections.[37]

But there is also a strong strain of authoritarianism that runs through modern Philippine history. Two leaders of the rebellion against Spain — Apolinario Mabini and Emilio Aguinaldo — advocated authoritarian rule. Later, Commonwealth president Manuel Quezon advocated "one party democracy" and Jose Laurel, the president of the Philippines during the Japanese occupation, looked to Japanese-style Fascism as the solution to the Philippines' underdevelopment. Even Benigno "Ninoy" Aquino, the leading opponent to Marcos's authoritarianism, is said to have believed that the successor to Marcos would need dictatorial power to rebuild the country.

There has often been a considerable discrepancy in the Philippines between the rhetoric of democracy and the willingness to actually practise it. Claro Recto noted the discrepancy between the ideal and the reality in 1952 when he said: "We must learn to make democracy more than a word, a slogan, a fetish, and to look upon it as a dynamic thing, a practical business".[38] Consequently, many of the same Filipinos who proclaim the Philippines' commitment to democracy also admit that there is a national tendency to over-indulge in the superficial trappings of democracy. The charge is frequently made that politicians and elected officials indulge in "too much politics". Both Ferdinand Marcos in 1972, and Gregorio "Gringo" Honasan, the leader of the August 1987 and December 1989 coup attempts, justified their extra-constitutional actions on the grounds that democratic politics as they were being practised at the time were excessive and irresponsible.

Unrequited Nationalism

The nationalist movement in the Philippines was co-opted by the fundamentally conservative native élite that had developed during the latter half of the nineteenth century. The élite sought greater equality and opportunity *vis-à-vis* the Spanish; but it had no desire to overturn an economic system that was proving to be so lucrative. It was selectively reformist rather than revolutionary, and was inclined towards compromise rather than conflict. By 1896 the élite was torn between accepting the reactionary and ham-handed Spanish regime and supporting a more "popular" revolutionary movement called the Katipunan. The revolt in 1896 and the subsequent struggle against

American imperialism temporarily divided the élite. But by 1901 the majority of them had accepted the American presence, seduced as it was by the "attractionist" policies of the American colonial administration, which accorded the élite the power and prestige it had craved under the Spanish.

In 1916 the U.S. Congress promised eventual independence for the Philippines. The question of the timing and terms of independence, however, continued to dominate Philippine politics until 1934. Reflecting a mixture of genuine nationalism and political opportunism, political leaders such as Manuel Quezon, Sergio Osmena, and Manuel Roxas pressed in public for early independence even though they privately questioned the country's readiness for it. The continual focusing of public attention on independence was done at the expense of attending to other, more difficult, socio-economic issues, such as the development of agriculture and industry. Moreover, the independence issue frequently was used by Filipino politicians to further their own political careers, often at the risk of damaging prospects for the independence for which they clamoured.[39]

The peaceful transition from American colony to commonwealth to independent nation has left Philippine nationalism uncertain and unfulfilled. And if independence came too easily, then America's neo-colonial influence has remained too durable. Post-independence economic and military ties with the United States have perpetuated Philippine dependency on that country. Filipino historian Teodoro Agoncillo has written that, "It was precisely when the Filipinos had won their political independence that their nationalism suffered an atrophy".[40] And according to Recto, "The world was thus presented with the admirable phenomenon of a new nation more dependent, and more willingly dependent, on its former sovereign after independence than before".[41]

The Philippines' economic and military dependency on the United States has led Filipino nationalists on an understandable but somewhat quixotic quest for "true" independence — something that is difficult if not impossible to achieve in an increasingly interdependent world. To the credit of Filipino nationalists, this search has resulted in a more sophisticated, independent, and balanced foreign policy. But it has also contributed to a naive desire for economic and military–political isolation. Furthermore, during the 1950s the nationalist belief that

Americans sought to keep the Philippines as a producer of raw materials contributed to the impetus for rapid, top-down industrialization. This had the unfortunate effects of encouraging the neglect of agricultural development and of locking the country into a strategy of inefficient industrial growth based on import substitution. Variants of this deep-rooted strain of economic nationalism continue to exist today.

In sum, nationalism "can give cohesion to people, but it does not in itself supply direction".[42] Philippine nationalists, unable to reach a consensus on what the national interest is and how it can best be achieved, have sometimes diverted their energies into issuing increasingly outdated and parochial critiques of foreign "domination". Consequently, the nationalist vision today remains as unfulfilled as it is potentially powerful.

Conclusion

The Philippines is a geographically fragmented and ethnically and culturally diverse country in which family, linguistic, and regional loyalties have traditionally dominated. The country's history has compounded the complexity of its culture by adding layer after layer of foreign influences. Consequently, the country suffers from a weak sense of national identity and unity.

Because of the diversity of Philippine society and the strength of traditional loyalties, politics are characterized by a high degree of particularism. They are also highly personalized, based on kinship, reciprocity and patron–client ties. These personal relationships have tended to mute class antagonisms – despite the country's highly skewed distribution of wealth and power. The personalized nature of politics, which tolerates favouritism and nepotism, has also resulted in pervasive skepticism about the fairness and equity of government institutions and the law. The importance of *pakikisama*, or smooth interpersonal relations, has placed a premium on appearance and ritual, rather than on substance, in political and social intercourse.

Finally, in apparent contradiction to the observations just made, the Philippines has a long and powerful tradition of nationalism and an equally long-standing tradition of electoral politics. But the nationalist tradition is muddied by the conservative élite's success at co-opting the nationalist cause and by the country's continued close ties with the United States. The tradition of electoral politics exists side by side with an ambivalence about the equity and efficacy of democratic politics as traditionally practised. It is this traditional brand of politics and government to which we now turn.

NOTES

1. Quoted in David Steinberg, *The Philippines: A Singular and Plural Place* (Boulder: Westview Press, 1982), p.129.
2. Ibid., p.26.
3. See John Leddy Phelan, *The Hispanization of the Philippines* (Manila: Cacho Hermanos, 1985); and Reynaldo Ileto, *Pasyon and Revolution: Popular Movements in the Philippines, 1840–1910* (Manila: Ateneo de Manila Press, 1989).
4. Frank Golay, *The Philippines: Public Policy and National Economic Development* (Ithaca: Cornell University Press, 1960), p.9.
5. Harold Crouch, *Economic Change, Social Structure and the Political System in Southeast Asia: Philippine Development Compared with the Other ASEAN Countries* (Singapore: Institute of Southeast Asian Studies, 1985), pp.10–14 and 42–43.
6. Peter W. Stanley, *A Nation in the Making: The Philippines and the United States, 1899–1921* (Cambridge: Harvard University Press, 1974), p.187.
7. For excellent descriptions of the colonial era, see ibid.; Theodore Friend, *Between Two Empires* (New Haven: Yale University Press, 1965); Daniel Doeppers, *Manila 1900–1941* (Quezon City: Ateneo de Manila University Press, 1984); Bonifacio Salamanca, *The Filipino Reaction to American Rule, 1901–1913* (Quezon City: New Day Publishers, 1984); and Stanley Karnow, *In Our Image: America's Empire in the Philippines* (New York: Random House, 1989).
8. Lucian Pye, *Asian Power and Politics: The Cultural Dimensions of Authority* (Cambridge: Harvard University Press, 1985), p.121.
9. Stanley, op. cit., p.235.
10. Ibid., p.25.
11. Steinberg, op. cit., p.54.
12. Amando Doronila, "The Transformation of Patron-Client Relations and its Political Consequences in Postwar Philippines", *Journal of Southeast Asian Studies* 16, no. 1 (March 1985):102.
13. Renato Constantino, ed., *The Recto Reader* (Manila: Recto Memorial Foundation, 1983), p.26.

14. Steinberg, op. cit., p.34.
15. Constantino, op. cit., p.26.
16. Frank Golay, "The Nature of Filipino Nationalism", in *Foundations and Dynamics of Filipino Government and Politics*, edited by Jose Abueva and Raul de Guzman (Manila: Bookmark, 1973), p.514.
17. Pye, op. cit., p.20.
18. Gabriel Almond and G. Bingham Powell, *Comparative Politics: A Developmental Approach* (Boston: Little Brown, 1966), p.50.
19. Frank Lynch and Alfonso de Guzman II, eds., *Four Readings in Philippine Values* (Quezon City: Ateneo de Manila University Press, 1981), p.6.
20. Bryan Johnson, *The Four Days of Courage* (New York: The Free Press, 1987), p.21.
21. Theodore Friend, "Philippine-American Tensions in History", in *Crisis in the Philippines: The Marcos Era and Beyond*, edited by John Bresnan (Princeton: Princeton University Press, 1986), p.24.
22. James Fallows, "A Damaged Culture", *Atlantic Monthly*, November 1987, p.56.
23. Golay, *The Philippines: Public Policy and National Economic Development*, p.15.
24. Philippine–American relations have also been viewed by most Filipinos as a patron–client relationship in which the United States (the wealthy and powerful patron) takes care of the Philippines (the needy client) in exchange for the Philippines' respect and loyalty.
25. Ian Buruma, "St. Cory and the Evil Rose", *New York Review of Books*, 11 June 1987, p.4.
26. Harry T. Oshima, "Postwar Philippine Economic Growth in Comparative Perspective: An Overview" (Makati: Philippine Society for International Development, 1982), p.32.
27. Resil Mojares, *The Man Who Would be President: Serging Osmena and Philippine Politics* (Cebu: Maria Cacao Publishers, 1986), p.159.
28. According to the Philippine Department of Social Welfare and Development. See the *Manila Chronicle*, 11 July 1987, p.3.
29. Carl Lande, *Leaders, Factions, and Parties: The Structure of Philippine Politics* (New Haven: Yale University Southeast Asia Studies Program, 1965), p.117.
30. James Rush, *Bringing Down Marcos: Part 3: Suspending Disbelief*, Report No.27 (University Field Staff International, 1986), p.4.
31. Lande, op. cit., p.80.
32. Constantino, op. cit., p.124.
33. Lande, op. cit., p.44.

34. See Benedict Kirkvliet, *The Huk Rebellion: A Study of Peasant Revolt in the Philippines* (Berkeley: University of California Press, 1977).

35. William Chapman, *Inside the Philippine Revolution* (New York: W.W. Norton and Co., 1987), p.17.

36. John J. Carroll, "Sources of Social Unrest", in *The Philippine Economy in the 1970s* (Quezon City: The Institute of Economic Development and Research, University of the Philippines, 1972), p.16.

37. Carolina Hernandez, "Reconstituting the Political Order", in *Crisis in the Philippines: The Marcos Era and Beyond*, edited by John Bresnan (Princeton: Princeton University Press, 1986), p.197.

38. Constantino, op. cit., p.134.

39. The most notable example was Manuel Quezon's opposition in 1933 to the Hare-Hawes-Cutting Act, which called for the creation of a commonwealth and established a timetable for independence. Quezon opposed the act, negotiated by Sergio Osmena and Manuel Roxas, because he feared its passage would bolster the prestige of Osmena and Roxas, his political rivals. Instead of supporting "their" act, Quezon travelled to Washington and in 1934 secured the passage of "his" act – the Tydings-McDuffie Act – which was essentially the same as its predecessor.

40. Teodoro Agoncillo, *Filipino Nationalism: 1872–1970* (Quezon City: R.P. Garcia Publishing Co., 1974), p.36.

41. Ibid., p.47.

42. Steinberg, op. cit., p.54.

chapter 2

Traditional Government, Politics and Economic Affairs

> . . . believing in the leadership of Governor Sergio Osmena Jr, and out of gratitude for him having sacrificed his personal interests to liberate the people of Cebu from Cuenco tyranny and oppression, and being indebted to His Excellency, President Quirino, for having supported Governor Osmena in his campaign to rid Cebu of terrorism, graft and corruption, and being an Osmenista at heart, out of loyalty to governor Osmena and since he is affiliated with the Liberal Party, do hereby affiliate with the Liberal Party as long as Governor Osmena remains with the Liberal Party. SO HELP ME GOD.
>
> — Oath of allegiance taken by
> Sergio Osmeña, Jr.'s followers in
> the 1953 presidential campaign.[1]

The oath of allegiance quoted above, and the circumstances that produced it, conveniently capture many key aspects of traditional Philippine politics. In the 1953 presidential campaign Sergio Osmeña, Jr., then governor of Cebu province and a member of the Liberal Party, backed Elpidio Quirino, the incumbent president and Liberal Party candidate, against the Nacionalista Party's highly popular candidate, Ramon Magsaysay. The oath of allegiance to Osmeña was needed to keep his followers from leaving the Liberal Party and jumping on the growing Magsaysay bandwagon. The oath is, as Resil Mojares has pointed out, "an undisguised declaration of personality oriented politics". It also reveals many other key aspects of traditional politics: the importance of gratitude, *utang na loob*, and loyalty; the family-cum-political feud between the Osmeñas and their rivals in Cebu, the Cuencos; the ever-present charges of graft and corruption; the transience of party affiliations (several months after the election, which Magsaysay won, Osmeña left the defeated Liberal Party and joined the triumphant Nacionalistas); and the importance of alliances between national and provincial leaders (Quirino desperately needed the votes of Osmeña's followers in Cebu, while Osmeña needed Quirino's help in his fight against the Cuencos).

This chapter presents a sketch of "traditional" government and politics in the Philippines — that is, the type of governance and politics that was dominant from independence in 1946 until the declaration of martial law in 1972. Brief attention will also be paid to the interaction of politics and the economy.

A familiarity with traditional government and politics is important for several reasons. First, assuming for the moment that the almost fourteen years of Marcos dictatorship was an aberration in Philippine politics, then the quarter century of traditional élite democracy preceding it can be viewed as the political "norm". As we will see, however, it was a norm that had many problems and was in the throes of change in the late 1960s and early 1970s. This process of change was abruptly terminated by Marcos in 1972, and democratic politics were, for the most part, suspended until the Aquino government came to power in 1986. Consequently, the democracy re-established under Aquino is rooted in and shaped by a pattern of political behaviour that is two decades old and that has been discredited in the eyes of many. This raises questions about the wisdom of reviving a troubled and possibly outmoded political system.

Secondly, a review of traditional politics provides important insights into both the causes of martial law and the reasons for its failure. There is no doubt that Marcos's lust for power was a key factor in his decision to declare martial law. However, his grab for power did not happen in a vacuum. Martial law was also at least partly in response to the political and economic problems that had grown under two and a half decades of élite democracy. And many of Marcos's early martial law policy initiatives were efforts to address problems that the traditional government and political élite had been unable or unwilling to tackle. Ultimately, martial law failed in part because Marcos and his government were not willing to jettison, or able to escape, traditional political values and practices.

Finally, looking to the future, it is clear that the legacy of Marcos's authoritarianism, significant as it is, will diminish in importance. Instead, increasingly at issue is the willingness and ability of the political leadership (and, by extension, the system of traditional democracy resurrected between 1986 and 1988) to find solutions to the many problems facing the Philippines. The success or failure of today's brand of traditional élite democracy in meeting the many challenges of the 1990s will determine if democracy will continue to be the "norm" in the Philippines or if the country will slide back into authoritarianism.

Traditional Politics: Élite Democracy

A college textbook on comparative politics written between 1946 and 1970 might have described the Philippines as a constitutional democracy with representative governmental institutions patterned on the American model, and with political competition expressed through elections contested by two political parties that had regularly alternated being in power.

A more insightful and accurate analysis would have noted that, in reality, Philippine democracy was élite democracy: political and economic power was held by a relatively small number of families whose wealth and power derived from their ownership of land and industry. The two major political parties, the Nacionalistas and the Liberals, were little more than shifting coalitions of these élite families and their factions, and did not differ ideologically in any significant way. And despite regular elections, economic inequality and the absence of effective mass organizations meant that the majority of the population had little influence on the determination of government priorities and policies.

Another important characteristic was the Philippines' unitary system of government. The national government in Manila had administrative control over almost all local governmental affairs. The 1935 Constitution, in effect until 1972, emphasized state supremacy over the individual and government control over national economic affairs. The national government exercised a high degree of regulation over the economy. At the same time, however, its initiatives in the area of social development programmes were limited throughout the early 1960s by an acute shortage of government revenues. This was caused by the domination of the Congress by conservative landowners, who blocked most calls for new taxes.

The overview of the key elements of traditional government and politics that follows will provide an insight into the myth and reality of democracy in the Philippines. How broad-based and deeply rooted was democracy? How popular or élitist was it? Whose interests did it serve? How well did it work? Did it provide responsive and effective government?

The Philippine Élite

The Philippine élite is the group that most Filipinos love to hate. The political left criticizes the élite for being "feudal exploiters of the masses" and "puppets of U.S. imperialism". The élite was also attacked by Ferdinand Marcos, who called its members "oligarchs" and blamed them for the backwardness and inequality of Philippine society. But despite these attacks from both the left and the right, the élite has endured and prospered, and continues to play an important role in politics. The Paternos and de Taveras, for example, two families that were among the first to co-operate with the Americans, are still politically prominent today. So too are many families that emerged during the pre-World War II period, such as the Aquinos, Laurels, Osmeñas, Sumulongs, Cuencos, Lopezes, and Ayalas. Who are these élite families and what has been and is the source of their dominance and longevity?

Some of the members of today's élite can trace their roots back to the *principalia*, the local officials during the Spanish era. Most of them, however, were Spanish or Chinese mestizos who became wealthy by accumulating land or (as in the case of some of the Chinese mestizos) in finance and commerce. Beginning in the latter half of the nineteenth century these families sent their sons to Europe for education, creating a new group of Filipinos that came to be known as the *ilustrados* ("enlightened ones").

The *ilustrados*, like nationalist Jose Rizal, were well educated, imbued with Western ideas, and ambitious. They chafed under the heavy-handed, antiquated, and racist administration of Spain. Some of the *ilustrados* became leaders of the uprising against Spain, but more welcomed the opportunity to share control of government, politics, and the economy with the Americans. While the American colonialists did not create the conservative native élite, their reliance on the *ilustrados* to administer the colony buttressed the latter's position as the dominant political and economic group.

The wealth of the *ilustrados* was based primarily on land ownership (and the income generated by tenancy) until World War II. Following the war they began to diversify into commerce, banking and industry, in large part because of the considerable incentives and protection offered by the government. During the 1950s and 1960s the basis of the élite's wealth gradually shifted from land ownership and agriculture to manufacturing and commerce based on, and made profitable by, import licences, foreign exchange allocations, and protective tariffs granted by the government.

The concentration of wealth in the hands of perhaps 400 families has allowed these families to dominate politics and government since independence. The élite families have traditionally controlled the votes of the tenants on their lands and employees in their factories. They have financed politicians (many of them from within the family), and political parties, and purchased the loyalty of government officials and military officers. They have owned and therefore manipulated the media. They have also supported and been supported by the Catholic Church. Some have even maintained their own private armies. Economist Frank Golay observed in 1960 that "income and wealth are concentrated, political power is highly correlated with wealth, and welfare goals are assigned a low priority".[2]

The élite, however, has been relatively open to accepting into its ranks (some would say co-opting) non-members who become wealthy or politically influential. Ramon Magsaysay and Juan Ponce Enrile are two notable examples. It has also been unified by its fear of agrarian radicalism or any reform that would erode its wealth and power. It was divided, however, by the controversy over collaboration with the Japanese during World War II and then by the diversification of the economy that began in the 1950s. The conflict over rival economic interests was dramatized by the economic debate in the 1950s over foreign exchange controls between the "sugar bloc" — a traditionally powerful pressure group representing sugar producers and exporters — and an emerging group of import substitution manufacturers.

Marcos, as we will see, cast himself as a populist dedicated to destroying the power of the traditional élite. In reality, however, he emasculated only those families that were political threats, co-opted the rest, and created a new élite dependent upon him.

The Importance of Local Politics

In the Philippines, local politics have traditionally been contests between two, or sometimes three, wealthy landed families. Control of local office is coveted for a number of reasons: the opportunity it offers for financial enrichment; the political power that comes with having control over the distribution of resources and patronage; the control of law enforcement; and because it deprives rival families of these same opportunities and benefits. The local élite families, therefore, have viewed direct or indirect control of local and provincial offices as critical to preserving or expanding their interests *vis-à-vis* other rival families. Moreover, the combination of a strong political and economic base at the provincial level is critical for members of the élite who have national political aspirations.

Local elections, then, have traditionally tended to be contests between the members of the wealthiest and most influential families, or their proxies. Local campaigns and voting have rarely, if ever, been influenced by ideology or national issues. Instead, they have emphasized local issues (such as the condition of schools and roads, the creation of jobs, and so forth) and personal relationships. Other voting considerations have included the perceived ability of the candidate to acquire funds or services for the locality, the strength of the candidate's connections in Manila (from where almost all funds flowed), and whether the candidate's long-term political fortunes were seen to be on the rise or in decline. The candidates mobilized the vote through a network of *liders* (precinct captains) who knew the voters personally, often because of their blood or ritual kinship ties. They secured votes by using a combination of family ties, *utang na loob*, loyalty, and promises of jobs, payments, or other material benefits. If necessary, they would also use threats and intimidation.

National political parties have traditionally been built from competing alliances of local leaders. Local elections, therefore, have been a test not just of the local candidates themselves, but also of the relative influence and vote-getting ability of Congressmen and other members of the national political élite. The candidates for local office need the support and superior resources of the provincial or national politicians, who, in turn, need the support of the local politicians in order to further their own provincial or national political aspirations. Consequently, local elections have had an important influence on the alliance building between the local and provincial politicians and the national political leadership.

Political Parties and Electoral Politics

In the light of the wealth and power held by the local and national élite, what role have political parties and elections played in Philippine politics? Have parties represented particular constituencies and interest groups, advocated distinctive ideologies and policies, and possessed a formal structure and organization? Have elections been a meaningful democratic exercise in which the Filipino people have changed their leaders and representatives? Or have politics merely been contests among the élite for control of government office to preserve or expand their economic and political power? The truth seems to lie somewhere in between.

Since World War II Philippine politics have been dominated by two national parties: the Nacionalista Party and the Liberal Party. These parties were, until 1972, remarkable in the developing world for their continuity and longevity. Even more remarkable, the two-party system persisted "despite fraud and the possibility of an attempted coup in 1949 . . . despite the Huk rebellion successfully seething not far from Manila in 1953; despite occasional public ruminations on the need for military or authoritarian efficiency in the late 1950s and the early 1960s".[3] During these years, the Nacionalistas and Liberals regularly contested elections – sometimes honestly and peacefully, sometimes not – for offices ranging from local mayor to the presidency.

The long-standing rivalry between the two parties, however, does not mean there were major ideological differences between them. Rather, the two parties were essentially identical. According to Jose Maria Sison, the founder of the Communist Party of the Philippines,

Philippine political parties are as alike as "the Democratic Party and the Republican Party or Coca Cola and Pepsi Cola are alike . . . . Their differences are at most factional and cliquish. They are preoccupied with quarrelling over the spoils of colonial office".[4] Nor does the longevity of the parties mean there was continuity in their leadership and membership. Instead, they were both little more than loosely knit and unstable alliances of factions. Their composition was shaped mostly by the local and national rivalries of élite families. They were held together by the ties of kinship and patron–clientelism, by the dispensing of patronage, and by shared economic interests. Finally, although the two parties were national in membership they were not national in their outlook. In fact, the concerns of the two parties were overwhelmingly local.

Despite their many weaknesses, the political parties played an important integrative role in many parts of the Philippines before martial law. William Overholt has noted that, "The democratic parties had deep roots in nearly every village and their patronage system integrated an extraordinary diversity of competing regional and ethnic groups".[5] Furthermore, the two party-system lent stability and continuity to Philippine politics. According to Lande, "the multiclass parties of the Philippines do satisfy most of the needs of members of all social strata, at least to the extent that the people themselves understand their needs".[6] But, as Lande has also pointed out, parties had to appeal to all classes, occupational and interest groups, and regions. Therefore, all national administrations were by necessity administrations of compromise. Consequently, they often lacked internal unity and a clear sense of direction.

As noted, the primary purpose of the Philippines' two parties has been to contest elections to control local and national offices and to protect and enhance their leaders' wealth and power. Consequently, Philippine elections have been "the focal area of political redistribution and exchange".[7] The no-holds-barred competition for political spoils has meant that violence and questions of legitimacy have shadowed Philippine elections. In the 1946 presidential elections, the supporters of Manuel Roxas threatened an uprising if he lost. After the fraud-ridden 1949 presidential elections, in which Jose P. Laurel never conceded defeat to Elpidio Quirino, the government had to suppress a minor revolt of Laurel's supporters in his home province of Batangas. In the wake of the fraud committed in 1949 the military was called out to guard the polling in the 1951 congressional elections. In the 1953 presidential contest Ramon Magsaysay's supporters planned a *coup d'etat* if he did not win. And in 1961 there was the threat of open violence when the incumbent, Carlos Garcia, considered not yielding the presidency to Diosdado Macapagal.[8]

Finally, at the very least, elections have served to "throw the bums out". Repeatedly, during the two and a half decades of post-war democracy, incumbent presidents lost to challengers — often because of the effectiveness of charges of corruption and nepotism. In the elections four years later the victor, in turn, became the vanquished.[9] This pattern of election followed by rejection was not broken until 1969 when Ferdinand Marcos spent tens of millions of dollars to win an unprecedented second term as president.

The Presidency

From 1935 until 1969, with the exception of 1942–45, during the Japanese occupation, Filipino voters regularly and enthusiastically went to the polls to elect a president.[10] The fierce and expensive competition for the presidency and the high degree of voter turn-out in presidential elections are reflections of the prestige and power Filipinos accord the office of the president. Until 1972, the power of the presidency was derived, in large part, from the 1935 Constitution, which gave the chief executive great prestige and considerable influence over economic policy and patronage. Consequently, the president was able to exercise substantial leverage over Congress, in large part because he controlled the disbursement of appropriations.

The constitutional powers of the presidency were enhanced by the prestige and authority that Manuel Quezon brought to the office from 1935 to 1941. During the post-war era, however, the relative power of the presidency rose and fell depending on who held office, and whether it was the beginning or the end of his administration. Presidents Quirino, Garcia, and Macapagal had limited success in asserting the power of the executive branch over the Congress. But Ramon Magsaysay, who had a relatively broad base of support (and strong American backing), and Ferdinand Marcos, who was especially adept at politics and governance, made the presidency relatively more potent. Every Philippine president, however, regardless of the strength of his personality, has been weakened by the absence of a strong and supportive political party structure, the presence of a typically contentious and ambitious Congress, and a relatively small government budget with which to fund programmes.[11]

Finally, because the presidency was at the top of the Philippines' political pyramid, the president was the focus of great, and often unrealistic, public expectations. He was expected to intervene in even the smallest of problems, including the allocation of patronage, distribution of "pork-barrel" funds, and resolution of local political disputes. The numerous and often conflicting demands placed on the president regularly far exceeded both his resources and his ability to mobilize the national government. In 1965 Carl Lande described the problem of unrealistic expectations in the following way:

> To the overwhelming majority of Filipinos. . .each presidential election campaign is but one more gamble on who, incumbent or challenger, will come nearer to fulfilling the ideal of the perfect president. As no mortal can fully achieve such an ideal, especially considering the myriad of pressures playing upon a Philippine chief executive, Filipino voters have turned against their presidents, even those who rode into office as popular idols, with remarkable regularity and speed.[12]

A quarter of a century after Lande wrote this, Corazon Aquino has been a victim of exactly the phenomenon he described.

The Congress

The pre-martial law legislature was bicameral, as it is today, with 24 senators elected in nation-wide polling, and 120 representatives elected by district. The Philippine Congress was authorized by the 1935 Constitution to 1) initiate all legislation; 2) approve the national government's budget (although the president also had funds at his disposal and could delay or selectively release congressional appropriations); 3) impose tariffs and quotas; and 4) review Cabinet appointments and senior military promotions. In addition, it had the sole power to declare war. All appropriations, revenue, and tariff bills originated in the House, while the Senate was solely responsible for ratifying treaties.

Because the twenty-four members of the Senate were elected in a national vote, the Senate was traditionally the home of the Philippines' most prominent politicians, and was viewed as a stepping stone to the presidency. Senators who went on to run for or be elected president included Carlos Garcia, Claro Recto, Raul Manglapus, Sergio Osmeña, Jr., and Ferdinand Marcos. The power held by the twenty-four senators and the lofty ambitions of many of its members made the Senate the centre of opposition to the president.

The House was dominated by members of landowning families or their representatives and was concerned primarily with family and local interests. Consequently, the vast majority of legislation considered in the House dealt with appropriations for local projects. There was an inherent logic to the local, "pork-barrel" concerns of the House, for as political scientist David Wurfel has written, "Aid to the constituent by means of national legislation would be depersonalized, and thus to most Congressmen, politically pointless".[13] Typically, the majority of bills was not acted upon until the very end of a session, resulting in considerable legislative "horse-trading" and the rapid passage of hastily written and frequently faulty bills. This led one Filipino political scientist to write, "There is little exaggeration in saying that the legislative process is virtually untouched by rationality, professional craftsmanship, and civic spirit".[14]

Because of the weaknesses of the Nacionalista and Liberal Parties there was little party discipline within Congress. Instead of being organized along party lines, the Congress was divided into, and legislative contests were shaped by, fluid "blocs" representing key economic interests: sugar producers, copra producers and millers, manufacturers, and exporters. There was competition — sometimes fierce — among these blocs for the beneficial economic legislation the Congress could enact. However, these blocs usually co-operated to stymie social legislation and occasional efforts to raise taxes required to finance social programmes. In 1960 Frank Golay observed:

> The competing racial and economic pressure groups are unwilling to expand governmental revenues and functions because of basic fears that social services will redistribute income in favor of some other element within society. The dominant economic groups compete for subsidies and concessions, but they present a united

front of opposition to economic leadership that proposes to utilize
government to promote social progress.[15]

The historical absence of progress made with land reform legislation
is perhaps the best example of the Congress' aversion to significant
socio-economic change. The promise of genuine land reform has been
a mainstay of Philippine politics since the creation of the Commonwealth. Like independence and democracy, no politician or government
official would dare to speak out against the principle of land reform.
Almost every Congress since independence has been able to boast
of passing laws ostensibly intended to improve agrarian conditions
and create a more just and equitable society. Most of this legislation,
however, was in response to the threat of agrarian unrest and was
disregarded as soon as the threat diminished. Almost all of it was
severely limited in scope, riddled with loopholes that were exploited
by landowners and their lawyers, and never implemented or enforced
by a Congress dominated by landowners.[16]

The Military

The Armed Forces of the Philippines (AFP) was created in 1935
in preparation for eventual independence, but there was little time
for it to become established before it was plunged into the chaos of
World War II. Following the war and independence, the Philippine
Constabulary (PC) was integrated into the AFP, giving the latter the
primary responsibility for defeating the Hukbalahap insurgency. With
the exception of limited participation in America's wars in Korea and
Vietnam, the Philippine military has been concerned with internal,
rather than external, security threats.

The Philippine military, modelled as it was on the U.S. Army, historically adhered to the supremacy of the civilian government and
was generally respected for its professionalism. But in the absence
of an armed struggle for national independence during the twentieth
century or serious external threats after World War II, it never acquired
a central political role or great public prestige. Because of this, the
Philippine élite traditionally has had little interest in a military career.
Instead, the AFP became a vehicle for the upward mobility of its
predominantly middle- and lower-middle class officers. These officers
took pride in the rigorous training they received at the Philippine

Military Academy (PMA), the local equivalent of West Point, and typically maintained close associations with their classmates. The importance of these associations became most evident in the mid-1980s when members of the PMA class of 1971 formed the core of the now-infamous Reform the Armed Forces Movement (RAM), the group that sought to overthrow first Marcos and then Aquino.

It has been suggested that the military traditionally looked to the president as its main ally against the legislature, and therefore has been extremely loyal to the commander-in-chief. But according to political scientist Francisco Nemenzo, presidents before Marcos were careful to control the military:

> Suspicious of the military, they checked every perceptible trend towards autonomy from civilian control. Congress was also apprehensive of the military. Defense budgets were always subjected to the minutest scrutiny. Officers kept a low profile because their promotion beyond the rank of major was subject to confirmation by the Congressional Commission on Appointments.[17]

Despite these constraints, the military's role grew gradually over time. Elements of the military backed Manuel Roxas in the 1946 presidential elections, and were active in the 1949 election victory of Elpidio Quirino.[18] During the 1951 elections the military was deputized by the Commission on Elections for the first time to guard the polls. President Magsaysay, who had been Secretary of National Defence, recruited a large number of military officers to head civilian offices and expanded the "civic action" functions of the army. Under Magsaysay the military was involved in projects for the rural population: digging artesian wells and constructing roads, bridges, irrigation ditches, school-buildings, and community centres. It participated in food production and was also active in providing free dental, medical, and legal services to rural dwellers.[19]

Ferdinand Marcos served as his own Secretary of Defence for the first thirteen months of his presidency. Under him, army civic action engineering battalions, strengthened as part of his agreement with the United States to send Filipino troops to Vietnam, were used in large numbers in road building and other community development projects. According to Amando Doronila, "This high visibility of men in uniform engaged in public works made the public accustomed to military involvement in civil affairs, let alone their involvement in counter-insurgency and law and order problems, and made their widening presence acceptable".[20] Beginning in 1972 the military was to play a key role in administering and defending Marcos's martial law regime.

The Political Economy

It is instructive that Frank Golay began his classic study of the Philippine economy with a chapter on the role of the state in the economy. Writing in 1960, he described the Philippine economy as being:

> essentially an enterprise type of economy with liberal rewards for entrepreneurial initiative. This is not to say that competition is the dominant characteristic of the economy but, rather, to emphasize the role of entrepreneurial initiative in organizing resources. The profit motive is the goad, but competition is not the regulator. Instead, the state by dispensing the largess inherent in its powers to tax and to spend − and in its equally important power, not to tax − tends to regulate the intensity of the profit motive.[21]

Because of the landed élite's control of the Congress, the Philippines' tax rates − especially land taxes − historically have been low (even for a developing country) and those taxes that are on the books have been poorly collected. As a result, government expenditure as a share of gross national product (GNP) in the Philippines averaged only 11 per cent in the 1950s and 1960s, versus about 20 per cent in Thailand and Korea, and 24 per cent in Malaysia. Moreover, gross investment by the government was only about a fifth of total government expenditure. Most of the government's expenditures (excluding those for education) were devoted to political patronage, so that there was little systematic attempt to use the government as a vehicle for national socio-economic development.

Golay also described an economic class structure in which dominant political and economic power was vested in the *cacique*, the land-based élite. Because their power and wealth derived from land ownership, they had little interest in technological improvements or entrepreneurship. They were a rentier class, interested in living off the income gained from the control of existing economic assets (primarily land and other natural resources), rather than in creating new sources of wealth. Consequently, Philippine agriculture has been characterized by:

- low productivity of land and labour;
- widespread absentee landlordism and high rates of tenancy;
- the organization of production into small-scale and technologically backward units; and
- relatively high land values because of rapid population growth and the closure of the frontier.[22]

In the 1950s the Philippines, like other less-developed Asian countries, sought to stimulate the growth of industry. And like most other Asian countries at the time, it adopted an approach based on import substitution. The Philippines' approach had two key dimensions to it. First, it relied on the export earnings of traditional agricultural and mineral commodities to finance the development of domestic industries. And secondly, it protected these "infant industries" from foreign competition through a combination of tariffs, import quotas, foreign exchange controls, and the overvaluation of the peso (until 1962).

Initially, the policy of import substitution produced the desired effect: the industrial sector grew by more than 8 per cent a year from 1949 to 1957. Per capita income also grew at an average annual rate of 3.6 per cent during the 1950s, a rate which rivalled that of most other countries in the region. Despite a decade of respectable economic growth, however, income distribution remained very uneven. In 1961, 20 per cent of the nation's total family income was earned by just 4.25 per cent of all families while, at the bottom of the socioeconomic pyramid, a similar 20 per cent of the nation's total family income was shared by 57 per cent of all families.[23]

By the late 1950s or early 1960s the industrial output of some of Asia's less developed countries was becoming more than enough to satisfy the limited domestic demand. Consequently, some Asian governments began to adopt new, export-oriented economic policies. They encouraged (and often subsidized) the export of manufactured goods, basing their ability to compete in the international market on their relatively inexpensive labour costs. In the Philippines, however, economic nationalism and the influence of import substitution industrialists caused the government to continue its policy of import substitution. The results for the Philippines were disastrous relative to the performance of other countries in the region. By the late 1950s the average annual growth of the economy had declined to only 4.2 per cent from 8.6 per cent in the early 1950s. The average annual growth of the industrial sector shrank to 3.7 per cent. The country suffered recurring balance of payments problems as the cost of imported materials far exceeded the earnings from traditional agricultural and mineral exports.

In 1962 President Macapagal abolished foreign exchange controls, which had the effect of devaluing the overvalued peso. This improved the Philippines' trade deficit by making the domestic cost of imports more expensive and the international price of exports more competitive. But the devaluation also caused a sharp rise in domestic inflation. To cushion the impact of the controversial decontrol, significant tariffs were imposed, thus preserving a high level of protection for increasingly inefficient local manufacturers.

Throughout the 1960s the economy continued to grow at an average annual rate of about 5 per cent. The manufacturing sector remained particularly weak. Few new jobs were created in the sector and only a handful of significant new export industries developed. The Philippines' average annual per capita GDP (gross domestic product) growth rate fell to 2.2 per cent during the 1960s, the lowest among all non-communist East and Southeast Asian countries. Moreover, little progress was made in improving income distribution. In 1971 20 per cent of the nation's total family income was earned by just 3.6 per cent of all families while, at the bottom of the pile, 20 per cent of the total family income was shared among 54 per cent of the nation's families.[24]

Conclusion: The Strengths and Weaknesses of Élite Democracy

The 1935 Constitution provided for a unitary state in which all power was vested in a regularly elected national government characterized by an American-style separation of powers. On paper, then, office holders were democratically elected and their policies were representative of the people's will. In practice, however, government on both the local and national levels was dominated by a small landed élite. It sought to use the government to preserve or enhance its own economic and political interests and emasculated the government's capabilities in the areas that did not serve its interests.

Traditional Philippine politics were characterized by the close correlation between landownership, wealth, and political power. Politics were driven by the rivalries between wealthy families and competing economic interests. Political affiliations and loyalties were determined primarily by family and linguistic ties, patron–client relationships, and patronage. Public office was seen as a vehicle for the control and allocation of privileges and government resources among competing élite factions and their followers.

Élite democracy, however, did have several strengths despite its many flaws. At the minimum, it produced a regular and relatively peaceful rotation of political leadership. It also required a degree of responsiveness on the part of the élite to mass concerns and needs — albeit generally on an *ad hoc* and self-serving basis. Furthermore, because the Philippines' social hierarchy was based primarily on the accumulation of wealth (as opposed to hereditary title, or civil or military rank), and because the American colonial period created a system of public education, there was a limited degree of social mobility in the Philippines. This, combined with a veneer of American-inspired equality, created a popular belief in upward mobility. During the 1950s and 1960s these factors provided something of a safety valve for mounting social, political, and economic pressures.

NOTES

1. Resil Mojares, *The Man Who Would be President: Serging Osmena and Philippine Politics* (Cebu: Maria Cacao Publishers, 1986), p.60.
2. Frank Golay, *The Philippines: Public Policy and National Economic Development* (Ithaca: Cornell University Press, 1986), p.11.
3. Theodore Friend, "Philippine-American Tensions in History", in *Crisis in the Philippines: The Marcos Era and Beyond*, edited by John Bresnan (Princeton: Princeton University Press, 1986), p.23.
4. Amado Guerrero (Jose Maria Sison), *Philippine Society and Revolution* (International Association of Filipino Patriots, 1979), p.116.
5. William Overholt, "The Rise and Fall of Ferdinand Marcos", *Asian Survey* 26, no.11 (November 1986):1139.

6. Carl Lande, *Leaders, Factions, and Parties: The Structure of Philippine Politics*, Monograph Series No. 6 (New Haven: Yale University Southeast Asian Studies Program, 1965), p.43.

7. Mojares, op. cit., p.159.

8. Ibid., p.155.

9. James Rush, *Bringing Marcos Down: Part 1: The Electoral Tradition*, Report no.3 (University Field Staff International, 1986), p.4.

10. In 1935 Manuel Quezon was elected the first President of the Philippine Commonwealth. During the Japanese occupation Jose P. Laurel served as President of the Japanese-appointed government in Manila, while Quezon and then, following Quezon's death in 1944, Sergio Osmeña Sr., served as President in exile in Washington. Manuel Roxas became the first elected President of the independent Republic of the Philippines in 1946. Roxas was followed by Elpidio Quirino (1948–53), Ramon Magsaysay (1954–57), Carlos Garcia (1957–61), Diosdado Macapagal (1961–65), and Ferdinand Marcos (1965–72). In 1969 Ferdinand Marcos became the first post-war president to be re-elected.

11. In response to these systemic contraints on the presidency, as well as because of an alleged cultural need for authority, some Filipinos have argued that the nation needs a presidential system that gives the chief executive almost unlimited power. Remigio Agpalo, a prominent Filipino political scientist during the Marcos era, argued that the nation required an authoritarian *pangulo* (literally "head") president who would act as a benevolent dictator.

12. Lande, op. cit., p.47.

13. David Wurfel, "Individuals and Groups in the Philippine Policy Process", in *Foundations and Dynamics of Filipino Government and Politics*, edited by Jose Abueva and Raul de Guzman (Manila: Bookmark, 1973), p.211.

14. O.D. Corpuz, "Political Trends in the Philippines", in *Trends in the Philippines*, edited by Lim Yoon Lin and M. Rajaretnam (Singapore: Institute of Southeast Asian Studies, 1972), p.42.

15. Golay, op. cit., p.30.

16. The implementation of land reform legislation, such as it was, moved at a glacially slow pace prior to the 1970s. David Wurfel has estimated that at the rate of progress maintained under Presidents Magsaysay and Garcia it would have taken approximately 700 years to repurchase and redistribute the 1.8 million hectares of tenanted agricultural land in the Philippines. Three years after the passage of the Land Reform Code of 1963, the most significant piece of land reform legislation up to that time, no agricultural land had been purchased. Consequently, the history of agrarian reform in the Philippines has been described by Wurfel

as being "a sadly monotonous one for a scholar, [but] a bitterly disappointing one for the hopeful tenant cultivator". See David Wurfel, "The Development of Post-War Philippine Land Reform: Political and Sociological Explanations", in *A Second View From the Paddy*, edited by Antonio Ledesma, Perla Makil and Virginia Miralao (Manila: Institute of Philippine Culture, 1983), pp.1–15.

17. Francisco Nemenzo, "Military Intervention in Philippine Politics", in *Diliman Review* 34, nos. 5 and 6 (1986):17.
18. See Richard Kessler, "Development and the Military: Role of the Philippine Military in Development", in *Soldiers and Stability in Southeast Asia*, edited by J. Soedjati Djiwandono and Yong Mun Cheong (Singapore: Institute of Southeast Asian Studies, 1988), pp.214–19.
19. See Felipe Miranda and Ruben Ciron, "Development and the Military in the Philippines: Military Perceptions in a Time of Continuing Crisis", in *Soldiers and Stability in Southeast Asia*, edited by J. Soedjati Djiwandono and Yong Mun Cheong (Singapore: Institute of Southeast Asian Studies, 1988), pp.168–74.
20. Amando Doronila, "The Transformation of Patron-Client Relations and its Political Consequences in Postwar Philippines", *Journal of Southeast Asian Studies* 16, no.1 (March 1985):112.
21. Golay, op. cit., p.xiii.
22. Ibid., p.266.
23. National Economic and Development Authority, *Philippine Statistical Yearbook 1987* (Manila: NEDA, 1988), p.114.
24. Ibid., p.114.

chapter 3

The Forces of Change

After decades of lethargy and improvisation, of short-term goals and stop-gap measures, the country was modernizing. It was moving toward sweeping change.

          — Ferdinand Marcos in 1971[1]

When Ferdinand Marcos, then a young and dynamic senator from the province of Ilocos Norte, was elected the sixth president of the Philippines in 1965, Philippine society was dualistic and transitional. Existing side by side were traditional and modern values and practices, and vastly different urban and rural societies. Although the national government was highly centralized, its ability to project its authority was weakened by its small revenue base and the control exerted by particularistic political and economic interest groups. A small industrial sector had developed, primarily to produce consumer goods for the protected domestic market. But the economy as a whole was still based on the relatively unproductive agricultural sector, and exports consisted mostly of unprocessed agricultural products and other raw materials.

The society was also experiencing swift and accelerating change. The population was growing rapidly, creating new demands on the government and economy. Urbanization and increasing levels of income and education contributed to rising expectations. New interest groups and constituencies began to emerge. New currents of nationalism surged forth. How did these changes affect the conduct of traditional politics as described in the preceding chapter? Were they pushing the Philippines towards chaos and revolution, as Marcos claimed when he declared martial law in 1972? Or were they merely the growing pains of a political system that was undergoing a transformation from élite democracy to a more pluralistic and participatory form of democracy? This chapter will examine these issues.

The Sources of Social Change

After two decades of high rates of growth, the Philippine population had become by the mid-1960s more youthful, demanding of education and other services, and expectant of progress. The economy had become somewhat more diversified, creating new economic interest groups. And in the countryside the land frontier was rapidly being reached, a trend that weakened the position of tenant farmers *vis-à-vis* landowners and contributed to rapid urbanization. Important changes also occurred within the Catholic Church.

Table 3.1
A Profile of Change: Selected Social Indicators

	1948	*1960*	*1970*	*1975*
Population (millions)	19.3	27.1	36.7	42.1
Population density (person/sq km)	64.1	90.0	122	140
% Urban/rural	28/72	30/70	33/67	33/67
Combined population of Metro Manila, Cebu & Davao (millions)	1.9	3.0	4.7	5.9
School enrolment (primary and secondary)	3.97[1]	4.76	8.69	9.55
Infant mortality[2]	101.63[3]	84.6	60.0	53.3

[1] 1954–55
[2] Deaths after 1 year per 1,000 live births
[3] 1950
SOURCE: NEDA, *Philippine Statistical Yearbook, 1987.*

Demographic Change

Post-war improvements in health, sanitation, and food production resulted in a rate of population growth of more than 3 per cent per annum during the 1950s and 1960s. Consequently, the population almost doubled between 1948 and the early 1970s, from under 20 million to nearly 37 million. As the population grew and became, on average, younger, it created a mounting demand for social services, particularly education, and for employment.

These demands in turn required the expansion of the national government's budget and bureaucracy. For example, between 25 and 30 per cent of national government expenditures had historically been devoted to public education. In the decade from 1960 to 1970 primary and secondary school enrolment almost doubled from 4.76 to 8.69 million. The literacy rate steadily grew, increasing from 72 per cent to 83 per cent during the same ten-year period, and the difference between urban and rural literacy declined.

Concurrent with the population explosion, increasing mechanization of agriculture and the reduced availability of virgin agricultural land were reducing the employment opportunities in the countryside, prompting migration to urban areas for employment. In 1950 only 5.6 million, or 28 per cent of Filipinos, lived in urban areas. By 1970 the urban population had more than doubled to 12 to 13 million, or 33 to 36 per cent of the total population. Between 1950 and 1970 the population of the metropolitan Manila region, the country's largest urban centre, doubled from under 2 million to almost 4 million.

Government, industry, finance and the media were concentrated in the cities, particularly in metropolitan Manila, and to a lesser degree, Cebu, Davao, Bacolod, and Iloilo. The expansion of both the government bureaucracy and industry stimulated the growth of a small, urban middle class that was largely divorced from traditional rural society. Frank Golay observed in 1960:

> Traditional patterns of kin-oriented behavior are eroding with internal migration, urbanization, and economic growth . . . . Preoccupation with the welfare of the extended family is lessening, and awareness of the community, of self-interest and the national interest is increasing.[2]

The Economy in the 1960s

The 1960s was a critical decade for the Philippine economy. At its outset the decade held the prospect of broad-based economic growth and development. A fledgling industrial sector had developed during the 1950s, the country had a variety of commodities to export, and Filipinos were well educated and entrepreneurial. But throughout the decade the economy remained trapped by policies that promoted import substitution and capital-intensive industrialization. As a result, the promise of the decade remained largely unfulfilled.

Table 3.2
A Profile of Economic Change: Selected Indicators

	1960	1965	1970	1975
GNP (billion pesos, 1972 prices)	30.2	39.5	50.0	68.5
Average annual GNP growth (preceding five years)	5.8	5.0	4.8	6.4
Per capita GNP (pesos, constant 1972 prices)	1101	1244	1358	1622
Average annual per capita GNP growth (preceding five years)	2.7	2.1	1.7	3.6
% GDP in				
Agriculture	34	34	29	27
Industry	23	24	29	33
Services	41	42	42	40
% employed labour-force in				
Agriculture	61	57	54	53
Industry	15	15	21	19
Services	23	28	25	28

SOURCE: NEDA, *Philippine Statistical Yearbook, 1987*.

During the 1950s and early 1960s the Philippine economy was notable for the considerable growth of relatively large and capital-intensive industries that produced and sold products for a protected and relatively small and poor domestic market. But by the early 1960s, as the demand of the domestic market was met, industrial growth slowed. Although the peso was devalued in 1962 and other steps were taken to reduce import substitution, many other biases remained and the economy was slow to develop non-agricultural exports. A major study conducted by the International Labour Organization (ILO) in 1974 concluded that import substitution had led to an attitude on the part of industrialists "which anticipated that inefficiencies would be permanently 'paid for' by the Government, by means of resources collected from the taxpayers, higher prices of consumer goods and, most important, lower real wages or under-employment".[3]

Consequently, by the late 1960s the Philippine economy had begun to reveal major structural problems. Productivity and real wages posted little growth. The share of employment in manufacturing remained flat at about 12 per cent of total employment. Total unemployment (open unemployment plus under-employment) was estimated by the ILO to be about 25 per cent. There were signs of a worsening distribution of income, especially in rural areas, despite aggregate per capita income growth. Forced to import expensive capital goods, the country suffered regular trade imbalances and a mounting balance of payments problem.

In the agricultural sector productivity increases during the 1960s were generally good, but according to the ILO study "most of the gain in agricultural income . . . accrued to landowners, whether landlords or owner-cultivators".[4] Moreover, the land frontier was reached in the 1960s, requiring that any further gains in agriculture be based almost entirely on improved productivity derived from higher yields and reduced spoilage.

A New Role for the Catholic Church

The Catholic Church has been described as "the most significant non-governmental linkage between the elite and the masses in the country".[5] Until the 1960s the Church generally shied away from political issues unless they threatened its own position or teachings. There were, however, some notable examples of early Church social activism. These included its support of the Federation of Free Workers, a moderate labour organization formed in 1950, and the Federation of Free Farmers, a reformist peasant organization founded by Jesuit-trained laymen in 1953.

The conclusion of the Second Vatican Council and the celebration of the quadricentennial of Christianity in the Philippines, both in 1965, marked the beginning of significant Church involvement in socio-economic issues.[6] The first significant manifestation was the formation of the National Secretariat for Social Action (NASSA) in 1968, which sought to change traditional Church values to emphasize social welfare and social action, particularly in the rural areas. By 1970, the Bishops were officially denouncing the exploitation of the poor, including the dispossession of farmers. The Church was now, as declared at the Asian Bishops Conference hosted in Manila that year, a Servant Church, the Poor Church of the Poor.[7] Although the Church was still far from the activist role of the early 1980s, the foundation for this was laid during the latter half of the 1960s.

Changes in Government and Politics

Social and economic change during the 1960s inevitably brought changes in government and politics. The traditional élite became more diverse and divided. The role of the national government expanded under Ferdinand Marcos. Respect for traditional politics declined. And a small but energetic leftist alternative emerged.

Diversification of the Élite

As we have seen, the élite, through its control of economic policy-making, created a highly protected and profitable economic environment conducive to élite entrepreneurship. As the Philippine economy grew and became more complex after the war, the activities and interests of the élite also became more diverse.[8] Moreover, while the degree of upward mobility into the élite had never been high, some upward mobility resulted from expanding education, the growth of the middle class, and increasing entrepreneurship. This added to further diversification of the élite.

This increased diversity heightened rivalry among them, particularly for control of the economy. Importers of finished goods, exporters of raw and processed goods, and protected manufacturers disagreed over exchange rate policy, taxes and tarriffs, and government incentives. In 1960 Frank Golay noted that: "The unity of the political elites has been permanently destroyed, and intense competition among the elites portends continued change."[9] As this competition intensified, it has been argued, the élite's commitment to traditional democracy waned, causing growing political instabilty in the early 1970s. One scholar noted the breakdown of intra-élite consensus by the late 1960s and wondered, "Would [their] democratic commitments be sufficiently strong to curb the temptation of one or another faction to seize uncontested control of a now more active state?"[10] To some observers, Marcos's declaration of martial law in 1972 represented the culmination (and termination) of élite competition.

The Growing Scope and Power of the National Government

The early post-war national government was characterized by a small revenue base which limited social expenditures to little more than education and *ad* hoc infrastructure projects. At the same time, the national government had a constitutional claim on all major sources of revenue, so that provincial and municipal governments were heavily dependent upon the national government for revenues. About half of their revenues came from the national government, making local government finances precarious and highly vulnerable to a reduction in national government support.[11] Furthermore, the flow of most national government resources to the provincial and local levels went through the Congress, which spent most of its time passing laws appropriating funds for specific schools, markets, roads, and buildings.

This began to change in 1965 with Marcos's election as president. In the face of congressional unwillingness to increase tax-based expenditures, Marcos resorted to internal and external borrowing to finance an unprecedentedly large programme to build roads, bridges, and markets. Marcos's four-year Infrastructure Development Programme had a positive impact on the economy, particularly in backward rural areas. It also had important consequences for government and politics. His programme eroded congressional control of the distribution of infrastructure and patronage benefits and began to centralize control of national government resources in the presidency. According to Amando Doronila:

Marcos built a new vehicle with which to bypass members of Congress in the distribution of projects direct to the rural electorate, carrying further the process in which the links between provincial leaders and their rural constituencies had already been made tenuous. . . . By 1969, Marcos, backed by state and private resources, had built an extensive patronage machine of a scale unmatched in post-war years. Clientelism had been so transformed that a giant patron state with a leadership more paternalistic than any landlord had emerged, with direct links to the Filipino masses. [12]

The Marcos presidency, then, reflected the transitional nature of the Philippines in the latter half of the 1960s. On the one hand, Marcos was both a product and practitioner of traditional élite politics. On the other hand, his presidency was characterized by the growth in the scope and power of the state, and by the more effective use of media and ideology to promote his policies and increase his own power.

Declining Respect for Traditional Politics

The 1960s was characterized by growing discontent with traditional politics and government among urban-based students and academics, the media, and other opinion leaders. This was stimulated by resurgent nationalism, including economic nationalism; intensified political rivalry within the élite; and the growth of anti-establishment movements in the United States, Europe, and the People's Republic of China. The result was greater political awareness and activism among university students, new and highly critical academic analyses of the shortcomings of Philippine political institutions, and heightened stridency in the media.

The awakening of student activism in the 1960s mirrored what was happening in other countries around the world. The students, many of whom were from middle class and upper middle class families, adopted Marxist–Leninist–Maoist analysis to criticize Filipino "feudalism" and American "imperialism". They also developed ties with workers and farmers groups in order to participate in, and learn from, the struggles of these "people's organizations". This new and more sophisticated activism fuelled recurring anti-government and anti-American demonstrations in Manila beginning in the mid-1960s.

The students' views were reflected in, and encouraged by the increasingly anti-establishment orientation of some of Manila's largest and most influential newspapers – which were owned by leading members of the élite. These included the *Manila Times* (owned by the influential Roces family and supported the then Senator Benigno Aquino), the *Manila Chronicle* (owned by the wealthy Lopezes, the family of Marcos's vice-president) and the *Free Press* (owned by the Locsin family). Many of the newspapers' scathing criticisms of the Marcos government, the political process, and the economic and political élite were accurate, and some were undoubtedly genuine. But often, the criticism pandered to sensationalism in order to increase sales, and some of it, particularly in the Lopez and Roces papers, was designed to embarrass Marcos and bolster his opponents.

Disgust with traditional politics may have reached a high point in 1969, with the infamous presidential contest between Ferdinand Marcos and Sergio Osmeña, Jr. Marcos handily won a second term, but only after spending so much government money that he created a financial crisis. According to Resil Mojares, the unprecedented level of vote buying in the 1969 elections demonstrated that the electorate had "grown tired of and cynical of machine politics. Trends pointed to the need for more distinct policy alternatives and sharper ideological focus".[13] The sour taste of the 1969 elections lasted, student protests grew in frequency and intensity, and in 1970 widespread dissatisfaction with the existing political order resulted in agreement to assemble a convention to draft a new constitution.

The Emergence of the Radical Left

The clearest rejection of traditional élite democracy came from the political left, which in the early 1960s consisted primarily of nationalistic and increasingly Marxist university faculty members and students in Manila. In 1964 Jose Maria "Joma" Sison, a student leader and member of the almost defunct pro-Moscow Partido Komunista ng Pilipinas (PKP) created the militant student organization, Kabataang Makabayan (Nationalist Youth, or KM), which organized the first major anti-American demonstrations in Manila in 1965. In 1968 Sison formed the Movement for the Advancement of Nationalism (MAN), which sought to include other progressive sectors of Philippine society in its effort to advance the nationalist cause.

Sison's view of politics went far beyond the calls for reform by traditional nationalists such as Claro Recto, Jose Diokno, and Lorenzo Tanada. Indeed, Sison's revolutionary zeal — and his own ambition — greatly exceeded that of his tired and discredited elders in the PKP. So in December 1968 Sison and ten other members broke with the PKP and founded the Communist Party of the Philippines (CPP) along doctrinaire Maoist principles. According to Sison, the eleven founders represented a total party membership of seventy-five, mostly students.[14] Sison and Bernabe Buscayno, a former Huk guerrilla also known as Kumander Dante, then formed the New People's Army (NPA), the military arm of the CPP, in March 1969, with Dante as commander. Dante brought to the cause thirty-seven Huk guerrillas and about as many guns. The creation of the CPP and NPA provided a radical alternative to both the Huks, who had degenerated into little more than bandits, and to the discredited and co-opted PKP.

In 1970 Sison published *Philippine Society and Revolution* (*PSR*) using the pseudonym Amado Guerrero. *PSR* scathingly attacked the "revisionist" PKP leadership, and offered a Marxist–Leninist–Maoist analysis of Philippine society. According to Sison, Philippine society was "semi-feudal" (with a small class of landowners and compradors exploiting and subjugating the mass of poor Filipinos) and "semi-colonial" (with U.S. imperialism controlling the Philippine economy, politics, culture, and foreign relations). The government, according to Sison, was nothing more than a "bureaucratic-capitalist" puppet of the Philippine élite and the United States.

Equally important, *PSR* presented an explicit Maoist blueprint for revolution in the Philippines, calling for a protracted guerrilla war in the countryside that would eventually engulf the cities and topple the government. Sison saw the Philippines in the 1960s as being like reactionary China in the 1920s and 1930s, and so the CPP was dogmatically Maoist (and pro-Chinese) throughout the 1970s. It was also fiercely anti-Soviet Union, because of both China's anti-Soviet line and Soviet ties to the disdained PKP. (Only later, in the 1980s, did the Sandinista experience in Nicaragua become the admired model of the CPP, and in 1982 the CPP stopped parroting China's anti-Soviet rhetoric.) *PSR* became the bible of the radical left and the guiding document of the CPP/NPA.

Another radical group, Christians for National Liberation (CNL), consisting of priests and sisters led by Father Edicio de la Torre, was formed in February 1972 — the centennial of the execution by the Spanish of three Filipino clerics, Fathers Burgos, Gomez, and Zamora. The CNL was Marxist and revolutionary from the outset. Revolution, the group asserted in its second national congress, was a "Christian imperative", and advancing the revolution would help to "build God's kingdom".[15] Its underground activities focused primarily on the political organization of peasants.

The radical left was small and isolated at first. It faced the formidable challenges of operating in a traditional, conservative, and predominantly Catholic culture, and of opposing a government and military with some experience in counter-insurgency. But the left also had a dedicated and intelligent leadership, an attractive and persuasive ideology that capitalized on growing nationalist fervour, and a blueprint for the future that promised sweeping, revolutionary change rather than reforms and palliatives. In the context of the tumultuous 1960s and 1970s this combination would provide a potent and persistent formula for rebellion.

The Philippines on the Eve of Martial Law

Ferdinand Marcos's 1971 prediction that the Philippines was "moving toward sweeping change" was accurate but understated. By 1971 the country was already in the midst of change and turmoil. Philippine society was modernizing and becoming more diverse and complex. As this happened, its politics were becoming increasingly polarized between a conservative élite, itself increasingly divided, and emergent forces calling for political, social, and economic change. It was a period marked by both rising popular expectations and deteriorating national consensus.

In retrospect, the rapid-fire sequence of dramatic events from 1970 to 1972 seemed to be moving the country inexorably towards not just "sweeping change", but on to a major upheaval of some sort. This section summarizes the progression of events before the imposition of martial law.

Political Turmoil and Economic Problems

The lead up to martial law began, ironically, with Marcos's re-election in 1969. The controversial 1969 presidential contest between Marcos and Osmeña began a period of political turmoil that continued unabated until the imposition of martial law three years later. At the same time, the Philippine economy was buffeted by a series of internal and external shocks. Agricultural harvests in 1970 and 1971 were poor because of typhoons and severe floods. The peso, floated in February 1970 in response to a balance of payments crisis caused by huge government spending for the 1969 election, had devalued by 42 per cent against the U.S. dollar by mid-1973. This fuelled rapid inflation, causing consumer prices to rise 32 per cent from 1970 to 1972.

On the political front, the 1969 presidential election was a clash between two experienced politicians with impressive political machines: Ferdinand Marcos and the Nacionalistas against Sergio Osmeña, Jr. and the Liberals. The election was the dirtiest and most expensive presidential contest the country had ever experienced. Marcos and the Nacionalistas spent between 800 and 900 million pesos (about US$200 million in 1969), about half of which came from government sources, to defeat Osmeña by an unprecedented margin of almost 2 million votes. The Nacionalistas also dominated the Senate contests, winning 7 of 8 seats. According to Resil Mojares:

> The election of 1969 was a culmination of sorts. It raised elite competition for power to a higher level of contradiction. Marcos, through his exploitation of state power, was a key figure in this development. He was not, however, its sole author. Such men as Serging Osmena were part of the whole process.[16]

By defeating Osmeña, Marcos became the first president of the republic to be re-elected. But his victory began a political backlash that reached its peak during the 1971 senatorial elections. The election added fuel to the student demonstrations that had begun in the mid-1960s. The inauguration of Marcos in January 1970 started the famous "First Quarter Storm" of student protests. A nearly successful student assault on Malacañang Palace (which became known as the Battle of Mendiola Bridge) in the days after the inauguration left four students dead. A year later students took over the Diliman campus of the University of the Philippines and declared the "Diliman Commune" for nine days. Students also supported the growing militancy of labour, particularly Manila's bus and jeepney drivers, which resulted in a series of strikes in the capital in 1970. The rise of violent student and labour protests, according to Amando Doronila, "symbolized the start of the rapid disintegration of consensus politics in the Philippines [and] signalled the intensification of the politics of the streets in which social grievances were being vented outside the parliamentary arena".[17]

The political turmoil that began with the 1969 presidential campaign resurfaced during the 1971 senatorial campaign. The November elections became a test of the popularity of Marcos and his Nacionalista Party. In August 1971 two grenades exploded at a crowded Liberal Party rally held in Manila's Plaza Miranda. At least 9 spectators were killed and 100 wounded. Eight Liberal Party senatorial candidates were injured, including Senators Jovito Salonga, Raul Manglapus, Eva Kalaw, and John Osmeña. Another leading member of the Liberal Party, Senator Benigno Aquino, had not yet arrived at the rally. President Marcos blamed the communists, while the Liberals accused Marcos and his followers. The perpetrators, however, were never identified or arrested, and Marcos used the incident to suspend the writ of habeas corpus for six months.[18]

In the wake of the Plaza Miranda bombing, the Liberal Party senatorial candidates won 6 of 8 seats in the November elections, eroding what had been the near total domination of the Senate by the Nacionalistas. The Nacionalista defeat was seen by many as a strong rejection of Marcos and a call for change. It may have prompted Marcos to begin to seriously consider extra-constitutional means for remaining in power when his term expired in early 1974.

The Constitutional Convention Controversy

By the end of the 1960s there was a widely shared sense in metropolitan Manila that the 1935 Constitution, written under American tutelage prior to the Philippines becoming a commonwealth, should be replaced with a truly Filipino charter reflecting the politics and government of an independent nation in the 1970s. Furthermore, according to Jose Abueva, who served as the secretary of the Constitutional

Convention: "The view prevailed that the old constitution somehow had resulted in the ills of Filipino democracy: oligarchal rule, political abuses, corruption, worsening social injustice, persistent underdevelopment."[19] It was widely hoped that a new constitution could establish a new set of principles and laws that would cure the country's ills.

In 1970 a law was passed calling for the holding of a Constitutional Convention (known as the "Con Con"), and in June 1971 the freshly elected delegates to the Con Con convened in Quezon City. The Con Con was divided from the start between those who sought the maintenance of the status quo and those who sought varying degrees of change. According to historian Lewis Gleeck:

> The idealists hoped for a reform of society through constitution-writing; the traditional politicians, who were forbidden to run [for a seat in the Convention], made sure that they would be represented by clients or relatives; the revolutionaries, certain of its failure, planned to use it as a forum for denunciation; a few professionals, skeptical but willing to try anything that theoretically promised reform without revolution, did their pragmatic best to make the exercise meaningful.[20]

At the inaugural meeting, which Marcos addressed, 17 of the 320 delegates walked out to protest Marcos's influence and interference, foreshadowing the controversy that would continue to surround the convention. The Con Con was also divided between those delegates who wanted the new constitution to explicitly ban Marcos from another term in office (in keeping with the 1935 Constitution, which limited a president to two terms), and those who supported Marcos and wanted a new constitution that would enable him to remain in power. In order to circumvent the ban on a third term, Marcos and his followers sought to do away with the presidential system and replace it with a parliamentary one to enable him to become prime minister. Marcos was rumoured to have tried to influence delegates through bribes, blackmail, and promises. "The cream of the national political elite", according to William Overholt, "proved extraordinarily vulnerable to personal pressures and frequently valid accusations of felony".[21] As a result of Marcos's influence and the low repute of the old Congress, the "ban Marcos" movement was narrowly defeated, and a parliamentary system was adopted — but only following the declaration of martial law.

The Growing Spectre of Martial Law

Tension continued to mount in 1972 as a spate of small bomb explosions racked the capital, including two at the Con Con in September. Most of the blasts were for political impact, occurring at times and places that minimized human or economic damage. Responsibility for the blasts, as for the Plaza Miranda bombing before them, was attributed to the communists, rightist extremists, and Marcos. Whoever was responsible, the growing climate of violence and chaos benefited all extremists. In July 1972 a ninety-ton ship, the *Karagatan*, was found off Isabela Province north of Manila, reportedly with a cache of 3,500 firearms on board. Marcos claimed they were destined for the NPA. Although his charge was doubted by many at the time, it has recently been convincingly asserted that the weapons were indeed a bungled shipment intended for the NPA that had originated in the People's Republic of China.[22]

By mid-1972 Marcos was regularly citing the growing violence in Manila as evidence of an impending communist uprising. He also claimed that the CPP and NPA planned to assassinate him and that Benigno Aquino and other Liberal Party leaders had held meetings with CPP head Jose Ma. Sison to establish a "united front" against his administration. Marcos often suggested he would not hesitate to "use the powers at his disposal to defend the republic". On 13 September 1972 Liberal Party senator Benigno Aquino fuelled further speculation about the imposition of martial law when he exposed "Oplan Sagitarius", which he claimed was a plan by Marcos to place the country under the control of the Philippine Constabulary as a prelude to martial law.

Finally, on 21 September 1972 Marcos signed Presidential Proclamation No. 1081 declaring martial law. It was not until the evening of 22 September, however, that he used the pretext of a staged ambush on Defence Minister Juan Ponce Enrile to publicly declare martial law. That night, fifty-three leading opposition figures were arrested, and the following day the military padlocked the Congress and shut down the media. Democracy in the Philippines had come to an abrupt end.

An "Illusory" Crisis?

By 1972 there was a growing sense of crisis, primarily in metropolitan Manila. It was a climate that Marcos undoubtedly helped to cultivate in order to further his own political ambitions. But the cause of the crisis included more than the cynical machinations of one man. Also contributing to the crisis were increased political violence, intensified ideological extremism, growing social and political polarization, and a declining sense of confidence in the Philippines' political and social institutions. One journalist has suggested that "a mood of collective flagellation took hold and a chase began to point out new instances of national failure".[23] But, was the nation on the verge of chaos or revolution as Marcos claimed?

Although the situation in 1972 was serious, it was not verging on revolution. One study, citing 1969 surveys that showed high levels of public satisfaction and participation, concluded that the situation was non-revolutionary. A poll taken at the height of the student demonstrations in 1970 revealed that less than 3 per cent of people polled identified themselves with "radical" issues such as anti-imperialism and social injustice while more than 80 per cent sought reform through the existing political structure.[24] Another report, by the Rand Corporation in 1970, concluded that the perception of a crisis was an "illusory" one confined mostly to metropolitan Manila, and that stability and popular satisfaction were much greater than the Philippine press and government portrayed. In 1971 a Philippine senate committee report described the communist insurgency as a growing problem, but concluded that it did not pose a serious military threat. Finally, even if the NPA actually had the 1,028 armed guerrillas Marcos claimed they had in 1972, it is unlikely that any but the most wishful rebels actually thought they had sufficient force to topple the government at that time.

Conclusion: A Failure of Philippine Democracy?

Did the imposition of martial law in 1972 represent the abrupt end of a functioning and viable democracy in the Philippines? Or did the tumult of the late 1960s and early 1970s indicate that Philippine democracy had already failed? There are a number of different views. They are worth considering not just from a historical point of view, but also because they raise important questions about the future viability of democracy in the Philippines.

One school of thought maintains that true popular democracy never really existed because of the political and economic dominance of the

U.S.-backed élite. Proponents of this view see the conditions resulting in martial law as having been caused by three related developments: an accelerating level of conflict within the élite, mostly over control of the economy; growing popular opposition to both the traditional élite and traditional politics; and the desire of the United States to protect its investments and military installations in the face of mounting nationalism. According to this view, martial law was the predictable reaction of the state to the dual threat of divisive intra-élite competition and mounting popular opposition.[25]

A second view argues that although an impressive effort was made to transplant democratic values and behaviour to the Philippines, democracy was never viable because of cultural and socio-economic conditions. The cultural conditions often cited include a natural predisposition to authoritarianism, excessive respect for hierarchy, and the predominance of kinship ties. The socio-economic conditions seen as being unconducive to democracy include the "feudal" nature of the society, the domination of the élite, and the pervasive poverty and inequality. According to one prominent proponent of this view at that time, the late Carlos Romulo:

> It became clear that the old order was no longer workable. Seventy-five years of experiment in classical Western democratic forms, it was sadly admitted, had failed and threatened disastrous consequences for the country unless a way could be found to restore its dynamism and vitality.[26]

A third and related view is that liberal democracy was a luxury a developing country like the Philippines could not afford. According to this view, the country's unruly democracy was responsible for many of its problems. Furthermore, democracy made it difficult, if not impossible to find solutions to many of these problems. Although not an advocate of martial law, William Overholt has accurately described the poor performance of the country's democratic institutions:

> The U.S. style judicial system, with an adversary process that emasculated the poor, and complex procedures that endlessly delayed decisions, could not cope with justice and crime.... Private weapons were more widespread than in any other country.... The democratic patronage system inhibited removal of corrupt and incompetent civil servants....Democracy directly

inhibited measures to ameliorate some of the world's worst social inequality ... and economic growth slackened.[27]

A fourth view maintains that democracy worked for a while, in an élite form, but could not survive either because of the heightened demands for broader political participation or because of the predations of the Filipinos themselves. The former is embraced by political scientist O.D. Corpuz who in 1971 pointed to a breakdown of consensus in Philippine society and the growing relevance and importance of the left. In the face of these disturbing developments, he wrote that traditional political parties were "utterly incapable of adopting and implementing a program of genuine socio-economic change".[28] The alternative "predatory" view is reflected in Lewis Gleeck's colourful description of Philippine society in 1972. According to Gleeck, traditional democracy was "tottering along in a kind of semi-anarchy as militant students, warlords and oligarchs' goons, bus and jeepney drivers, rice speculators and vicious media representatives repeatedly lamed, tormented and wounded it until it was moribund".[29]

Finally, there is a school of thought that maintains that an imperfect form of democracy was, on balance, working, and it was purposefully undermined by Marcos so that he could remain in power. According to political scientist David Wurfel:

> Filipino democratic institutions did not break down, either in the sense of an inability to maintain order or a failure to respond to changes within the society. The rising political violence after 1969 was to a considerable degree the creation of Marcos himself, first in trying to get himself re-elected and then in preparing a justification for martial law. And the legislation as well as the Constitutional Convention elections during the same period gave new opportunities to the under-privileged and under-represented to put their mark on political processes and government programmes. If allowed to complete its task, the Con Con would probably have produced a document that opened up government to new social forces on a permanent basis. It was a classic case of intra-élite conflict benefiting mass participation.[30]

This view is also shared by Resil Mojares, who has written:

> Widespread disaffection with traditional politics, with its anti-democratic orientation and neo-colonialist bias, had given rise

> to mass movements and politicized sectoral groups. . . . These
> groups exerted new pressures which promised to revise reigning
> political equations in the country. Invoked as an extraordinary
> measure 'to save democracy', martial law may in fact have come
> at that time when, for the first time, democracy was beginning
> to work.[31]

Each one of these schools of thought contains elements of truth, but not one is entirely correct. There were (and continue to be) important cultural and socio-economic impediments to democracy in the Philippines; but there was also a fairly strong tradition of commitment to the ideal, if not the practice, of democracy. Traditional democratic politics did not result in a government that made particularly rational or effective policies beneficial to the majority of Filipinos. But it was a system that even the poorest and most uneducated Filipino felt a part of. Paradoxically, although Philippine democracy was élitist, it was so personalized and idealized that tens of millions of Filipinos accepted the system with all its faults. And while élite rivalry had reached a feverish and irresponsible level, there remained strong adherents to democratic principles within the élite (although Marcos was not one of them).

In sum, at a minimum there was a considerable loss of faith in the ability of the existing democratic institutions to cope with the immediate and longer term challenges facing the country. But to the extent that there was a failure of democracy, it was a failure not of the institutions *per se*, but rather of the commitment of the political élite to make those institutions work. It is intriguing but futile to speculate if democracy could have survived. In the face of an extraordinary attack on it by Marcos, it would have taken equally extraordinary leadership and a national consensus to defend it. Both were lacking in 1972.

NOTES

1. Ferdinand Marcos, *Today's Revolution: Democracy* (Manila, 1971), p.iv.
2. Frank Golay, *The Philippines: Public Policy and National Economic Development* (Ithaca: Cornell University Press, 1968), p.416.

3. International Labour Organization, *Sharing in Development, A Programme of Employment, Equity and Growth for the Philippines* (Geneva and Manila: ILO, 1974), p.31.
4. Ibid., p.18.
5. David Wurfel, "Martial Law in the Philippines: The Methods of Regime Survival", *Pacific Affairs* 50, no.1 (Spring 1977):17.
6. Wilfredo Villacorta, "The Catholic Church in Contemporary Philippine Politics" (undated mimeograph), p.2.
7. James Rush, *The Philippine Church, Part 1*, Report No.31 (University Field Staff International, 1984), p.4.
8. Kit Machado, "Philippine Politics: Research 1960–1980: Areas for Future Exploration", in *Philippine Studies: Political Science, Economics and Linguistics*, edited by Donn Hart (Northern Illinois University Center for Southeast Asian Studies, Occasional Paper No.8, 1981), p.32.
9. Golay, op. cit., p.415.
10. Machado, op. cit., p.6.
11. Raul de Guzman, "Philippine Local Government: Issues, Problems and Trends", *Philippine Journal of Public Administration* 10, no.2–3 (April–July 1966):231.
12. Amando Doronila, "The Transformation of Patron-Client Relations and its Consequences in Postwar Philippines", *Journal of Southeast Asian Studies* 16, no.1 (March 1985):113–14.
13. Resil B. Mojares, *The Man Who Would be President: Serging Osmena and Philippine Politics* (Cebu: Maria Cacao Publishers, 1986), p.131.
14. William Chapman, *Inside the Philippine Revolution* (New York: W.W. Norton, 1987), p.77.
15. *Manila Chronicle*, 13 December 1987, p.18.
16. Mojares, op. cit., p.143.
17. Doronila, op. cit., p.115.
18. Reporter Gregg Jones convincingly shows that the communists were responsible for the Plaza Miranda bombing. His claim that the communists planned the bombing in order to trigger a political crisis beneficial to them is supported by Victor Corpuz. See Gregg Jones, *Red Revolution: Inside the Philippine Guerrilla Movement* (Boulder: Westview Press, 1989), chapter 5; and Victor Corpuz, *Silent War* (Manila: VNC Enterprises, 1989), pp.13–17.
19. Jose Abueva, "Ideology and Practice in the 'New Society'", in *Marcos and Martial Law in the Philippines*, edited by David Rosenberg (Ithaca: Cornell University Press, 1979), p.37.
20. Lewis Gleeck, Jr., *President Marcos and the Philippine Political Culture* (Manila: Loyal Printing, 1987), p.109.

21. William Overholt, "The Rise and Fall of Ferdinand Marcos", *Asian Survey* 26, no.11 (November 1986):1139.
22. Jones, op. cit., p.51.
23. Chapman, op. cit., p.91.
24. See Eduardo Lachica, *Huk: Philippine Agrarian Society in Revolt* (Manila: Solidaridad Publishing, 1971), pp.193–94.
25. See Stephen Shalom, *The United States and the Philippines: A Study of Neocolonialism* (Quezon City: New Day Publishers, 1986), pp.161–69.
26. Ferdinand Marcos, *The Democratic Revolution in the Philippines* (Manila: The Marcos Foundation, 1977), p.16.
27. Overholt, op. cit., p.1138.
28. O.D. Corpuz, "Political Trends in the Philippines", in *Trends in the Philippines*, edited by Lim Yoon Lin and M. Rajaretnam (Singapore: Institute of Southeast Asian Studies, 1972), p.50.
29. Gleeck, op. cit., p.98.
30. Wurfel, op. cit., p.5.
31. Mojares, op. cit., p.156.

PART TWO

The Authoritarian Experience, 1972–86

chapter 4

Authoritarianism and Its Impact

> Martial law, together with the New Society that has emerged from its reforms, is in fact a revolution of the poor, for it is aimed at protecting the individual, helpless until then, from the power of the oligarchs. Martial law was therefore a blow struck in the name of human rights.
>
> — Ferdinand Marcos, 1977[1]

The declaration of martial law on 22 September 1972 ended over a quarter century of robust, if often irresponsible and élitist, democratic politics. It began a period of more than thirteen years of one-man rule that included more than eight years of martial law (until January 1981), and five more years during which Marcos continued to exercise complete power under the amended 1973 Constitution.

Marcos's authoritarianism initially promised a dramatic departure from the fractious élite democracy that had preceded it. The divisions between the executive and legislative branches of the government that so often seemed to paralyse the government would be ended by the creation of a monolithic and omnipotent state (headed by Marcos, of course). The past emphasis on "pork-barrel" and patronage would be replaced by technocratic efficiency. The political and economic dominance of the traditional élite or "oligarchy" would be broken. Economic policies and programmes that enriched the few would be replaced by an economic development programme that would benefit the majority of poor Filipinos. Particularistic interests would be replaced by a new sense of national unity and purpose.

Yet, by the time the Marcos regime collapsed in early 1986 the country had suffered through several years of the worst political and economic crises in its history. The government had forfeited virtually all of its legitimacy and credibility; corruption and favouritism had spread throughout government and society like cancer; the economy had been ravaged by greed and mismanagement; the welfare of most Filipinos had declined significantly; the communist threat cited by Marcos as a reason for imposing martial law had grown ominously; and society was polarized as never before.

It is against the backdrop of the initial promise of martial law (and of Marcos as a leader) and its ultimately disastrous consequences, that the authoritarian experience will be viewed and assessed. The dismal condition of the Philippines at the end of the Marcos era is a powerful and indisputable indictment of the consequences of authoritarianism. Still, there are many important questions about the Marcos regime that need to be answered. What were the sources of support for authoritarianism? Why did it last as long as it did? What role did the military play? How violent and repressive was the regime? What explains the regime's rampant corruption and mismanagement of the economy? What caused the regime to collapse when it did?

Imposition of Martial Law

Martial law was publicly declared on 22 September 1972, but it was based on Presidential Decree No. 1081 dated 21 September. The declaration had an immediate and profound impact on political life. Beginning on the night of 22 September, according to an account by Jose Abueva:

> . . . the army closed down all radio and television stations and newspaper offices and arrested prominent publishers, journalists, and commentators critical of the president, including a few who were allegedly involved in a conspiracy against him and the government; several opposition senators, a number of opposition delegates to the Constitutional Convention, a governor, and a congressman known to be close to the president but suspected of arms smuggling; labor leaders; and thousands of activists

and protesters. Notorious criminals at large were rounded up. Checkpoints were established, and soldiers inspected all vehicles, padlocked the Congress building, and guarded the schools, which were closed down for a few weeks. . . .

The army next cracked down on the so-called "political warlords" and their "private armies" all over the country. A thorough and effective campaign for the surrender of privately held firearms yielded over half a million weapons, according to the president and the military. Military tribunals were created to process the martial law detainees. For months, news and rumors circulated about the arrest of suspected subversives and criminals. To dramatize the seriousness of law enforcement by the authorities, a convicted Chinese drug pusher was executed by a firing squad. Presidential decrees, orders, proclamations, and instructions issued forth in rapid succession, as if to underscore the will of the president, with the assistance of the military, to strengthen their control on the conduct of the citizenry. Some agencies, including a few strategic private enterprises and public utilities, were placed under military direction or supervision. Military intelligence spread its surveillance far and wide, especially in the colleges and universities, which had been well known for their radicalism. . . .[2]

Some 30,000 people were initially detained under martial law. The total number of detainees swelled to 50,000 before it rapidly declined. By 1975 it was estimated that some 6,000 people were still being detained. Most of the initial detainees were "traditional" opponents, such as Benigno Aquino and Jose Diokno, student and labour activists, and war-lords, and criminals. A number of Marcos's political opponents such as Sergio Osmeña, Jr., Raul Manglapus, and Jovito Salonga left the Philippines to escape arrest and detention. Few, if any, known communists were arrested at the outset of martial law, but soon after its imposition, the military began a series of successful offensives against communist guerrilla forces in the provinces north of Manila.

In late November 1972 the final draft of a new constitution, establishing a parliamentary form of government, was overwhelmingly approved by the now intimidated and acquiescent Constitutional Convention. By creating, at least on paper, a parliamentary system, the new document gave Marcos a constitutional basis for remaining in power beyond the expiration of his second term as president. Under the transitory provisions of the new constitution Marcos became both president and prime minister until such time as he decided to convene an Interim National Assembly (which he did not do until June 1978). The constitution's provisions effectively made Marcos's orders and decrees the law of the land, and stated that they would remain in effect even after the lifting of martial law.

The legitimacy of the new constitution was one of a number of issues voted on by a public show of hands in about 40,000 hastily convened citizens' assemblies held across the country in mid-January 1973. These meetings were held in lieu of a plebiscite required by the 1935 Constitution. Based on this haphazard and largely undocumented vote, Marcos announced on 16 January that the new constitution had been ratified by over 95 per cent of the population (hence it is referred to as the 1973 Constitution). He also announced that "the people" had decided that Congress should not be reconvened. In March 1973 the Supreme Court recognized its own impotence in the face of martial law by ruling in *Javellana vs Executive Secretary* that the new constitution "was not validly ratified in accordance with . . . the 1935 Constitution [but that] there is no further judicial obstacle to the new Constitution being considered in force and effect". Thus, within six months, the limited legal effort to challenge martial law was defeated and Marcos was able to claim that he was exercising "constitutional authoritarianism".

The Shifting Ideology of Authoritarianism

As a skilled lawyer, shrewd politician, and savvy statesman, Marcos made it a point to give authoritarianism a legal and ideological under-pinning. It is impossible to know exactly how much Marcos believed his own ideological pronouncements. It is possible that some of his statements reflect a genuine ideological commitment, particularly at the outset. But many of them clearly were self-serving and used to generate domestic support and blunt foreign criticism.

Over the nearly fourteen years of authoritarianism the ideological justification for one-man rule shifted, reflecting the changing interests and objectives of the regime as well as the changing conditions within the country. Ultimately, the justification for the regime came full circle from 1972 to 1985–86. By 1985 Marcos was making the same claim he had made in 1972 – that he was the only leader capable of saving the Philippine government and society from crisis and civil war.

Marcos, writing in 1981 about the situation in 1972, totally rejected the idea that constitutional democracy could have survived and functioned. He wrote:

> When one looks back in contemplation of the choices laid before the country – the alternatives to martial law – the following possibilities come to mind. A rightist coup would have brought with it violence at the outset, reconstitution and reinforcement of the established political and economic order, and a feigned attempt at social reform. The election of the Liberal Party with Aquino as President would have been followed by the declaration of martial law and the subsequent strengthening of the exploitative oligarchical order. A communist takeover would have meant revolutionary violence, a totalitarian regime, a complete uprooting of the social order, and the loss of individual freedoms.[3]

As this passage indicates, Marcos and the supporters of martial law portrayed the Philippines as a nation in the midst of a grave crisis. They claimed that the democratically-elected government and the nation's democratic institutions were under attack, primarily by the communists, and secondarily, by conservative extremists within the traditional "oligarchy". They further claimed that the traditional methods of democratic government and politics were unable to cope with these extremist challenges. Therefore, martial law was necessary to cope with the national crisis and defend Philippine democracy from threats from the left and the right.

Although Marcos discounted the future of traditional democracy in the Philippines, he also rejected the notion that martial law meant the end to constitutionalism or the beginning of military rule. From the beginning of martial law until his final "inauguration" in February 1986 Marcos sought to cloak his authoritarian regime in a veil of constitutionality and legality – what he called "constitutional authoritarianism". He sought to establish and then maintain the legitimacy – or at least the nominal legality – of his regime through a series of five referenda and plebiscites between 1973 and 1981. These exercises included referenda in 1973 and 1975 that "approved" the continuation of martial law; a constitutional plebiscite in 1976 that approved Amendment 6, which gave Marcos the power to legislate by decree; a 1977 referendum that allowed Marcos to serve as both president and prime minister of the Interim Batasang Pambansa (National Assembly); and a 1981 constitutional plebiscite that approved a variety of amendments designed to maintain Marcos's power following the formal end of martial law.

These referenda and plebiscites were all, to greater or lesser degrees, carefully managed by the government. The government unilaterally determined the types of questions that were asked and tallied the responses. It also controlled the media and restricted public debate and the presentation of opposing views. Consequently, while these referenda initially provided some legitimacy to the regime, over time they became less and less credible. And with each additional revision of the constitution it became more evident that Marcos was simply adjusting the document to fit his needs and interests, like a man having his favourite pair of slacks taken in and let out in response to his changing waistline.

Martial law was portrayed as the beginning of a revolution in Philippine politics and society. But, according to Marcos, it would be a "revolution from the centre", by which he meant both the centre of the political spectrum (as opposed to the extreme left and right), and the centre of society, which he saw as the state. In other words, it would be a revolution that he controlled. Martial law was also "revolutionary" in its professed desire to change Filipino values and behaviour. Marcos claimed that martial law would replace the Filipino's self-interest with national interest, passivity with action, and inferiority with self-confidence. According to Jose Abueva: "The intended changes are summarized in the term *disiplina* (discipline), which was the ubiquitous early exhortation and warning of martial law authorities".[4]

Marcos also cultivated the image that he was a populist, as the quote at the outset of this chapter shows. He claimed that his policies were, for the first time in Philippine history, for the benefit of the masses rather than the traditional élite. His professed commitment to economic and governmental reform did generate considerable initial public support and was particularly important in mobilizing the commitment of the "technocrats" of the public planning sector and the entrepreneurs of the private business sector to the New Society.[5]

By September 1976 the government was claiming widespread success in restoring peace and order, culminating in the capture of two top leaders of the communist New People's Army and the signing of the Tripoli Agreement that promised to defuse the Muslim insurgency. In the absence of a potent threat to the Marcos regime's security, "developmental authoritarianism" became the dominant ideological justification for the perpetuation of martial law. Marcos increasingly based his regime's legitimacy on its ability to promote national economic development. In 1980 he wrote:

> The credibility of government does not turn on our having periodic elections, not on the working of an uninhibited press, but on what the government means to the people. The credibility of government is determined by the jobs and opportunities, such as education and social services it makes available to the poor.[6]

Unstated in this quote was the key corollary proposition that development required a powerful government and political stability that came only with continued authoritarianism.

Developmental authoritarianism remained the operative ideology until it was completely undermined by the realities of the economic crisis of the early 1980s. Consequently, by 1983 Marcos's justification for continued authoritarianism had reverted to that used a decade before: the communist insurgency and economic problems were so great that only someone of his experience could possibly lead the country and solve its pressing problems. For more than a decade, then, the rationales for authoritarianism shifted, and ultimately came full circle. But the dictator remained the same.

Initial Impact of Martial Law

The imposition of martial law caused the immediate, dramatic, and unprecedented curtailment of civil liberties in the Philippines. The Congress was closed; real or potential opponents were arrested, or forced to go underground, or leave the country; political activities were banned; and the media were silenced. These changes were just the beginning of a process that resulted in a major, and ultimately disastrous, reshaping of Philippine society and politics.

For the first three or four years of martial law, however, an argument could be made that the benefits of authoritarianism outweighed the loss of democratic freedoms. Initially, martial law provided stability and hope where previously there had been conflict and uncertainty. According to William Overholt:

> the vast majority of Philippine society strongly supported Marcos. Most of the rest acquiesced in his reforms. Most people were convinced that Philippine democracy could not in any case long survive the perpetuation of crime, inequality, poverty and incoherent economic policy.[7]

This section describes the major changes initially wrought by martial law.

Concentration of Power in Marcos

Martial law resulted in the unprecedented centralization of state power in the executive branch, and specifically in the hands of Ferdinand Marcos. All authority flowed from Malacañang, the presidential palace, expanding dramatically the tradition of centralized government in the Philippines. Marcos became responsible for all law-making and all important administrative and judicial decisions as well. All government expenditures were determined by the executive branch. All local officials, judges, ambassadors, and military officers served at the president's pleasure.

The centralization of authority in the office of the president was illustrated by the scope of responsibilities of Marcos's Executive Secretary, Alejandro Melchor. According to the *Far Eastern Economic Review*, Melchor was responsible for

> everything from the general strategy for countering the Muslim insurgency to programming the development of non-petroleum sources of power generation. Melchor coordinated the development of the heavy industrial zone in Northern Mindanao, as well as the development of urban renewal for Manila's slums. He was in charge of the dam projects in Northern Luzon and bridges in the Southern-most island of Tawi-Tawi. . . . Foreign embassies considered his opinion on diplomatic matters of more consequence than any opinion coming from the Department of Foreign Affairs.[8]

Marcos centralized his control by making a variety of significant administrative changes. These changes were made in the name of increasing government efficiency. But they also strengthened the Marcos government's control over national affairs and helped to balance his dependency on the military.[9] These changes included:

1. grouping the country's 73 provinces into 13 administrative regions;
2. creating a Department of Local Government to oversee the activities of local government;
3. forming the Metro Manila Commission to co-ordinate the policies and activities of the 12 cities surrounding Manila;
4. creating a Ministry of Human Settlements (MHS) to oversee Imelda Marcos's various social programmes;
5. reorganizing the Philippine Constabulary (PC) into 13 Regional Unified Commands (RUCs); and
6. organizing the local police into an Integrated National Police (INP) force under the control of the PC.

Following, as it did, years of bickering, inefficiency, and corruption within the government, the centralization of power in the executive held the promise of quick decision-making, rational planning, and effective implementation. And at first it appeared that this promise would be realized.

Emasculation of the Traditional Élite

Claiming that he sought to smash the self-serving power of the traditional élite or "oligarchs", Marcos moved quickly to weaken the political and economic power bases of his rivals. The greater the perceived threat they presented to his regime, the fiercer was his attack. Consequently, he stripped wealthy families such as the Lopezes (the powerful clan of his vice-president) and the Jacintos of most of their assets. He jailed or exiled political rivals and forced other, less threatening families to divest some of their assets, but not so much that they lost their stake in the new order.

Many of the policies implemented by the Marcos government had the intended effect of weakening the traditional élite. Marcos's land reform programme broke up large rice and corn landholdings. The government took over two of the most important sources of élite wealth — sugar and copra procurement and marketing — and improved tax collection. It issued decrees forcing certain family-owned corporations to go public. Finally, local élites were also stripped of virtually all their local power and autonomy by the centralization of the national government, increased influence of the military, and the elimination of local elections, traditionally their source of leverage *vis-à-vis* the national government.[10]

An Enlarged Role for the Military

Disdainful and untrusting of the government bureaucracy, Marcos needed another national institution to enforce and administer his policies. He naturally looked to the military, which was not "tainted" by traditional politics or closely associated with the traditional political élite. Moreover, in the event that he encountered opposition to martial law, he needed the armed forces' fire-power to enforce his decrees. He also saw the military's organization, discipline, and efficiency as an antidote to many of the weaknesses which he felt afflicted Philippine society.

Marcos, therefore, carefully cultivated the military, gave it new responsibilities, and entered into an interdependent relationship with it. Officers were promoted for reasons of political loyalty, and loyal generals were allowed to extend their service. The size of the Armed Forces of the Philippines (AFP) more than doubled between 1972 and 1976 (the height of the Muslim insurgency) from 62,715 men to 142,450 men. Appropriations grew from P900 million in 1972 (1.7 per cent of GNP) to P6.9 billion (5.2 per cent of GNP) in 1976.[11]

One of the first tasks of the military after the declaration of martial law was to restore order. A national curfew was imposed and 500,000 guns allegedly were collected. But the military's efforts to disarm the civilian population also triggered the intensification of hostilities by the Muslims in the south. This began a bloody conflict between the AFP and Muslim secessionists in the south that would rage for more than four years.

The role of the military, however, quickly went well beyond preserving law and order. The military's National Intelligence and Security Authority (NISA) grew into a full-blown national intelligence network while Marcos's private security force, the Presidential Security Guard (PSG), also dramatically increased in size and power. In 1975 the Integrated National Police was fused into the Philippine Constabulary, removing the control of the police from civilian officials. In addition to this, military officers replaced many civilian officials at the national and local levels. According to Francisco Nemenzo:

> The Armed Forces of the Philippines assumed judicial powers through the military tribunals which had jurisdiction over a wide range of cases. Officers in active service were named to sensitive diplomatic posts. A number of colonels and generals were appointed to the directorates and management staffs of developmental agencies and government-controlled corporations. Two provincial commanders became concurrent provincial governors. . . . With the civilian politicians sidelined, the local commanders became the chief dispensers of political patronage.[12]

Finally, the military also assumed a new and important role in the economy. A series of presidential decrees and letters of instruction gave the military administrative power over the media, public utilities, and other government-controlled companies. Industries such as the steel industry were deemed to be important to national security and were placed under military supervision.[13] The influential positions occupied by many senior military officers provided them with opportunities for graft and corruption. According to two students of the military, "Prime real estate, imposing residences, luxury cars, high living and other forms of conspicuous consumption indicated a lifestyle which only Marcos loyalists within the military could affect."[14]

At the same time that Marcos expanded the role of the military, he was also careful to keep it from becoming too powerful. According to political scientist Richard Kessler:

> During his first two terms in office, a strong military was an important counterbalance to his political opposition, but after eliminating his political opposition with martial law, the military became the greatest threat to his power. Thus, he followed a policy of divide and conquer.[15]

By employing this policy, Marcos succeeded in keeping the military both under his control and loyal until the mid-1980s. But by playing off one military group against another he also created a high degree of factionalism that eventually contributed to his downfall and threaten to do the same to the Aquino government.

Rise of the Technocrats

The technocrats were, after the military, the second key group in the early martial law years. They were Western-educated economists and managers who were without independent political bases and political ambitions. They included Rafael Salas, Alejandro Melchor, Cesar Virata, Vicente Paterno, and Jaime Laya. They were, for the most part, among the "best and the brightest" the Philippines had to offer.

Marcos was not the first Philippine president to include techno-crats in his Cabinet, but the centralization of power under martial law gave them unprecedented authority – at least during the first few years. The relatively greater expertise and influence of the tech-nocrats resulted in improved government financial planning; increased revenue collection; larger and somewhat better planned national development programmes; increased rice production under the Ma-sagana 99 programme; and the introduction of a national family planning programme.

Perhaps equally important, the participation of these internationally known and respected managers in the martial law government gave the regime considerable credibility with the domestic and international business communities, foreign governments, and international de-velopment and commercial banks. The technocrats spoke the same language as foreign officials, their plans and presentations were impressive, and they were confident that they would succeed. For the first several years it appeared that they might.

Rapid Economic Growth

Thanks to increases in international commodity prices, and guided, in part, by the technocrats, the Philippine economy posted generally impressive growth until 1978. In 1973 GNP grew by 10 per cent and there was a current account surplus. In 1975 there was an investment boom and 1976 was notable for some success in controlling inflation. Exports grew dramatically in 1973 and 1974 and by 1977 the country had successfully begun to diversify its exports to include garments, electronic goods, and non-traditional agricultural products such as bananas. Overall, from 1972 to 1977 the economy sustained real GNP growth that averaged over 6.5 per cent per annum, despite the oil crisis, world inflation, and a recession in the major developed economies. This steady growth, coupled with a slight slowing of the population growth rate (from a five-year average of about 3 per cent to about 2.7 per cent) resulted in an average annual expansion of per capita GNP of almost 3.9 per cent from 1972 to 1977.[16]

During the first years of martial law agriculture benefited from extensive infrastructure development (particularly irrigation and electrification), cheap credit, and subsidized fertilizer prices under the Masagana 99 programme, and good weather conditions. The result was an average annual increase in agricultural value-added of 5 per cent between 1972 and 1976 and the achievement of rice self-sufficiency for the first time ever in 1976.

Marcos's second martial law declaration proclaimed that the entire country was subject to land reform. A subsequent decree, Presidential Decree No. 27 (PD 27), issued in October 1972, began a process of land reform that promised to transfer ownership of tenanted rice and corn lands to those who tilled the land. The programme set a retention limit of 7 hectares, but it exempted the country's many large sugar and coconut holdings on the questionable grounds that economies of scale are needed with these crops. It began by redistributing the largest landholdings, and within two years most holdings of 24 hectares or more had been redistributed. At this point, however, the programme began to meet the resistance of the small landowners, many of whom were government officials, teachers, and other members of the middle class who had invested their savings in land.

The early economic policies of Marcos were well received by a number of key groups. The urban middle class and the co-opted members of the traditional élite generally benefited from the growth and diversification of the economy. Although limited to rice and corn lands, PD 27 held out to the small tenant farmer the promise of land ownership. Domestic and foreign investors and international bankers appreciated the improvements in law and order, the government's receptiveness to foreign investment, and the marginal improvement in government efficiency. The ambitious multi-year development plans of the technocrats impressed international development agencies like the World Bank and the United States Agency for International Development (USAID).

At the same time, however, there were a number of causes for concern. The manufacturing sector posted moderate growth, but did not generate enough new jobs to absorb the rapidly growing urban labour force. The surplus of labour, combined with government policies designed to control wages, resulted in declining real wages for most Filipinos. Moreover, in an effort to manage economic growth and development, the government increased its regulation of and intervention in the economy. Finally, the Marcos government also began to rely on external borrowings to finance its infrastructure expenditures, which were creating increasingly large budget deficits. Initially, the reliance on borrowing made sense, for between 1974 and 1978 the interest rates charged were low, and even negative after deducting for inflation.[17] But it established a dependency on borrowing that the government was unable to reduce in later years, when interest rates shot up. These and other problems eventually would come back to haunt, and ultimately ruin, the Philippine economy.

Impact on the Communist Movement

In late 1972, when Marcos cited the threats of communist revolution and Muslim secession as the primary reasons for declaring martial law, there were about 1,000 armed members of the communist New People's Army (NPA) operating in central and northern Luzon and parts of Mindanao, and perhaps 14,000 armed Muslims in Southern Mindanao. The imposition of martial law temporarily set back the military expansion of the communist insurgency, but it caused the simmering discontent of the Muslims in the south to burst into open revolt.

The declaration of martial law both helped and hurt the communists. First, there was a surge in membership as many political and social activists (some of whom were not necessarily communists) were forced to go "underground" in the cities or "into the hills" in the countryside. The increase in party membership was so great following the declaration of martial law that the CPP and NPA had to turn recruits away because of an inability to train and arm them.

In response to the new political opportunities and challenges created by martial law, the CPP founded the National Democratic Front (NDF) in April 1973. The NDF sought to build a "popular front" of "progressive" groups opposed to the Marcos regime. It became reponsible for most urban organization and propaganda work, and sought to penetrate and influence non-communist organizations including labour unions and Catholic Church social action organizations.

But the CPP and NPA had difficulty in further expanding their membership following the initial surge. There was hardly any net growth of the party or the NPA between 1973 and 1976, during which time party membership remained stagnant at about 3,000 people, of which about half were NPA regulars.[18] Martial law also damaged the communists' urban movement, which had depended on many now-banned "front organizations" such as labour unions and student groups. During the first four years of martial law the NPA, which established a Maoist "base area" in Isabela province north of Metro Manila, was pursued doggedly by government troops and suffered serious military set-backs at their hands.[19] The communists were dealt two more blows when NPA chief Bernabe Buscayno, also known as Kumander Dante, was captured in 1976, and CPP founder and leader Jose Ma. Sison was captured in November 1977.

Effect on Muslim Secessionism

Marcos declared martial law at a time when there was growing discontent among the more than two million Muslim Filipinos living on the islands of Mindanao, the Sulu chain, and Palawan. The Muslims had never been fully integrated into the Philippine nation, and they felt long ignored and often insulted by the predominantly Christian government in far away Manila. Their resentment had been intensified by the national government's policies during the 1950s encouraging Christian migration to the Muslim areas of Mindanao. This triggered an increase in bitter land disputes, and ultimately left the Muslims as a majority in only three provinces in the south.

By the late 1960s growing Christian–Muslim animosity had produced a series of bloody incidents between heavily armed groups on both sides. Government forces in Mindanao, at best, were unable to control the mounting violence and, at worst, sided with the Christian

groups. The mounting violence and insecurity led to severe disloca-
tions in some parts of Mindanao. By the end of 1971 there were at
least 100,000 refugees in Cotabato and Lanao provinces, most of
whom were Muslim.[20] The conflict was further intensified and complicated by traditional political and ethnic rivalries, and by religious
and generational differences among the various Muslim groups.

The imposition of martial law, and in particular the military's collection of personal weapons, ignited the long simmering discontent of
many Muslims. In late 1972 the secessionist Moro National Liberation
Front (MNLF) and its military arm, the Bangsa Moro Army (BMA),
were formed by Nur Musuari, a former professor of political science.
The armed forces of the MNLF, which grew to some 20,000 by 1975,
fiercely fought the AFP, using a combination of conventional and
guerrilla tactics.

By 1975 about three-quarters of the AFP's combat troops were
deployed in Mindanao, creating an uneasy military stalemate. But
politically, the MNLF was successful at bringing the Filipino Muslims'
grievances to the attention of influential Muslim oil-producing countries (such as Libya and Saudi Arabia) and the Organization of Islamic
Conference (OIC). This pressure, and the growth of the communist
insurgency in other parts of the country, forced Marcos in 1976 to
enter into peace negotiations with the MNLF under the auspices of
Libyan leader Moammar Gadhafi. In December 1976 Imelda Marcos
visited Libya and signed the Tripoli Agreement, which called for an
immediate cessation of all hostilities and pledged "autonomy" for
thirteen provinces in Southern Mindanao and Palawan. But the next
year, in what the MNLF claimed was a breach of the agreement,
Marcos held a referendum on the agreement. As ten of the thirteen
provinces were predominantly Christian, the agreement was rejected.
The situation in Mindanao deteriorated again.

Creation of a Filipino Ideology?

Ferdinand Marcos sought to engender a new sense of nationalism
among Filipinos, in part to co-opt the nationalist fervour that had
been on the rise prior to the imposition of martial law. He supported
his nationalist rhetoric by broadening and balancing somewhat the
nation's foreign relations and allowing Imelda Marcos to become a

prominent figure at international gatherings. But Marcos also sought to manipulate and channel nationalism to further his own ends – to foster support for his regime and strengthen his position *vis-à-vis* the United States. Other nationalistic forces that did not share his particular vision, such as leftist student organizations and labour unions, were outlawed, emasculated or co-opted.

The "New Society" Marcos sought to create was based on an ideology that emphasized individual and national discipline and the sacrifice of personal liberties for economic development. Martial law, he claimed, was a "revolution from the centre" that would create a more unified, prosperous, and egalitarian nation, and one that Filipinos could take new pride in.

For roughly the first five years of the martial law regime – until 1977 – it looked to many as if Marcos's grandiose promises were more than just rhetoric. Law and order were restored, though at the expense of civil and political rights. The military appeared to have the communist insurgents on the run, and a peaceful settlement of the Muslim conflict seemed to be in prospect. The economy registered healthy growth and apparently weathered the first "oil shock" fairly well. The government's national development efforts were centralized under the control of an impressive group of technocrats and land reform was being implemented. In the wake of the American defeat in Vietnam an effort was made to diversify Manila's foreign relations to include China and the socialist bloc. For all these reasons, Marcos's claim that he and he alone could lead the country down the path to the "New Society" was believed by many, though certainly not all, Filipinos.

After 1977, however, the promise of a Marcosian "New Society" began to fade quickly. The regime's rhetoric diverged from the increasingly grim reality, and ultimately Marcos's persistent promise of a "New Society" became instead a perverse and painful joke. It is this decline that we now examine.

Subsequent Impact of Marcos's Rule

The Marcos regime's initial gains could not be sustained. The over-centralized national government began to atrophy. In the absence of any accountablity, government policies affecting the entire nation were increasingly shaped by narrow self-interest. Favouritism and venality became rampant. The economy began to reveal the effects of mounting corruption and mismanagement.

Ironically, the regime's weaknesses and failures became more pronounced at about the same time that Marcos permitted a partial, though still tightly controlled, resumption of political activity. In 1978 Marcos began a process of political "normalization" designed to establish an acceptable (at least to him and his foreign supporters) institutional and political framework that would permit the lifting of martial law. The first step was the election and convening of a powerless Interim Batasang Pambansa in 1978. This was followed by local elections in 1980, and finally, in 1981, by the lifting of martial law and a sham presidential election.

Despite the rhetoric of political "normalization", the 1978 Batasan elections demonstrated that Marcos was not prepared to tolerate meaningful parliamentary opposition to his regime. In Metro Manila, where Imelda Marcos was leading the pro-Marcos slate, ballot-box stuffing, vote buying, and other "anomalies" were used to defeat the entire slate of 21 opposition Laban Party candidates led by the still-imprisoned Benigno Aquino. Only 13 oppositionists in the Visayas and 1 in Mindanao won seats.

Possessing lots of money and being the only national political party at the time, the supporters of Marcos also triumphed in the 1980 local elections. The dominance of the Marcos machine and continuing divisions within the opposition prompted a fairly successful boycott movement during the 1981 presidential election. It was not until the 1984 Batasan elections, after the assassination of Benigno Aquino, that a significant portion of the opposition would again participate in a Marcos-dominated electoral exercise.

Over-Centralization of Executive Power

In the absence of any institutional checks and balances, Ferdinand Marcos (and increasingly his ambitious and extravagant wife, Imelda) came to control virtually every important aspect of Philippine government and society. One leading Filipino businessman later likened government ministries under Marcos to the spokes of a wheel, with Marcos as the hub. All the spokes were attached to the hub but none of them knew what the others were doing. As the government became more centralized under Marcos the number of spokes grew, making it impossible for Malacañang to effectively manage and control everything.

First Lady Imelda Marcos increasingly participated in the accumulation of power, and as she did her husband's vaunted technocrats were increasingly by-passed. In 1975 she was appointed governor of Metro Manila, the new conglomeration of eleven cities making up the metropolitan Manila area. In 1978 she was made head of the Ministry of Human Settlements, a "super ministry" created to fund and administer her hodgepodge of pet "human development" projects. In addition to holding these positions, Mrs Marcos often conducted high-profile diplomatic missions on behalf of her husband. She was also the driving force behind expensive cultural and medical projects in Metro Manila, such as the Philippine Cultural Center. According to one informed estimate, by 1981 she was controlling public and private funds equal to 50 per cent of the total government budget, much of it sucked from other ministries' programmes and administered with little accountability.[21]

Malacañang Palace, as we have seen, also asserted its control over provincial and local government. The 1975 referendum gave Marcos the authority to reappoint or replace all provincial and local officials whose elective terms had expired in December 1973. Marcos also established the *barangay* as the smallest unit of local government. The *barangay*, like the barrio that preceded them, consisted of the inhabitants of a small rural village or, in urban areas, a neighbourhood. The *barangay* was created ostensibly to broaden citizen participation in the "New Society". But instead of creating an upward flow of political participation and ideas, the result of these actions was a downward flow of central government authority. Provincial and local governments became nothing more than agencies for implementing national policy.[22]

These and other policies prompted Jose Abueva to write in 1976:

> Political and economic initiative continues to come from the center. Not only is the Marcos regime concentrating and mobilizing wealth, it is also concentrating and mobilizing other instruments of political power, in particular the military, the mass media,

and foreign resources. These instruments of political power constitute a technologically modernized form of élite domination.[23]

The concentration of power in the hands of the Marcoses, however, did not translate automatically into a stable institutional base for the regime. To create this, in 1978 Marcos formed the New Society Movement (Kilusang Bagong Lipunan or KBL), a national political party-cum-machine. The KBL's membership included government bureaucrats, members of the business community, and the thousands of local leaders annointed by Marcos.[24] The combination of Marcos's leadership, large amounts of money at its disposal, and control of both the national and local government apparatus made the KBL a formidable political machine in its early years.

The KBL was formed in advance of the April 1978 elections for the Interim Batasang Pambansa. Despite the convening of the 200-seat assembly, the power and cohesiveness of the government remained rooted in the person of Marcos and not in institutions or laws. Under Amendment 6 of the 1973 Constitution Marcos was empowered to legislate by decree, even after the assembly convened. The KBL became another vehicle (along with the military and *barangay* councils) for Marcos and his followers to manipulate the partial resumption of local politics.

By the late 1970s the regime had a shrinking base of organized mass support. And in the event of the demise of Marcos, there was no established procedure for succession. More and more, Marcos depended on his ability to control or retain the support of key groups, particularly the military, government bureaucrats, local officials, international lenders and investors, and the U.S. Government.[25] By the early 1980s the government's ability to provide basic services to the countryside had deteriorated because of the lack of government funds, corruption, and the growing presence of the NPA. The over-centralized government increasingly became like a paralysed octopus, whose tentacles had a frozen stranglehold on local government.

Decline of Judicial Independence

While Marcos used military tribunals for the trial of "subversives" until the end of martial law in 1981, he retained the civilian judicial system, in part to maintain the illusion that his regime respected the law. In reality, however, the decline of judicial independence began shortly after the declaration of martial law, when the Supreme Court declared that although the 1973 Constitution had not been validly ratified, there was "no judicial obstacle to its implementation".

Shortly after he declared martial law Marcos ordered all judges except those on the Supreme Court to submit letters of resignation. These were held by Marcos until the passage of a Judiciary Reorganization Act in 1983. Thus, according to the Lawyers Committee for Human Rights, "for over a decade the nation's judges rendered decisions under the pervasive threat of removal".[26] With the reorganization in 1983 every sitting judge owed his or her appointment to Marcos, prompting the Lawyers Committee to note in 1985, "the effects of that debt are evident in the quality of judicial performance".[27]

Judicial authority was particularly constrained in the area of human rights. Even after the formal end of martial law in 1981 Marcos maintained the right to arrest and detain anyone considered to be a "subversive" without warrant or trial under Presidential Detention Authorizations (PDAs). In 1985 the Supreme Court ordered the release on bail of two people detained under PDAs. But, according to the Lawyers Committee:

> This modest assertion of power ran up against an unflinching military, which refused to release the two detainees. Minister of Defense Enrile asserted that "Only the President can lift the PDA". President Marcos finally ordered the two temporarily released on the grounds that they "no longer pose any appreciable danger to national security and public order". His action left no uncertainty that he continued to regard himself, and not the nation's highest court, as the only authority empowered to release persons held persuant to a PDA.[28]

Destruction of Democratic Institutions and Politics

Besides emasculating the judiciary, Ferdinand Marcos destroyed all of the other traditional checks and balances in Philippine politics. He effectively abolished traditional political institutions (such as the Congress and political parties); he brought under his control other important institutions such as the once respected Commission on Elections (COMELEC); and he created new institutions to give the appearance of democracy, such as the Interim Batasang Pambansa and local *barangay* governments. He also restricted most other forms of political participation (such as student demonstrations and labour strikes), and controlled and manipulated the media.

Not surprisingly, there was a significant curtailment of political pluralism and participation. As political scientist Kit Machado has noted:

> some institutional positions and power bases that formerly gave individuals influence were eliminated or undermined, and some new ones emerged. Some groups were suppressed or had their autonomy reduced. Others emerged under state sponsorship. Uncontrolled mass participation was greatly restricted. The number of individuals and groups able to influence the political process became smaller, and the points of access became fewer.[29]

For the first five years of martial law the only options open to the traditional opposition were silence, co-optation, fleeing the country, or going underground. Until 1978 traditional political parties − never organizationally strong to begin with − continued to exist, but in little more than name only. With the traditional opposition broken and silenced, the relative influence of the radical left, which was already underground, increased.

Another consequence was that "the defunct democratic patronage system no longer ameliorated strong conflicts among ethnic and regional groups, so regional antagonisms surfaced with a vengeance".[30] The residents of Ferdinand Marcos's home province of Ilocos Norte and of Imelda Marcos's home province of Leyte benefited from a disproportionate share of infrastructure projects and government jobs.[31] Conversely, the provinces of political rivals, such as Tarlac, the home of Benigno Aquino, were often denied government largess. Most of the resource-rich island of Mindanao was at best ignored, and at worst exploited, by the national government.

Politicization and Deterioration of the Military

In the years from 1972 to 1985 the size of the Armed Forces of the Philippines more than doubled. But starting in the late 1970s, because of budget constraints and the politicization of the military leadership, the quality and effectiveness of the AFP began to deteriorate — at the same time that the communist insurgency was growing and becoming more sophisticated.

Between 1972 and 1985 the size of the AFP, including the Philippine Constabulary, increased 2.5 times, from 62,715 to 159,466. The paramilitary Civilian Home Defense Force (CHDF) grew from 200 in 1972 to 35,000 in 1979.[32] The Presidential Security Command (PSC) and military intelligence services were also dramatically expanded. Appropriations for the military increased by a factor of seven, from P879.4 million to P6.132 billion.

The buildup of the military was most marked between 1972 and 1976, reflecting the imposition of martial law and the intensification of the Muslim insurgency. Expenditures then flattened out and were a déclining percentage of the national budget from 1977 until 1981. Significantly, military expenditures did not rise dramatically from 1982 to 1985, despite the dramatic increase in the strength of the NPA. As a result, by 1986 military pay was, in real terms, 38 per cent to 45 per cent less than 1972 levels, even though nominal pay had risen by over 300 per cent. By 1985 the average appropriation per soldier had declined to less than one-third of the level in 1977 and two-fifths of the 1972 level.[33] The result was poor training and professionalism; inadequate food, health care, and supplies; and shoddy or non-existent equipment.

As the AFP grew in size, the definition of its mission in society also expanded dramatically. Its role in administering martial law has already been noted. In addition to this, according to the *Far Eastern Economic Review*, "Normal constabulary duties became confused with counter-insurgency, and the Integrated National Police, the civilian police force, became subordinate to military direction. Even the country's fire-fighting services and prison custodial guards were put under military control".[34] In the early 1980s the AFP also became responsible for administering government development programmes such as the huge P3 billion Kilusang Kabahayan at Kaunlaran (KKK) livelihood project.

As Marcos's base of public support began to erode, he increasingly relied on a small group of his most loyal generals. In 1981 Marcos selected General Fabian Ver, his cousin and former bodyguard, as Chief of Staff over General Fidel Ramos, a West Point-trained "professional". In 1983 General Ver created the Regional Unified Command (RUC) system, which made all regional commanders report directly to him, effectively excluding both Defence Minister Enrile and Vice-Chief of Staff Ramos from the chain of command. The ascendance of General Ver – particularly given the absence of an established mechanism for presidential succession – sharpened factional differences within the military and signalled that what mattered was political connections, not professionalism.

These factors combined to cause a gradual deterioration in the AFP's fighting capabilities after 1976. This deterioration, however, did not become obvious until the end of the decade, when the NPA's fighting capabilities improved significantly. The AFP's decline became painfully apparent to the junior officers who bore the burden of fighting the insurgency with poorly trained and paid troops, shoddy equipment, and inadequate supplies. It was these officers, far removed from the intrigues of the capital, who were most directly affected by factionalism, unprofessionalism, and corruption of the senior military leadership. Many of these disenchanted junior officers eventually became the key players in the February 1986 revolt against Marcos and in subsequent attempts to unseat the Aquino government.

Mounting Human Rights Violations

The government and the media it controlled sought to portray the Marcos regime as practising "authoritarianism with a human face". By 1980, for example, the Marcos government boasted that there were less than 1,000 political prisoners in its jails. It pointed out that political opposition was tolerated and Marcos had ordered the execution of only one person since the imposition of martial law, a notorious Chinese drug peddler.

While it is true that the Marcos regime was relatively less brutal than some authoritarian regimes, it is also true that the "human face" of martial law masked many inhumane activities. From the outset Marcos relied on a sophisticated and subtle mix of real and threatened harrassment, intimidation and violence. This ranged from legal, financial, and personal harrassment by the government, to revoking passports and other travel rights, to threatening arrest and imprisonment, to detention, torture, and murder. It appears that initially the more extreme and violent abuses of human rights were not widespread or systematically undertaken by the government, particularly in urban areas. But by the late 1970s, the situation began to change for the worse.

The increase in serious human rights violations in the late 1970s was caused by a convergence of several factors. At the top of the list was the deterioration and growing incompetence of the government security forces including the army, constabulary and paramilitary Civilian Home Defence Force. Accustomed to being the enforcers of martial law, the security forces tended to view the Filipino people with suspicion and hostility. Any opposition to the government was interpreted as being "subversive", as was any effort to redress the country's growing social problems through non-governmental channels. The influential and increasingly critical Catholic Church was also viewed with great suspicion.

Other important forces were also at work. First, the communist rebels were gaining the support and assistance of increasing numbers of people in the rural areas. They were also procuring more weapons and becoming more sophisticated and dangerous in their military capabilities. The combination of political and military success by the CPP and NPA posed a serious challenge to the government and the armed forces – a challenge that few officers or local government officials were willing or able to combat effectively.

At the same time, as the national government began to suffer financial problems in the early 1980s, political control at the provincial and local levels increasingly reverted to pro-Marcos politicians, many of whom were prepared to use intimidation and violence to preserve their positions. There had been plenty of political violence before martial law, especially at the local level. But under Marcos the local "warlords" were not subjected to the scrutiny of a free press or the threat of legal action by an independent judiciary. They were accountable only to Marcos, and they had little to worry about as long as they helped to preserve his position.

These factors led to the gradual escalation in political violence in the late 1970s and following the lifting of martial law in 1981, particularly in remote rural areas where government control was being challenged by the insurgents.[35] The major types of abuses included the following:

1. Arbitrary arrest and preventive detention of opponents of the regime. Using Presidential Commitment Orders (PCOs) and Presidential Detention Authorizations (PDAs) Marcos and the military could arrest and detain people indefinitely merely by labelling them "subversives". Using the same authority, the regime could also prevent their release, even following an acquittal or dismissal of charges by a civilian court.

2. Torture, including inhumane confinement, and subjection to beatings and burns, and sexual abuse. According to a 1983 report of the Lawyers Committee, torture "appears to have become a standard operating procedure of security and intelligence units in the Philippines".[36]

3. Political killings or "salvagings" of suspected "subversives", usually by military or paramilitary forces. The most common targets of salvagings were human rights, peasant, and labour activists; suspected communists and their sympathizers; and the relatives and friends of suspected communists.

4. Beginning in 1981, "strategic hamletting", or the forced resettlement of entire villages in order to isolate rebels. Forced hamletting deprived villagers of their rights, caused large losses of property and crops for those who were forced to move, and often involved intimidation and abuse by the military.

Marcos also played a shrewd on-again-off-again game of intimidation with the media. Formal censorship had been quickly ended under martial law. But in its place, Marcos's family and cronies took control of most media outlets. Those that were not controlled directly were forced to practise self-censorship if they wanted their licences renewed (and keep their owners and staff out of jail). After loosening media control somewhat following the lifting of martial law in 1981, Marcos cracked down again in late 1982, closing the critical publications *We Forum*, *Malaya*, and *Philippine Times* and arresting their publishers and staff members.

Prior to 1983 the most brutal human rights violations occurred largely in the countryside, out of the public's sight, and away from the attention of the domestic and foreign media in Manila. Moreover, for the most part these abuses did not involve well-known political figures. The government could thus claim with some success that abuses, particularly by the military, were the unavoidable by-product of the war against the communist insurgency. All this changed with the assassination of Benigno Aquino on the tarmac of the Manila International Airport in 1983.

Politicization of the Catholic Church

The Catholic Church in the Philippines was one of the few traditional institutions that increased in importance during the Marcos era. The imposition of martial law and its subsequent abuses caused the Church to emerge as one of the most important, though cautious, sources of opposition to authoritarianism. According to Lande, "The Church, against its wishes and tradition, was propelled into an active though changing political role".[37]

The assumption of this political role dramatically redefined the Church's traditional place in Philippine society. Benigno Aquino observed in 1983:

> When all the political parties were banned . . . the traditional channels for redressing grievances disappeared. The politician who was the middleman between the governor and the governed lost his standing. Suddenly the local Catholic priest found himself ministering not only to the spiritual needs of his community, but more and more, his temporal needs [sic]. When villagers were abused they went to their parish priest. When husbands disappeared or were arrested, the wives and children went to their parish priest. . . .[38]

The Church, however, was a diverse and extended family divided into conservative, moderate, and progressive blocs. The imposition of martial law intensified divisions within the Church just as it did in Philippine society at large. As a result, the Church faced the challenge of preserving its institutional unity at the same time that both it and society were threatened by polarization and disintegration.

In the years prior to martial law the Catholic Church had been in the early stages of transition from a basically conservative institution that reinforced the political and socio-economic status quo to one that was actively involved in temporal as well as spiritual affairs. The impetus for change was the Second Vatican Council of 1962–65. Vatican II, as it became known, formulated the Church's response to the poverty, inequality, and oppression that pervaded most of the Third World. It proclaimed that the Church and its priests had an obligation to serve the poor, not just spiritually, but also in their struggle to overcome poverty and oppression. This seemingly simple reorientation had a profound effect on the role of the Church in society, first in Latin America, and then in the Philippines.

An important outgrowth of Vatican II was the spread of liberation theology in the late 1960s. The original proponents of liberation theology were priests from poor Latin American countries. They adopted Marxist class analysis to explain the causes of poverty and oppression and advocated that priests actively assist their followers in efforts to improve their lot in life. Liberation theology "conferred on the priest the right — even the duty, some contended — to engage in social revolution".[39]

The spread of liberation theology in the Philippines resulted in increased social activism among priests and nuns and the setting up of hundreds of Basic Christian Communities (BCCs) during the 1970s. In its most extreme form, liberation theology also provided the ideological underpinning for revolutionary groups such as Christians for National Liberation (CNL), the religious arm of the communist National Democratic Front. Thus, the Church became increasingly divided between an older and more traditional leadership that sought to minimize the Church's involvement in temporal affairs, and a younger and more progressive (though not predominantly communist) group of priests who felt strongly that the Church had a responsibility to promote much needed social change in the Philippines.

The Church hierarchy's response to martial law further stimulated internal divisions. The Church leadership, as represented by the Catholic Bishops Conference of the Philippines (CBCP), quietly accepted the imposition of martial law in 1972. However, the more progressive wing of the Church, as represented by the Association of Major Religious Superiors created Task Force Detainees (TFD) in 1973 to monitor human rights abuses. With the first detentions of clergymen in 1974 the CBCP, led by the new Archbishop of Manila, Jaime Cardinal Sin, adopted a policy of "critical collaboration" *vis-à-vis* the martial law regime, mixing dialogue and co-operation with criticism and calls for change.

Sin's vacillating policy was criticized by both the conservatives in the Church (who did not want the Church to become involved in political issues) and the progressives (who sought an outright condemnation of the Marcos regime). But it succeeded in holding the Church together. As a result, as David Wurfel noted in 1977, the Church provided the:

> most effective leadership for mass discontent against the martial law regime, and only a small portion of its potential has been realized . . . the legitimacy of its leadership is probably more widely respected today than is that of the government, and the contents of its vast communication network more widely trusted.[40]

By 1977 the mounting abuses of power and obvious failures of the Marcos regime prompted a widening recognition among all but the most conservative elements of the Church hierarchy that the Church had to speak out more forcefully. The Church became progressively more concerned with human rights abuses by the military and called for their end. It called for the freeing of political detainees. Cardinal Sin became more and more critical of corruption and the failure of government policy-making, particularly with regard to socio-economic development. By 1978 pastoral letters and statements, whether issued individually or collectively by the CBCP, had moved from the identification and condemnation of specific acts and policies to a call for the end of martial law.[41] By 1982, in the face of stepped up hostility from the government and military, Cardinal Sin said the Church's relationship with the Marcos government had become "more critical than collaboration".[42] In February 1983 the CBCP issued a pastoral letter that called for the restoration of human rights and urged Filipinos to protect them; criticized government corruption and development policies; and called upon the government to seek out the root causes of the country's social problems instead of offering promises and propaganda.

In sum, by the early 1980s a combination of events and conviction had made the Church increasingly united and outspoken in its opposition to the Marcos regime. The centre of gravity within the Church hierarchy had shifted in the direction of the centrist activists led by Cardinal Sin. Although they were not the most progressive members of the Church, they nevertheless felt that the Church had a critical role to play in resolving the mounting polarization of Philippine politics and society.

From Corruption to "Kleptocracy"

The financial aggrandizement of political leaders traditionally has been an integral part of Philippine politics and government. Few Filipino politicians have left office without having significantly increased their wealth. Money is needed to acquire and hold public office, particularly national office. Indeed, one of the perceived benefits of the regularity with which presidents were replaced after one term (until Marcos was re-elected in 1969) was that it kept any one group of politicians from draining the public coffers for too long.

The magnitude of corruption, however, increased exponentially under Marcos, to the point where U.S. Congressman Stephen Solarz, a long-time critic of Marcos, described the regime as a "kleptocracy". By this he meant that the greed of Marcos, his family, and his cronies far surpassed traditional levels. There are numerous reasons for this. One explanation is the Marcos family's seemingly insatiable appetite for money. They came to view the government and the entire economy as vehicles for increasing their own fortunes, regardless of the larger consequences for the nation. A second reason is simply that the unprecedentedly long duration and absolute power of the Marcos regime gave it far more opportunities than earlier regimes. But there are also several other reasons which provide additional insights into the nature of the regime.

Marcos saw quite accurately that political power was intimately linked to wealth. He therefore sought to amass his own fortune, and equally important, to make sure that potential political rivals were deprived of an opportunity to amass wealth that might be used against him. To do this he sanctioned the creation or take-over of businesses by family members and friends and created government monopolies in key areas of the economy, such as sugar, coconut, and flour milling.[43] He also directed the allocation of government credit to his "cronies". The government-owned Development Bank of the Philippines (DBP) virtually became a private bank for Marcos's cronies, making loans for uneconomical projects (such as new sugar mills) and injecting funds into crony companies when they failed.

As the ultimate patron in the clientelistic political system, Marcos had many more clients than any previous leader. Hundreds if not thousands of military officers, senior officials, cronies, and local leaders had to be kept satisfied. Corruption was the only way that sufficient resources could be generated to keep all his clients loyal and willing to do his bidding.

Another factor is the traditional blurring of the distinction between what is public and private in the Philippines. This is a long-standing element of the political culture, but it became much more pronounced under Marcos because of his predilection to control virtually every aspect of society. Thus, the resources of both the government and private sectors were viewed by the Marcoses as being available for their use. The budgets of government ministries were regularly tapped to finance Imelda's extravagant trips and parties, and businesses were expected to make contributions and/or offer shares of ownership to family members.[44]

Finally, the mid- and late-1970s saw a dramatic increase in the availabilty of foreign loans as international banks sought to recycle Organization of Petroleum Exporting Countries' (OPEC's) newly acquired petro-dollars. International credit was available and relatively cheap, and a "borrow to grow" policy was accepted by creditors and debtors alike. This huge inflow of credit presented new and unprecedented opportunities for official and private corruption.

Given this combination of factors, therefore, it is not surprising that the amount of wealth amassed by Marcos, his family, and his followers was unprecedented. It was rumoured that Marcos had become a billionaire even before he declared martial law in 1972. Today, estimates of the fortune accumulated by the Marcoses range from US$5 to 10 billion.

Marcos and his cronies used a variety of schemes to amass their fortunes.[45] None of these techniques were particularly new to the Philippines. But the scope of corruption, the magnitude of the amounts involved, and the damage done to both the government and the economy make the corruption of the Marcos regime a singular, and one would hope, unique, experience in Philippine history.[46]

The seemingly insatiable greed that characterized the members of the Marcos family and their closest associates had a number of profoundly negative consequences for the nation. It further undermined the low respect for government traditionally held by many Filipinos and further legitimized the narrow self-interest that Marcos had been so critical of in earlier years. It contributed to the spread of lower level corruption in the bureaucracy and military. It also discouraged and alienated both the non-crony indigenous business class and foreign investors. Finally, it resulted in serious distortions in economic policy-making, and the misappropriation and waste of limited economic resources.

Failure of Economic Policy-Making

Behind the veneer of modest GNP growth during the late 1970s and early 1980s hid a situation where real income for most families was falling, productivity in agriculture and industry was stagnating, and little or no structural transformation towards an industrial economy was occurring.[47] What caused this reversal of the country's economic prospects?

There are four major reasons for the loss of the economic gains achieved during the first five years of martial law. The first was the government's excessive intervention in the economy. The second was the increasing politicization and corruption of economic policy-making. The third cause was the government's failure to sustain its gains in agricultural development. The fourth was an increasingly disadvantageous international environment. These four factors combined to have a disastrous effect on the economy and welfare of the average Filipino.

As we have seen, government intervention in the economy and concentration of economic power have been hallmarks of the Philippine economy since World War II. But under Marcos the level of government intervention and the concentration of economic power in the hands of a few were unprecedented. A 1984 report by a group of economists at the University of the Philippines (UP) noted:

> the main characteristic distinguishing the Marcos years from other periods in our economic history has been the trend towards the concentration of power in the hands of the government, and the use of the governmental functions to dispense economic privileges to some small factions in the private sector.[48]

The UP report listed some 688 presidential decrees and 283 letters of instruction issued from 1972 to 1979 which represented government intervention in the economy in one form or another.

Another study, by the U.S. Agency for Internatioal Development, captures the extent of government intervention in the economy. According to USAID, the Marcos government:

> increased its interventions in setting exchange, wage and interest rates; food pricing; and rent and tuition controls. Low interest credits, guaranteed by the government, became easy to obtain for public and favored private corporations. Duty-free and tax exemption privileges were granted to a number of industries. Entrepreneurs were successful in securing continued government protection so as to maintain and expand profits without having to become innovative and cost-effective as should be the case with "infant" industries. Monopoly and monopsony power in certain industries and imported commodities were created through presidential decrees (coconut, sugar, rice, wheat, feed grains, tobacco, meat, fish, etc.).[49]

Hand in hand with the enlarged role of the government in the economy came the politicization and corruption of economic policy-making. The roots of this can be traced back to the demise of the power of the "technocrats" which some say was signalled by Imelda Marcos's successful sacking of Executive Secretary Alejandro Melchor in November 1975. The result, ironically, was that, "having freed his technocrats from interference by members of the Congress he [Marcos] permitted his kinsmen and cronies to interfere instead".[50] Increasingly, decisions concerning the economy were made by friends and supporters of the Marcoses, only a very small number of whom proved to be competent businessmen. According to Belinda Aquino:

> Before long, large portions of the economy came under the effective control of Marcos cronies. Roberto Benedicto monopolized the sugar industry. He also shared control over the mass media with Benjamin Romualdez. Eduardo Cojuangco and Juan Ponce Enrile had cornered the coconut industry . . . .[51]

Marcos claimed that the enlarged role of the government was necessary to achieve economic growth and development, and that the concentration of economic power increased economic efficiency. But according to William Overholt, he substituted a "ruthless elite for a merely inefficient one". Most of the crony businesses were dependent upon cheap government loans, government-decreed monopoly or monopsony power, or other government-decreed preferences. Consequently, many businesses grew too rapidly and were not competitive or financially sound. The fragility of the financial system was revealed in early 1981, when Dewey Dee, a prominent Chinese businessman skipped the country, leaving behind debts of between US$65 and US$100 million. The Central Bank had to step in to avert a serious run on investment houses and Chinese banks. The weakness of the country's crony-dominated manufacturing sector was dramatically highlighted a few months later when the government financed a P5 billion (US$635 million) bail-out of the huge Construction and Development Corporation of the Philippines (CDCP), the Herdis Group, the Disini Group, and other crony manufacturing firms that were faltering. The foundering of large firms with government guarantees soon made the government the owner of 230 firms. Henceforth, government budgets were grotesquely unbalanced by the cost of subsidizing these firms.[52]

Finally, the Marcos government increasingly relied on domestic and foreign borrowing to finance its deficit-generating expenditures. According to the UP report:

> the accumulation of debt accelerated with such rapidity that the debt accumulated from 1979 to 1982 exceeded all debts accumulated during all previous years. . .as a result of a tightening of international credit markets and lower world inflation since 1979, as well as the country's own large exposure to international banks, it had to pay a higher real interest rate on new borrowings and get them on increasingly shorter terms.[53]

Decline of the Agricultural Sector and Failure of Agrarian Reform

Marcos claimed that his regime modernized the agricultural sector and initiated the most far-reaching land reform programme in the country's history. He also took credit for improving rural infrastructure such as roads, irrigation, and electrification and for achieving self-sufficiency in rice production for the first time in 1976. The Marcos government deserves some credit for these accomplishments, but this praise needs to be heavily qualified.

The centre-piece of Marcos's efforts to increase agricultural productivity was the Masagana 99 programme, which provided cheap credit to farmers so that they could purchase and grow genetically altered varieties of rice that were faster growing and could be grown almost the whole year round. The introduction of these high yielding varieties (HYVs) resulted in a near doubling of rice yields between 1973 and 1985. However, while the HYVs were sturdy and quick growing, they also required greater inputs of expensive fertilizers and pesticides than traditional varieties. Consequently, only relatively richer farmers could afford to plant HYVs, and their higher yields were offset, to varying degrees, by higher production costs. By the early 1980s agricultural productivity was further threatened by a deterioration in the rural infrastructure (including the rural banking system), which had begun to show signs of neglect, mismanagement, and corruption.

The agricultural sector also was negatively affected by the creation of coconut and sugar monopolies controlled by Marcos's cronies. The 1984 UP report estimated that sugar producers were deprived of between P11.6 billion pesos and P14.4 billion pesos from crop year 1974 to 1983.[54] Coconut farmers were paid 9 to 15 per cent less by UNICOM, the private milling and marketing company controlled by Eduardo "Danding" Cojuangco, which had a monopsony over copra purchasing.[55]

Finally, the Marcos land reform programme was, at best, an extremely limited success. While he was the legally elected president, Marcos had shown little interest in or commitment to genuine land reform. It was only after he declared martial law that he became an outspoken supporter of land redistribution as a way to both legitimize his regime and weaken his landowning opponents. Four days after declaring martial law, Marcos issued his second presidential decree which declared the entire Philippines as subject to land reform.[56] A month later Marcos issued Presidential Decree No. 27, which subjected all tenanted rice and corn landholdings of more than 7 hectares to government purchase and redistribution. It also declared that all share tenants would become leaseholders under Operation Leasehold and promised that all tenants working land of up to 5 hectares would become amortizing owners of that land under Operation Land Transfer. Landlord compensation, for the first time, was not to be based on the market price of land, but instead was to be equivalent to two and a half times the annual harvest. In announcing PD 27 Marcos boldly asserted that "land reform is the only gauge for the success or failure of the New Society. If land reform fails, there is no New Society".

As decreed, Marcos's land reform programme was the most ambitious ever attempted in the Philippines, and Marcos's power to implement it was unprecedented. In reality, however, his programme was considerably more limited in scope. To begin with, all sugar and coconut lands were exempted from the programme. Consequently, Operation Land Transfer was limited to only 400,000 out of a million rice and corn tenant farmers. Of those who actually became amortizing owners, almost 90 per cent eventually defaulted on their payment obligations. "The net result", according to David Wurfel, "was to put more than 86,000 tenants on the road to ownership (with only 2 per cent completing the process); while this was less than 9 per cent of a very conservative estimate of all rice and corn tenants, it was, nevertheless, a greater accomplishment than in any previous administration".[57] It also gave Marcos a solid base of grass-root peasant support in the provinces of Central Luzon, where the policy was most fully implemented. However, in regions where implementation was flawed or incomplete, the programme contributed to agrarian unrest by raising and then dashing hopes.[58]

The impact of Marcos's land reform programme was limited for a variety of reasons, not the least of which was Marcos's lack of commitment to its implementation. David Wurfel suggests that Marcos "simply lost his originally keen interest after the owners with more than 100 hectares had been dispossessed".[59] But perhaps more importantly, Marcos, like preceding presidents, was unwilling to alienate the Philippines' many medium-sized landowners. By December 1977 a seminar conducted at the Rand Corporation concluded that land reform was "a failing program" due to small-landlord opposition, tenant reluctance, and lack of political will by Marcos.

The Marcos programme also encountered a number of other problems inherent to any agrarian reform programme. First, designing a successful agrarian reform programme is an extremely complicated conceptual undertaking. In the process, a number of complex questions must be addressed, many of which have no easy answers. What is the trade-off between productivity and equity? What is the most appropriate land retention limit? Should it be uniform, or should it vary depending on region and crop? Should export-oriented and plantation-based agribusinesses be subjected to reform? How are land values calculated and landowners compensated? How does the government pay for the redistribution? Even the best intentioned technocrats within the Marcos government could not fashion a programme that successfully addressed these fundamental and complex issues.

Secondly, the bureaucratic challenge of administering a land transfer programme is huge and it proved to be overwhelming in the Philippines. For the Marcos programme to work it had to be explained to isolated and uneducated peasants; its provisions had to be enforced; land had to be surveyed and ownership had to be determined; ownership documentation had to be produced and distributed; compensation had to be administered; and disputes over ownership and compensation had to be resolved. The number, magnitude, and cost of these functions were simply beyond the administrative capabilities of the Philippines' sleepy and poorly financed bureaucracy.

Finally, even a well designed and effectively administered land reform programme, by itself, could not change the fact that there simply was not enough land left to distribute. The Philippines' agricultural land frontier had been reached by the late 1960s. After that time, the increase in the total area of cultivated land came primarily from the cultivation of relatively unproductive and non-sustainable upland areas. The rural population continued to grow, however, creating a burgeoning population of landless agricultural workers. Marcos's land reform programme, with its focus on tenant farmers, failed to address this fundamental problem.

The deterioration of the agricultural sector during the later years of the Marcos regime is most clearly seen when viewed in a comparative context. From 1973 to 1979 the Philippines' total gain in agricultural production exceeded that of Indonesia, Malaysia, or Thailand. But from 1980 to 1985 the size of production gains in the Philippines declined, so that by 1985 the country's total gain in agricultural production for the 1975–85 period was less than that of the three above-mentioned countries, as well as Vietnam and Burma (see Table 4.1). By the early 1980s the Philippines' agricultural productivity was low compared to

Table 4.1
Index of Agricultural Production
(1974–76 = 100)

	1973	1975	1979	1985
Burma	98	101	116	164
Indonesia	95	100	114	150
Malaysia	91	98	115	135
Thailand	95	101	116	146
Vietnam	95	96	120	162
PHILIPPINES	86	102	122	133

SOURCE: NEDA, *Philippine Statistical Yearbook, 1987.*

other countries of Southeast Asia. In the case of rice, average yields in 1981 were only 2.2 tons/hectare, compared to 2.8 tons/hectare in Malaysia and 3.7 tons/hectare in Indonesia.[60]

Economic and Human Consequences

The Marcos government's policies resulted in an economy that, by 1980, was weakened by excessive government intervention, heavy foreign borrowing, inefficient industry, and lagging agricultural growth. These structural weaknesses, combined with the corruption of economic policy-making, made it considerably more difficult for the Philippines to adjust to the second round of international economic shocks caused by the oil price rise of 1979. The oil price rise triggered an international economic malaise characterized by high global inflation and interest rates; recession among the developed countries; and sharp drops in coconut, sugar, copper, gold, and other commodity prices.

Each of these conditions had serious repercussions for the Philippines. The hike in oil prices increased the country's import bill at the same time that the global recession caused the demand and prices for most of its exports to decline, creating a growing trade deficit. Rising interest rates made the Philippines' foreign debt burden more costly and eventually unpayable. Higher prices of oil and other manufactured imports fuelled domestic inflation, undermining the real value of wages and salaries. The combination of these conditions resulted in the collapse and government bail-out of crony firms beginning in 1980 and 1981; large capital flight in 1981 and 1982; a virtual standstill in economic growth by 1982; and an inability to pay its foreign debt in 1983.

For the average Filipino, the result of corruption, cronyism, and economic mismanagement was a noticeable decline in incomes and standards of living between 1970 and 1980. According to the UP report, real earnings of salaried employees in 1980 were only 93 per cent of their 1972 earnings and the real earnings of wage workers were only 87 per cent of their 1972 level.[61] The number of people underemployed tripled in five years, from 1.6 million in 1978 to 5.6 million in 1983.

The reduction in incomes caused by declining real wages and increasing underemployment affected nutrition and health levels, particularly among children. The percentage of children under seven years of age who were moderately or severely underweight for their age declined from 22 per cent in 1978 to 17 per cent in 1982, but then climbed back to 22 per cent in 1985.[62]

Along with declining real incomes came a worsening distribution of income. Census figures show that the poorest 60 per cent of all Filipino households received 25 per cent of the nation's total income in 1971. By 1979 their share of national income had shrunk to only 22.5 per cent.[63] The rich were in fact becoming richer while the poor were becoming poorer.

The decline in the economy and in the well-being of most of the people did not go unnoticed. A poll taken by the Development Academy of the Philippines in April 1984 found that 51 per cent of those polled said that the quality of their lives had deteriorated from a year earlier. (Only 12 per cent said their lives had improved.)[64] The social and political consequences of this economic decline were serious:

> As people's livelihoods have worsened, traditional loyalties, social relationships, and patron-client ties have disintegrated. The government has been unable or unwilling to fill the vacuum, but the communists have keyed their efforts toward these socially displaced people.[65]

As the next section will show, beginning in the late 1970s the communists successfully capitalized on declining economic and social conditions, particularly in the countryside.

Expansion of the Communist Insurgency

As we have seen, in 1977 it appeared that the communist movement had been effectively contained by Marcos. But in reality the movement had already passed through its worst period and was beginning to lay the groundwork for the dramatic growth that would occur during the first half of the 1980s. The growth of the communist insurgency after 1976 was due to five factors:

1. the polarization and radicalization of politics caused by the closing of all legal avenues of political dissent;
2. the decline in government efficacy and legitimacy on both the national and local levels;
3. the deterioration of the economy after 1979;
4. increasing human rights abuses, particularly by the military; and
5. the increased political and military sophistication and effectiveness of the communists.

In 1976, in an effort to reverse the dismal situation it was in, the leadership of the CPP had issued a new game plan for the future, entitled "Our Urgent Tasks". The new strategy called for the NPA to avoid military action as much as possible and concentrate instead on developing a "mass base" of rural supporters. As a result, the relative lull of the late 1970s was misleading. According to Gareth Porter:

> While the Armed Forces of the Philippines was busy fighting the MNLF in Mindanao during the mid- and late 1970s, the CPP/NPA cadres were quietly establishing political bases in the non-Muslim areas of Mindanao and on the islands of Panay, Samar, and Negros in the Visayas. For several years they avoided military operations altogether, giving the impression to the Marcos regime that the revolutionary organization was dormant. The primary objective during the late 1970s was to expand the number and size of "guerrilla fronts" — areas stretching across a number of municipalities and including CPP, NPA and mass organizations. From

1976 to 1980, the number of fronts increased from 135 to 376, according to CPP figures.[66]

Additionally, beginning in 1977, the National Democratic Front (NDF) was reinvigorated by the CPP. Although the NDF had been formed in 1973, prior to 1977 it had not mounted a serious effort to form a genuine "united front" with non-communist opponents of the Marcos regime. But in 1977 the Party sought to make the NDF more attractive to these neglected non-communist "middle forces" by introducing the notion of a post-Marcos "democratic coalition government" of anti-Marcos and anti-imperialist groups. The idea, according to one observer, was: "sign up now and reserve your seat in the new parliament".[67] The support of the non-communist middle forces, however, remained elusive until 1985.

After labouring for several years to build a strong mass base, the CPP and the NPA "took off" in 1979–80. Rudolfo Salas became party head in early 1978. (He remained its head until he was captured in late 1986.) Under his leadership the CPP and the NPA set out to aggressively expand its membership. In 1980 CPP membership totalled about 8,000 cadres and the NPA had about 3,500 armed guerrillas. Under Salas, the CPP called for a tripling of party membership, a doubling of the size of the NPA within three years, and the expansion of guerrilla fronts in Mindanao from five to fourteen.[68] There was also a major policy change in favour of stepping up the pace of the insurgency by freeing many NPA units from their propaganda duties so that they could devote all of their time to military operations. This led to heightened military activity by the NPA and a growth in encounters with the AFP.[69] By October 1982 the size of the NPA had almost doubled to 6,000 and they claimed to be operating in 43 out of 72 provinces.

The growth in the scope and sophistication of the communist movement was accurately described by *Ang Bayan*, the official CPP newspaper. According to the paper:

> By the end of 1981, the requirements of the early substage of the strategic defensive stage of our people's war had been fulfilled: NPA guerrilla fronts and zones were firmly in place in all major strategic areas in the country. And as the Party accelerated the establishment of territorial organs and mass organizations,

guerrilla units were gradually relieved of the main responsibility for mass work, enabling them to devote most of their efforts to military work. Where there used to be only armed propaganda units (APUs), there were now platoons and companies of full fledged guerrilla units.[70]

Conclusion: Explaining the Decline of the Marcos Regime

Ferdinand Marcos's early martial law accomplishments were significant. They included restoring law and order, improving the planning and implementation of government programmes, building rural infrastructure, promoting agricultural development and agrarian reform, encouraging manufacturing and diversifying exports, formulating a somewhat more multi-dimensional foreign policy, and generating a new sense of national pride.

As we have seen, however, Marcos was unable or unwilling to sustain his initial successes. More and more, his considerable talents were channelled into the maintenance of his power rather than restoring political participation and sustaining economic development. Increasingly, his policies were perverted by self-interest, corruption, and venality. His vision became distorted by years of self-serving deceptions, so much so that by the mid-1980s one wondered if he could distinguish between truth and falsehood, between reality and the fantasy world that increasingly existed in Malacañang Palace. His great self-confidence, based on years of successful manipulation of Philippine politics and society, eventually developed into supreme arrogance.

What explains the depths to which the Marcos regime and the country sank? Perhaps the single most important explanation is the ambition, arrogance, and greed of Marcos and his family. Marcos's successful political career, which culminated in his winning the 1965 presidential election, demonstrated his self-confidence, intelligence, and political skill. His excessive use of money and fraud to secure his re-election in 1969 was a preliminary indication of the size of his ambition. After establishing himself as the Philippines' premier politician, Marcos easily convinced himself that only he could lead the country. And after successfully imposing martial law, Marcos undoubtedly felt it was in his power to single-handedly control and transform Philippine society. He assumed that he alone knew what was best for the Filipino people, that they lacked the discipline and direction which only he could provide, and failing that, that he could easily deceive and intimidate them.

Marcos probably genuinely believed in the need to transform and modernize Philippine society, at least during the early years of martial law; but ultimately, he became a captive of the country's traditional political culture. Despite his disdain for traditional politics, the involvement in the government of numerous members of the Marcos-Romualdez clan took traditional family-based politics to new heights. Even if Marcos had wanted to, it is doubtful that he could have changed the personalistic and particularistic political system. And for all his talk of modernizing the economy, he ended up trusting and relying on his cronies more than his technocrats. In the end, many of the entrenched traditions and patterns of behaviour that Marcos sought to change under martial law contributed to his failure.

There are, however, several other important factors that contributed to the dismal failure of the Marcos regime. First, the Filipino people must share a portion of the blame. Many Filipinos responded positively to the powerful image that Marcos projected, reflecting a traditional Filipino tendency to respect and be attracted to those with power (those who are *malakas*). In addition, many Filipinos tolerated the regime's nepotism and corruption, accepting them as part and parcel of Philippine politics. Secondly, the over-centralization of the government, the absence of any meaningful checks and balances, and the lack of accountability increased the probability of bad decision-making. Thirdly, Marcos's suppression of most political opposition stunted the development of moderate political alternatives and made his claim that only he could rule the country a self-fulfilling prophecy. And finally, a portion of the responsibility must also be shared by the U.S. Government, for its tolerance of the regime's excesses, and later on, for its unrealistic expectations of the regime's willingness and ability to reform itself.

Some observers have identified 1976 – the year after Alejandro Melchor, Marcos's Executive Secretary and chief technocrat, was forced to resign by Imelda Marcos – as the year that the tide turned and the regime began its long, slow deterioration. Others point to 1978 or 1979, when the economy began to show the first signs of extensive corruption and mismanagement. But as late as 1981, when Marcos formally ended martial law and was re-elected president, the regime still appeared to be firmly in control, and it looked as if there was some chance of improvement. According to William Overholt:

> While Marcos retained most of the apparatus of martial law, there was significant liberalization. Rule by decree dwindled (although for some time decrees were backdated). Somewhat greater press freedom and political organization was permitted. In August the right to strike was returned, subject to revocation if the government declared national security to be involved.[71]

As late as 1981 Marcos was still able to manipulate Philippine government and politics with impunity, although in ways that had become transparently self-serving. The Interim Batasang Pambansa was dominated by members of the KBL, and was viewed as little more than a rubber stamp intended to legitimize the Marcos regime. Similarly, the 1980 local elections resulted in a near total sweep by the KBL. The ninth revision of the Constitution – which created a French-style presidential–parliamentary system – was approved by a plebiscite in April 1981 with the "usual irregularities". And the June 1981 presidential election was accepted as a farce by almost everyone, with the notable exception of George Bush, the then U.S. vice-president, who attended Marcos's inauguration and commended him on his "adherence to democratic principles and the democratic process".

The appearance that existed as late as 1982 that Marcos still had complete, if increasingly less effective, control over Philippine politics disguised what William Overholt has called the "de-institutionalization" of Philippine politics and government under Marcos. The traditional government and political institutions were abandoned or undermined, almost all state power still resided in the persons of Ferdinand and Imelda Marcos, there was no accepted formula for succession, and the "legitimate" opposition was weak and divided.

Furthermore, by the late 1970s the regime's political base had begun to erode. According to Lela Noble:

> The effort to include the common man, exemplified by the agrarian reform program and by "barangay democracy" in the early years of martial law, showed few signs of existence, let alone

success. Medium and small scale landowners, however, seemed solidly supportive. . . . And [for officials outside of Metro Manila] . . . patronage apparently produced loyalty. The military also appeared loyal, though undisciplined at lower levels and fraught with factional rivalries at the top . . . . In Manila, meanwhile, the technocrats seemed increasingly isolated.[72]

Nor could Marcos's outward appearance of invincibility hide the reality of his declining health caused by an on-again, off-again battle with *lupus erythematosus*, a chronic kidney disease. Marcos's uncertain health weakened his control over the government (and over his ambitious wife) and emboldened the opposition. Finally, and perhaps most significantly, by 1982 Marcos could not disguise the fact that the economy was in serious and growing trouble.

NOTES

1. Ferdinand Marcos, *The Democratic Revolution in the Philippines* (Manila: The Marcos Foundation, 1977), p.1.
2. Jose Abueva, "Ideology and Practice in the 'New Society'", in *Marcos and Martial Law in the Philippines*, edited by David Rosenberg (Ithaca: Cornell University Press, 1979), pp.35–36.
3. Ferdinand Marcos, *Progress and Martial Law* (Manila: The Marcos Foundation, 1981), p.34.
4. Abueva, op. cit., p.35.
5. David Rosenberg, "Creating a 'New Society'", in *Marcos and Martial Law in the Philippines*, edited by David Rosenberg (Ithaca: Cornell University Press, 1979), p.17.
6. Ferdinand Marcos, *An Ideology for Filipinos* (Manila: The Marcos Foundation, 1980), p.19.
7. William Overholt, "The Rise and Fall of Ferdinand Marcos", *Asian Survey* 26, no.11 (November 1986):1142.
8. Quoted in Lewis Gleeck, *President Marcos and the Philippine Political Culture* (Manila: Loyal Printing, 1987), p.144.
9. Raul de Guzman and Mila Reforma, *Government and Politics of the Philippines* (New York: Oxford University Press, 1988), p.56.
10. Kit Machado, "Philippine Politics: Research 1960–1980: Areas for Future Exploration", in *Philippine Studies: Political Science, Economics and Linguistics*, edited by Donn Hart (Northern Illinois University Center for Southeast Asian Studies, 1981), p.33.

11. Felipe Miranda and Ruben Ciron, "The Philippines: Defence Expenditures, Threat Perception and the Role of the United States", in *Defence Spending in Southeast Asia*, edited by Chin Kin Wah (Singapore: Institute of Southeast Asian Studies, 1987), p.136.

12. Francisco Nemenzo, "Military Intervention in Philippine Politics", *Diliman Review* 34, nos.5&6 (1986):17.

13. P.N. Abinales, "The Philippine Military and the Marcos Regime", mimeographed (Quezon City: University of the Philippines Third World Studies Center, undated), p.12.

14. Felipe Miranda and Reuben Ciron, "Development and the Military in the Philippines: Military Perceptions in a Time of Continuing Crisis", in *Soldiers and Stability in Southeast Asia*, edited by J. Soedjati Djiwandono and Yong Mun Cheong (Singapore: Institute of Southeast Asian Studies, 1988), p.176.

15. Richard Kessler, "Development and the Military: Role of the Philippine Military in Development", in *Soldiers and Stability in Southeast Asia*, edited by J. Soedjati Djiwandono and Yong Mun Cheong (Singapore: Institute of Southeast Asian Studies, 1988), p.222.

16. See Vicente Jayme, "The Philippine Economy: An Evolving Economic Structure", in *Trends in the Philippines II*, edited by M. Rajaretnam (Singapore: Institute of Southeast Asian Studies, 1978), pp.75–104.

17. Emmanuel de Dios, ed., *An Analysis of the Philippine Economic Crisis* (Quezon City: University of the Philippines Press, 1984), p.4; hereafter referred to as the "UP Report".

18. See Ross Munro, "The New Khmer Rouge", *Commentary* (December 1985), p.25; and Larry Niksch, *Insurgency and Counterinsurgency in the Philippines* (Washington, D.C.: Library of Congress, Congressional Research Service, July 1985), p.36.

19. See Gregg Jones, *Red Revolution: Inside the Philippine Guerrilla Movement* (Boulder: Westview Press, 1989), chapter 4.

20. Cesar Majul, "The Moro Struggle in the Philippines", *Third World Quarterly* (April 1988), p.905.

21. Overholt, op. cit., p.1148.

22. Machado, op. cit., p.18.

23. Jose Abueva, quoted in Gleeck, op. cit., p. 145.

24. The KBL also drew the more pragmatic members of both the old Liberal and Nacionalista parties, such as Salvador Laurel and Emmanuel Pelaez.

25. Machado, op. cit., p.9.

26. The Lawyers Committee for International Human Rights, *The Philippines: A Country in Crisis* (New York: The Lawyers Committee for International Human Rights, 1983), p.181.

27. Ibid., p.181.
28. Ibid., pp.185–86.
29. Machado, op. cit., p.25.
30. Overholt, op. cit., p.1147.
31. There are, however, conflicting claims about the extent to which Marcos filled the army with Ilocanos. See Miranda and Ciron, "Development and the Military in the Philippines", p.209.
32. Kessler, op. cit., p. 222.
33. Miranda and Ciron, "The Philippines: Defence Expenditures, Threat Perception and the Role of the United States", pp. 135–36 and 141.
34. *Far Eastern Economic Review*, 9 October 1987, p.19.
35. See Amnesty International, *Report on an Amnesty International Mission to the Republic of the Philippines* (London: Amnesty International, 1982); and The Lawyers Committee for International Human Rights, op. cit.
36. The Lawyers Committee, op. cit., p.7.
37. Carl Lande, "The Political Crisis", in *Crisis in the Philippines: The Marcos Era and Beyond*, edited by John Bresnan (Princeton: Princeton University Press, 1986), p.121.
38. Statement of Benigno Aquino before the Subcommittee on Asian and Pacific Affairs, in *United States-Philippines Relations and the New Base and Aid Agreement* (Washington, D.C.: U.S. Government Printing Office, 1983), p.82.
39. William Chapman, *Inside the Philippine Revolution* (New York: W.W. Norton, 1987), p.200.
40. David Wurfel, "Martial Law in the Philippines: The Methods of Regime Survival", *Pacific Affairs* 50, no.1 (Spring 1977):17.
41. Lela Noble, "Politics in the Marcos Era", in *Crisis in the Philippines: The Marcos Era and Beyond*, edited by John Bresnan (Princeton: Princeton University Press, 1986), p.106.
42. *New York Times*, 12 December 1982, p.4.
43. One study done in the early 1980s concluded that the Marcos family controlled at least 48 corporations in 1979, and the Romualdezes controlled another 68. See Belinda Aquino, *Politics of Plunder: The Philippines Under Marcos*, Occasional Paper No. 87-1 (Quezon City: University of the Philippines College of Public Administration, January 1987), p.25. One Marcos crony, Jose Campos, claimed that he set up and ran at least 34 companies for Marcos. See the *Asian Wall Street Journal*, 12 February 1987, p.8.
44. Imelda Marcos's extravagance was legendary. The money she spent on parties, clothes, jewellery, and art came from the budgets of other government departments. For example, documents found after the 1986

revolution reportedly show that some of Mrs Marcos's shopping trips to New York were paid for from an account with the government-owned Philippine National Bank intended to finance the government counter-insurgency effort. See the *Asian Wall Street Journal*, 12 February 1987, p.1.

45. See Belinda Aquino, op. cit., chapters 4 and 5, for a detailed and comprehensive description of the "dynamics of plunder" during the Marcos era.

46. For example, by the time Marcos and his cronies fled the country, sugar producers had lost perhaps P12.7 billion (about US$635 million), and P9.7 billion (about US$485 million) were missing from coconut-monopoly funds. See the *Asian Wall Street Journal*, 12 February 1987, p.8.

47. U.S. Agency for International Development, *Country Development Strategy Statement for the Philippines, FY 1986–90* (Manila: USAID Mission, 1985), p.6; hereafter referred to as the USAID CDSS.

48. UP Report, p.10.

49. USAID CDSS, p.3.

50. Carl Lande, "Philippine Prospects After Martial Law", *Foreign Affairs* 59, no.5 (Summer 1981):1159.

51. Belinda Aquino, op. cit., p.32.

52. Overholt, op. cit., p.1150.

53. UP Report, p.15.

54. Ibid., p.45.

55. Ibid., p.49.

56. David Wurfel has characterized the pace of land redistribution during the Marcos presidency as follows: "Though slightly above the pace of activity of Macapagal's last two years in office, this was only ⅓ of the annual average during the Magsaysay/Garcia years". See David Wurfel, "The Development of Post-War Philippine Land Reform: Political and Sociological Explanations", in *Second View from the Paddy*, edited by Ledesma, Makil and Miralao (Manila: Institute of Philippine Culture, 1983), p.6. Indeed, the most important action taken on land reform during the Marcos presidency was a series of amendments made in 1971 to the Land Reform Code of 1963. According to Wurfel, these amendments did not originate from Malacañang Palace, but instead were initiated over the opposition of Marcos by a group of middle-class legislators seeking to woo an organized peasantry.

57. Ibid., p.9.

58. David Wurfel, "Land Reform: Contexts, Accomplishments and Prospects Under Marcos and Aquino" (Paper prepared for the Association of Asian Studies annual meeting, 25–27 March 1988), p.6.

59. David Wurfel, "The Development of Post-War Philippine Land Reform: Political and Sociological Explanations", p.8.
60. USAID CDSS, p.12.
61. UP Report, p.22.
62. USAID CDSS, p.37.
63. UP Report, p.20.
64. Larry Niksch, *Insurgency and Counterinsurgency in the Philippines* (Washington, D.C.: Library of Congress, Congressional Research Service, 1985), p.19.
65. Ibid., p. 19.
66. Gareth Porter, *The Politics of Counterinsurgency in the Philippines: Military and Political Options*, Occasional Paper No.9 (Honolulu: University of Hawaii Center for Philippine Studies, 1987), p.4.
67. Chapman, op. cit., p.222.
68. Munro, op. cit. p.31.
69. In 1981 the NPA also received one shipment of about 200 rifles, reportedly sent from the Palestinian Liberation Organization through South Yemen.
70. *Ang Bayan*, March 1986, p.7.
71. Overholt, op. cit., p.1150.
72. Noble, op. cit., p.101.

chapter 5

The Decline and Fall of Marcos, 1983-86

> Tama na! Sobra na! (Enough! Too much!)
>
> — Aquino-Laurel campaign slogan during the 1986 presidential election.

It is easy, with the benefit of hindsight, to identify signs in the late 1970s and early 1980s that pointed to the decline and eventual collapse of the Marcos regime. The over-concentration of power in the person of Marcos; the increasing corruption and "cronyism"; the deterioration of the military and the economy; and the growth of the insurgency were all evident. But until 1983 the regime's weaknesses and failures were somewhat obscured by the "Marcos factor" — the perception, if not the reality, that Marcos could run circles around his critics (whether Filipino or American); that his control of the government and the KBL was so absolute that nothing could unseat him; and that the United States and the rest of the international community would continue to support his government in the absence of other alternatives. In a testimony to the U.S. Congress just over two months before his assassination, Benigno Aquino acknowledged Marcos's skill. He said that Marcos had survived in office for so many years because "he has used his awesome powers rather sparingly. [He] would rather persuade before he bribes; bribe before he threatens; threaten before he arrests; arrest before he kills".[1]

What then was it that caused Marcos's fall in February 1986? Why did it not come sooner? Or later?

To some observers, the Marcos regime was inherently unviable. David Wurfel, taking a long-term perspective on Marcos's rule, wrote in 1977, "the task he has set himself – the long-term maintenance of one-man rule in a relatively well educated society with over 50 years of experience with free, competitive politics – is an impossible one."[2] Philippine Marxists also predicted the eventual demise of the regime, but for different reasons. To them, the feudalism, oppression, and imperialism of the "U.S.-Marcos dictatorship" would lead inexorably to class conflict and eventual revolution. But these perspectives, while correctly identifying long-term trends, do not help to explain why the regime collapsed when it did.

At the other extreme, there are those who attribute the demise of Marcos almost exclusively to the political and economic crisis created by the August 1983 assassination of opposition leader Benigno Aquino. They point to the assassination's effect in intensifying and mobilizing both domestic and international opposition to the regime, and the equally dramatic and undermining collapse of the economy following the assassination. This view also has a considerable element of truth. But it ignores the fact that the regime had been in serious decline since 1981, and it does not explain why it took another two and a half years after the assassination for the regime to be toppled.

The crisis caused by the Aquino assassination took place in the larger context of the developments described in the last chapter. The erosion of Marcos's credibility, the decline of the government's legitimacy and effectiveness, the faltering of the economy, and the rise of traditional and radical opposition all set the stage for the final scene played out from late 1983 to early 1986. This chapter will describe the causes and consequences of this drama.

The Aquino Assassination and Its Aftermath

The political and economic insecurity the Philippines was experiencing in the early 1980s grew to crisis proportions on 21 August 1983. On that date, former senator and exiled opposition leader Benigno "Ninoy" Aquino was killed by a single shot in the head as he disembarked from an airliner at Manila's international airport. Although the Marcos regime was able to weather the political and economic storm that raged in the months after Aquino's murder, the assassination permanently energized the existing opposition, politicized new sectors of society, and placed the regime on the defensive as never before. It also prompted Washington to begin a long and sometimes halting process of distancing itself from the Marcos government. For all these reasons Aquino's mother, Dona Aurora Aquino, was correct when she said at his funeral that "Ninoy accomplished more in death than he would have in life".

Brash, articulate, energetic, and a consummate politician, Ninoy Aquino was a rising star in Philippine politics during the 1950s and 1960s. By 1971 Aquino had become a leading senator from the Liberal Party and a vocal critic of Marcos. It was anticipated that Aquino would run for president in the 1973 elections. The elections were never held, of course, and instead Marcos jailed Aquino immediately after declaring martial law. Marcos freed Aquino in May 1980 so that he could have heart surgery in the United States. Aquino, his wife, Corazon or "Cory", and their family remained there for the next three years. But by mid-1983 he felt compelled to return to the Philippines for a variety of reasons – despite warnings that he would be re-arrested or even killed. Aquino felt increasingly isolated from developments in Manila, particularly in the light of Marcos's declining health and the mounting political and economic uncertainty. Specifically, he wanted to return in order to prepare for the parliamentary elections scheduled for May 1984. But Aquino was also concerned that the country was in danger of splitting apart (particularly if Marcos died and his wife succeeded him) and he believed that Marcos had to be persuaded to begin a peaceful transition back to democracy. Aquino, of course, saw himself playing a leading role in the post-Marcos era, and wished to return in order to re-establish his leadership in preparation for that new era.

Ninoy Aquino was murdered as he was being escorted by soldiers down a stairway from the airplane to a security van waiting on the airport tarmac. While Aquino was on the stairway, he was out of the sight of the other passengers and the crowd of supporters and journalists waiting in the arrival terminal. There was an initial shot and then a burst of gun-fire. When it ended Aquino was face down on the tarmac, killed by a bullet in his head. Several feet from him was the dead body of Rolando Galman, the man the government would claim shot Aquino on the orders of the NPA.

The government's explanation of the assassination suffered from many inconsistencies, however, and the general public's reaction was an equal mixture of disbelief and rage. Few Filipinos believed that the communists had ordered the assassination, or that they could have carried it out, given the high level of security at the time of Aquino's arrival. Indeed, because of the tight security, most Filipinos believed the military killed Aquino, presumably on orders from General Fabian Ver or other senior officers close to the president. At the same time, few Filipinos thought that Marcos was ruthless or stupid enough to order Aquino's assassination (at least using such a questionable plan). But many suspected that Imelda Marcos might have ordered the murder while her husband was incapacitated with one of his bouts of lupus.

In the days following the murder, large numbers of Filipinos, perhaps in the hundreds of thousands, filed by Aquino's open coffin to see the bloody and bloated body of the new martyr. Ten days later, an estimated two million people witnessed Aquino's funeral procession. On 14 September the first anti-Marcos rally involving the previously timid middle and professional classes was held in the Makati business district, and on 21 September, the eleventh anniversary of martial law, there were violent anti-Marcos protests in Metro Manila.

Why was there this deeply felt and widespread reaction to the murder of Aquino? There is, after all, a long tradition of political violence in the Philippines.[3] Despite Aquino's intelligence, charisma, and courage during his eight years of captivity, he was, in many ways, still the consummate traditional politician – ambitious, smooth-talking, and unscrupulous. In addition to this, he was a member of the traditional élite, having married into the Cojuangco family, one of the wealthiest landowning families in the country.

The reasons for the popular reaction to the Aquino assassination, therefore, are complex. First, although political violence was a fixture in Philippine politics, traditionally national political leaders were exempted as targets of this violence. The murder of Aquino broke this unspoken rule. Secondly, the murder underscored the harsh reality of the Marcos regime's willingness to resort to violence to control political opposition. Thirdly, the murder heightened concern that Marcos was no longer in control and that Malacañang was being run by two even greater evils: Imelda Marcos and General Fabian Ver. Fourthly, the bravery that Aquino demonstrated by returning despite the threats against him forced many Filipinos to confront their own lack of courage in challenging the Marcos regime. And finally, the Christ-like martyrdom of Aquino in the name of the Filipino people (in 1980 he made a speech in which he said that the Filipino "is worth dying for") had an immediate and potent religious significance for devoutly Catholic Filipinos.

Although Marcos was ill at the time of the assassination, in the weeks and months that followed he mounted an effective effort at damage control. In his news conferences and speeches he steadfastly portrayed the murder as having been ordered by the communists – even before ballistics tests had been concluded and the alleged murderer's identity became known. In response to the mounting demonstrations he mixed the promise of reconciliation with the threat of reprisals, including the re-imposition of martial law. In October he was forced to appoint an independent commission to investigate the Aquino and Galman murders, but he appointed as head of the commission a relatively unknown judge, Corazon Agrava, and selected as its other members people not known to be critical of the government. Although the Agrava board would eventually surprise most people (including Marcos) with its independence, initially it was used by Marcos to counter the opposition's calls for justice, and as such helped him to defuse the time bomb created by the assassination. Finally, he granted a series of interviews with the international media designed to restore foreign (and particularly U.S.) confidence in his ability to control the situation.[4]

Despite Marcos's considerable efforts, however, the Aquino assassination set in motion political and economic forces that even he could not control or finesse. The most important political force was the growth of both "traditional" and "non-traditional" opposition groups.

Traditional or party-based opposition to Marcos, which had been largely dormant and ineffective throughout most of the 1970s, began to revive between 1980 to 1982. After the lifting of martial law in 1981, non-traditional "cause-oriented" and "mass-based" opposition groups also began to grow. But it was the Aquino assassination that energized both traditional and non-traditional opposition to Marcos. Following the assassination the level and intensity of the opposition to Marcos grew dramatically, despite the absence of a single leader capable of unifying the many divided and often rancorous opposition groups.

The revival of the opposition was supported by the Catholic Church and by Church-affiliated groups like the Bishops-Businessmen's Conference for Human Development (BBC). Beginning with its coverage of the Aquino assassination and continuing through the February 1986 revolution, Radio Veritas, the Church-owned radio station, became the leading source of accurate news and information nation-wide. This crack in the regime's control of the media was followed by the revamping of a Church-funded weekly newspaper, *Veritas*, which began to publish a steady stream of critical articles and commentaries.

The opposition was also supported by the increasingly politicized urban middle class and business community, particularly in Metro Manila. Previously complacent society matrons began to volunteer their time and energy to opposition activities. Middle-level executives with MBA degrees contributed their analytical, managerial, and marketing skills. A growing number of senior executives, disgusted with economic mismanagement and cronyism, first quietly supported the opposition and later became outspoken in their criticisms.

The Revival of "Traditional" Opposition

The activities of traditional political leaders who opposed Marcos, as we have seen, had been severely curtailed for the better part of a decade. For the first six years of martial law, they were largely immobilized. A number of the legal opposition's leaders, including Benigno Aquino, were arrested and detained, while others lapsed into passivity or collaborated with the regime. As a result, "in the absence of a politicized mass base or a reliable middle layer of leadership, which the electoral parties failed to acquire prior to martial law, the legal opposition collapsed".[5]

The resurrection of traditional opposition was slow and, until 1983, largely in response to Marcos's political manoeuvrings. Lakas ng Bayan (strength of the nation), abbreviated to its acronym, Laban (fight), was formed by Benigno Aquino to contest the 1978 Batasan elections; and the United Nationalist Democratic Opposition (UNIDO), an alliance of eight moderate opposition groups, was formed in 1980 by Aquino, Salvador Laurel, and Gerardo Roxas to pressure Marcos to end martial law.[6] A consensus was reached within the opposition to boycott the 1981 presidential elections. Laban and the Pilipino Democratic Party (PDP) joined to become PDP-Laban in 1982 in preparation for the 1984 Batasan elections.

The revitalization of traditional opposition also brought back many of the divisive personal and political rivalries that had long been dormant among many of the traditional political leaders. UNIDO was wracked by rivalry for control between Salvador Laurel and Eva Kalaw. Within PDP-Laban, tension existed because of differences between the younger, more ideologically inclined members on the one hand, and the more traditional politicians on the other.[7] The old Liberal Party also was divided by factionalism and was shorn of its traditional leadership (such as Aquino and former Senator Jovito Salonga, who was in exile in the United States).

Once it was clear that Marcos would weather the storm caused by the assassination, the traditional opposition set its sights on the May 1984 Batasang Pambansa elections. To some members of the opposition (and the U.S. Government) the elections were viewed as an opportunity for Marcos to take the first meaningful step towards the restoration of democracy. But to others, the elections were the "last chance" for a return to democracy before Philippine society became irreparably polarized and radicalized. UNIDO was the only opposition party given official status as a national political party for the elections. Consequently, a number of members of PDP-Laban and smaller regional parties ran under the UNIDO banner, which was an important step towards opposition unity. Among the traditional opposition, only the Liberal Party decided to boycott the elections, a mistake that would set them back for several years to come.

The government party, the KBL, enjoyed an overwhelming advantage in the elections because of the financial resources at its command and the government's control of the Commission on Elections (COMELEC), the military, almost all local officials, and most of the media. But the opposition mounted an active and extensive national campaign led by Salvador Laurel and Benigno Aquino's widow, Corazon. The opposition was aided by increasing support from the business community and the middle class, and by the growth of an opposition press following the Aquino assassination. Equally important was the creation of the National Movement for Free Elections (NAMFREL), a Church-backed organization of volunteers dedicated to watching polling places, guarding ballot boxes, and monitoring the government's vote counting.

Although marred by vote buying, intimidation, fraud, and a delayed vote count, the elections on 14 May were the fairest electoral contest since the 1971 elections. To the surprise of most observers, the opposition won 61 of the 183 elected seats in the 200-member Batasan, and it might have won a majority if the vote counting had been completely honest. In the critical Metro Manila contests, the opposition won 16 of 21 seats. Of the winning opposition candidates, close to a third were members of UNIDO, while the rest were members of PDP-Laban or other regional parties.[8]

The traditional opposition was emboldened by success in the May 1984 Batasan elections, but it remained disunified, despite efforts to unify it. A "Convenors Group" was established by Lorenzo Tanada, businessman Jaime Ongpin, and Corazon Aquino in early 1985 to establish a "fast track" process for quickly selecting a single opposition leader if Marcos called a "snap election" or died. UNIDO leader Salvador Laurel and Liberal Party stalwart Eva Kalaw balked at the prospect of not being selected, and formed the National Unification Committee (NUC). In June 1985 Laurel had himself selected by the NUC to run for president in the event that an election was called.

In the course of these efforts Corazon "Cory" Aquino gradually emerged as an important political figure. This happened in part because she was the widow of Ninoy Aquino, in part because of the absence of any other credible leader, and in part because of her own strength of character. A movement to draft Cory Aquino as the primary opposition leader grew in strength and by November 1985 1.2 million signatures had been collected on a petition urging her to run for president if an election were held. But one key signature was absent from the petition – that of Salvador Laurel – and without his endorsement of Aquino the opposition remained split.

The Rise of "Cause-Oriented" Opposition

Following the Aquino assassination there was also an explosion of non-traditional "cause-oriented", "sectoral", or "mass-based" groups. The cause-oriented groups were so named because of their concern with particular causes or issues (in contrast to the traditional political parties' avoidance of issue-oriented politics). The sectoral and mass-based groups included unions and labour federations, farmers' organizations, student and teachers' associations, women's groups, human rights lawyers, and other groups with memberships ranging from the urban poor to urban professionals.

Topping the list of demands of all these groups were a credible investigation of the Aquino assassination, the restoration of political freedoms, the end of U.S. support for Marcos, and the ouster of Marcos. They pressed these demands by staging *lakbayan*, or "people's freedom marches", and mass demonstrations, which soon became known as the "parliament of the streets".

The cause-oriented opposition grew so rapidly that at the anniversary rites for the Aquino assassination in August 1984, close to a million people marched in protest, many under the banners of specific opposition groups. In 1984 the first *welgang bayan* (people's strike) was organized in Davao City. The *welga* was a broad-based general strike designed to immobilize the city and show the weakness of the government. It was followed by similar strikes in the cities of Bacolod and Cebu. Towards the end of the year, the most prolonged and co-ordinated transport strikes since the 1940s paralysed major areas in Metro Manila and Central Luzon as well as key southern cities such as Davao, Butuan, Cagayan de Oro, Cebu, and Bacolod. In 1984 alone some 270 labour strikes rocked the industrial sector, more than in any previous year.[9]

By 1985 there were more than 100 mass and sectoral organizations that formed and re-formed ever shifting coalitions. The unity of the cause-oriented groups was fragmented by disagreements over tactical issues such as the acceptability of political violence and the value of parliamentary struggle; relations with the communist National Democratic Front; and a variety of ideological and policy issues ranging from economics to foreign relations. These and other differences were magnified by the highly personalized nature of many groups.

The major centre-left groups included those with significant business community leadership such as Kaakbay and Bandila and social democratic groups like ATOM (for August Twenty-one Movement), which was formed by Benigno Aquino's brother, Agapito "Butz" Aquino, and JAJA (for Justice for Aquino, Justice for All), which was formed after the Aquino assassination and became the first major coalition among left and centre forces. JAJA was superceded by the Coalition for the Restoration of Democracy (CORD) in preparation for the May 1984 elections.

To the left of these groups were more militant ones such as the Nationalist Alliance, the KMP (National Farmers' Movement), and the KMU (May First Movement) labour federation. In May 1985 Bayan (Bagong Alyansang Makabayan or New Nationalist Alliance) was formed in an effort to establish a unified command for all the left and centre-left cause-oriented groups. Bayan soon became the largest and best organized of these groups. By 1986 it claimed a national membership of about 2 million, comprising 600,000 KMU members, 100,000 KMP members and the rest from about 1,000 provincial-based organizations with which it was affiliated.

The goals of Bayan were fourfold. First, it demanded that the Marcos dictatorship be replaced with genuine "popular democracy". Secondly, it called for the achievement of "national sovereignty" by opposing all forms of foreign domination. Thirdly, it sought to promote "people's welfare and economic development" and to rid the country of economic inequality. And finally, it aspired to national unity, which it defined as "solidarity between all genuinely patriotic and democratic classes, sectors and forces of the Philippines".[10]

Bayan was created with strong backing from the NDF and opinions vary over how much autonomy Bayan actually had. The NDF saw Bayan as its vehicle for a "united front" of all nationalistic and anti-Marcos forces. But the NDF was not prepared either to make ideological compromises or to accept anything less than full control over the group. As a result, Bayan came to be viewed by many moderates as little more than a "front organization" for the NDF, prompting most of the centrist, pro-Aquino groups eventually to break with it.

The growth of cause-oriented groups from 1983 to 1985 reflected the politicization and mobilization of virtually every sector of Philippine society. Although some of these groups were controlled or heavily influenced by the far left, others were not. The growth of these progressive but centrist groups filled a dangerous void that existed between the radical left and the traditional political parties.

According to Emmanuel Soriano, a leader of Bandila (and later President Aquino's national security advisor):

> In '83 . . . you had a very highly organized Left and a very highly organized Right in the dictatorship, and a highly unorganized, fragmented middle. Our situation now is a more organized middle group in 1985 than in '83.[11]

By helping to politicize and organize the centre, or "middle forces" as they were called, the moderate cause-oriented groups provided an ideological and institutional alternative to the far left.

The cause-oriented groups also stimulated new groups of Filipinos to participate in the political process. According to journalist Lewis Simons:

> their demonstrations, marches, and pamphleteering kept the opposition alive during extended periods of lethargy. They drew the younger, formerly uninterested businessmen and technocrats into the political mainstream. The young, in turn, recruited the vitally needed big-business leaders and the top-rank academicians and clergy who had stayed out of the arena because they found all politicians distasteful, or the association with them unprofitable. Once these men began participating in earnest, they started a process of reform in Philippine politics that may, eventually, prove truly revolutionary.[12]

The Economic Crisis

As we have seen, the Philippines' economy steadily deteriorated during the early 1980s. Manufacturing declined, agriculture stagnated, the financial system was in disarray following the Dewey Dee crisis, the debt burden weighed heavily on the government, and the country's balance of payments worsened. Beginning in 1980, the rate of real GNP growth declined each year. In 1979 real GNP had grown 6.8 per cent. By 1981 GNP growth was only 3.7 per cent, and in 1983 the growth rate fell to 1.1 per cent, well below the rate of population increase.

As economic and financial conditions worsened during 1981 and 1982, the Philippines faced a serious balance-of-payments problem.

The country's current account deficit grew to more than US$2 billion in 1981 and then to US$3.2 billion in 1982. Capital flight increased, and in early 1983 many of the country's foreign creditors began to withdraw their lines of short-term credit to the Central Bank. There was increasing speculation that the government would be forced to declare a moratorium on debt payments.

Growing concern about the economy turned into a full blown economic crisis following the Aquino assassination. According to the 1984 UP study:

> Crisis of confidence seized foreign banks which refused to renew short term financing that the authorities had hitherto taken for granted. International reserves fell drastically from $2.54 billion at the start of 1983 to $1.43 billion by the end of September of that year. . . . In October 1983, the prime minister announced that international reserves had been reduced further to $430 million, owing to what was termed 'capital flight', although it was later learned that the level of reserves had been overstated.[13]

In response to the drain on foreign reserves, in October 1983 the government declared a commercial bank debt moratorium and imposed import controls. In 1984 it entered into prolonged negotiations with the International Monetary Fund (IMF) and the World Bank on a new Stand-by Loan Agreement and Structural Adjustment Programme, which were needed to improve the country's balance of payments and set the stage for a rescheduling of the country's commercial debt. The conditions the IMF attached to the loan programme were very tough: strict limits were set on government spending; new taxes were imposed; growth of money supply was tightly controlled; wage controls were imposed; and exchange rates, interest rates, and agricultural price controls were deregulated. These steps, while necessary to curb the government's fiscal profligacy, helped to plunge the economy into a deep recession.

In 1984 and 1985 the GNP shrank by 7.1 per cent and 4.2 per cent respectively. Real per capita GDP fell by 8.3 per cent in 1984, and another 6.7 per cent in 1985. Combined unemployment and underemployment rose from 15 per cent (2.3 million workers) in the first quarter of 1978 to more than 40 per cent (8.2 million workers) in the first quarter of 1984. In that year, inflation soared to 50 per cent, the highest level since World War II.

Confidence in the economy was further undermined by the mounting revelations of the rampant greed and corruption on the part of Marcos's family and friends. Articles substantiating the long circulating rumours of the huge "hidden wealth" of Marcos and his cronies (including government officials such as Defence Minister Juan Ponce Enrile, Energy Minister Geronimo Velasco, and Philippine Airlines president Roman Cruz, Jr.) appeared in the *San Jose Mercury News* in June 1985. These were followed by another in *Village Voice* claiming that the Marcoses owned real estate worth more than US$200 million in New York City.

The economic situation was so bad by the end of 1983 that almost 60 per cent of all Philippine families were living below the poverty line. Illustrative of this is that, even if both parents in a typical family worked and earned the legislated basic minimum wage (P42, or about US$2.50, per day in Metro Manila), a wage that was not paid by many of the smaller employers, they would earn only about 60 per cent of the income needed for their family to live above the poverty threshold.

Explosive Growth of the Communist Movement

Fuelled by the deepening national crisis, the CPP and NPA grew rapidly from 1982 to 1986. The ranks of the CPP roughly doubled in the five years from 1980 to more than 20,000 cadres in 1985. The number of full-time guerrillas in the NPA grew from about 7,500 in June 1983 to about 16,500 in 1985. In February 1985 the NDF claimed more than 6,000 "revolutionary mass organizations" and the CPP claimed it exercised leadership or effective influence over more than 350 factories and enterprises in urban areas and in 300 schools.[14] As many as 8,000 *barangay*, or 20 per cent of the total, were estimated to be influenced or controlled by the communists.[15] Unlike the Hukbalahap rebellion of the late 1940s and early 1950s, the communist movement of the 1980s had become national in scope, and had well-developed political and military strategies.

The communist movement in both urban and rural areas benefited from the Marcos government's preoccupation with the political and economic crisis that followed the Aquino assassination. The communists' urban organizations, particularly the NDF, capitalized on the politicization of the middle class and business community, the increased activism of cause-oriented groups, and the human suffering caused by the economic crisis. The rural movement benefited from the decline in government social services to the countryside, increasing anarchy and militarization, and the drop in copra and sugar prices.

The CPP-NPA was able to capitalize on the increasing discontent so effectively because of its emphasis on organizational work, which had produced a sizeable and growing "mass base" of support. According to William Chapman, the NPA had developed a "working formula" for building their mass base:

> The base grows as the NPA wins the people's trust and demonstrates its benefits for them in practical ways. The larger that base becomes, the more shelter and support it provides for the soldiers. The expanded mass base in turn expands the NPA. This intricate, mutually supporting relationship flourished in the 1980s. . . . [16]

By February 1985 the CPP claimed to have more than 60,000 "national democrat mass activists" throughout the country.[17] The religious arm of the NDF, Christians for National Liberation (CNL), was also actively trying to use the Catholic Church's national infrastructure and legitimacy to promote the left's cause. By 1985 CNL membership consisted of as many as 1,200 priests and nuns who formed secret cells inside the Catholic Church and its many organizations.[18]

But the expansion of the mass base was not done through persuasion alone. Chapman, writing in late 1986, noted that "The NPA had learned many lessons in its seventeen years, but none was so important as the fact that selective violence wins friends and builds support".[19] Many of the targets of the NPA's selective violence were local officials, 138 of whom were killed by the NPA in 1984, according to the military.[20] In 1985, a U.S. government official observed that, "The guerillas are killing the worst and the best local officials. They don't worry about the mediocre ones; they know they'll go along".[21]

Another important reason for the rapid growth of the insurgency, however, was the inability and unwillingness of the Armed Forces of the Philippines to counter it. AFP Chief of Staff General Ver was not a professional soldier, and his primary concern was defending the Marcos regime and his own power. By 1985, 27 of the AFP's 60 generals were "overstaying" generals whose mandatory retirements had been postponed because of their loyalty to Marcos. In 1985 it was reported that General Fidel Ramos ordered tanks and infantry battalions lying idle in a Metro Manila suburb to be deployed to fight the insurgency, but the general commanding these forces went to President Marcos and was able to get fifteen of the tanks redeployed to protect Malacañang Palace instead.[22] Consequently, both the commitment of the military leadership to pursuing an aggressive counter-insurgency programme and the AFP's actual capabilities to carry out such a programme were lacking. In June 1983 Admiral Robert Long, the U.S. Commander-in-Chief for the Pacific reported that the AFP was "incapable of performing . . . organic functions that any armed force should be able to provide for its own self-defense".[23]

As the insurgency grew, the officers and troops in the field faced increasingly larger NPA units that were often better armed and trained than the government forces. This reinforced the military's inclination to adopt a fundamentally defensive approach to the insurgency based on garrisoning towns rather than aggressively pursuing the guerrillas. In 1984 the NPA had units in 63 of the 73 provinces and initiated 2,700 military encounters, compared to just 1,000 initiated by the AFP.[24]

The organizational success of the communists, combined with the military's own heavy-handedness, increased the hostility of the very citizens the military was supposed to be defending. This resulted in increasingly frequent and brutal human rights violations by the AFP and the poorly trained paramilitary Civilian Home Defence Force (CHDF). These violations, in turn, were used by the communists to gain more supporters.

Not everything was rosy for the communists, however. At about the same time that Bayan was being formed in 1985 the NPA in Mindanao was conducting a massive purge, dubbed "Operation Clean", of cadres suspected of being military plants or Deep Penetration Agents (DPAs). The purge, driven by fear and panic, rapidly spun out of control. According to one account:

> Suspected traitors were summoned to 'seminars' on topics such as human rights or the 1986 snap election called by Mr. Marcos. When the suspects arrived, they were arrested, interrogated and tortured . . . . The purge quickly spread beyond the control of the NPA leaders. Low-level bosses started their own purges. . . .[25]

The purge may have resulted in the killing of several hundred cadres and seriously hurt the NPA's operations in Mindanao. By January 1986 the purge had become so frenzied that the rebels had all but abandoned their military operations.[26]

Despite the problem in Mindanao, the prospects for the continued growth and success of the insurgency appeared excellent in 1985. So great was the CPP leadership's optimism that they began to predict that the armed struggle would reach the stage of "strategic stalemate" in three to five years. "In the months before the [1986] election", William Chapman noted, "the CPP found itself in a mood of extreme self-confidence bordering on euphoria. Never had its prospects seemed so brilliant. The early 1980s had been a period of rapid growth and it seemed, after the years of trial and error and near extinction, that destiny favored it at last".[27]

Growing Foreign Pressure

The Aquino assassination caused a dramatic increase in international attention on the Philippines. Following the assassination the international (but predominantly U.S.) media flocked to the Philippines and began scrutinizing the Marcos regime as never before. The rapid growth of the communist insurgency and the potential threat it posed to the U.S. bases in the Philippines worried U.S. military strategists. The economic crisis caused international bankers and business executives to take a new and much more critical look at the regime they had dealt with for so long. International human rights groups, such as Amnesty International and the Lawyers Committee for Human Rights, stepped up their monitoring of human rights abuses.

In Washington, the U.S. Congress passed a joint declaration condemning the assassination and calling for a complete and credible investigation. The U.S. Administration had no choice but to cancel a visit to Manila by Reagan scheduled for November 1983. Increasingly concerned about the deteriorating situation, the Administration became more candid in its public descriptions of the Marcos regime's shortcomings and called for political, economic, and military reforms. Along with Congress it pushed, with mixed results, for a full investigation of the Aquino assassination, the retirement of Chief of Staff Ver, free and fair Batasan elections in 1984, military reform, and a panoply of economic reforms. At the same time the U.S. embassy in Manila distanced itself somewhat from the regime and expanded its contacts with the moderate opposition.

After visiting Manila in early 1984, the U.S. Commander-in-Chief of the Pacific, Admiral William Crowe, gave a highly critical and pessimistic briefing on the Philippines to President Reagan. This heightened concern within the Administration led to an inter-agency review of U.S. policy in early 1985. In October 1985, Reagan's close friend, Nevada senator Paul Laxalt, visited Manila to convey personally to Marcos Reagan's concern about the situation. Laxalt claims that he suggested that Marcos should hold elections to re-establish his mandate but that Marcos had rejected the idea.

Reagan, however, was not about to abandon his old and trusted friend in the Philippines. The Administration continued to view the co-operation of Marcos as the key to the success of the reforms Washington was calling for. By maintaining this approach it indulged in wishful thinking that Marcos was willing and capable of making reforms that would further undermine his already weakened position.

The Beginning of the End

Marcos successfully rode out the storm following the Aquino assassination, but not without losing considerable public and international support. The growing size and frequency of anti-Marcos demonstrations, swelling numbers of communists and communist sympathizers, increasing outspokenness of Church and business leaders, and expansion of a small but influential opposition press were all clear indications of Marcos's declining popularity. But the mounting political opposition to him was confined for the most part to the major urban centres. Outside the politicized minority in the cities and those affected by the communist insurgency in the countryside it was business as usual for the majority of poor Filipinos who were just trying to make ends meet.

The glacial pace of the erosion of support for Marcos has been described by public opinion analyst Felipe Miranda:

> One may say that survey results over the past two decades project an image of Filipinos who by 1970 reflected much optimism about themselves and their country's capability to progress in life; who in the early years of martial law administration were ready

to see national welfare being served ahead of their personal welfare; who even by 1981 were liberally granting their political system and government the benefit of the doubt and, on balance, were still supportive of government and other political institutions; but who, by 1984–85, had largely lost confidence in their political institutions and ruling authorities and, in crisis, anticipated with great uncertainty and anxiety more threatening economic and political developments.[28]

Viewed another way, by 1985 the foundations of the Marcos regime had been seriously eroded. Assessing the situation in mid-1985 William Overholt has written that:

the Marcos regime had a weak and fearfully divided executive leadership, a collection of emasculated institutions, and a social base confined to the few remaining cronies who weren't bankrupt, senior military officers who were increasingly unsure of the loyalty of their troops, a nervous network of political officials who knew they had no future after Marcos, and Ilocano communities for whom ethnic ties remained paramount. . . . In short the Marcos regime was a hollow shell.[29]

It was this hollow shell of a regime that Marcos sought to breath new life into by calling for a "snap" presidential election.

The 1986 "Snap" Presidential Election

Faced with growing political opposition, an economic crisis, an expanding insurgency, and mounting American pressure for reforms, Marcos sought to regain the initiative. In a characteristically surprise move, during an interview on American television in early November 1985, he announced that there would be a "snap" presidential election in early 1986 to settle the question of his government's mandate.

The fact that he made the announcement on American television suggests the election was called as much for U.S. Government consumption as for domestic political reasons. In addition to seeking to silence his American critics, however, there were a number of other reasons for his dramatic announcement. One was the growing likelihood that the ruling KBL would suffer significant losses in the local elections then scheduled for May 1986. Such losses would have diminished the KBL's ability to deliver the vote for Marcos if the presidential election went ahead, as originally scheduled, in 1987. A second factor was Marcos's supreme confidence that the divided opposition would not be able to field a unified ticket against him, and that even if they did, none of the likely opposition candidates would be a match for him. And finally, it is likely that Marcos anticipated that his health would continue to decline, so it made sense to hold the presidential election sooner rather than later.

On 2 December the court trying the Aquino-Galman murder case declared General Fabian Ver innocent of the murder of Benigno Aquino. The next day Corazon "Cory" Aquino announced her long-awaited decision to run against Marcos. But so did Salvador "Doy" Laurel, and for the next week it appeared that the opposition would be split, just as Marcos had expected. However, on 11 December, the last day for candidates to register, a "shot gun wedding" was arranged between the two opposition candidates following the intervention of Archbishop Jaime Cardinal Sin. Laurel accepted the vice-presidential slot and Aquino, for her part, agreed to run under the banner of Laurel's UNIDO party and give him a prominent say in the composition of the new government if they won. To the surprise of most observers – and perhaps Marcos most of all – a united and potentially powerful opposition slate had been forged.[31]

The snap election presented a vexing problem for the leftist opposition to Marcos. Within Bayan there was serious disagreement over whether to boycott the election or support the Aquino–Laurel slate. Those advocating a boycott were skeptical of the opposition slate's commitment to progressivism, and viewed the elections as inherently unfair and unwinnable. The far left also hoped to build upon the anticipated failure of the presidential election to generate support for Bayan candidates in the local elections scheduled for May 1987. After considerable internal debate the advocates of a boycott ultimately prevailed, and the official Bayan position supported an "active and militant" boycott of the elections. With this decision the left forfeited the opportunity to have an influence on the most important political event since the declaration of martial law. In doing so they ceded centre stage to Ferdinand Marcos and Corazon Aquino and were relegated to watching from the wings as the drama unfolded.

The 1986 presidential election was similar to past elections in so far as it was primarily a contest between personalities and less a public debate over issues. But the 1986 contest was unique in the degree of contrast between the two candidates and what they represented, and by the great differences in the power and resources of their respective political organizations.

The Marcos campaign slogan, "Marcos, now more than ever" encapsulated his message — the country faced problems (somehow not of his making) that only he could solve. In contrast to this, the Aquino slogan, "Enough! Too much!", emphasized how unbearable the situation had become under Marcos, and demanded he be replaced.

Although sixty-nine years old and suffering from bouts of lupus, Marcos remained the undisputed and unrivalled master of the Byzantine world of Philippine politics. When his illness was not debilitating he exuded self-confidence and bravado; and even when he was in a physically weakened state he still possessed the shrewdness and mental agility that had been his trademarks for the last twenty years. He hammered away at Aquino's lack of experience, calling her a mere housewife who was better suited for the kitchen than for the presidential office. He invoked the spectres of a communist take-over, Muslim secession, and civil war if Aquino was elected. And as an enticement to vote for him — as well as a reminder of his virtually unlimited power — he issued countless presidential decrees raising salaries, lowering prices, giving land, granting new loans and writing off old ones.

But Marcos's regal performance could not erase the deepening sense shared by many Filipinos that his time had come, that his failing health was a reflection of the failure of his policies, and that he was a captive of his own corrupt system, unable to reform it even if he wanted to. Moreover, his selection of Arturo Tolentino, a KBL stalwart, as his vice-presidential running mate did little to give the ticket a reformist cast.

In stark contrast to the wily and almost larger than life Marcos stood fifty-three-year-old Corazon Aquino, the well-bred widow of Benigno Aquino, and the hesitant inheritor of the mantle of her husband's anti-Marcos crusade. A self-proclaimed political neophyte, she came to represent morality, courage, and change. As someone who had personally suffered at the hands of Marcos, she embodied the nation's suffering under the Marcos regime. Although a small and soft-spoken woman, her willingness to stand up to the "macho" Marcos made her a symbol of courage to people who perhaps felt that they had been too timid for too long. But most of all, she offered the hope of change, reconciliation, and redemption.

Equally contrasting were the resources at the command of the two opposing camps. Marcos had at his disposal the almost unlimited resources of the government as well as the KBL's well entrenched, if somewhat rusty, nation-wide political machine. The KBL, though not monolithic, controlled 69 of 73 provincial governments, 53 of 59 city governments, and the large majority of municipal and *barangay* posts across the country. Marcos controlled directly or indirectly all of Metro Manila's television stations and most of the radio stations and newspapers as well. He also had appointed the majority of the commissioners of the Commission on Elections, the body responsible for overseeing his tailor-made election code. Once the voting was finished, the KBL-controlled Batasang Pambansa was responsible for canvassing (certifying) the election returns and proclaiming the winner. Finally, Marcos could count on his hand-picked judiciary to be unresponsive to any election protests filed by the opposition.

Aquino and Laurel mounted a tireless campaign against this intimidating array of political weapons. Deprived of equal access to the media, and unable to rely on a national political machine to deliver the vote, they took to the road. By late January they had visited 50 of 73 provinces and by election day they had covered 68.

Aquino's campaign emphasized the continuation of her husband's cause, her sincerity, and her honesty. She underscored her courage in standing up to Marcos in the hope others would stand up too. Her positions on major issues were moderate, but lacking in detail. She pledged to restore democracy and human rights, end corruption, pursue a peaceful solution to the insurgency, encourage a free but equitable economy, and honour the military bases agreement with the United States until its expiration in 1991.

But it was her righteousness and courage more than her policies that held such strong appeal to the average Filipino. Responding to Marcos's charges that she was just an inexperienced housewife, she countered that the country's many problems were attributable to Marcos and his twenty years of "experience". She struck at his "macho" image by challenging his war record and calling him a coward for not visiting the strongly oppositionist island of Mindanao for ten years. She painted him as an inveterate liar and described his government as "a dictatorship cleverly crafted by an evil genius".

Although clearly the underdogs, Aquino and Laurel were able to draw on a number of important sources of support for their uphill fight. These included the Catholic Church, the National Movement for Free Elections, a coalition of small parties and moderate cause-oriented groups, and the international media. Of these, the roles of the Church and NAMFREL were particularly important.

Cardinal Sin, according to his spokesman, viewed the Aquino–Marcos struggle as "a fight between the forces of good and the forces of evil, a fight between the children of the light and the children of darkness". In such a fight, Sin believed the Church could not be neutral. "How can I be neutral in the face of evil?" he asked.[32] It is not surprising, therefore, that Cardinal Sin played an important role in forging the Aquino–Laurel coalition. Nor is it surprising that the Church-owned Radio Veritas and *Veritas* weekly newspaper provided extensive coverage of the Aquino–Laurel campaign when much of the rest of the Marcos-controlled media would not.

As the election approached and Cardinal Sin's fear of massive fraud grew, he issued a pastoral letter on 19 January in which he warned of "a sinister plot by some people and groups to frustrate the honest and orderly expression of the people's genuine will". He also called for all voters to "vote for people who embody the Gospel values of humility, truth, honesty, respect for human rights and life" and urged them not to be "corrupted by money or other immoral considerations. . . ."[33] In late January the Catholic Bishops' Conference of the Philippines (CBCP) urged Catholic voters to combat a "conspiracy of evil" that threatened to thwart the people's will during the election. And on 5 February, just two days before the election, Cardinal Sin virtually endorsed Aquino, saying that she would make a good president if elected.

NAMFREL, with its close ties to the Church and the business community, served as a critical independent election "watch-dog". It recruited and trained more than 500,000 volunteers who monitored the voting and vote count in about 90 per cent of the country's precincts. On the local level the NAMFREL presence before and on election day created outposts of accountability that helped to offset the dominance of the local KBL machine. On the national level, the NAMFREL computerized "quick count" of election returns was viewed by many Filipinos as being more credible than the Marcos-controlled COMELEC count. As the discrepancy between the two counts grew after the election, the NAMFREL count, which showed Aquino and Laurel winning, seriously undermined the claims made by Marcos that he had won, and won legitimately.

Despite the efforts of the Church and NAMFREL to discourage election fraud, the magnitude of the cheating that occurred on election day and afterwards exceeded the opposition's worst expectations. Francis Clines of the *New York Times* elegantly described the scene:

> The day dawned at crescendo, the complaints of fraud and ballot thievery pouring in as a single tide from the scores of thousands of island precincts: ballot boxes allegedly stuffed with Marcos votes even before the polls opened; voting precincts suddenly moved overnight; "goon" intimidators loitering in the path of voters; tally sheets reportedly missing; mercenary voters allegedly commuting across a swatch of precincts to vote early and often.[34]

What Clines described were the results of a massive and carefully premeditated effort by Marcos and the KBL to assure the victory of the Marcos–Tolentino team. This effort was detailed in a report on the election released by NAMFREL after the February revolution. According to the NAMFREL report, the government relied on a strategy of "subtraction" designed to disenfranchise significant numbers of voters in Central Luzon, Metro Manila, and the Southern Tagalog region – areas known to be heavily pro-Aquino. To do this, voter registration lists were tampered with, voided or misplaced; ballot boxes were snatched; people were paid not to vote; and opposition ballots were undercounted. Consequently, voter turn-out averaged slightly under 80 per cent nation-wide, lower than the turn-out for the 1984 elections. But in Metro Manila, a heavily pro-Aquino area, the turn-out was only about 73 per cent because many voter registration lists had been tampered with, which made it difficult or impossible for many Manileños to vote.

The "subtraction" strategy was complemented by more traditional vote "addition" and "substitution" efforts. An estimated one million votes were cast by "flying voters" (voters who registered and voted in more than one precinct), votes were bought, ballot boxes were stuffed, and returns were miscounted. NAMFREL concluded that only 41 per cent of the country's 91 electoral districts were unaffected by the government's strategy of subtraction, addition, and substitution. According to NAMFREL, "With exceedingly high incidence of disenfranchisement of voters in opposition strongholds and abnormally high voter turn-out in KBL bailiwicks, the net effect was the minimization of UNIDO's gains in opposition-leaning areas and the maximization of KBL margins in its own bailiwicks."[35]

The disenfranchisement, vote buying, fraud, and violence of election day were followed by a more subtle but equally serious form of cheating as the votes were counted. On 8 February, the NAMFREL tally showed Aquino leading by nearly one million votes. COMELEC, however, showed Marcos with a slight lead. From that point on, the difference between the two counts continued to grow, eventually prompting thirty COMELEC computer operators to walk out on the evening of 9 February to protest discrepancies between what they were inputting and what COMELEC was posting publicly.

By 10 February the gap between the two counts had widened considerably. The COMELEC count, which had stopped following the walk-out, had counted only 28 per cent of the vote and had Marcos winning 51 per cent of the votes counted. NAMFREL, however, had counted 48 per cent of the votes and had Aquino winning 53 per cent of it. Over the next two days the percentage of the votes counted by COMELEC edged up to about 50 per cent and the portion of the total vote counted by NAMFREL reached about 70 per cent. But the difference between the two counts remained more or less constant. COMELEC claimed that Marcos and Tolentino had won over 53 per cent each, while NAMFREL showed Aquino and Laurel each winning about 52 per cent. Stalemated, COMELEC washed its hands of the mess and on 12 February the KBL-dominated Batasang Pambansa began to canvass the election results provided by COMELEC.

On 15 February, amid growing domestic and international outrage, the Batasan declared Marcos the winner, with 53.8 per cent of the votes as against Aquino's 46.6 per cent, representing a difference of about 1.5 million votes. The Batasan decree was based on 20.1 million votes counted, or only 77 per cent of registered voters. (In the May 1984 Batasan elections, with some voters participating in a boycott, the voter turn-out was 89 per cent). Particularly damaging to the Aquino vote count – and damning to the credibility of the Batasan decree – was the fact that only 71 per cent of the Metro Manila vote was counted.

The numerous reports of fraud and intimidation, the suspiciously low turn-out in opposition areas, the delay in the COMELEC counting, the glaring discrepancy between the COMELEC and NAMFREL counts, and the Batasan's heavy-handed canvassing of the results all combined to form a powerful indictment of the Marcos government's handling of the election. On 14 February the Catholic Bishops' Conference of the Philippines expressed its outrage, calling the fraud "unparalleled" and condemning the KBL's tactics as "a criminal use of power to thwart the sovereign will of the people". On 15 February President Reagan reversed his early judgement that election fraud had been committed by both sides, and echoing the findings of American and international observer missions, said the election abuse was "so extensive that the election's credibility has been called into question".

But most important of all, Mrs Aquino refused to accept the Marcos "victory", and on 16 February she announced that a campaign of peaceful civil disobedience would begin with a nation-wide general strike and the boycott of government and crony-owned businesses. Marcos, it appeared for the moment, had "won" the election, but at the considerable cost of losing the last vestiges of his credibility and legitimacy.

From Snap Election to "Snap Revolution"

Aquino's decision to reject the election results and continue her campaign against Marcos was fraught with danger. As James Rush has noted, "For Mrs. Aquino and the forces of the center, embarking upon a national campaign of non-cooperation was full of risk, not the least of which was unleashing other social and political forces which they could neither control nor contain".[36] The left, realizing that their boycott of the election had removed them from the forefront of the struggle against Marcos, sought to regain some involvement in and control over the mounting protest. Bayan and the NDF offered to participate in Aquino's strategy of non-cooperation, but their offers were rejected.

But less than a week after Aquino announced her campaign of civil disobedience, the focus of the anti-Marcos struggle shifted dramatically away from the civilian opposition and moved to the military. On 22 February Minister of Defence Juan Ponce Enrile, Vice-Chief of Staff General Fidel Ramos, and several hundred troops loyal to them suddenly and unexpectedly broke with Marcos, locked themselves in the military headquarters in Camps Crame and Aguinaldo in Metro

Manila, and in so doing, became the catalysts for the collapse of the
Marcos government three days later.

The EDSA "Revolution"

The dramatic four-day EDSA "revolution" (EDSA is the acronym for the
highway running between the two military camps where the revolt took
place) was televised globally, and there are now several excellent published accounts available, so only a sketch will be provided here.[37]

The February revolution is often described as a "civilian-backed
military revolt". More accurately, it began as a hastily planned action
by Enrile and a small group of "reformist" military officers loyal to
him. These officers, apparently with Enrile's knowledge and support,
had planned to attack Malacañang Palace, capture the Marcoses, and
force them to step down (or, presumably, kill them, if necessary). Their
plans were discovered by General Ver, however, who began to arrest
the reformists suspected of involvement in the coup plot. Learning of
the imminent round-up Enrile and about 300 members of the Reform
the Armed Forces Movement (RAM) barricaded themselves in Camp
Aguinaldo on the afternoon of 22 February, and called on General
Ramos to join them. Ramos, who probably was not a party to the details
of the coup plan, agreed to join the revolt, most likely out of exaspera-
tion with Marcos and Ver, but perhaps also because of the personal
opportunity it presented.[38] Enrile and Ramos announced their resignations from the Marcos government, denounced the election as a
fraud, and called on Marcos to step down.

That evening Cardinal Sin broadcast a message over Radio Veritas
urging people to go to Camps Crame and Aguinaldo to protect the
rebels and give them food. In response to Sin's call, tens and then hundreds of thousands of civilians congregated at EDSA in what became
known as "people power". The crowds of civilians surrounding the
rebels effectively immobilized the military forces loyal to Marcos by
making it impossible for them to stage an attack on the rebels without
causing a civilian massacre. There were several tense confrontations
between civilians and troops sent to attack the rebels, but in the end
the troops retreated and a blood letting was avoided. Moreover, the
demonstration of "people power" was proof to most foreign governments that the regime had lost the last vestiges of its legitimacy. Faced

with stubborn civilian opposition, a growing number of defections in the military, and mounting pressure from Washington, Marcos finally agreed to leave Malacañang Palace on the evening of 25 February.

At 10:00 a.m. on 25 February, Corazon Aquino had taken the oath of office as the seventh president of the Philippines "in the name and will of the Filipino people". Also sworn in were Salvador Laurel as vice-president and foreign minister, Juan Ponce Enrile as defence minister, and Fidel Ramos as Chief of Staff of the "New" Armed Forces of the Philippines. Enrile had urged Aquino to hold the ceremony in one of the military camps, but Aquino and her advisors were intent on having it held in a non-military location to emphasize the primacy of the civilian government. Consequently, the inauguration was held at Club Filipino, an exclusive club that has long been a gathering place for the country's élite. As Robert Shaplen first pointed out, it was ironic and perhaps indicative of things to come that the ceremony was held at an élite club so soon after the triumph of "people power".[39]

At noon that same day Ferdinand Marcos had also taken an oath as president in a melancholy ceremony at Malacañang Palace. Conspicuously absent were his vice-presidential running mate, Arturo Tolentino, and Cesar Virata, Marcos's chief technocrat, who had served as prime minister and finance minister. But even as Marcos was being sworn in, preparations were being made to leave the palace. In the early evening Marcos informed the U.S. ambassador, Stephen Bosworth, that he would relinquish office, but that he wished to go home to the province of Ilocos Norte. At about 9:00 p.m. four U.S. helicopters picked up Marcos, his family, General Ver and about thirty others and flew them to Clark Air Base, north of Metro Manila, where they spent the night. Early the following morning, his request to remain in the country having been denied by Aquino, Marcos and his party of about fifty-five were flown first to Guam and then to Hawaii. On board the plane were US$1.1 million in newly minted pesos and jewelry and other assets reported to be worth US$30 million. The Marcos government had come to an end after more than twenty years of increasingly corrupt, authoritarian, and damaging rule.

Causes of the EDSA "Revolution"

The EDSA "revolution" began as a military revolt, but it is unlikely that it would have succeeded without the participation of Metro Manila's citizenry. The uprising was, therefore, a direct continuation of the heightened political participation stimulated by the February presidential election, and reflected the public's rejection of the fraudulent election results.

The presidential election had generated an unprecedented level of political participation in the Philippines. A number of prominent business leaders broke with tradition and boldly proclaimed their support for Aquino. Previously apolitical middle-class Filipinos became volunteers in NAMFREL and joined more overtly partisan campaign organizations such as "Cory's Crusaders". There were also reports that among the poorest voters a significant number became sufficiently politicized so that they voted on the basis of their beliefs rather than for bribes (although the smart ones took the money too). For the first time in a very long time people felt they had a say and a stake in the outcome of the election. When it became clear that "Cory" Aquino had been cheated, they felt *they* had been cheated.

But the EDSA uprising was also the result of a convergence of several other factors, most of which had been developing since 1983. First was the organization and mobilization of centrist opposition groups with the support and encouragement of the Church and the business community. Most of the centrist cause-oriented groups that had originally been formed to protest the assassination of Benigno Aquino became important actors in the Aquino–Laurel campaign and subsequently mobilized their followers to participate in the EDSA demonstration.

At the same time that centrist groups were becoming stronger, the left found itself largely relegated to the sidelines by its decision to boycott the presidential election. In January 1986, *Ang Bayan*, the CPP newspaper, called the snap election a "grand deception − a trap that aims to tighten [the Filipino people's] chains under the rule of the US–Marcos fascist dictatorship". It also predicted that "the election is virtually over in favor of the US-Marcos clique, with the US accepting Marcos's 'victory'". According to political scientist Alex Magno:

> By insisting on a vanguardist role [the left] tailed in the events.
> Trapped in dogmatic visions of what revolution should be like,
> the hour of rising found them wandering about in the side streets.
> They who fought the hardest and contributed the most martyrs

to the cause of freedom now contemplate on the callous ironies
of history.[40]

A third critical factor was the unprecedented role played by the
Catholic Church in the events following the election. On 14 February,
the 103-member Catholic Bishops' Conference of the Philippines had
issued a statement charging the government with "unparalleled" fraud
and stating that "a government that assumes or retains power through
fraudulent means has no moral basis". In addition to repudiating the
election results, the Church also supported Aquino's call for non-violent
civil disobedience. On the evening of 22 February, Jaime Cardinal Sin
took the bold and risky step of calling the citizens of Metro Manila
into the streets to support the Enrile–Ramos revolt.[41]

The disunity and rivalry that had become endemic to the Marcos
government by late 1985 was a fourth important ingredient in the EDSA
success story. Within the government, Ferdinand and Imelda Marcos,
General Fabian Ver, and their closest cronies had been concerned
above all else with the survival of the regime, and the protection of
their power and privileges. But the expectation that Marcos's ambitious
wife would attempt to succeed her ailing husband caused the palace
to be divided into factions loyal to the president and the first lady.
At the same time, the loyalties of the AFP's senior officers were divided
among Ver, Enrile, and Ramos. It is likely that this complex web of
loyalty, rivalry, and suspicion complicated the decision-making process
within Malacañang Palace.

Whose "Revolution" was it?

The most immediate and dramatic consequence of the EDSA revolt was,
of course, the downfall of the Marcos regime. But the unique nature
of the "civilian-backed military revolt", as it was frequently referred
to in the press, also influenced the composition and character of the
Aquino government and the political environment in which it operated.
Most immediately, the leading role played in the revolt by Enrile and
Ramos guaranteed the two men, and the Philippine military, an important
role in the new government and dramatically changed the nature of
civilian–military relations. Conversely, the lack of participation by the left
meant that it was closed out of a potential role in the new government.

While these changes alone make the importance of the February revolt indisputable, there has been considerable disagreement over the meaning and significance of other aspects of the event. For instance, who could claim primary responsibility for the success of the uprising: the military, the moderate opposition, or the left? Was it just a spontaneous uprising against Marcos or the culmination of a process of mass politicization and mobilization? Was it just a "revolt" against a hated ruler or the beginning of a genuine "revolution"?

The significance of these questions is more than just historical, for the differing answers reflect the important disagreements that existed among key groups following the fall of Marcos. These differences would influence many aspects of government and politics during the first two years of the Aquino era. For this reason the question of "whose revolution was it?" deserves further examination.

Both the supporters of Aquino and the military jealously claimed responsibility for the success of the February revolution, as did the radical left, although in a more indirect way. According to Aquino's supporters, the EDSA revolution was an extension of the struggle of the Aquino forces against Marcos that had begun with her campaign for the presidency. Aquino's supporters also claimed that the military revolt started by Enrile and Ramos would not have succeeded without the protection and legitimation provided by "people power". The EDSA revolution, therefore, was a popular rejection of the claims to leadership of both the extreme left and right (including Marcos and the military). Consequently, the new Aquino government based its claim to legitimacy not on the fraudulent presidential election, but rather on the public's repudiation of Marcos at EDSA.

The military participants in the revolt, however, held the view that EDSA was primarily a bold military strike against the dictatorship and only secondarily a civilian uprising. They chose to interpret "people power" as being a sign of public support for the military rebels as well as for the civilian opposition. Although this distinction may seem trivial, it took on considerable significance a year and a half later, when Colonel Gregorio "Gringo" Honasan and other military dissidents claimed that their August 1987 coup attempt was the continuation of the revolution that *they* had started in February 1986.

The radical left, having boycotted the presidential election, could not and did not claim a leading role in the EDSA revolution. *Ang Bayan* grudgingly acknowledged that the EDSA revolution was "the biggest political event since the imposition of martial law in 1972".[42] It also conceded that "although the national democratic movement played a major role in politicizing the broad masses of the people towards the level of struggle attained in February 22–25, it had limited influence in the uprising, particularly in Metro Manila which was the center of the action".[43] The left, however, did claim responsibility for leading the anti-Marcos struggle in the difficult months and years prior to the February uprising.

Which of these three claims is most accurate? The left has a valid claim only to an indirect role in the uprising. Bayan and other progressive cause-oriented groups were at the forefront in organizing and mobilizing opposition to Marcos. Their use of mass political mobilization was the predecessor of what Aquino came to call "people power". But the "people power" exhibited at EDSA was characterized by the moderation of the middle class – not the militancy of the extreme left. It was influenced by the Church, pro-Aquino politicians, and other moderates – not by Bayan or the NDF. Indeed, the essentially moderate uprising prevented a resurgence of the left's participation in the anti-Marcos struggle. According to James Rush, if the EDSA revolt had not happened when it did,

> the well-organized and adamant forces of the left would have inevitably regained the momentum they had lost by boycotting the election campaign . . . . At the grass roots level only the mass organizations and trade unions of the left had the infrastructure and discipline needed to execute massive shutdowns. The impressive regional general strikes of 1985, the *welgang bayan*, had been organized by Bayan, not by opposition politicians.[44]

The military's view is also true, but only up to a point. Enrile, Ramos, and the members of RAM must be credited with breaking with Marcos in the face of considerable odds against them. Without "people power", however, their action might have gone down in the history books as an attempted military coup bloodily quashed by Marcos and Ver. And while the military revolt served as the catalyst to the broader civilian uprising, it should be remembered that the military rebels' original objectives were not to lead a popular uprising in favour of Corazon Aquino. Instead, they sought to establish a civilian-military "committee" including Aquino, Enrile, Ramos, Sin, and several other leading Filipinos.[45] But because of the need to generate civilian support for the military revolt, Enrile felt compelled to announce his support for Aquino during the first press conference at Camp Aguinaldo on 22 February.

In the final analysis, therefore, the EDSA phenomenon was fundamentally a moderate, civilian-based uprising against Marcos. Clearly, the withdrawal of support for Marcos by elements of the armed forces was critical to the regime's downfall. By Aquino's own admission, if it were not for the military revolt begun on 22 February she might have spent weeks and perhaps months leading a dangerous and uncertain national campaign of civil disobedience against Marcos. But it is unlikely that Enrile's hastily concocted revolt would have survived a military reprisal by forces loyal to Marcos, or would have received the support of most military officers, if the Church and the civilian population had not intervened to support it. According to James Rush:

> The timing of the long-hoped-for change of government, in short, pre-empted extreme alternatives and gave new life to the political center, the undeniably elite-led center with its complex democratic vision of itself and its fervent belief that elections can bring things aright.[46]

Myths, Realities, and Expectations of the EDSA Revolution

Myths — regardless of whether they are centuries old or brand new — are an important part of every country's political culture. They shape people's views of national history and can provide a unifying heritage; they influence people's sense of national identity; they contribute to a common set of values and attitudes; and they affect people's views of the present and their expectations for the future.

The EDSA revolution quickly assumed mythical dimensions for many Filipinos. To many, it demonstrated the deep- rooted courage, love of freedom, and non-violent nature of Filipinos. It proved that Filipinos of all classes and backgrounds could unify and work together. It underscored the important role of religion and faith in determining the destiny of the nation. And it held the hope of a new and better era in Philippine politics and society. These myths, though rooted in truth to varying degrees, were similar in that they all influenced popular perceptions and expectations in the months following the revolution.

The first myth was that the non-violent nature of the EDSA revolution was uniquely "Filipino" and it demonstrated that peaceful change was possible in the Philippines. Because the EDSA revolution was largely non-violent, deeply infused with religiosity, and at times even fiesta-like, some Filipinos have concluded that the Philippines has a uniquely peaceful approach to "revolutionary" change. But while the uprising was non-violent, the myth overlooks the reality that there were numerous situations where massive violence was narrowly avoided, and that if it was not for a few key decisions (and mistakes), events could have run a much bloodier, and ultimately more extreme, course.[47] A second dimension of this myth — that the EDSA experience demonstrated that the country's problems could be solved peacefully and to everyone's satisfaction — was in many ways a reflection of the wishful thinking of a conservative élite and middle-class threatened by the prospects of a revolutionary communist movement.

A corollary to the myth of "peaceful revolution" was the myth that the EDSA uprising resulted in the unification of all classes and sectors of Philippine society. Following the uprising, the wealthy residents of Manila's affluent suburbs liked to talk about how they mingled with the masses and how everyone shared food and a common cause. In reality, however, the turn-out at EDSA was predominantly middle class and urban. Solidarity, to the extent that it existed, was based more on shared opposition to Marcos than on a common vision of a more unified and egalitarian society.

A second powerful myth with important consequences was that EDSA was a "people powered revolution". People power protected the military rebels from the forces loyal to Marcos and resulted in the collapse of the dictatorship. Many Filipinos hoped that the use of people power would begin a new era of popular, rather than élite, politics in the Philippines. They hoped to institutionalize the direct mass action of people power as a counter-balance to the more traditional forms of representative or indirect government. The goal was to give "the people" a greater and more direct influence on a traditionally élitist government.

Initially, the belief in people power did not seem completely naive. The Aquino government based its claim to legitimacy on the February uprising rather than on the disputed election. A public opinion poll taken in June 1986 showed that the public shared this interpretation:

people power was overwhelmingly considered the source of the Aquino government's legitimacy rather than an electoral victory.[48]

But the concept of people power remained vague, especially concerning how it could be institutionalized. It was also easily co-opted by different groups and corrupted by some. According to Lewis Simon, the RAM rebels had planned all along to use mass support to protect themselves.[49] In the months following EDSA, many traditional politicians (including Mrs Aquino) adopted the rhetoric of people power at the same time that they rejected the idea of creating "people's councils" or any other significant mechanisms for ensuring non-traditional political participation. Aquino's abandonment of "people-power" would become one of the major criticisms of the new government by the left.

A third important myth was that EDSA signalled the collective redemption of the military. Because of the military's role in sparking the EDSA uprising, some Filipinos concluded that the military as a whole had redeemed itself by rejecting Marcos's authoritarianism. According to this view, the military leadership had demonstrated its commitment to democracy and could be relied on to protect the democratic gains made in February. Referring to the military, one leading communist conceded: "Overnight they have turned from villains to heroes. From fascists, they have suddenly become 'liberators'".[50] This observation was later substantiated by a public opinion poll in June 1986 showing that a majority of respondents thought the military had improved in the three months following the revolution and that the AFP would be loyal and obedient to Aquino.[51]

In reality, however, the support for the uprising within the military was neither universal nor overly enthusiastic. The EDSA uprising was begun by a small group of officers and troops whose loyalties were more to Enrile and the cause of a stronger military than to Aquino and democracy. Consequently, the intervention of people power protected the rebels; but according to Francisco Nemenzo, it also "contained the mutiny, preventing it from developing into a coup d'etat that would have either installed a military dictator or a civilian government chosen by a military junta".[52] And although a number of key military officers eventually threw their support behind the anti-Marcos rebels over the four-day uprising, many others "sat on the fence", waiting to see which side would prevail – just as they would during the August 1987 and December 1989 coup attempts.

Significance of the EDSA Revolution

The EDSA revolution was predominantly Metro Manila-based, middle class, and moderate. It succeeded in toppling Marcos because of both the defection of key members of the military leadership and the protection provided by massive civilian support. It freed the Philippines of Marcos's one-man rule and installed a popular leader at the head of a disparate and inexperienced coalition government. It also gave new life to centrist, moderate politics in a society that had been on the brink of splitting apart. Reflecting the diminished appeal of extremism, a public opinion poll taken three months after the revolution showed that 54 per cent of respondents thought that the CPP should not be legalized, as opposed to only 34 per cent a year before.[53] Finally, the uprising gave most Filipinos, at least temporarily, a new sense of national pride, unity and hope.

The unseating of the Marcos government in four relatively peaceful days was, in its own right, a major accomplishment. But the "revolution" did little to clarify the orientation and direction of the new government. As Alex Magno has observed: "The February Revolution was decided at the level of abstract symbolism and not on the terrain of competing alternative programs."[54] The reality is that the February 1986 uprising was a revolt against Marcos, not a revolution in Philippine politics and society. And once the Marcos government was gone, the question became: what would Corazon Aquino offer in its place?

Conclusion: The Marcos Legacy

Almost fourteen years of authoritarianism left a disturbing legacy that cast a long shadow over politics, government, and the economy. Marcos perverted most of the positive aspects of traditional democracy and reinforced most of the system's worst features. He further centralized the already over-centralized national government and deprived local governments of the little autonomy they once had. He replaced the intra-élite political competition of the traditional system with managed or unfair plebiscites, referenda, and elections. He undermined the already discredited legislative tradition by creating a rubber stamp National Assembly. And he further weakened the legal system and the administration of justice by couching his dictatorship in legalisms and by corrupting the courts. Consequently, the accountability of the government, never great to begin with, sank to an all-time low.

Marcos's intolerance of political opposition during the first decade of his dictatorship caused the moderate traditional opposition to atrophy at the same time that it stimulated the growth of the radical left. Furthermore, the absence of political opposition and Marcos's control of the media caused a stultification of public debate of important national issues such as the nature of Philippine nationalism, economic policies, and relations with the United States. Eventually, however, Marcos's efforts to control Philippine society generated significant opposition. His efforts to control or suppress labour, peasant, and student unrest ultimately strengthened both the communist and non-communist left. His clashes with the Church politicized it and eventually unified it in opposition to him. The decline in the economy caused by cronyism and mismanagement and the growth in the communist insurgency gradually prompted the previously apolitical middle class and non-crony business leaders to join the opposition.

Marcos's reliance on the military, first to administer martial law, and then to defend his regime following the end of martial law, inevitably led to the politicization of the AFP. The importance Marcos placed on loyalty rather than on competence resulted in the ascendancy of General Fabian Ver and other trusted generals. The politicization of the senior officer corps and the resulting deterioration of the AFP's capabilities gave rise to the counter-politicization of members of the junior officer corps. The loyalty of these younger officers was to the military as an institution rather than to Marcos; but as we shall see, they were no less politicized (or ambitious) than their superiors.

The Marcos regime also took the tradition of government intervention in the economy to a new and unprecedented level. It is only a slight exaggeration to say that Marcos viewed the entire Philippine economy as a tool for the enhancement and preservation of his political power. Consequently, during the last four years of the Marcos regime the economy faltered and then collapsed under the weight of cronyism and mismanagement. As a result, the incidence of poverty rose from 49 per cent of families in 1972 to 59 per cent in 1985, and income distribution became even worse than it traditionally had been.

The inter-relatedness of the different elements of political and

economic decline were particularly evident on the local level. Mismanagement, corruption, and economic crisis resulted in the deterioration
of basic government services, especially in the countryside. Describing
the situation in the countryside *circa* 1985 one journalist noted its
"utter lawlessness and its remoteness from the normal workings of
government". He observed:

> The rural Philippines existed in a kind of civic vacuum . . . . Armed
> bandit gangs moved about the hills unhampered . . . . Agencies
> of law enforcement either could not or did not bother to help . . . .
> Welfare and other services came rarely and if they came at all
> they were manipulated for partisan uses by local politicians.[55]

A leading Filipino businessman described the situation another way
in January 1986. According to him:

> Locally the three people who used to convey values were the
> mayor, the teacher and the priest. The mayor has lost credibility
> and the teacher is no longer educated. The priest is the only
> one left.[56]

He might have added that in many areas the priest had been joined
by the NPA.

Given the decline in government effectiveness, the heavy-handedness
of the military, and the deteriorating economic security of many Filipinos it is not surprising that the communist insurgency grew rapidly.
By February 1986 membership in the CPP had reached the 30,000
mark. The NPA had over 20,000 full-time armed guerrillas and perhaps
another 10,000 in armed militia. The movement was active in 62 out
of 73 provinces. It controlled or influenced at least 20 per cent of all
barangay and claimed a mass base of one million people. The most
important communist gains, however, were political not military. As
William Chapman has written:

> Militarily, no terrain was taken, no strongpoints occupied, and the
> impression was left that neither side had won or lost . . . . This
> was classic guerilla war and, despite its growing numbers, the
> NPA in mid-1986 was not winning it. What it was winning . . . was
> the political war that received far less public attention. For nearly
> two decades, the cadres had worked in thousands of *barangays* and
> had won the allegiance of thousands of peasants, farm workers,
> fishermen, and those who lacked any livelihood.[57]

Finally, despite all Marcos's rhetoric about creating a "new society", his fourteen-year dictatorship reinforced many aspects of traditional Philippine political culture. Under Marcos the kinship-based and highly personalized nature of Philippine politics reached an all-time high. The interests and desires of the Marcos–Romualdez clan and its supporters were all that mattered – not institutions or laws. The line between public and private, always blurry in the Philippines, was completely erased. The greed demonstrated by Marcos's family and friends re-inforced the acceptance of self-interest, corruption and favouritism as norms in Philippine politics. The reliance on force and coercion strengthened the Philippines' propensity for political violence and weakened the nation's commitment to justice and human rights.

In the end Marcos became the archetypical ageing dictator: corrupt, discredited at home and abroad, and clinging to power. When he was finally deposed in February 1986 he hastily and ingloriously fled Malacañang Palace with only a small group of family members and close friends, their luggage stuffed with millions of dollars in cash, jewelry, and passbooks to foreign bank accounts. They left behind a deeply divided society, a bankrupt government, a severely damaged political system, and a battered and heavily indebted economy.

Deposing Ferdinand Marcos turned out to be a relatively easy task compared to the challenge of coping with the legacy of his regime. The agenda of the new Aquino government would be largely reactive – a response to the Marcos legacy. It would emphasize national recon-ciliation, the restoration of freedom and democracy, and economic recovery and reform. In the following chapters the fate of the Aquino agenda will be described and assessed.

NOTES

1. Statement of Benigno Aquino before the U.S. House of Representatives Subcommittee on Asian and Pacific Affairs, in *United States-Philippines Relations and the New Base and Aid Agreement* (Washington D.C.: U.S. Government Printing Office, 1983), p.78.
2. David Wurfel, "Martial Law in the Philippines: The Methods of Regime Survival", *Pacific Affairs* 50, no.1 (Spring 1977): 29.
3. A year before Aquino was killed, Emmanuel Pelaez, a former vice-president and member of the Batasan, narrowly missed being killed in

an assassination attempt presumed to be linked to his criticism of the crony-controlled coconut monopoly.

4. For an excellent account, see Lewis Simons, *Worth Dying For* (New York: William Morrow and Co., 1987), chapters 2,3,7, and 8.
5. Temario Rivera, *Political Opposition in the Philippines: Contestation and Cooperation*, Wisconsin Papers on Southeast Asia no.9 (Madison: University of Wisconsin, 1985), p.5.
6. UNIDO was formed in August 1980 as a coalition of the Liberal Party leadership, the anti-Marcos bloc of the Nacionalista party led by Jose and Salvador Laurel, and a number of predominantly regional parties. The Laurels had recently broken with Marcos and pulled their wing of the Nacionalista Party out of the KBL. The leadership of UNIDO included Salvador Laurel, Gerardo Roxas and Eva Kalaw of the Liberal Party, and in the United States, Raul Manglapus and Benigno Aquino.
7. Rivera, op. cit., p.11.
8. Ibid., p.9.
9. Ibid., p.2.
10. Max Lane, "The Urban Mass Movement in the Philippines" (1988), p.20.
11. *Diliman Review*, January–February 1986, p.7.
12. Simons, op. cit., p.55.
13. Emmanuel de Dios, ed., *An Analysis of the Philippine Economic Crisis* (Quezon City: University of the Philippines Press, 1984), p.17.
14. *Liberation*, January–February 1985, p.10.
15. See the U.S. Senate Committee on Foreign Relations, *The Situation in the Philippines* (Washington D.C.: U.S. Government Printing Office, October 1984); Larry Niksch, *Insurgency and Counterinsurgency in the Philippines* (Washington D.C.: Library of Congress/Congressional Research Service, July 1985); and Gareth Porter, *The Politics of Counterinsurgency in the Philippines: Military and Political Options*, Occasional Paper No.9 (Honolulu: University of Hawaii Center for Philippine Studies, 1987).
16. William Chapman, *Inside the Philippine Revolution* (New York: W.W. Norton, 1987), p.130.
17. *Liberation*, January–February 1985, p.10.
18. Ross Munro, "The New Khmer Rouge", *Commentary* (December 1985), p.26.
19. Chapman, op. cit., p.130.
20. According to the U.S. Defense Department, the Philippine Government claimed that 439 local officials were killed by the communists between 1981 and July 1985. See U.S. House of Representatives Subcommittee on Asian and Pacific Affairs, *Recent Events in the Philippines, Fall 1985* (Washington D.C.: U.S. Government Printing Office, 1985), p.74.

21. Quoted in Ross Munro, op. cit., p.21.

22. *Asiaweek*, 24 May 1985, p.16.

23. House of Representatives Subcommittee on Asian and Pacific Affairs, *United States–Philippines Relations and the New Base and Aid Agreement* (Washington D.C.: U.S. Government Printing Office, 1983), p.66.

24. House of Representatives Subcommittee on Asian and Pacific Affairs, *Recent Events in the Philippines, Fall 1985* (Washington D.C.: U.S. Government Printing Office, 1985), p.78.

25. *Asian Wall Street Journal*, 25 May 1987, p.9.

26. Ibid., p.9.

27. Chapman, op. cit., p.238.

28. Felipe Miranda, *The Political System and Nation-building in the Philippines* (Quezon City: Social Weather Stations, Inc., January 1987), p.53. See also the Bishops-Businessmen's Conference, "Nationwide Sociopolitical Opinion Surveys" of 1984 and 1985, August 1985, and the September 1985 Philippine Social Science Council public opinion poll.

29. William Overholt, "The Rise and Fall of Ferdinand Marcos", *Asian Survey* 26, no.11 (November 1986): 1160.

30. Portions of this section were first published in my chapter entitled "Unfinished Revolution: The Philippines in 1986", in *Southeast Asian Affairs 1987* (Singapore: Institute of Southeast Asian Affairs, 1987).

31. Also contesting the elections were former senator Eva Kalaw, who ran for vice-president under her wing of the Liberal Party, and Ruben Canoy, who ran for president under the Social Democratic Party.

32. Quoted in the *International Herald Tribune*, 18 June 1986, p.4.

33. *Bulletin Today*, 19 January 1986, p.10.

34. *New York Times*, 8 February 1986, p.10. See also Robert Shaplen, "A Reporter at Large: From Marcos to Aquino", *The New Yorker*, 25 August and 1 September 1986.

35. National Movement for Free Elections (NAMFREL), *The NAMFREL Report on the February 7, 1986 Philippine Presidential Elections* (Manila: NAMFREL, 1986 or 1987), p.3.

36. James Rush, *Bringing Down Marcos: Part IV: Conclusion*, Report No.2 (University Field Staff International, 1986), p.3.

37. See Lewis Simons, *Worth Dying For*; Bryan Johnson, *The Four Days of Courage* (New York: The Free Press, 1987); Asia 2000, *Bayan Ko!* (Hong Kong: Asia 2000, 1986); Al McCoy, Gwen Robinson and Marian Wilkinson, "How the February Revolt was Planned", in the *Philippine Sunday Inquirer*, 5 and 12 October 1986; and Robert Shaplen, op. cit.

38. By joining Enrile, Ramos, who was respected for his professionalism and honesty, greatly enhanced the credibility of the revolt in the eyes

of the Catholic Church, among key members of the Philippine military, and within the U.S. Government.

39. Robert Shaplen, *The New Yorker*, 1 September 1986, p.52.
40. Alex Magno, "The Anatomy of Political Collapse", in *The February Revolution: Three Views* (Quezon City: Karrel, Inc., 1986), p.8.
41. It was also reported that Cardinal Sin had established "close links" with the members of the RAM reform group within the military and had promised to support them in the event of reprisals against them. See *Christian Science Monitor*, 6 February 1986, p.12.
42. *Ang Bayan*, March 1986, p.1.
43. Ibid., p.12.
44. Rush, op. cit., p.9.
45. Simons, op. cit., pp.266–67.
46. Rush, op. cit., p.9.
47. See Bryan Johnson, *The Four Days of Courage* (New York: The Free Press, 1987), especially chapters 8–12 and 14.
48. Ateneo-Social Weather Stations, *Public Opinion Report: June 1986* (Quezon City: Ateneo de Manila University and Social Weather Stations, 1986), p.33.
49. Simons, op. cit., p.281.
50. *New York Times*, 27 February 1986, p.14.
51. Ateneo-Social Weather Stations, op. cit., p.28.
52. *Kasarinlan* 2, no.1 (third quarter 1986):30.
53. Ateneo-Social Weather Stations, op. cit., p.29.
54. *Business Day*, 20 February 1987, p.5.
55. Chapman, op. cit., p.19.
56. Meeting with Bien Tan, Jr., January 1986.
57. Chapman, op. cit., p.15.

PART THREE

Democracy Restored

chapter 6

The Politics of Survival, 1986–88

Now for the hard part

— Cover of *Time* magazine,
10 March 1986

This chapter reviews political developments in the Philippines from the beginning of the Aquino government in late February 1986 through the local elections in January 1988. These two years were full of promise and uncertainty, exhilaration and frustration, and high expectations and bitter disappointments. It was a period in which Filipinos revelled in and tested the limits of their political freedom after almost fourteen years of authoritarianism under Marcos. And it was a period that began with all the uncertainty and instability usually associated with an abrupt regime change, but ended with many of the major contours of Philippine politics having been established.

It was also during this period that the inexperienced and eclectic coalition government of Corazon Aquino endeavoured to restore democracy — at the same time that it faced a variety of serious challenges to its very survival. As we will see in this and subsequent chapters, the threats the government faced during this period had an important effect on the character of the democratic institutions and processes that emerged. Therefore, to understand why the Aquino government acted as it did, it is necessary to understand the political environment in which it existed and the flow of events that affected its behaviour.

This chapter provides a brief account of events from early 1986 to early 1988. This chronological approach is intended to show the relationship between the many important developments during this period. It also serves to set the stage for more in-depth analyses of the process of redemocratization (Chapter 7), the role of the military and other key political actors (Chapter 8), the role of the communist and non-communist left (Chapter 9), and lastly, the government's economic policies, including agrarian reform (Chapter 10).

From "Revolution" to Restoration

The EDSA "revolution", we have seen, was more an uprising against the failed Marcos dictatorship than a fundamental social or political upheaval. The predominantly middle-class participants in the revolt demanded the ouster of Marcos, the empowerment of Aquino, and a return to democracy. But few Filipinos had given much thought to how democracy would function after the fall of Marcos. Would it be traditional élite democracy or would it be a more "popular" style of democracy? Was the Philippines really ready for truly pluralistic politics? How committed would the government be to promoting the socio-economic equality necessary to make democracy work? What was the appropriate mix of "checks and balances" within the new government? What role would the military, Catholic Church, and media play? What would be the nature of the non-communist opposition? How would the democratic government's response to the communist challenge differ from that of the Marcos government? In late February 1986 there were few, if any, complete or widely accepted answers to these questions.

There was, however, at least one thing widely shared by most Filipinos in late February — high hopes and expectations. Most hoped that the demonstration of "people power" at EDSA would be the beginning of truly participatory democracy in the Philippines. It was also hoped that the average Filipino, having been politicized by the presidential election, would become a more conscientious and active participant in the political process. There were expectations that Corazon Aquino would somehow establish a new moral order for Philippine politics and society. There were also expectations that the military would complete the process of redemption begun at EDSA and become a loyal defender of the government and people. It was hoped that the new government would find a peaceful solution to the communist and Muslim insurgencies. Finally, there were expectations that the change in government would result in a rapid improvement in the economy and a flood of new foreign aid and investment.

Most of these hopes and expectations would have been unrealistic under the best of circumstances. Given the difficult circumstances facing the Aquino government, most of them bordered on fantasy. Upon taking her oath as president, Corazon Aquino became the head of a bankrupt and divided government that was, at best, only partially in control of a divided and traumatized nation. The Aquino government had to fend off threats from the extreme left and right and preserve its own fragile unity. At the same time, it sought to restore democratic institutions, revive the economy, and seek a peaceful solution to the communist insurgency without alienating key groups, particularly the military.

The number and magnitude of the challenges facing the inexperienced and divided Aquino government quickly placed it on the defensive. The government found itself with a popular leader, but with few other sources of tangible political support. In order to survive extremist challenges to its existence, the government sought the support of the traditional political and economic élite by restoring its prerogatives and backing away from policies that might result in fundamental social and political change. The result was the restoration of most of the main elements of pre-martial law traditional democracy.

The First One Hundred Days of President Aquino[1]

The first challenge President Aquino faced was to form a Cabinet that was both satisfactory to the disparate groups that had shared a role in overthrowing Marcos, and at the same time one that could agree upon a set of policies to redress the long list of problems facing the nation. The fragility of the coalition government was evident from the outset. The Aquino–Laurel ticket, it will be recalled, was a "shotgun wedding", having been formed only after considerable bargaining between the two principals and the intervention of Cardinal Sin. The coalition was further divided by the inclusion of three Marcos-era hold-overs, Juan

Ponce Enrile, Fidel Ramos, and Central Bank Governor Jose Fernandez. Finally, the coalition was weakened by its multi-party composition, with considerable (and eventually irreconcilable) ideological differences among its most prominent members.

Consequently, the original Aquino Cabinet consisted of a volatile mix of personalities and political persuasions. These included, to the left of centre, Joker Arroyo, a human rights lawyer and close friend of Aquino, in the traditionally powerful position of Executive Secretary; Jose Diokno, former senator and human rights lawyer, as head of the Presidential Commission on Human Rights; and Augusto "Bobbit" Sanchez, another human rights lawyer, as Minister of Labour. In the centre were a number of forceful personalities such as Aquilino Pimentel, a former member of the National Assembly and founder of the Pilipino Democratic Party (PDP), as Minister of Local Governments; Jovito Salonga, a former senator and Liberal Party leader, as head of the Presidential Commission on Good Government; Jaime Ongpin, a prominent business executive, as Minister of Finance; Jose Concepcion, a businessman and NAMFREL head, as Minister of Trade and Industry; and Solita Monsod, an economist from the University of the Philippines, as Minister for Economic Planning. And to the right of centre were Vice-President and Foreign Minister Salvador Laurel, and Minister of National Defence Juan Ponce Enrile. This disparate mixture of personalities and political views made disagreements and disunity within the Cabinet inevitable. Consequently, in many areas the president and the executive branch moved slowly, if at all, despite the virtually unlimited power it had.[2]

The first challenge to this shaky coalition was the continued existence of the Marcos political apparatus. Though leaderless, this once-formidable machine still remained intact and possessed the ability, it was feared, to thwart the new government's initiatives. Still in place at the national level were the KBL-controlled Batasang Pambansa, the Marcos-appointed judiciary, many generals who had loyally served Marcos, and a bureaucracy filled with officials who owed their jobs to Marcos or other members of the KBL. Equally disconcerting was the near total control of provincial and local governments by KBL officials. Under the existing election code, these officials' term of office did not expire until June 1986.

The Aquino government moved rapidly to dismantle the most tangible of these aspects of the Marcos legacy. It restored the writ of habeas corpus; created a Presidential Commission on Human Rights (PCHR) to investigate human rights abuses; established the Presidential Commission on Good Government (PCGG) to identify and retrieve the "ill gotten" and "hidden wealth" of the Marcos family and their cronies; and officially retired General Fabian Ver and twenty-two of Marcos's "overstaying generals". In the first week in office, over the objections of Enrile and the military, the government began to release about 500 Marcos-era political prisoners including Jose Ma. Sison, the CPP founder; Bernabe Buscayno, alias "Kumander Dante", the NPA founder; and Father Edicio de la Torre, a founder of the Christians for National Liberation. In the weeks that followed Aquino offered an amnesty to the communist rebels and called for the CPP-NPA to lay down their arms and enter into peace talks with the new government.

Shortly thereafter, Local Government Minister Aquilino Pimentel announced that some 14,000 local officials would be subject to replacement by government-appointed "Officers in Charge" (OICs) until new local elections could be held. The decision to effect a wholesale replacement of local officials was made for at least three reasons. First, there was concern that the sitting officials, most of whom had been elected under the KBL banner or appointed by Marcos, would remain loyal to Marcos (or to Marcos's associates such as Eduardo "Danding" Cojuangco) and might attempt to undermine the new government. Secondly, the Aquino government wished to have loyal followers in place at the local level before it conducted a constitutional plebiscite or national elections. Finally, patronage considerations and a sense of vengeance on the part of some also contributed to the decision.

Pimentel's announcement triggered a major controversy and created the first crack in the government coalition. The KBL claimed that the replacement of the duly elected officials was unconstitutional and amounted to "revolutionary terror". But the real reason its members were upset about the appointment of OICs was that it meant a sweeping transfer of power at the local level from the KBL to the supporters of the new government. As previously noted, the control of local government office is critical to the local élite to preserve or enhance their political and economic power. Furthermore, the past "official" activities of outgoing KBL officials would become subject to the scrutiny of the incoming OICs, making the former officials vulnerable to charges of corruption and misuse of office. And finally, local offices are the building blocks of the national government and political parties. National leaders are dependent upon local officials to deliver the vote in national elections. Because of the political importance of the local office, therefore, the KBL was joined by Vice-President Laurel and other UNIDO stalwarts in criticizing Pimentel's decision to appoint new officials. Laurel complained that the majority of the appointments were going to members of PDP-Laban, rather than to UNIDO members.

In a page right out of the pre-martial law era, a dispute over patronage – and not policies – became the first major political issue in the post-Marcos era. As a result, in many provinces around the country there was confusion about who was in charge, and in some there were physical stand-offs between incumbents, who would not leave office, and the incoming OICs. For example, the governors of Tawi Tawi, Sulu, and Basilan in Mindanao set up barricades, and in Danao, Cebu, the OIC mayor was barred from entering the city hall to take over office from his nephew.

The situation in Masbate province, though worse than most, illustrates many of the problems encountered with the appointment of the OICs. The first OIC governor was replaced after a month by Julio Fernandez, a pro-Aquino political figure. According to the *Asian Wall Street Journal*:

> Three months later Mrs Aquino announced that Mr Fernandez was being replaced and she named a third governor. Her reasons for doing so are unclear. But Mr Fernandez refused to go and for six days the province had two governors. The rivals flew to Manila to be interviewed by Mrs Aquino, who then relented and allowed Mr Fernandez to stay in office. Critics, quoting alleged witnesses, say Mr Fernandez was reinstated because he cried before the president. . . .
>
> However, to placate the loser, Mrs Aquino allowed him to appoint 10 of the province's 21 mayors, which he proceeded to do. . . . But the 10 mayors called upon to step down, all of whom were appointed by Mr Fernandez, refused to do so. For several weeks the province's 21 towns had 31 mayors. . . .[3]

The Aquino government then dealt with the important issues of the future of the Marcos-shaped 1973 Constitution and the 200-member

Batasang Pambansa. The two were inextricably linked, for if Aquino claimed victory in the February 1986 presidential election as the basis for her government's legitimacy, then she implicitly accepted the continued validity of the 1973 Constitution (under which the election was held), and therefore the continued legitimacy of the Batasan. Consequently, on 25 March, one month after taking office, Aquino issued Presidential Proclamation No. 3, the preamble of which stated that "the new government was installed through a direct exercise of the power of the Filipino people assisted by units of the New Armed Forces of the Philippines" and that "the heroic action of the people was done in defiance of the provisions of the 1973 Constitution". This preamble made it clear that the basis of the government's legitimacy was the February revolt rather than the presidential election. According to Justice Minister Neptali Gonzales, the Aquino government was "revolutionary in origin, democratic in essence and transitory in nature". In the place of the 1973 Constitution the proclamation established an interim "Freedom Constitution" giving Aquino virtually unlimited power comparable to what Marcos had exercised, abolished the Batasan, and removed security of tenure for most civil servants. The Freedom Constitution would remain in effect until a constitutional commission could be convened and a new constitution drafted and ratified.

In response to their sudden unemployment and emasculation, a group of KBL and UNIDO members of the Batasan announced their intention to convene a "rebel Parliament" in April. Blas Ople, a former Batasan member and labour minister under Marcos, proclaimed, "This is an act of revolt and we are ready to be arrested and jailed". But his bravado, and the self-righteous cries of injustice coming from the same legislators who had proclaimed Marcos president rang hollow to most Filipinos and the rump parliament movement eventually fizzled out.

In mid-April, Aquino moved to cleanse another Marcos-tainted institution by swearing in ten new Supreme Court justices and beginning a review of all judicial appointments. On 25 May, three months after coming to power, she announced the appointment of forty-four people to a commission to draft a new constitution.

Thus, by June the character of the Aquino government had begun to emerge. But so too had many of its problems and shortcomings. To its credit, the administration had faithfully restored individual, political, and press freedoms. With the initiation of the Constitutional

Commission it had also begun the process of building new democratic institutions. On 5 June, the one-hundredth day of the administration, the communists announced their willingness in principle to negotiate with the government for a cease-fire. In Mindanao, a temporary truce was fashioned with the Moro National Liberation Front (MNLF), but government efforts to bring the Muslims to the negotiating table produced few results, in part because the Muslim insurgents remained divided into three warring factions. On the economic front the gov- ern ment moved quickly to dismantle repressive labour laws and government control of the sugar and copra markets.

The Aquino government, however, often seemed paralysed by inde- cision and internal disagreements. Tensions mounted between Defence Minister Enrile and liberal Cabinet ministers like Executive Secretary Joker Arroyo over the government's conciliatory policy towards the communist insurgents. Important differences of opinion within the Cabinet also emerged on critical economic issues such as the hand- ling of foreign debt, trade liberalization, and land reform. Additionally, the rift continued to grow between Vice-President Laurel, who sought a larger role for himself and UNIDO, and the members of PDP-Laban, who jealously guarded Aquino's and PDP-Laban's pre-eminence within the coalition.

It also became clear that a number of Aquino's campaign pledges would be delayed or abandoned. Rhetoric calling for the institutionaliza- tion of "people power" remained just that − rhetoric. The government's economic development plan called for "people-powered development", but there was no sign of any action in one critical area − agrarian reform. Although the government's economic programme called for a reduced government role in the economy, it became clear that the government would have to play a major role for the foreseeable future by "priming the pump" and overseeing the disposition of hundreds of government and crony-owned firms.

Coping with the Military and the Communists

If the first half of 1986 was marked by the efforts of the new govern- ment to consolidate its power against the challenge of remnant Marcos forces, the second half of the year was dominated by a search for a *modus vivendi* between the civilian government and the military.

The Aquino government included a number of former political activists and human rights lawyers who instinctively viewed the military as untrustworthy, undemocratic, and dangerous. Under Marcos, the AFP had become accustomed to having an influential role in government policy-making, particularly in the area of national security, and many officers doubted the competence and judgement of the new civilian leaders. The rapidly shifting allegiances within the military between officers loyal to Aquino, Marcos, Enrile, and Ramos further added to the uncertainty and volatility of civilian–military relations.

The lingering distrust that existed between the new civilian leadership and the military was a powerful undercurrent influencing events. The focal point of civilian–military tensions, however, was the civilian leadership's conciliatory approach to the communist insurgency, particularly after the beginning of negotiations between the government and the communists in early August.

The AFP frowned upon Aquino's decision to release all political prisoners and was concerned about the Presidential Commission on Human Rights' investigations into military abuses during the previous regime. It was also strongly opposed to Aquino's efforts to negotiate a settlement with the communist insurgency. General Ramos, with the support of Enrile, pressed Aquino to adopt an integrated counterinsurgency plan that ignored negotiations and emphasized instead the defeat (as opposed to reassimilation) of the NPA through co-ordinated military and civilian programmes.[4] The military's plan would have devoted a larger share of the government budget to the counter-insurgency effort and given the military greater influence over local officials in determining counter-insurgency policies and programmes. But Aquino rejected the plan, reportedly so as not to jeopardize the prospects of a peaceful settlement with the insurgents.[5] In May, in what the military viewed as a further concession to the communists, Aquino decided that the military would not be directly involved in the initial peace talks.

The AFP's growing dissatisfaction with the Aquino government remained relatively muted until July. On 6 July, following a weekly rally of Marcos loyalists in Manila's Luneta parade ground, Arturo Tolentino, Marcos's vice-presidential running mate, proceeded to the nearby Manila Hotel, where he took an oath as vice-president and declared that he would be acting president in the absence of Marcos. The supporters of Marcos and Tolentino occupied the venerable hotel and were quickly joined by several hundred troops led by Brigadier General Jaime Echeverria and Colonel Rolando Abadilla, who established a perimeter around the hotel. These troops, in turn, were quickly surrounded by troops loyal to the government, and a stalemate ensued.

During the next two days little happened while Defence Minister Enrile negotiated a face-saving settlement in the absence of Chief of Staff Ramos, who was travelling with President Aquino in Mindanao. On the third day of the siege Tolentino and his civilian supporters were allowed to disperse, and the rebel troops were "punished" with thirty push-ups and allowed to rejoin their units.

The "Manila Hotel incident" publicly revealed for the first time the depth and breadth of discontent within the military. Many of the soldiers who participated in the affair said they did so to protest the government's policies towards the communists, which they thought were too lenient and exposed the military to communist attacks. The incident also highlighted for the first time several other disturbing aspects. First, the way the incident ended – with the rebel troops being reincorporated without punishment – revealed the very fragile unity within the military. Secondly, the incident demonstrated that Chief of Staff Ramos had less-than-total control over his factionalized officers and troops. Most of the soldiers who participated in the affair were members of the "Guardian Brotherhood" fraternity within the AFP. Their action was premeditated, but had not been detected (or at least reported) by military intelligence. Finally, the incident illustrated the influence of Enrile within the military. Some of the rebel soldiers claimed they had joined the coup because they had heard Enrile was one of its leaders. Enrile, it was rumoured, knew of the plan in advance but did not stop it, and instead manipulated it to his own advantage.

On 5 August, after months of secret and informal communication, the government and the communists (represented by the National Democratic Front) began formal talks on forging a cease-fire. President Aquino and some of her closest advisors initially viewed the insurgency primarily as a response to the poverty and injustice of the Marcos era. They believed that the combination of reforms promised by the government, an amnesty programme, and the threat of a more effective military would bring all but the most hard-core of the insurgents "down from the hills". After several months, however, the continuation, and in some areas intensification, of NPA attacks on the military soon underscored the reality that the insurgency would not end quickly or peacefully.[6] This realization bolstered the position of other Aquino advisors who were less optimistic about the willingness of the insurgents to abandon their struggle. Increasingly, the government viewed the peace talks as being necessary to legitimize a more aggressive counter-insurgency policy once the talks failed (as some in the government were certain they would).

In the face of Aquino's popularity and apparent sincerity the communists did not want to be perceived as spurning her olive branch. Moreover, the left recognized the precarious position of Aquino *vis-à-vis* the military and did not wish to seriously undermine her position. Equally important, the peace talks provided them with unprecedented visibility and legitimacy. Although the communists' efforts to receive belligerent status were not successful, the fact that the government was prepared to negotiate with them gave them a stature and respectability that was unthinkable while Marcos was still in power.

An additional reason for entering into the talks was the government's progress in negotiating with the Muslim insurgents in the South. On 5 September Aquino made an unprecedented visit to the predominantly Muslim city of Jolo in Mindanao. There she met Moro National Liberation Front chairman Nur Misuari, who had recently returned to the Philippines from thirteen years of exile in Libya and Saudi Arabia. In Jolo, they agreed to enter into negotiations over Muslim autonomy and to continue the cease-fire that the Muslim rebels had informally observed since February.[7]

Thus, both the government and the communists felt that they would benefit from the talks — even if neither side was particularly sanguine about the prospects for a lasting settlement. The same was true of the prospective cease-fire itself. The Aquino government saw it, at best, as the beginning of a gradual demilitarization of the conflict; or, at worst, as a needed respite that would give the government and the armed forces time to prepare for the resumption of hostilities. The communists also felt that a cease-fire would be to their advantage, judging from their willingness to moderate a number of their demands and to press ahead with the negotiations even after the capture of CPP leader Rodolfo Salas in late September and the brutal murder of leftist labour leader Rolando Olalia in mid-November. For the communists, the primary potential benefit of a cease-fire seemed to be in the area of political propaganda and organization.

The "Cory Constitution"

While the government and communists were talking about a cease-fire, a 48-member Constitutional Commission, or "Con Com", appointed by Aquino was slowly piecing together a document that, if ratified, would replace the temporary Freedom Constitution and define many of the future contours of Philippine government and politics. It was "an act of creative restoration" based on a collective desire of the majority of the commissioners to "reconstruct pre-Martial Law political structures and also to reform and improve them based on the hard lessons of the Marcos years".[8]

The Con Com was dominated by moderates who supported Aquino or could be expected to be sympathetic to the new government's needs and interests. Nearly two-thirds of the commissioners were law graduates, many of them lawyer-politicians in the traditional Filipino mould. But the body also included several prominent jurists, legal scholars and political scientists, and economists.[9] There were only small minorities on both the right (led by Blas Ople) and the left (led by peasant leader Jaime Tadeo), which prompted three of the left-leaning commissioners to stage a walk-out in early September to protest the "tyranny of the majority". The Catholic Church was well represented by four commissioners with direct or indirect Church affiliations. The Commission became the focus of considerable lobbying, most notably by Bayan and other leftist cause-oriented groups, pro-family groups, and anti-nuclear groups. On 12 October, a month and a half after the deadline originally set by Aquino, the Commission approved the 109-page final version by a vote of 45 to 2 (one commissioner had resigned from the commission in protest).

The new Constitution reflected the moderate and tradition-oriented views of the majority of the commissioners. It narrowly rejected a parliamentary system in favour of a presidential form of government with a bicameral legislature similar to that which had existed before martial law. In reponse to the abuses by Marcos it made the declaration and use of emergency powers more difficult and provided greater judicial independence. Its more progressive provisions included a bill of rights, a call for land reform, the creation of a commission on human rights, and universal high school education. More traditional elements included a highly centralized government, emphasis on the family as the basis of society, prohibitions of divorce and abortion, and the protection of private property.

The constitutional commissioners had sought to bridge (if not reconcile) a number of fundamental differences in Philippine society, resulting in a document that was often ambiguous and sometimes contradictory. Political commentator Alex Magno summed up the document's somewhat jumbled, but generally centrist, nature when he described it as:

> . . . a conscious repudiation of the preceding dictatorship. . . .
> There are flashes of surprising progressivism . . . . But these are
> reined in by the phraseology of conservative restraint . . . . All
> potentially explosive provisions were left to the Congress to sort
> out . . . . It is as if the conservatives and progressives intentionally
> left things hanging so that they could clash another day.[10]

And clash they would. But the battle did not wait for the convening of the new Congress. Instead, it began with the campaign leading up to the constitutional plebiscite in February 1987.

November: The Enrile Challenge and the Cease-fire

By September Defence Minister Enrile had begun to openly express his dissatisfaction with the Aquino government, particularly its willingness to negotiate with the communists while the NPA continued to attack government forces. He publicly disclaimed any desire to replace Aquino as president, but he envisioned himself as a key power broker in the Cabinet because of his considerable following among the right and the military. However, as the months passed, there were reports that Aquino's inner circle of advisors — and specifically Joker Arroyo — had shut Enrile out of the decision-making process. His growing attacks on the Aquino administration were partially in response to his ostracism and frustration. But they were also clearly intended to force a change in the Cabinet and its policies — particularly with regard to the handling of the insurgency. They may also have been the first step in a calculated plan to seize power.

Not coincidentally, in October rumours swirled around Manila of an imminent coup, called "God Save the Queen", being planned by members of the RAM faction associated with Enrile. These "RAM-boys" sought the elimination of "leftist" influences in the Cabinet, the restoration of the Batasang Pambansa, and, especially, more power and a greater role in decision-making for Enrile. Under the RAM plan Enrile would become prime minister and Aquino remain in office as president, but as little more than a figure-head (hence the reference to "the Queen" in the coup's name).

By November Enrile had begun to publicly challenge the legitimacy of the Aquino government in what appeared to be an effort to provoke a showdown. Ironically, the month started auspiciously. On 1 November the communists made a major concession to the government by expressing their willingness to agree to a temporary cease-fire in advance of "comprehensive negotiations" and by tabling a proposal for a 100-day cease-fire beginning on 10 December. But as prospects for a truce brightened (and with it the vindication of Aquino's approach) disgruntled elements in the military and other extremist opponents intensified their efforts to destabilize the government. November began to resemble the chaotic period just before the imposition of martial law in 1972. A spate of bombings in Manila was followed by three political assassinations (killed were labour leader Rolando Olalia; David Puzon, an associate of Enrile; and Muslim leader Ulbert Ulama Tuguny); the kidnapping of a senior Japanese business expatriate; and a series of leftist demonstrations. Meanwhile, continuing rumours of a coup attempt by members of the RAM group added to the atmosphere of crisis and loss of control.

Events came to a head on 22 November when Ramos received reports that at least 100 members of RAM were preparing to take over the Batasang Pambansa building and key military and communications facilities, reinstate the legislature, and call for new presidential elections. Ramos went on national television and radio to notify all military personnel to disregard any orders that did not come from the normal chain of command, and particularly any orders from Colonel Gregorio "Gringo" Honasan, a leader of RAM and a close associate of Enrile.

On 23 November Aquino called an emergency Cabinet meeting at which it was decided that the entire Cabinet would tender their resignations. Later in the afternoon, Aquino met with Enrile, who had not attended the earlier meeting, and told him: "We can't work together anymore". Enrile resigned and was promptly replaced as defence minister by General Rafael "Rocky" Ileto, Enrile's deputy and a respected former ambassador. Following Enrile's peaceful departure from the government Metro Manila breathed a collective sigh of relief. The following day the relief turned to euphoria with the announcement that the communists had agreed to a sixty-day cease-fire (they had wanted a longer one, but the military had objected). Three days later, on 27 November, an agreement was signed calling for the cease-fire to begin on 10 December.

The pre-empted coup indicated that the Ramos faction within the military had cast its lot with President Aquino and was ascendant over the Enrile/RAM group. This appeared to reduce the threat of Enrile and RAM, but it also made Aquino more dependent upon General Ramos. Moreover, in order to satisfy Enrile's supporters within the military, the dismissal of Enrile had to be balanced by the dismissal of Cabinet members the military viewed as "leftist and incompetent". This forced Aquino to accept the resignations of two ministers suspected of over-indulgence in corruption, the removal of Pimentel as local government minister and the eventual dismissal of the controversial labour minister, Augusto Sanchez.[11]

February 1987: Voting for Cory and her Constitution

The draft constitution quickly became a partisan political issue, and the 2 February constitutional plebiscite became a test of Aquino's popularity and legitimacy. According to opposition politician Renato Cayetano, the plebiscite was an "opponent-less presidential campaign masquerading as a plebiscite".[12] But the plebiscite was more than just a popularity poll. It was also the first national test since the February 1986 elections of the popularity and organization of the reconstituted and realigned political parties. It was viewed as a dry run to register voters and mobilize support for the May congressional elections.

President Aquino, of course, praised the document, saying that "Democracy is safe with this constitution". Cardinal Sin also gave his blessings to it, calling it "unique, perfect and beautiful". However, others were less enthusiastic. After characteristic vacillation, vice-president Laurel and UNIDO gave their qualified support to the charter. Enrile and the right opposition, recognizing that acceptance of the new Constitution would firmly establish the Aquino government until 1992, condemned it as partisan, socialistic, and pacifist. From the military came grumblings about the abolition of the death penalty and a provision to phase out the CHDF. Leftist groups such as Bayan, the KMU labour federation, and the KMP peasant federation, which had lobbied unsuccessfully to have "democratic nationalist" provisions written into the document (so that they could not be blocked by future Congresses), criticized the charter's ambivalent provisions on land reform, foreign ownership, and the U.S. military bases.

The Aquino government sought a large "yes" vote as a reaffirmation of support for the government and its policies. The administration's message basically was: if you like Cory you should like her constitution. This highly personalized approach to the plebiscite was reflected in government banners which read: "Yes to Cory, Yes to Country, Yes to Democracy, Yes to Constitution". Aquino's supporters formed Lakas ng Bayan (Strength of the Nation) or Lakas as an umbrella organization to co-ordinate the coalition's campaign. Aquino herself campaigned vigorously for the charter. But rather than focusing on the substance of the new Constitution, Aquino chose instead a more traditional approach to campaigning that emphasized the tangible benefits her government had provided to the province or city she was in. In return for a "yes" vote she promised more and better roads, schools, and irrigation.

On 22 January 1987, just over a week before the plebiscite, Philippine policemen opened fire on a large group of peasant demonstrators who sought to march to Malacañang Palace to present their demands for land reform to the president. When the shooting and chaos at the Mendiola Bridge ended, some 19 demonstrators had been killed and about 100 wounded. Exactly who triggered the firing probably will never be known, but it is likely that the violence was provoked by either the extreme right or the extreme left (and perhaps by both) with the hope of destabilizing the government before the Constitution could be approved. To some, the "Mendiola massacre" was bloody proof that the Aquino government was just as brutal and reactionary as its predecessor. The NDF, for example, used the incident as further justification for its decision to abandon the peace talks with the government. To others, however, the massacre was a tragic mistake and a sobering reminder of the deep divisions within Philippine society.

The "Mendiola massacre" was followed by a poorly planned and executed military revolt on 25–27 January led by Air Force Colonel Oscar Canlas. Some 500 mutineers attacked military installations and the Channel 7 television station in Quezon City, but succeeded only in taking the television station. After almost three days of a stand-off, a face-saving compromise was reached. The rebels surrendered to General Ramos, but were allowed to keep their weapons as they left the station and boarded buses to take them back to military camps in Metro Manila. Although almost comic, the revolt was intended to be the first stage of a plan for Marcos to return to the Philippines. The plan was foiled in Hawaii, when the U.S. Government thwarted Marcos's attempt to return in a private jet. According to one reporter, "When it became apparent that the other attacks had failed the rebels quickly replaced the pro-Marcos posters with anti-communist slogans and signs".[13]

In the wake of the Mendiola and Channel 7 incidents the constitutional plebiscite increasingly came to be seen as a test of whether Filipinos wanted stability or more change. The unequivocal answer was stability. The "Cory Constitution" was approved by 76 per cent of almost 22 million votes cast (out of about 25 million registered voters). As expected, support for the Constitution mirrored support for Aquino. However, it was approved by only 55 per cent of military voters and was rejected by narrow margins in the Marcos-Enrile strong-holds of Ilocos (where 52 per cent were negative votes) and Cagayan Valley.[14]

The large "yes" vote was interpreted as a vote for Aquino as much as for the new charter. As such, it was an important confirmation of her popularity and strengthened her hand in dealing with the left. It was also interpreted by many as a sign of the desire of the population for a return to normalcy and stability.[15] Alex Magno noted that ratification indicated the public's desire for and expectancy of stability, but he also cautioned against complacency, warning that "ratification *per se* does not imply stability. Substantial policy initiatives will have to be undertaken to address the political sources of instability."[16]

Five days after the Constitution was ratified the cease-fire with the communists formally ended, although negotiations had been suspended by the communists in late January. Following the end of the cease-fire, the government adopted a more hardline public stance concerning the insurgency. On 18 February, under pressure from the military, Aquino ordered the Presidential Commission on Human Rights

(PCHR) to expand its investigations to include atrocities committed by the insurgents. In a speech at the Philippine Military Academy in March Aquino said that the time had come "to take up the sword of war" and mount a "string of honorable victories".[17]

The AFP's ability to achieve "honorable victories", however, had already been called into question by the uncovering of a massacre by the military of some eighteen peasants near Lupao, Nueva Ecija province, in mid-February. Further doubts about the government's ability to conduct a responsible and effective counter-insurgency effort arose with the emergence and rapid growth of vehemently anti-communist "vigilante groups" in Mindanao and other parts of the country. Many of these groups used intimidation and violence to root out and "neutralize" suspected communists and their sympathizers, often with the support of the military. To Filipino human rights and social activists it was becoming more and more difficult to see any change in the military under Aquino.

On 28 February, after a long delay because of fear that it would increase military discontent, Aquino proclaimed a six-month amnesty programme that granted a "full and complete" amnesty for those who broke laws for political beliefs. (The amnesty was later extended for an additional six months.) The programme earmarked some US$50 million to establish "national reconciliation" centres to process, train, and find land or jobs for rebels who surrendered. The NDF, however, rejected the amnesty as a "bribe". NEDA head Solita Monsod claimed in late 1987 that almost 8,850 rebels applied for amnesty and more than 5,700 had been placed in the government's National Reconciliation and Development Programme.[18] The *Far Eastern Economic Review* reported that more than 7,000 regulars had surrendered by February 1988. But it also observed that, "For many returnees, life after amnesty has been marked by lack of livelihood, housing, food, and security".[19]

April and May 1987: Election Fever

The first genuinely free congressional elections since 1971 were scheduled for 11 May 1987. At stake were 24 seats in the Senate, each elected in a national vote, and 200 seats in the House of Representatives. The elections were the first test of electoral politics under the restored democratic system. They were also another test of President Aquino's popularity, and the relative strength of emerging political groupings on both the left and the right.

The Aquino government sought the election of as many of "Cory's candidates" as possible so that Aquino would have a friendly and supportive legislature. To this end a coalition of pro-administration parties was formed under the Lakas banner. Aquino campaigned vigorously for Lakas candidates, and particularly for the twenty-four-member Lakas senatorial slate, which included a mixture of traditional political figures, moderate progressives, and some new faces.

The moderate right opposition formed a seven-party coalition called the Grand Alliance for Democracy (GAD). Leading the GAD senatorial slate were Juan Ponce Enrile, Blas Ople, Arturo Tolentino, and Eva Kalaw. The more extreme right opposition included die-hard Marcos loyalists such as Rafael Recto, Marcos's lawyer, and Nicanor Yniguez, the former head of the Batasan, under the Union for Peace and Progress-KBL (UPP-KBL). Comprised of unrepentant Marcos "loyalists", the UPP-KBL had as one of its campaign pledges to bring back the deposed president.

The left participated in the elections for the first time since the 1946 elections. They formed the Alliance for New Politics (ANP) as an umbrella for Partido ng Bayan (PnB), Bayan, and Volunteers for Popular Democracy (VPD). The ANP fielded a seven-member senatorial slate that included three former communists, and sponsored more than 100 candidates for the House.

The congressional campaigns quickly took on a traditional cast, with the candidates and voters concerned more with personalities and "pork-barrel" than with issues. In the face of President Aquino's popularity, the opposition avoided criticizing her directly and instead attempted to discredit her relatives and closest advisors. Only the left made a concerted effort to focus on issues during the campaign, a tactic which ultimately proved to be unsuccessful.

On election day some 85 per cent of the country's 26 million registered voters went to the polls. There was relatively little election-related violence and the casting and counting of ballots were relatively clean. The Lakas slate won 22 of 24 Senate seats, with former senator and PCGG head Jovito Salonga topping the voting with almost 13 million votes. Nominally pro-Aquino candidates for House seats won about 150 seats, or 75 per cent of all elected seats. From among the opposition senatorial candidates only two were placed among the top twenty-four: Joseph Estrada, a film star and former mayor, who was placed fourteenth, and Juan Ponce Enrile, who eventually finished twenty-fourth. None of the left's senatorial candidates scored in the top fifty. The best vote-getter, Horacio "Boy" Morales received only 1.3 million votes and only two ANP candidates won their contests for seats in the House.

The right opposition fared better in contests for the House than for the Senate. Twenty-eight KBL or GAD candidates and 19 former KBL members who ran as independents won seats in the House. Another 21 former KBL members ran under one of the pro-Aquino parties and won, according to a study done by the Institute for Popular Democracy, a left-leaning research organization.[20] The result was some 70 representatives, or 35 per cent of the House, who potentially could coalesce in opposition to the Aquino government.

In another ritual of Philippine politics, Enrile and the GAD quickly declared the election a "failure" – after only 2 per cent of the vote had been counted. GAD indignantly announced, "We are not going to be party to this farce. We reject the flawed results as being fabricated by the Aquino administration and we will hold it reponsible for the consequences of its act".[21] On 24 May 15,000 to 20,000 GAD and KBL supporters led by Enrile staged their own version of people power, dubbed "EDSA II", to protest the election results. At the protest rally there were signs that said "Enough is enough, Mrs President. You'd better step down or else . . ." and "Look up young soldiers, look up. The Ilocos king [Marcos] is coming back".[22]

The latter placard reflected more than just the wishful thinking of Marcos loyalists. In early July, two weeks before the Congress was scheduled to convene, it was reported that Marcos was once again making preparations to return to the Philippines, lead a military force to overthrow the Aquino government, and take Aquino hostage. For the second time in 1987 Marcos's plans to return were thwarted by the U.S. Government, which made it clear that Marcos was to stay put.

The New Congress Convenes

The convening of Congress in late July meant the end of Aquino's law-making powers. The *Far Eastern Economic Review* offered this description of Aquino's wielding of power:

> During her 478 days of "revolutionary" power she issued 302 decrees. Most of them fell into the category of government "housekeeping", but some others, notably the family code, an investment code and an outline for a "Comprehensive Agrarian Reform Program" were broad in scope. As the days ticked down to the convening of Congress, the paper flow from Malacanang increased; on the last day before Congress met Aquino signed 42 orders.[23]

The new Congress convened on 27 July. After the joint opening session the House met in the former Batasang Pambansa building in Quezon City, built by Marcos to house his rubber stamp parliamant. The Senate convened in the old Congress building in Manila, which had been padlocked by Marcos when he declared martial law fifteen years earlier.

Aquino used the opening of Congress to give her first State of the Nation address. In her speech to the joint session she focused on the insurgency and the nation's external debt problem (after, it should be noted, a restructuring agreement had already been laboriously negotiated), rather than setting out a legislative agenda or emphasizing the importance of land reform. She said foreign creditors "took undue and unfair advantage of the internal difficulties" in the Philippines in order to force the government to come to an agreement. Aquino's focus on the foreign issue had the intended or unintended effect of diverting public attention from other critical but divisive domestic issues such as land reform.

The newly elected members of the Senate and the House busied themselves with the tasks of organizing committees, establishing parliamentary procedures, recruiting staffs, and drafting legislation and resolutions. But as they did, acts of political violence continued to threaten the government and undermine the foundations of democracy. In early August Jaime Ferrer, the Secretary of Local Government, became the first Cabinet member in Philippine history to be assassinated when he was gunned down near his home in suburban Metro Manila. Before the month was over, on 28 August dramatic events occurred that came perilously close to overthrowing the Aquino government and all that it had built.

The 28 August Coup Attempt

The final third of 1987 was dominated by the Aquino government's efforts to restore its stability and reorient its policies following a military coup attempt on 28 August. Although unsuccessful, the coup attempt was a serious blow to Aquino's leadership and the government's stability. It resulted in the removal of the remaining "controversial" members of the Cabinet, heightened the influence of Chief of Staff Ramos and the "constitutionalists" in the AFP, and triggered efforts by the government to regain support of traditional sectors of society, such as the business and local political élites.

The coup came in the midst of mounting political violence in Metro Manila and on the heels of a government decision in early August to raise fuel prices by about 20 per cent. On 21 August, the anniversary of the murder of Benigno Aquino, 5,000 leftists had marched to Malacañang Palace to accuse Aquino of "betraying the legacy" of her husband. A strike had been planned by the major labour unions to protest the announced increase in oil prices. The day before the strike, the government panicked and backed down, and promised a price roll-back. But the leftist KMU still called for a strike. A spokesman for the KMU said: "It is high time we gave this government a lesson".[24] On 26 August the strike crippled Metro Manila and the cities of Cebu, Davao, and Bacolod. Troops fired on demonstrators in Metro Manila, wounding four, and some 240 strikers and labour leaders were arrested.

Early on the morning of 28 August troops under the command of RAM founder Colonel Gregorio "Gringo" Honasan entered Metro Manila from a military camp north of the city.[25] Several hundred rebels attacked Malacañang Palace, but were repulsed by the Presidential Security Guard. Another 1,000 or so attacked Villamor Air Base, the headquarters of the Philippine Air Force; Camp Aguinaldo, the headquarters of the AFP; and television stations in Quezon City. During the morning Ramos was reported to be isolated in Camp Crame, across from Aguinaldo, unable to communicate with his commanders and unsure who remained loyal to him and who did not.[26] Outside Metro Manila, rebel soldiers temporarily succeeded in taking control of bases in Quezon, Cebu, and Cagayan provinces. In Baguio City, the entire cadet corps of the Philippine Military Academy was reported to have withdrawn its support for Aquino, and troops at Camp Olivas in Central Luzon sided with the rebels.

Initially, the rebels were successful in holding their positions. But by mid-afternoon, once Ramos had ascertained who was on his side and was fortified by reinforcements of loyal marines, the tide turned and the government began to reassert its control. In the process of dislodging the rebels from Camp Aguinaldo the General Headquarters building was set on fire. When the day's shooting was over, 53 civilians and soldiers had died and several hundreds had been wounded. Honasan and an unknown number of his troops escaped. Another 1,000 were captured or surrendered.

The coup caught the civilian government, General Ramos, and the U.S. Government by surprise and came very close to succeeding. It failed for three reasons, according to political scientist P.N. Abinales. First, the rebels failed to capture Malacañang Palace, which would have had a big psychological impact on those officers and troops "sitting on the fence". Secondly, the rebels failed to get complete control of Villamor Air Base, which would have been used as a landing area for additional support from the provinces and as a staging area for air attacks. Finally, they failed to capture the AFP communications centre at Camp Crame, making it much harder to communicate with supporters outside Metro Manila.[27] (The nearly successful coup attempt in December 1989 demonstrated with devastating effect that Honasan and his followers had learned from the mistakes made in August 1987.)

President Aquino, whose son was seriously injured in the attack on Malacañang, branded the rebels "traitors and murderers of unarmed civilians who called themselves idealistic". But Cardinal Sin, Vice-President Laurel, and other leaders avoided equally harsh criticism of the rebels, suggesting a degree of sympathy for the rebels' cause, if not the coup itself. Bayan described the coup attempt as "a deadly gang war between two distinct camps within the same AFP".[28]

On 9 September, in what Press Secretary Teodoro Benigno called a "spontaneous combustion", the Aquino Cabinet resigned *en masse* in response to the crisis of confidence, paving the way for a Cabinet revamp. Ultimately, however, only Salvador Laurel's resignation as Secretary of Foreign Affairs was irrevocable, and only three other resignations were accepted by Aquino. But they were three of her closest advisors: Executive Secretary Joker Arroyo, Finance Secretary Jaime Ongpin, and presidential speech-writer and advisor Teodoro "Teddy Boy" Locsin.

In announcing his decision to resign as Secretary of Foreign Affairs (but not as vice-president), Laurel cited "fundamental differences of opinion" with Aquino. He also claimed, with some validity, that Aquino reneged on a pre-election pledge to let him play a leading role in the government, including naming 25 to 30 per cent of the Cabinet. Another reason for his break, however, was that the PDP-Laban and Lakas members of the government had successfully restricted the amount of patronage available to Laurel to dispense to his UNIDO followers, thus undercutting his leadership within his own party. Laurel's resignation was a calculated effort to reclaim his own political independence and identity at a time when it appeared that the Aquino government might not survive.

Following the coup attempt Laurel also made a characteristically opportunistic effort to curry favour with the military and the opposition.[29] Laurel toured fourteen military camps where he talked with troops and expressed sympathy for their grievances. Laurel's behaviour during these "dialogues" was hardly designed to strengthen the military's support for the Aquino government. According to *Malaya*, the meetings went as follows:

> Reading from a questionnaire, Laurel asked the soldiers to shout out their answers so that, he said, the leadership could determine the sentiments of the military.
>
> "Should President Aquino change members of the cabinet?" Laurel asked.
>
> "Yes!" answered thousands of soldiers and policemen. . . .
>
> "Should the President remove the communists in government?" Laurel asked. "Yes!" answered the soldiers.[30]

The following month, in a further bid to win the support of the military, Laurel called on Aquino to grant amnesty to the coup participants. He also said he was willing to head a military-backed government, but only if the military would "go back to the barracks" after deposing Aquino and installing him.[31]

The resignations of Arroyo, Locsin, and Ongpin were accepted in mid-September. Arroyo, known as "the little president", was a devoted human rights lawyer (he had defended Benigno Aquino). He, and to a lesser degree, Locsin, were viewed by the left as nationalist counter-weights to church-influenced technocrats inside Aquino's government. The right and the military, however, viewed them as, at best, critics of the military, and at worst, communist sympathizers. In any event, Arroyo and Locsin were generally considered to be abrasive, overly-protective of Aquino, unwilling to make political compromises, and lacking in administrative abilities.

Reflecting the disappointment of the left, *Malaya* commented that Arroyo's departure represented a political watershed:

> The revolution has turned full circle, losing the last of the liberal faces that gave the first Aquino cabinet its pro-people character. Now the political right has taken over.[32]

This assessment was something of an overstatement, for the Cabinet still contained a number of moderates and was freed of Laurel's conservatism. Moreover, Arroyo's resignation did exorcise another controversial and disruptive influence from the Cabinet, in the same way that Enrile's departure did in late 1986. However, without Joker Arroyo as her lightning rod, Aquino would have to take more direct responsibility (and criticism) for her policies.

Secretary of Finance Jaime Ongpin was also considered to be abrasive and controversial, but for different reasons. As a successful and respected business executive Ongpin was not at home in the highly politicized and publicized world of government. This led to heated disputes with other Cabinet members (such as Arroyo and Monsod) and with the press. But more importantly, Ongpin had been one of the chief architects (with Central Bank Governor Jose Fernandez) of a controversial debt rescheduling agreement signed in early July 1987. The agreement had been attacked by economic nationalists and was implicitly criticized by Aquino in her State of the Nation address to Congress in July 1987. Consequently, Ongpin was sacrificed to placate the left. Three months later he committed suicide.[33]

The resignations following the August coup attempt eliminated most of the remaining sources of controversy and disagreement within the Cabinet, resulting in a Cabinet that was more unified and centrist-conservative in its political orientation. It was the third Cabinet reshuffle in eighteen months (the first was in November 1986, and the second was before the May 1987 elections), and further weakened the continuity of government policy-making and implementation.

Throughout September Metro Manila seemed to be bordering on complete chaos. There were daily reports of "Honasan sightings" and frequent rumours of new military coup attempts. On 19 September Leandro Alejandro, the 27-year-old Secretary General of Bayan, was murdered. Rumours circulated that *habeas corpus* would be suspended or that some form of martial law would be re-imposed. Many observers described the situation as being worse than 1972, and one journalist wrote that "republican institutions are a facade for a democracy that is faltering".[34]

The chaos caused by the coup attempt revitalized the right opposition, which began to act as if the collapse of the Aquino government was imminent. Francisco Tatad – a gifted writer who had served under Marcos, broken with him, supported Aquino, and then joined GAD – predicted the government's collapse in four to six months. Blas Ople, in a Marcos-like attempt to cloak a power grab in legalistic niceties, spoke of the likelihood of a "constitutional coup" in which Aquino would be forced to resign and Salvador Laurel, in his capacity as vice-president, would constitutionally succeed her as president. Laurel, for his part, was more than happy to bolster his standing with the right by charging that the Aquino government had suppressed a list of 40 to 100 (the number kept changing) known communists or communist sympathizers holding positions in the government. In an imitation of American-style McCarthyism, Laurel promised to expose "the list". However, "the list" turned out to be a file of old and often inaccurate intelligence reports on "leftists" that included five senators, fifteen congressmen, and ninety-seven local government officials.

The NPA was also quick to take advantage of the post-coup attempt confusion in government and military circles by mounting attacks in Quezon and Negros provinces and in the Bicol region. The legal left, through the KMU, likewise put pressure on Aquino by planning a series of *welgang bayan* (people's strikes) to begin in mid-October to protest the inadequacy of the proposed minimum wage increases and government lay-offs. In response, Aquino indefinitely deferred further government lay-offs and asked Congress to increase the minimum wage by P8 to P10 per day. Unplacated, the KMU continued to call for a general strike, but given the already high level of political insecurity, the October *welgang bayan* failed to receive the level of public support that the August *welgas* had received.

The Aquino government struggled to counter the widely held belief that it was disunited and tottering on the brink of collapse. It tried to prove its ability to fight the communists by claiming (falsely) large victories against the insurgents in the Bicol region. Aquino began to enforce greater Cabinet discipline and demonstrated her accessibility and confidence by travelling to several provinces and meeting with local civilian leaders and troops. The coup attempt also forced Aquino and the Congress alike to take the military's grievances more seriously, prompting across-the-board pay increases and an even stronger anti-communist stance. According to the *Philippine Daily Inquirer*:

> The way many administration officials and congressional leaders have been racing with each other to come up with measures to appease the apparently restive military gives the impression that Honasan had actually obtained his objectives.[35]

To a large degree he had.

Coup jitters, rumours of an Enrile-Laurel "constitutional coup", and talk of imposing martial law continued in Metro Manila until late October. On 20 October Aquino finally rebounded with a "get tough" speech to businessmen in which she vowed to crack down on illegal strikes and improve basic infrastructure and services. The rightist opposition continued to call for Aquino's resignation, but in the face of her continued popularity and American support there was little more they could do. And the radical left overplayed its hand. On 28 October three low ranking American servicemen were gunned down in Angeles City, the home of Clark Air Base, in what appeared to be an NPA attack. Initially, the communist assassination squad, the Alex Boncayao Brigade (ABB), denied responsibility for the killings, perhaps fearing an adverse public reaction. Only later did the communists reverse themselves and take responsibility for the murders. But by early November – even though Honasan was still on the loose – it was clear that the government had weathered the crisis.

The January 1988 Local Elections

On 18 January 1988 elections were held for more than 14,000 four-year positions, including provincial governors, city mayors, and town councillors. The local elections were the first since January 1980 and the first genuinely free local elections since 1971. They were also the last step in Aquino's process of restoring democratic institutions. They took on added importance as a result of the blow to the government's stability caused by the 28 August coup attempt. They were also an important indicator of the relative strength of the political families or "dynasties" that traditionally dominated local politics, and of the alliance building abilities of the national political leadership. As such, they were an important catalyst to the realignment of political parties. Finally, they were important as a test of the local strength of the communist and non-communist left.

The ruling PDP-Laban and Lakas coalition agreed on common gubernatorial candidates in 56 of the 75 provinces, 20 of whom received President Aquino's public endorsement. The Liberal Party, headed by Senator Jovito Salonga, sought to use the local elections to strengthen its position as a centrist alternative to the Aquino coalition. By comparison, UNIDO, the Grand Alliance for Democracy, and the Nacionalista Party participated on a much more limited, *ad hoc*, and regional basis.

The left, for the most part, had come to reject the value of the "electoral struggle" after its poor showing in the May 1987 congressional elections and in the face of mounting harrassment by the military and vigilantes. Consequently, the Partido ng Bayan/Alliance for New Politics fielded slates of candidates for local office only in areas where the communist presence was strong, or had their candidates run under the banner of Lakas or other centrist parties. The CPP and NPA used the elections to generate revenues by charging candidates in communist-controlled areas for the assurance that they could campaign safely.

In the local elections, personal connections with candidates (or with their family or supporters) were much more important than party affiliations. In most municipalities and provinces around the country, the 1988 local elections revolved around the expansion or protection of long-existing family-based "political dynasties". In only a handful of contests did ideology and party platforms play a significant role in determining the results.

The Commission on Elections took control of 24 provinces and 14 cities and towns. Elections in 13 provinces (mostly where there was heavy NPA or MNLF influence) were postponed up to two weeks to allow COMELEC to shift scarce personnel to trouble areas. By 16 January about 98 people had been killed in election-related violence (38 of them were candidates), 12 were wounded (including 8 candidates), and 34 had been kidnapped (including 20 candidates).[36] This compared with 905 people who died in 1971, 410 in 1980, and 104 in the May 1987 congressional elections. In a sad and telling irony, more Filipinos were killed in the January 1988 exercise in electoral politics than were killed in the February 1986 "revolution" that deposed Marcos.

Conclusion: Coming Full Circle

The disparate coalition of forces that coalesced around Corazon Aquino to contest the 1986 presidential election came to power abruptly and with almost no time to prepare for the sweeping change in leadership that followed the EDSA uprising. According to William Overholt:

> Cory Aquino moved into an organizational vacuum. Her new regime . . . did not have a unified executive leadership or effective institutions, such as a reliable military, a unified national political party, or competent civil administration. It was, in short, the beneficiary of a vacuum, not a functioning machine.[37]

It was no small feat then for the Aquino government to survive the political sniping by Marcos loyalists, the subsequent and more serious challenge from the Enrile camp, and numerous planned or attempted coups by disaffected members of the military. The government's ability to survive was all the more notable given that it was also faced with two armed insurgencies and a devastated economy. Despite these challenges President Aquino honoured her pledge to restore democratic institutions and processes. If the February 1986 presidential election is included, Filipinos went to the polls a record four times in the two years from February 1986 to January 1988. A new Constitution was drafted and promulgated, and congressional and local elections were held. The holding of local elections in January 1988 completed the process of democratic restoration.

Because of these accomplishments, and despite many other problems and failures, President Aquino has remained very popular. As the public opinion poll results in Table 6.1 show, Aquino's popularity remained unprecedentedly high during the first year of her presidency but declined to a more normal level following the August 1987 coup attempt.

Table 6.1
President Aquino's Popularity Ratings

	1986		1987		1988
	May	*October*	*March*	*September[1]*	*February*
Satisfied	60	78	76	55	76
Dissatisfied	7	6	7	24	12
Undecided	29	15	17	21	12

[1] The September poll was taken in Metro-Manila only. All others are national.
SOURCE: Ateneo-Social Weather Stations, *Public Opinion Reports*, October 1986, March and October 1987, February 1988.

But given the many challenges the Aquino government faced, its survival and success required more than just the passive support of the Filipino people. President Aquino, however, was unwilling or unable to transform her personal popularity into an organized base of active support for her policies.

The fundamental instability of the Aquino coalition was reflected in the three major Cabinet revamps that occurred between late 1986 and early 1988. In less than two years there were three ministers or secretaries of national defence (Enrile, Rafael Ileto, and Fidel Ramos); three ministers or secretaries of local government (Aquilino Pimentel, Jaime Ferrer, and Luis Santos); two ministers or secretaries of foreign affairs (Laurel and Raul Manglapus); and two ministers or secretaries of finance (Ongpin and Vicente Jayme). Most of these changes were in response to three key dynamics. The first was the basic need for a greater degree of unity within the Cabinet. The second was the need to placate the military. The third was the desire to strengthen Aquino's uncertain base of political support in both the executive and the legislative branches. These shuffles disrupted government policy-making and implementation, especially during the crucial first year. The final result was a more unified, if conservative, Cabinet.

The real and perceived insecurity of her government reinforced President Aquino's conservative and risk-averse nature. In 1987 the

Far Eastern Economic Review observed that: "The main objective . . . has remained the government's consolidation, not its exposure to further dangers by creating new enemies".[38] Consequently, at the same time that traditional democratic institutions and processes were being restored, less traditional concepts of "people power" and "new politics" were jettisoned by the government. This was glaringly evident during the local elections, when the Aquino coalition formed alliances with many former associates of Marcos in order to broaden and strengthen the government's shaky foundation of support. The government also backed away from its strong commitment to controversial and potentially divisive issues such as the prosecution of human rights abuses by the military, extensive land reform, and reducing the size of the government bureaucracy.

Finally, in order to enlist and maintain the support of General Ramos and other "constitutionalists" in the military, the Aquino government was forced to make numerous concessions to the AFP, particularly in its response to the communist insurgency. It is an overstatement to say that the military controlled the civilian government, but as we will see in Chapter 8, it did establish control over national security policy-making. And as we shall also see, this is one of the most significant changes in Philippine politics in the post-Marcos era.

NOTES

1. Portions of this chapter are taken from my chapter entitled "Unfinished Revolution: The Philippines in 1986", in *Southeast Asian Affairs 1987* (Singapore: Institute of Southeast Asian Studies, 1987).
2. Laurel was also appointed Prime Minister, a position that ceased to exist when Aquino abolished the Batasang Pambansa a month later.
3. *Asian Wall Street Journal*, 26 January 1987, p.1.
4. Gareth Porter, *The Politics of Counterinsurgency in the Philippines: Military and Political Options*, Occasional Paper no.9 (Honolulu: University of Hawaii Center for Philippine Studies 1987), p.59.
5. Ibid., p.60.
6. The AFP reported that 912 soldiers, 1,070 members of the NPA, and about 1,000 officials and civilians were killed from late February to mid-December 1986. The military also claimed that only 342 NPA regulars and 766 "activists" surrendered in 1986. See the *Philippine Daily Inquirer*, 8 February 1987, p.1.

7. In January 1987 the government and the MNLF held talks in Jeddah, Saudia Arabia, at which the MNLF dropped its demand for full independence and agreed to negotiate for Muslim autonomy. In February, preliminary negotiations began in Manila, but the talks were quickly deadlocked due to differences over the degree of autonomy and the government's insistence that any agreement providing for autonomy be consistent with the new Constitution and subject to a plebiscite. The talks collapsed in May.

8. James Rush, "The Cory Constitution", UFSI Report No.4 (University Field Staff International, 1987), p.3.

9. Ibid., p.2.

10. Alex Magno in *Newday*, 10 November 1986, p.4.

11. Despite the removal of some of the more disparate and controversial members of the Cabinet, bickering continued until after the 28 August coup attempt. In mid-March 1987 newspapers reported a rift between Arroyo and the members of the "Council of Trent", the Jesuit-trained, market-oriented businessmen and technocrats led by Finance Secretary Jaime Ongpin. Ongpin reportedly criticized "serious delays" in implementing financing and tax programmes and lack of co-ordination by Arroyo. Arroyo lashed out at the new taxes, saying, "Government can not tax people without consulting them. That's basic in a democracy." He also chided Ongpin for "agreeing to impositions of the World Bank and IMF". See *Asiaweek*, 29 March 1987, p.23.

12. *Far Eastern Economic Review*, 29 January 1987, p.20.

13. *Washington Post*, 30 January 1987, p.1. The take-over of Channel 7, which followed on the heels of the Mendiola shootings, was another example of a growing pattern of military coup attempts immediately following some other political crisis. The October-November 1986 "God Save the Queen" coup plan followed the murder of leftist leader Rolando Olalia, the kidnapping of a Japanese businessman, and a spate of bombings in Metro Manila. The August 1987 coup attempt followed the same pattern, coming on the heels of a *welgang bayan* called to protest oil price rises.

14. *Bulletin Today*, 8 February 1987, p.1.

15. With the ratification and adoption of the new Constitution government ministries became departments and ministers became secretaries.

16. Alex Magno in *Businessday*, 13 February 1987, p.4.

17. Office of the President, *Speeches of President Corazon C. Aquino* (Quezon City: Philippine Information Agency, January-March 1987), p.102. Several days before she gave her speech at the PMA a bomb exploded in the reviewing stand, killing 4 workers and injuring 43.

18. *Bulletin Today*, 25 November 1987, p.1.
19. *Far Eastern Economic Review*, 4 August 1988, p.14.
20. Institute of Popular Democracy, *Political Clans and Electoral Politics: A Preliminary Research* (Quezon City: Institute for Popular Democracy, 1987), p.99.
21. *Asiaweek*, 24 May 1987, p.12.
22. *Washington Post*, 25 May 1987, p.A21.
23. Far Eastern Economic Review, *Asia 1988 Yearbook* (Hong Kong: Review Publishing, 1988), p.215.
24. *Washington Post*, 26 August 1987, p.4.
25. The rebels entered Metro Manila in a convoy of trucks and buses with headlights on and red lights flashing. Their approach to the capital went unreported – despite a red alert being in effect. The *Far Eastern Economic Review* noted that Honasan's "access to the AFP headquarters and ease of movement within central Luzon bespoke of compliant senior officers willing to stand back and watch to see what happened." See the *Far Eastern Economic Review*, 10 September 1987, p.13.
26. Although it appeared that the U.S. embassy had as little advance knowledge of the coup as the Aquino government, it was subsequently reported that the U.S. military attaché had close ties with Honasan and was at Camp Aguinaldo during the coup. This provoked a storm of criticism that led to the replacement of the military attaché.
27. P.N. Abinales in *Economic and Political Monthly* 1, no.6 (University of the Philippines Third World Study Center, September 1987):3.
28. *Malaya*, 7 September 1987, p.7.
29. In 1978 Laurel had joined the KBL in order to win a seat in the interim Batasang Pambansa. Two years later he left the KBL, allegedly because Marcos had thrown his support behind the Laurel family's rivals in Batangas province, the Leviste family.
30. *Malaya*, 7 September 1987, p.1.
31. *Straits Times* (Singapore), 20 October 1987, p.9.
32. *Malaya*, 19 September 1987, p.4.
33. See Claudia Rossette's thoughtful series, "Aquino's Embattled Democracy", in the *Asian Wall Street Journal*, 29 February, 1 and 2 March 1988.
34. *Manila Chronicle*, 22 September 1987, p.1.
35. *Philippine Daily Inquirer*, 6 September 1987, p.4.
36. *Daily Globe*, 17 January 1988, p.1.
37. William Overholt, "The Rise and Fall of Ferdinand Marcos", *Asian Survey* 26, no.11 (November 1986):1163.
38. *Far Eastern Economic Review*, 13 August 1987, p.17.

The Restoration of Democracy under Aquino

> I believed that I was called to the Presidency to reestablish democracy and secure our freedoms by the separation of the powers that had come into my hands. . . To that end, I bent all my efforts, convinced that that was what our people wanted first and foremost: a true democracy. . . .
>
> — Corazon Aquino
> 26 March 1987

During the first two years of her administration, Corazon Aquino pursued her calling – the re-establishment of democracy – with almost single-minded intensity and dedication. Her commitment to the democratic process kept her from abusing the near total power she held under the interim Freedom Constitution. Her belief in political freedom prompted her to release political detainees, and kept her from suspending the writ of habeas corpus or declaring martial law in response to the instability that followed the August 1987 coup attempt.

As president, Aquino did not have the power nor the inclination to single-handedly decree new policies, the way Ferdinand Marcos did. Even when she possessed decree-making power under the Freedom Constitution, her use of it was limited by her disinclination to rule by fiat, by divisions within her government, and by the pressure brought to bear by other groups, particularly the military.[1] It is therefore difficult to differentiate between the policy outcomes Aquino wanted, those she tolerated, and those she was forced to accept.

To begin to explain and assess the Aquino government's policies we must begin with a description of Corazon Aquino's personality and priorities. President Aquino's personality is, by most accounts, fairly straightforward: she is intelligent, religious, honest, kind, calm, and reserved. In short, she made the perfect complement to her late husband's egotism and flamboyance. To this list of traits must also be added several more that she developed over the course of her husband's long incarceration, the tragedy of his assassination, and her emergence as a leading figure in the anti-Marcos opposition. These include toughness, quiet self-confidence, loyalty towards friends, and a stubborn commitment to freedom and democracy.

Her political persona, however, is much more complex, and in some ways contradictory. She is a member of one of the Philippines' wealthiest families and when she married Benigno Aquino she married into one of the nation's most famous political families. This fusion of land-based wealth and political power makes her, in many ways, the personification of the traditional élite. At the same time, however, the personal angst the Marcos dictatorship caused her produced in her a strong commitment to democracy, at least as it existed before martial law. In the course of running against Marcos she adopted many reformist policies. And the mass support that ultimately swept her into power imbued her with populist inclinations similar to Ramon Magsaysay's.

As a leader and policy-maker Aquino has preferred to achieve a consensus when possible, but she has also shown that she is prepared to make tough decisions when all other options have been exhausted. On issues she feels strongly about she has acted decisively and confidently, often to the surprise and regret of her opponents. But on the many issues about which she knows little or is ambivalent, she has often been excessively cautious and tentative. She can be highly principled (concerning the restoration of democracy, for example) or very pragmatic (as when she reconciled with pro-Marcos politicians).

President Aquino's democratic vision is a simple and powerful one. She sees democracy as the antidote to the ills of the Marcos era and as the *sine qua non* for national unity and recovery. But her vision is also a limited and limiting one, for she has been unable or unwilling to envision and create a form of democracy different from that which existed prior to martial law. Given the weaknesses and failures of traditional élite democracy, an important question arises whether President Aquino's restoration of democracy has resulted in the creation of the "true democracy" she spoke of in the quote above.

This chapter describes in greater detail the restoration of democratic institutions and processes under Aquino, and assesses the quality of the democracy she played a major role in establishing. It seeks to answer questions such as: how free and fair were the contests for national and local political office? How effective and equitable were democratic institutions in responding to the needs of the Filipino people? What were the achievements and failures of the democratic system after two years? To what extent did Aquino restore traditional pre-martial law government and politics? With what consequences?

To answer these questions this chapter will examine in some depth the following components of democratic government and politics: 1) the 1987 Constitution; 2) the 1987 congressional and 1988 local elections; 3) the quality of justice and human rights under Aquino; 4) the challenge of decentralization; and 5) the problem of government corruption and ineffectiveness. The next chapter describes and assesses the impact of a variety of other actors on the democratic process, including the military, the Congress, political parties, and the Catholic Church.

The 1987 Constitution

The Aquino government, as we have seen, was quick to discard the 1973 "Marcos" Constitution in favour of a provisional Freedom Constitution until a new charter could be drafted and ratified. The "Cory Constitution" was drafted during the latter half of 1986 by a Constitutional Commission hand-picked by Aquino, and was overwhelmingly ratified in February 1987.

According to its preamble, the Constitution was promulgated "in order to build a just and humane society". Its Bill of Rights guarantees, *inter alia*, rights to assembly, to information and access to official documents, to form unions, to collective bargaining, and to strike. The Constitution also establishes a number of fundamental principles and "state policies", including the following:

- Civilian authority is, at all times, supreme over the military.
- The separation of Church and State is "inviolable".
- The State will promote a "just and dynamic social order" and will ensure "social justice in all phases of national development".
- The State is committed to the "sanctity of family life" and will protect and strengthen the family as "a basic autonomous social institution".
- The Philippines will pursue an "independent" foreign policy.

The 1987 Constitution, like its predecessors, establishes a unitary state, although with some provisions for the devolution of power to local governments. It also restores a tripartite separation of powers among the executive, legislative, and judicial branches of government. The Constitutional Commission narrowly agreed to a U.S.-style presidential system with a bicameral legislature rather than a parliamentary system. Under this system the president, vice-president and twenty-four senators are elected in national elections for six-year terms (with the president and vice-president limited to one term only). The members of the 250-seat House of Representatives serve for three-year terms. The independence of the judiciary is guaranteed and the Supreme Court is vested with the exclusive right to rule on the constitutionality of laws.

The Constitution includes a number of other important provisions:

- It limits to sixty days the period the president can suspend the writ of habeas corpus or impose martial law, and makes both subject to congressional revocation.
- It gives Congress the task of devising a system of popular legislative initiative and referendum.
- It strengthens judicial independence by providing fiscal autonomy and creating a council to screen judicial appointments.
- It establishes the rights of non-governmental, community-based, and sectoral organizations to pursue and protect the people's welfare and interests.
- It proclaims all types of crop-lands subject to land reform (but left the critical details of implementation to Congress).
- It prohibits capital punishment and abortion and guarantees universal high school education.
- Finally, it states that the Philippines "consistent with the national

interest, adopts and pursues a policy of freedom from nuclear weapons in its territory" and requires that any future agreement permitting foreign military bases in the Philippines be ratified by the Senate.

Also notable is what is not contained in the 1987 Constitution. First, the Constitutional Commission rejected any significant devolution of the national government's power to the local or provincial levels. Excluded from the Constitution is language from the preamble of the 1973 Constitution that had been interpreted as a Philippine claim to the Malaysian state of Sabah. Also excluded was a provision in the 1973 Constitution that gave the state responsibility for setting and achieving population growth targets, a reflection of the strong influence of the Catholic Church in the Commission. Finally, the majority of the commissioners also rejected "nationalist" efforts to forbid or significantly reduce foreign ownership in certain industries; guarantee "direct and indirect protectionism" for Philippine industry and agriculture; and ban foreign military bases.

In sum, the 1987 Constitution reflects the interests and philosophies of the forty-eight commissioners who drafted it in 1986, and the many competing groups that tried to influence it (such as the Church, farmers and landlords, and cause-oriented groups). Edicio de la Torre, speaking in early 1987, observed, "the Constitution can only reflect the present balance of forces within the government. Hence, it is strong on human rights, but weak on social and nationalist areas".[2] The document also reflects the pervasive and powerful desire that existed at the time to make the Constitution a bulwark against the political (and to a lesser degree, economic) abuses of the Marcos era. The president's ability to assume extraordinary powers was limited; non-traditional mechanisms for broader representation were endorsed; the judiciary's independence was strengthened; and a commission on human rights was created.

In the years to come it will be increasingly difficult to determine the original intent of the Constitution's framers because much of the language they used is intentionally ambiguous and sometimes contradictory. But in the final analysis, the Constitution is just a document. The language contained in it can and will be re-interpreted, circumvented or changed, reflecting prevailing political interests and values. It will be up to the political leadership of the Philippines, as well as the Supreme Court, to determine and enforce the original intent of the Constitution and to ensure that the document continues to be both relevant and respected.

The May 1987 Congressional Elections

Elections for the Senate and the House of Representatives were held on 11 May 1987. A total of 84 candidates ran for 24 senatorial slots and some 1,890 candidates vied for 200 House seats. The May elections were an important indicator of the political concerns of the nation, the popularity of President Aquino, and the relative strength of recently created political parties and coalitions. The elections were also the first test of the fairness and honesty of the democratic process restored by Aquino. Finally, they were a test of whether or not there had been any change in the voting behaviour of the Philippine electorate. Would the campaigns and voting proceed along the lines of traditional élite democracy that emphasized personal relationships and patronage over issues? Or would there be support for the issue-oriented and mass-based "new politics" of the left?

The elections demonstrated that traditional élite politics still reigned in most parts of the country. Many of the candidates for the House were members of families that had dominated local politics before or during the Marcos era. The elections became the arena for long simmering rivalries between influential local families — rivalries that had been dormant or muted under Marcos. According to the Institute for Popular Democracy:

> The political vacuum created by the downfall of the Marcos regime and the subsequent replacement of the local officials by the OICs upset the status quo previously enjoyed by the dominant clans. The new situation forced them to adapt to the changing political scenery by forming new alliances and local political parties.[3]

The 1987 campaign had all the excitement and excess of traditional campaigns. Campaign posters blanketed walls, buildings, traffic signs, and trees. Campaign speeches were filled with flowery rhetoric, unrealistic promises, and outrageous charges against rivals. Money flowed, promises were made, deals were struck, alliances were formed and broken, and numerous "debts of gratitude" were called in. And like traditional campaigns, personalities and not issues dominated.

The May elections differed from past contests, however, in several important ways. First, the elections were a genuinely multi-party contest, with the spectrum of candidates ranging from Marcos loyalists on the right to former communists on the left. Moreover, they came at a time when political parties were still in the process of regrouping, so that many candidates ran under multiple party affiliations. Because of this, the party affiliations of most candidates (with the exception of the candidates of the left and the KBL-UPP) had relatively less significance than in past elections.

Secondly, the elections were held just over a year after the beginning of the Aquino presidency, while Aquino had unprecedented popularity, but at a time when her administration was still poorly established. They were also elections to fill a totally new Congress. Thus, they were focused less on the past record of the Congress (there was none) but were more a referendum on the Aquino government. In particular, they became a test of whether the government would be given the chance to pursue its policies with a supportive Congress, or whether people felt a significant opposition was needed to "fiscalize" (to scrutinize and counter-balance) the Aquino government. President Aquino campaigned vigorously for her coalition's candidates (particularly in the Senate), defended her administration's record, and promised more and better government services, roads, schools, and markets.

Thirdly, the congressional elections preceded the election of local officials and came at a time when all local offices were in the hands of Aquino-appointed OICs (officers-in-charge). In theory, the control of local offices worked to the benefit of the administration's candidates, but in practice other factors were more important on the local level.

The parties that made up the pro-Aquino coalition — PDP-Laban, Laban, UNIDO, the Liberal Party, and several smaller regional parties — campaigned together under the banner of Lakas ng Bansa, or Lakas, which was managed by Paul Aquino, the president's brother-in-law. The Lakas senatorial slate, which was hand-picked by the president, included many well-known centrist political figures such as Jovito Salonga, Raul Manglapus, Ernesto Maceda, Aquilino Pimentel, Agapito "Butz" Aquino, and John Osmeña. But it also included non-traditional politicians such as Alberto Romulo, Rene Saguisag, Leticia Shahani, Augusto Sanchez and Wigberto Tanada. Prominent Lakas candidates for the House of Representatives included Ramon Mitra, Francisco Sumulong, Antonio Cuenco, and several members of the Aquino and Cojuangco families. In general, the list of the Aquino coalition's candidates for the House was shaped by a perceived need to form alliances with the traditional local élites and had much less to do with the individual candidate's political record or beliefs. For example, at least nineteen former KBL Ministers of Parliament, two ex-Marcos Cabinet members, and six former KBL provincial governors ran under the Aquino coalition's banner.[4]

President Aquino announced that "an opposition is not needed in the Senate". The opposition, however, did not agree with her judgement. The non-loyalist right opposition formed the Grand Alliance for Democracy (GAD), a seven-party coalition which included KBL remnants such as Arturo Tolentino and Blas Ople, Nacionalista Party members such as Juan Ponce Enrile, Liberal Party members such as Eva Kalaw, UNIDO members such as Rene Espina, and Christian Democrats such as Francisco "Kit" Tadad. On the far right, the die-hard Marcos loyalists rallied together under the banner of the Union for Peace and Progress-KBL (UPP-KBL). Its senatorial slate of seventeen included former Batasan speaker Nicanor Yniguez and Marcos's personal lawyer, Rafael Recto.

As noted in the previous chapter, the legal left participated in the elections for the first time since 1946. The Alliance for New Politics (ANP) was formed as an umbrella for the Partido ng Bayan, Bayan, and Volunteers for Popular Democracy. The ANP's senatorial candidates included Bernabe "Kumander Dante" Buscayno, founder of the NPA, Horacio "Boy" Morales, a former leader of the NDF, Jose Burgos, the publisher of *Malaya*, Crispin Beltran, Chairman of the KMU, and Jaime Tadeo, head of the KMP. The ANP also fielded 104 candidates for the House, including Bayan secretary-general Leandro Alejandro.

The Lakas campaign had the advantages of greater financial resources and superior organization provided by the Aquino-appointed OICs and the combined network of the PDP-Laban, UNIDO, and Liberal Parties. It also benefited from the support of Jaime Cardinal Sin, who endorsed ten senatorial candidates – all on the Aquino slate.

The Association of Major Religious Superiors in the Philippines supported twenty-four candidates, including three ANP candidates. The Iglesia ni Kristo endorsed fourteen government and ten opposition senatorial candidates.[5]

The Lakas coalition's most important advantage, however, remained President Aquino's popularity and seemingly unsulliable image. Polls taken by the Lakas campaign showed that most people would vote for candidates endorsed by the president. Therefore, according to Paul Aquino, the Lakas campaign manager, "Immediately we abandoned the issue-oriented type of campaigning and decided to pound on the president's popularity. The campaign line was simply: 'I am a candidate and I am Cory's candidate'".[6] Lakas candidates, therefore, stressed two simple themes. The first was the need to support Cory Aquino and provide her with an overwhelming legislative majority. The second was the continuing threat posed by Marcos and the right opposition's past and continuing association with him.

The right opposition also recognized that people had developed "protective instincts" for Aquino and, therefore, avoided attacking her directly. Instead, they accused the Aquino administration of being soft on communism, and they resorted to traditional *bomba*, or exposé politics, claiming, for example, that Aquino's sister-in-law, Margarita "Ting-Ting" Cojuangco, a beautiful and wealthy socialite, absconded with jewellery Imelda Marcos had left behind when she fled from Malacañang Palace. In an ironic effort to equate the Aquino government with the Marcos government, the opposition charged the ruling Lakas coalition with abuse of power, and made dire predictions that the government would resort to widespread election fraud.

On election day, 85 per cent of the Philippines' 26 million registered voters turned out to cast their ballots. The elections were marked by relatively little violence. About 90 people were killed in 153 election-related incidents, which compared favourably with the approximately 150 election-related deaths in both 1986 and 1984, and the more than 900 in 1971.[7] The elections were also relatively clean. An international observer team and most reporters found no evidence of systematic cheating, although there were many isolated incidences of intimidation, vote-buying, and ballot-box stuffing. Delays and mistakes in vote counting also raised some disturbing questions about the impartiality and competence of both COMELEC and NAMFREL.

But, on balance, COMELEC Chairman Ramon Felipe was accurate when he described the elections as "the most peaceful, honest, and orderly since the end of the war".

The result was a resounding victory for the Aquino coalition, which won 22 of 24 Senate seats and over 150 of 200 elected seats in the House. Former senator and Liberal Party leader Jovito Salonga topped the vote, followed by President Aquino's brother-in-law, Agapito "Butz" Aquino. In the House, leading supporters of Aquino such as Ramon Mitra, Jose "Peping" Cojuangco, and Francisco Sumulong all won seats. (All told, six of Aquino's relatives won seats in the new Congress.) Lakas senatorial candidates received, on average, about 60 per cent of the national vote.[8]

Among the GAD candidates for senator only Joseph Estrada, a popular film star and former mayor, and Juan Ponce Enrile were placed in the top twenty-four. Enrile's margin, however, was so narrow that he was not confirmed until August. Overall, GAD senatorial candidates averaged about 25 per cent of the national vote. (Only in Northern Luzon, the home of Marcos and Enrile, did the vote for GAD candidates match the vote for Lakas.) Among absentee balloting, however, of which 90 per cent were military votes, Enrile was placed first and GAD candidates won 16 of 24 slots, indicating significant discontent with the Aquino government within the military.[9] No one from the UPP-KBL senatorial slate was placed in the top thirty, in large part because of their close and unabashed identification with Marcos. UPP-KBL senatorial candidates received only about 5 to 8 per cent of the national vote.

The right opposition fared better in the House contests, however, with twenty-five GAD or UPP-KBL candidates and twenty independents who had formerly been members of the KBL. Another twenty-one former KBL members ran under the Lakas banner and won.[10] Winners in the House who were closely associated with Marcos included Marcos's Minister of Tourism, Jose Aspiras; the son and grandson of former Minister of Agriculture Conrado Estrella; former Local Government Minister Jose Rono; two members of the powerful Singson family in Ilocos Sur; Cebu war-lord Ramon Durano; and in Mindanao, Lanao del Norte, war-lord Ali Dimaporo and his son.

None of the ANP senatorial candidates were elected and the two most popular ANP candidates, Horacio "Boy" Morales and Bernabe

Buscayno, each won only about 1.3 million votes. In the House elections only two ANP candidates were elected and about twenty other non-ANP candidates who had been endorsed by the ANP won congressional seats. Overall, the ANP's share of the national vote (about 8 per cent) was much smaller than expected, but the voting also demonstrated that the ANP had pockets of support in almost all parts of the Philippines.

Following the election, the ANP joined the right opposition in accusing the government of resorting to "fraud and terrorism" and dismissed the elections as "nothing more than a costly and noisy extravaganza meant to resuscitate the old, decrepit, and bankrupt political system".[11] The characterization of the elections as a "costly and noisy extravaganza" was certainly correct. But the description of the electoral process as "old, decrepit, and bankrupt" was only partially correct. For while the process certainly was antiquated, and indeed may have been bankrupt, the ANP's defeat demonstrated that it was not nearly as decrepit as the left had thought. Nor was the electorate as ready for change as the left had hoped.

The January 1988 Local Elections

The 18 January 1988 local elections were the first since 1980 and the first completely free local elections since 1971. They also provided Filipinos the first opportunity to pass judgement on the OICs appointed by the Aquino government in early 1986. The 1988 local elections were supposed to be the final "jewel" in the crown of democracy, legitimacy, and stability that Aquino hoped to fashion. They took on added importance because of the blow to the government's stability caused by the 28 August coup attempt. This blow prompted the Aquino government to use the local elections to mend its relations with traditional political leaders on the local level, many of whom had been associated with the Marcos regime. In some areas the elections were also an indicator of the direct or indirect control and influence of the legal and communist left. The presence of a leftist alternative in these areas made the elections a test of the Aquino administration's acceptance of "new politics", as opposed to traditional élite politics.

Finally, for national leaders such as Senator Jovito Salonga and

Representative Jose "Peping" Cojuangco, the 1988 local elections laid the foundation for the 1992 presidential and congressional elections. The competition was particularly fierce between Salonga's resurrected Liberal Party and the Aquino- and Cojuangco-dominated PDP-Laban/ Lakas coalition. The Liberal Party emerged as a serious challenger to PDP-Laban/Lakas while, at the same time, both the right opposition and the legal left failed to mount major election campaigns.

At stake were more than 14,000 four-year positions ranging from the mayor of Manila to some 12,000 town councillors across the country. Also included in this total were 75 provincial governorships and vice-governorships, 450 provincial board memberships, and about 1,555 mayoral and vice-mayoral positions. About 155,000 candidates ran for office – an average of about ten candidates for every position or one out of every 180 Filipinos registered to vote. In one district in Davao City, for example, there were some sixty candidates for eight councillor slots. In the Metro Manila suburb of Paranaque, five members of the Ferrer family had declared their candidacy for mayor at one point in the campaign.

The incumbents in the election were the OICs appointed by the Aquino government in 1986. Most of them had opposed Marcos, but a significant number had co-existed comfortably under the Marcos regime in earlier years. Some were traditional politicians from dominant local families, but others were businessmen or lawyers who had not been professional politicians. Some had proven to be effective, honest, and popular leaders, but almost as many had adopted traditional approaches to government and politics that involved favouritism and corruption.

The majority of incumbent OICs sought election to their office or to a higher one. Many, but not all, of the OICs received the endorsement of one or both of the parties in the Aquino coalition. In many places two or more of the rival candidates claimed to be the candidate endorsed by PDP-Laban or Lakas. But unlike traditional elections, the incumbency did not necessarily bring a decided advantage. Some OICs had been in office long enough to be blamed for all the local problems, but not long enough to be able to do anything about them. Some were inexperienced and incompetent. Some lacked a local base of political and financial support. Finally, some were resented because they were appointed.

The ruling PDP-Laban/Lakas coalition agreed on common gubernatorial candidates in 56 of 75 provinces. The Liberal Party fielded
candidates in about half of the contests. Salvador Laurel and the
remnants of UNIDO went into the elections in a much weaker condition due to the perceived decline in Laurel's political fortunes, which
had caused defections to either the Liberal Party or GAD. Enrile and
GAD were notable more for their inability to mount a nation-wide
slate of candidates. This prompted one reporter to call the opposition
"a motley crowd of political-has-beens feebly trying to regain the power
and prestige they lost after Cory Aquino assumed the presidency".[12]

The legal left decided to limit its participation in the elections
because of its poor performance in May, and because of increased
intimidation by the military and vigilante groups. Partido ng Bayan
(PnB) secretary-general Fidel Agcaoili explained:

> We've learned our lesson, elections are the game of the elite. . . .
> We're still availing ourselves of the democratic space, but we
> don't have much hope. . . . We don't expect our legal status to
> last long. The government is going to declare us illegal.[13]

Consequently, the PnB fielded candidates only in areas where the
NPA was strong, such as in parts of Pampanga, Bulacan, Samar, and
Mindanao. All told, the PnB supported about 350 candidates nation-
wide. But only about 130 candidates in 19 provinces and 42 towns
were officially under the PnB flag. The other PnB endorsed candidates
ran under other party affiliations.[14]

The CPP and NPA used the elections to attack candidates on the
extreme right and receive payments and concessions from more
acceptable candidates. The NDF chief for the Visayas said that the
NPA exacted fees from candidates wishing to campaign in communist-
controlled "red zones". A "permit-to-campaign" pass cost from P4,000
to P5,000 (US$200 to US$250). The funds were to be used for "bigger
and more spectacular" NPA offensives after the elections. In other
areas traditional politicians were rumoured to have provided food
and medicine to the NPA in order to be allowed to campaign. One
gubernatorial candidate in the Bicol region – a former KBL member –
was rumoured to have given the NPA both money and ammunition.

As expected, issues and ideology had relatively little appeal or influence in the elections, although this was not entirely true in contests

where the PnB ran candidates. To the extent that candidates emphasized issues, they were traditional ones such as corruption, law and order, and the provision of infrastructure, jobs, and basic services. There were, however, some relatively less traditional campaign issues. For example, some candidates were accused of being disguised communists. Others were accused of perpetuating traditional "political dynasties". But other seemingly important issues — such as positions on land reform and the appropriate role of the military — were rarely raised.

President Aquino, herself a member of the country's leading political family, was unwilling to speak out against the re-emergence of local political dynasties. Instead, her response was, "Let the people decide". She also tried to avoid becoming involved in the Byzantine complexity of the local elections. She said she would only endorse those candidates who ran under the joint PDP-Laban/Lakas banner. Otherwise, she said half jokingly, all her time would be taken in photo sessions with local candidates. Eventually, she succumbed to pressure and ended up endorsing more than twenty candidates for governor and a number of mayoral candidates.

If an Aquino endorsement was not available, the next best thing was to be tagged as the "official" candidate of PDP-Laban or Lakas. This was especially important in the many areas where there were numerous candidates claiming to support Aquino. The scramble for the endorsement of the leaders of the parties became the source of numerous complex and confusing disputes among the candidates over who was the "official candidate". These, in turn, intensified inter- and intra-party tensions among the PDP-Laban and Lakas coalition members.

PDP-Laban, headed by President Aquino's brother, Representative Jose "Peping" Cojuangco, supported almost any candidate who was a proven vote-getter. In many areas this meant supporting former KBL officials, including a number of people closely associated with the abuses of the Marcos era. Examples of pro-Marcos politicians supported by PDP-Laban included Roque Ablan of Ilocos Norte, the Singsons in Ilocos Sur, Alfredo Maranon in Sagay, Negros, and Raul Lee in Sorsogon. Commenting on this, Amando Doronila wrote: "Like Faust, the Aquino Government has made its pact with the devil, representing its shift to the right".[15]

Jose Cojuangco claimed that these politicians were "moderate" forces needed to defend the government against the left and the right.[16] Other members of the ruling coalition justified the support of Marcos "war-lords" as being part of Aquino's policy of "reconciliation". Paul Aquino, Aquino's brother-in-law and head of Lakas was somewhat more straightforward. He acknowledged that the Aquino government had no choice but to bring the old war-lords back into the ruling circle. Others portrayed it as a defensive manoeuvre designed to provide the government with much needed local support. It was also suggested that the Marcos supporters were brought on board in order to keep them from supporting the military. According to this argument, it was necessary to give the Marcos-era politicians a stake in the system so that they would help to defend it against any future coup attempts by the military.

Traditional and Non-Traditional Contests

Most of the contests in the local elections involved a bewildering number of candidates and parties. The configuration of these contests – that is, the number and types of candidates and their party affiliation(s) – had little to do with party platforms or issues. Instead, the key factor shaping most of the local contests was the revival of competition among the small number of families that typically dominate local politics. Many of these rivalries had been frozen or seriously cowed under Marcos because of his near total control of local politics. With the restoration of democracy, these "dynastic" rivalries resurfaced with a vengeance. As with past local elections, these local rivalries were fuelled by the support of provincial and national politicians seeking to extend their political alliances to the local level.

Most local contests, therefore, involved a complicated set of factors including long-standing political and personal rivalries and alliances; hastily-constructed short-term tactical alliances; an overlay of local, provincial, and national political party rivalries; and the lingering influence of the May congressional elections. The relative importance of each of these factors varied from place to place and from contest to contest. Most of the contests, however, can be grouped into four categories: a) traditional rivalries between dominant local families;

b) traditional local rivalries that were proxies for provincial or national rivalries; c) non-traditional ideological contests; and d) other non-traditional contests. The first two categories of traditional contests were by far the most common, but the existence of the two categories of non-traditional contests were reflective of changes occurring on the local level.

1. *Traditional rivalries between (and within) dominant local families.* In the 1988 local elections long-standing inter-family contests for political supremacy on the local or provincial level resurfaced across the country. Typically, these rivalries were between two or three leading families, although there were some important intra-family rivalries as well. Some of the more prominent examples of the effort to re-establish or protect local, family-based "political dynasties" include the following: in Tarlac, where several Aquinos ran for a variety of offices; in Cebu, where Osmeñas and Cuencos tried to re-establish their historical dominance; and in Ilocos Sur, where six members of the Singson family vied for various posts.

2. *Traditional local rivalries that were proxies for provincial or national rivalries.* Two notable examples of "proxy wars" during the January elections occurred in Rizal and Batangas provinces. The gubernatorial contest in Rizal province was between two dominant families — the Sumulongs and the Salongas — and their respective political parties. The contest was a continuation of a Salonga–Sumulong provincial and national rivalry that went back to the 1950s. In the 1987 congressional elections Jovito Salonga was elected senator while Francisco Sumulong and his nephew, Egmidio Tanjuatco, won two House seats. The 1988 local elections in Rizal became an important test of the popularity and power of Salonga and his Liberal Party relative to that of the Sumulongs and the PDP-Laban/Lakas coalition. Salonga, the Liberal Party president and a possible presidential aspirant, used the Rizal gubernatorial contest to challenge the political influence of Sumulong, an influential member of the House, and the PDP-Laban/Lakas coalition to which he belonged. Salonga charged that the Sumulongs and Tanjuatcos were attempting to create a "political dynasty" in Rizal. He implied that their attempt was part of a larger effort master-minded by Jose Cojuangco and others close to

President Aquino to create a national political dynasty. The result: Salonga's "anti-dynasty" campaign was successful and his candidate for governor, a relatively unknown physician, defeated Francisco Sumulong's nephew.

The gubernatorial elections in Batangas province, the provincial base of the Laurel family, became the focal point of a political battle between UNIDO and PDP-Laban, both nominally part of the Aquino coalition. Jose Cojuangco sought to erode Vice-President Salvador Laurel's power base by supporting the opponent of Laurel's nephew, Benjamin Laurel, in the gubernatorial race. Cojuangco was successful and Laurel's nephew lost, dealing a blow to the Laurel family's (and therefore UNIDO's) national political standing.

3. *Non-traditional ideological contests.* There were two types of non-traditional ideological contests: those dominated by vocal anti-communists and those in which leftist candidates ran.

Davao City, the birthplace of vigilante groups, provided the setting for one of the most colourful anti-communist campaigns. One of the three leading candidates for mayor in Davao was Jun Pala, a popular, controversial, pistol-packing radio announcer who became legendary for his verbal attacks on the communists and any group he thought was at all sympathetic to the left (including the Church, human rights groups, and the media). His campaign capitalized on the widespread anti-communist sentiment in Davao City and the growth of vigilante organizations. But Pala was also perceived as something of a populist and had name recognition because of his radio broadcasts and general notoriety. Initially, his two, more traditional opponents, the mayor and vice-mayor, were put on the defensive by Pala, and had to match his strident anti-communist stance. In the end, however, the moderation, political machine, and money of the more traditional politicians prevailed. The incumbent vice-mayor, backed by many of Davao's traditional politicians, won. Pala was placed a respectable third.

At the other end of the political spectrum was a small group of candidates supported by the Alliance for New Politics, the Partido ng Bayan, and other "progressive" groups. The ANP and PnB fielded candidates in selected areas where there was a significant communist presence such as in Samar, Pampanga, and parts of Mindanao. In other areas, leftist candidates ran under traditional party banners.

The left sought control of selected municipalities so that they could develop concrete examples of the benefits of progressive "people's" governments for propaganda use. They also sought to win local government offices in order to reduce the effectiveness of the military and vigilantes. According to Jackie Sebastian, NDF Chairman for the Eastern Visayas, "Local officials are crucial in the counter-insurgency warfare. It is thus imperative for us to prevent Rightist officials from setting the low intensity conflict into high gear in the region".[17]

The province of Pampanga, north of Metro Manila, is an example of an area where the left chose to contest the local elections. Pampanga is a historic centre of agrarian radicalism. The town of Santa Ana (population 40,000) was one of the strongholds of the Huks in the 1950s. It has been heavily influenced by the CPP and NPA since the late 1970s. The ANP chose to field a full slate for mayor, vice-mayor and councillors in Santa Ana. Agapito Gaddi, the ANP mayoral candidate, was one of eight candidates. Gaddi was considered one of the leading contestants, in part because he came from a traditionally influential family (his grandfather was mayor and his father was a judge) and in part because he enjoyed the support of well-developed local chapters of Bayan and PnB, farmers' groups, and perhaps the CPP as well. His campaign platform was progressive – he called for immediate land reform, the creation of people's organizations, and "true democracy". But he employed traditional campaign techniques, including motorcades and reliance on the vote-getting ability of about 100 *liders* (ward healers). In his printed flyer he made it a point to stress his family's historic commitment to public service in Santa Ana; he denied being a communist or a member of the NPA; he stressed that he and his family were devoted Catholics; and he closed by acknowledging, in advance, his debt of gratitude to those who would vote for him.

Gaddi was confident of victory, but on the night after the elections ballot boxes from four barrios, containing 4,000 of the 12,000 votes cast, were snatched, causing COMELEC to schedule a re-vote in these four barrios in early February. In the week following the first election, government troops moved into the area around Santa Ana and had two encounters with NPA guerrillas. In the face of the growing military presence in the area, the ANP withdrew from the re-election, claiming that the military's presence would "terrorize voters and stifle freedom and exercise of suffrage and force them to vote for the candidates of the powerful". His campaign lost, and concerned about his safety, Gaddi fled Santa Ana for the relative security of Metro Manila. Santa Ana remained in the hands of traditional politicians.

4. *Other non-traditional candidates.* The final category includes two other types of non-traditional candidates: active military officers and non-professional politicians. A small number of active military officers chose to run for governor or vice-governor. Military candidates included Colonel Rodolfo Aguinaldo in Cagayan province, Rolando Abadilla in Ilocos Norte province, and Orlando Dulay in Quirino province. All three had become well known for their opposition to the Aquino government (which included supporting some of the coup attempts against the government) and for their fierce anti-communism. They capitalized on strong anti-government sentiment in their provinces (particularly in Ilocos and Cagayan), and on the organizational strength and influence of the military. Aguinaldo, Abadilla, and Dulay all won. The success of their candidacies indicated the high degree of politicization within the military, the level of their discontent with the Aquino government, and the considerable popularity the military enjoyed in northern Luzon, the home of Marcos and Enrile.

Finally, there were also several notable victories by non-professional politicians. These included Daniel Lacson in Negros Occidental province and Roberto Pagdanganan in Bulacan province. Lacson, who was from a prominent family with interests in sugar and shipping, became involved in civic affairs when the sugar-based economy of Negros collapsed in the early 1980s. Pagdanganan, like Lacson, came from the private sector and was appointed by Aquino as OIC governor in early 1986. Both did such respectable jobs that they ran virtually unopposed and were elected in the 1988 elections. Lacson has become nationally and internationally known for his reformist policies, effective management, and ambitious plans to diversify the Negros economy.

The Big Winner: Traditional Politics

In most parts of the country the local elections were successfully held, which is to say that vote-buying, fraud, and violence before and on election day did not exceed historical norms.[18] Some 135 people were killed or wounded in election-related incidents. The *relative* tranquillity of the elections was an accomplishment, given the magnitude of the exercise, the nearly twenty intervals since the last free local elections, and the intensity of many of the contests. Still, it is a sad irony that the deaths of more than 90 people during the local elections were accepted as part of a democratic electoral process by the same nation that, less than two years before, had prided itself on ousting a dictator through a non-violent revolution.

Who won? Could any one party claim victory? A partial listing of the affiliations of the gubernatorial winners, though impressionistic at best, suggests the relative strengths of various parties in the Philippines. The affiliations of fifty-eight winning governors whose party affiliations were on record at COMELEC in late 1988 are shown in Table 7.1.

While PDP-Laban and Lakas combined won about 55 per cent of the governorships, the parties of the Aquino coalition were hurt by the "dynasty issue" and by their support of some Marcos-era political

Table 7.1
Party Affiliations of 58 Winning Governors in the 1988 Local Elections[1]

	Governorships Won	
Party	*Number*	*Percentage*
PDP-Laban	12	21
Lakas	12	21
PDP-Laban and Lakas	8	14
Liberal Party	7	12
UNIDO	5	9
Independent	5	9
Nacionalista, KBL or other parties	9	14
Total	58	100

[1] Available COMELEC records listed Party affiliations for only 58 of 75 governorships.

SOURCE: Commission on Elections records.

bosses. These issues were exploited by the Liberal Party, and to a lesser degree by UNIDO. Consequently, the local elections were significant because they revealed the emergence of Jovito Salonga's Liberal Party as a significant rival to the PDP-Laban/Lakas grouping headed by the Aquinos and Cojuangcos. According to political commentator Francisco Tatad:

> It is obvious Mrs. Aquino did her best to install her relatives and friends in order to establish a broad dynastic grassroots base for her reelection bid. And Mr. Salonga did his best in raiding all the other parties to protect his local turf and his Senate presidency and to project himself for the next presidential contest.[19]

The results, however, were less an indication of grassroots sentiment either in favour of or against the Aquino government than they were a reflection of the changing fortunes of the local and provincial political élites. Many traditional political dynasties were restored or strengthened, such as those of the Aquinos, Singsons, Salongas, Villafuertes, and Osmeñas. But some other notable ones were weakened, such as the Sumulongs and Laurels.

The conduct and results of the 1988 local elections revealed the persistence and vitality of traditional politics in the Philippines. Most candidates came from traditionally dominant families. Most campaigns focused on the character of the respective candidates, their power and connections, and their ability to provide jobs or a new road or school. Voting in most areas, and particularly in rural areas, was heavily influenced by direct or indirect personalistic ties, promises of patronage or other benefits, and explicit or implicit threats of punishment.[20] On the national level, members of the Aquino coalition, including President Aquino herself, forgot their former distaste of Marcos-era politicians and supported many candidates formerly associated with Marcos. Traditional politics triumphed. Philippine politics had come full circle.

Justice and Human Rights

The Philippine judicial system has a history of being slow, cumbersome, and subject to manipulation and abuse. These shortcomings antedate the Marcos era. Under Marcos, however, the judicial system lost whatever vestiges of credibility it once had. Marcos's "constitutional authoritarianism" perverted both the theory and practice of rule by law rather than by men. Moreover, the favouritism and corruption that existed under Marcos made a sham of the concept of equality under the law. The use of force by pro-Marcos war-lords and the military also made a mockery of the notion of law and order. The problem was compounded by the deterioration in the government's efficacy, legitimacy, and authority under Marcos.

As a result of these abuses, Corazon Aquino inherited a society sceptical of the judicial process and suffering from high levels of lawlessness and violence. On one level the task of reforming the judicial system was relatively simple. The laws and institutions that had been ignored or abolished by Marcos could be restored with relative ease. But on another level the challenge was considerably larger and more difficult, for the judicial system had to be remade from the bottom up. In order for the judicial system to work new procedures and institutions had to be created, and even more difficult, new norms and standards of justice had to be established and enforced. The Aquino government was considerably more successful with the former challenge than with the latter.

The Restoration of Rights and Judicial Reform

Two of Aquino's first acts as president were the restoration of the writ of habeas corpus that had been denied under Marcos and the release of all political prisoners, including alleged leaders of the CPP and NPA. By early March 1986 more than 500 prisoners had been freed and by mid-June 1986 the total had reached 563.[21] In March, Aquino also established a Presidential Commission on Human Rights (PCHR), headed by former senator and human rights lawyer Jose Diokno, to investigate past and continuing human rights abuses by the government. She also abolished Marcos era decrees that allowed indefinite detention under "Preventative Detention Actions" or "Presidential Commitment Orders".

The Aquino government's early commitment to human rights and justice was also reflected in the 1987 Constitution, which included many references to the state's role in promoting justice. For example, it called for the state to promote "a just and dynamic social order" and for "social justice in all phases of national development". The Constitution's Bill of Rights guaranteed due process, equal protection under the law, free access to the courts, "adequate" legal assistance to the poor, and a speedy trial. The Constitution also created a permanent Commission on Human Rights to succeed the Presidential Commission on Human Rights.

Aquino also undertook a judicial reorganization that included appointing 11 of 15 Supreme Court justices, 9 new judges to the Sandiganbayan (a special court created to handle cases of government graft and corruption), and 42 of 51 judges in the Court of Appeals.[22] Judicial independence was also strengthened by constitutional provisions that forbade the executive or legislative branches from reducing judicial appropriations, created a Judicial and Bar Council to nominate lists of potential candidates for all future judicial appointments, and gave the Supreme Court administrative supervision over all the lower courts.

These reforms represented an important break with the Marcos era, and were a necessary first step in improving the independence and fairness of the judicial system. However, they have had only limited impact on the functioning of the judicial system, for the provision of justice requires that reforms and resources be directed to the lower levels of the system. The Philippines is a highly litigious society, but the process of litigation favours the wealthy and the educated. Lawyers are typically paid by the court appearance rather than by the case, so that they have an incentive to maximize the number of court appearances by stretching cases out for as long as possible. Appealing a case is difficult and costly as both the Supreme and Appelate Courts are located in Metro Manila. Judges are over-burdened, inadequately trained, and poorly paid. Trial by jury is not practised, and so judges become the targets of political influence and bribery.

Adding to the problem is the prison system, which is old, decrepit, and overcrowded. Typical of prisons in the Philippines was one provincial jail visited in 1987. Some 800 inmates – including a number of children – were housed in a facility designed to accommodate 250 people. Two-thirds of them had not been convicted of any crime, but were there awaiting trial. Some had waited one and a half to two years for trial for petty crimes, mostly theft, for which the sentence, if they were convicted, probably would be less than the time they had already spent in jail awaiting trial. One inmate spent four years in jail waiting for a decision on robbery charges. He claimed that he had not seen his lawyer for more than three years and did not know whether he was dead or alive.[23]

The public's faith in the legal system and in the dispensation of justice was further undermined by the Aquino government's inability to curb, solve, and punish politically motivated acts of violence. The most notable of these were the slayings of labour leader Rolando Olalia, Bayan head Lean Alejandro, and local government minister Jaime Ferrer; the attempted murders of two other prominent leftists, Bernabe Buscayno and Nemenzo Prudente; and the mass killings at the Mendiola Bridge, and in Lupao, Nueva Ecija. In the wake of each incident special "task forces" were set up to identify the assailants, but typically little progress was made. Political assassination had become cheaper and easier than non-violent political rivalry.

Human Rights Abuses under Aquino

The above-mentioned acts of political violence were tragic and deplorable. But of even greater concern was the continuation of, and in some cases increase in, organized violence and intimidation, much of it condoned, if not actually sanctioned, by the Aquino government. For every attack on a prominent political leader there were numerous attacks on innocent citizens, journalists, lawyers, policemen, soldiers, and low level government officials. The most disturbing of these were the "salvagings" (politically motivated murders), disappearances, torture, and intimidation by members of the military and paramilitary and vigilante groups. The NPA also violated human rights in the name of its cause. As we will see in Chapter 9, the NPA had its own concept of "revolutionary justice" under which it meted out punishment, often including death. According to the military, eighty-eight policemen, soldiers, and civilians were killed by the NPA in the Metro Manila area alone in the first ten months of 1987.[24]

Task Force Detainees (TFD), the Catholic Church's human rights monitoring group in the Philippines, claimed there were 59 disappearances, 208 salvagings, and 512 cases of torture in the first eleven

months of 1987.[25] Many of these human rights violations were attributed to members of the paramilitary Civilian Home Defence Force
(CHDF). The CHDF was intended to provide a locally recruited and
trained militia to support the army and constabulary. But the CHDF
became known during the 1980s for its indiscriminate recruitment,
deficient leadership and training, and poor discipline. As the presence
of the NPA expanded during the early 1980s, members of the CHDF
increasingly became the targets of the NPA "sparrow squads" (small,
urban-based assassination units), intensifying the CHDF's hostility
towards the population they were supposed to protect. Under the best
of circumstances the members of the CHDF were poorly educated
and trained, with little if any ability to distinguish a communist from
a non-communist social or political activist. At their worst, they were
armed thugs sanctioned by the government to use force to carry
out the biddings of local landowners and politicians, regardless of
their legality.

The army and the Philippine Constabulary (PC) also have been
blamed for many human rights abuses. The deep-seated anti-communism of many members of the military led them to suspect almost
any individual or group that agitated for social change or criticized
the military. Consequently, the military (and the paramilitary CHDF)
were hostile towards most peasant and labour organizers, politically
active priests, human rights lawyers, members of Basic Christian
Communities and other non-governmental organizations promoting
social change.

Some military abuses were due to poor training and discipline,
which led to the unnecessary use of force. Sometimes the inherent
uncertainty of fighting a guerrilla war in which civilians and insurgents
were indistinguishable led to tragic mistakes. But more often, military
abuses were due to the indiscriminate use of military force and a
heavy-handed approach to waging counter-insurgency operations.
The use of torture, violence, and even murder was seen by some
members of the military as a necessary part of the counter-insurgency
effort. Some used violence against those suspected of aiding the
insurgency in a calculated effort to punish, intimidate, and gather
information.

The problem of human rights abuses was not confined to the
countryside. In 1987 and 1988 the military and police regularly made

armed sweeps of slums in Metro Manila in search of communists, rounding up and arresting suspects based on hearsay and informer's tips. In early November 1987 they twice raided the government-run Polytechnic University of the Philippines and arrested 39 communist suspects. They also sought the arrest of its president, Nemenso Prudente, a former student activist, on suspicion of harbouring communists. (Several days later Prudente was seriously wounded in an ambush for which a shadowy anti-communist group took responsibility.) But usually these raids netted few, if any, communists, and indeed there are stories that the military usually released the true insurgents, suggesting just how arbitrary and ineffective these sweeps were.

In the face of these continuing abuses, the Aquino government was unwilling to make human rights violations a major focus, primarily out of fear of alienating the military leadership. As a result, the Presidential Commission on Human Rights, which had no power of prosecution and could only make recommendations to the President, made little headway in its investigation of human rights abuses. The Commission's annual report for 1986 listed 708 complaints filed with the PCHR, of which 225 concerned alleged violations during 1986, and 483 before 1986. Most cases involved salvaging, disappearance, or torture. The PCHR report indicated that only 23 cases were "resolved" in 1986, although it was not stated how they were resolved.[26] No action was taken on the Commission's recommendation that it clear officers and government employees eligible for appointment or promotion to ensure that they were not respondents in cases filed with the PCHR. Furthermore, the PCHR was not assigned to investigate the Mendiola shootings in January 1987, probably at the insistence of the military, which feared an independent investigation. Consequently, most of the PCHR's members resigned and its effectiveness and stature were further diminished by the death of its chairman, Jose Diokno, in February 1987.

The PCHR was succeeded in May 1987 by the constitutionally mandated Commission on Human Rights (CHR), which was tasked with investigating "all forms of human rights violations". These were interpreted to include violations by the government and communist rebels alike. By the end of 1987 the military had presented more than 100 complaints of NPA abuses to the CHR for investigation. Like the PCHR, the CHR was empowered only to investigate violations, not to prosecute them. According to Amnesty International, "as of the end of January 1988, not a single military or police officer had been convicted and sentenced for such political killings – or indeed any other serious human rights offence – since the Aquino government came to power."[27]

Even when there was a commitment to investigate and prosecute abuses, there were numerous obstacles to successful prosecution. According to Amnesty International:

> In the few cases where court proceedings have been initiated, witnesses have been harrassed, arrested, or even killed. In many cases witnesses are afraid to come forward to identify their assailants. Victims or their families have withdrawn cases under pressure. Arrest warrants are not served. Military personnel accused of offences are sometimes allowed to remain on active duty, bearing arms. Investigators often cannot obtain military records. Frequently the investigation of human rights offences appears to collapse before the prosecution stage is ever reached.[28]

Human rights abuses are, in a sense, just the most recent manifestation of a long and sad tradition of localized violence in the Philippines. They are also a reflection of the national government's limited ability to establish its authority nation-wide, particularly in remote rural areas. But the abuses are also a product of the polarization and militarization of local communities caught in the conflict between the radical left on the one hand and the military, paramilitary, and vigilante groups on the other. Whatever the combination of causes, the credibility of both the Aquino government and the judicial process were undermined by the continuation of human rights abuses.

The Challenge of Decentralization

The Philippines is a unitary state in which all power is invested in and flows from the national government. Subnational units of government – provinces, cities, municipalities, and *barangay* – are the creation of the national government and possess power only to the extent that it is granted by the national government. As we have seen, historically this has produced a highly centralized, but weak, government.

The signs of excessive government centralization are widespread. Teachers, policemen, and firemen are employees of the national government. All but the very smallest public works projects are planned and funded by national departments. The provincial or regional heads of these departments are responsible to officials in Metro Manila rather than to the governors of the provinces in which they operate. Provincial and local governments have very limited opportunities to raise revenues by taxation. Consequently, most local government officials spend much of their time in the capital lobbying congressmen and bureaucrats to secure or release funds and to influence personnel appointments. In addition to this, the administration of higher justice is geographically centralized, with the Appelate and Supreme Courts located in Metro Manila. Finally, the regulatory bureaucracy is also located in Metro Manila, which has contributed to the concentration of business in Metro Manila and the provinces adjacent to it at the expense of more geographically balanced economic development.[29]

As a result of this centralization, the call for decentralization or greater local autonomy has been a recurring theme in Philippine politics. The first local autonomy legislation was passed in the 1950s. During the martial law period Marcos promised more local autonomy, but actually did just the opposite. The Aquino government, as we will see, has acknowledged the need for greater decentralization, but like its predecessors it has been unwilling or unable to delegate significant authority or resources to local government units.

At issue are two types of decentralization. The first and most important is political decentralization, which involves the devolution of political power to local governments so that they can plan and decide on policies affecting their locality and control financial resources. The second type, administrative decentralization, involves transferring a share of the functions and decision-making authority lodged in national departments to their regional and provincial offices.[30] We will focus here on political decentralization because changes in this type of decentralization have an important influence on the pace and responsiveness of policy-making and on the distribution of government resources. The debate over political decentralization pits congressmen and elements of the executive branch against mayors and provincial governors. Consequently, it reveals a great deal about political relationships and the distribution of political power.

The Philippines' tradition of centralized government exists alongside two other somewhat paradoxical political traditions. The first, as we have seen, is the highly particularistic nature of Philippine politics. National political organization, to the extent that it exists in the form of political parties, traditionally has been based on the coalescing of local factions. Consequently, there is a continuing tension between the extremely centralized structure of the national government and the particular concerns of the politicians who control the government.

The second tradition concerns the limited scope and resources of the national government. Although all Philippine constitutions have accorded the national government great power, in reality the conservative élite that has controlled it since the creation of the commonwealth has sought to limit the government's size and scope. This is seen in the ruling élite's traditional aversion to taxation. Philippine tax revenues as a percentage of the government budget have historically been lower than most other developing countries. Even Marcos preferred to finance his government by borrowing from abroad rather than significantly increasing taxes, although he did improve collections. Consequently, national government revenues have tended to be inadequate to support an effective bureaucracy or to fund large national social programmes (excepting primary education). As a result, the national government has had difficulty in effectively or consistently reaching down to the local level. At the same time, however, local and provincial governments, devoid of any significant authority to raise revenues, and controlled by the local landed élite, have been unable or unwilling to fill the vacuum.

This has created a situation in which provincial and local politicians are dependent upon the executive branch and Congress to provide the funds, projects, and patronage opportunities they need. The president and Congress, in return, are politically dependent upon the local politicians to deliver votes in the next election. As a result, the executive branch actively intervenes in local affairs, particularly in the area of appointments. The Congress, not to be outdone, spends much of its time passing countless minor bills to fund local "pork-barrel" projects and resolutions renaming government buildings, in order to gain the support of local officials and voters.

Under Marcos, the government's excessive centralization sapped what little local initiative existed and reinforced the traditional tendency to "look to Manila" for guidance and resources. By the early 1980s, however, corruption, the mounting political and financial problems of the national government, and the growth of the communist insurgency combined to cause a serious deterioration in the government's ability to provide basic services on the local level. This, in turn, caused the proliferation of a wide variety of non-governmental organizations (NGOs), ranging from left-leaning social action groups, to church- and business-supported economic development groups, to right-wing vigilante groups.

During her campaign for the presidency, Corazon Aquino had been critical of the over-centralization of the Marcos dictatorship and called for the revitalization of local governments as a necessary element of redemocratization. However, when Aquino assumed power, her immediate concern with local government was not decentralization *per se*, but rather the loyalty of the approximately 14,000 provincial and municipal officials elected under or appointed by Marcos. Her decision to replace them with her own appointments amounted to an act of extreme centralization. According to Alex Magno, the appointment of OICs, most of whom were members of the local political élite, "simultaneously asserted the centrality of the Manila-based power stucture and marginalized the mass organizations and grassroots institutions that had developed during the period of popular resistance to the dictatorship".[31] The decision also became regrettable for other reasons. It ignited a political storm in hundreds of governors' and mayors' offices across the country as well as within her fragile coalition government. It caused her to spend countless hours resolving disputes over appointments. The replacement of a number of capable "Marcos" officials with inexperienced or incompetent OICs did considerable damage to many local governments. Finally, the inability or unwillingness of some OICs to work with the local military commanders (many of whom had not been replaced following the change in government) became an early irritant between the military and the civilian government.

Perhaps because of her unpleasant experience with the OICs, Aquino avoided the thorny issue of political decentralization during 1986 and 1987 and instead focused on administrative decentralization. She began a reorganization of the Marcos bureaucracy that was supposed to result in greater administrative decentralization, but most of the members of her Cabinet resisted efforts to reduce their departments' control over local affairs. Some of their resistance was due to a desire to preserve their institutional power and prerogatives (including patronage opportunities). Some of it, however, was rooted in a justifiable concern about the ability of many local and provincial governments to honestly and effectively administer programmes. Whatever their motivation, Aquino's decision to postpone local elections until January 1988 meant that she did not have to face a group of independently elected local officials until after the elections. Consequently, the issue of the relationship between the national government and local government units was left to the Constitutional Commission.

The constitutional commissioners did not change the fundamental dominance of the national government, but they did offer some potentially significant improvements in the authority of local governments. Partly in response to the decline of local government under Marcos, the 1987 Constitution calls for the Congress to enact a local government code which "shall provide a more responsive and accountable local government structure instituted through a system of decentralization . . . . "[32] It also states that local governments shall have a "just share" of national taxes and that they are entitled to "an equitable share in the proceeds of the utilization and the development of the national wealth within their respective areas".[33] The Constitution leaves it to the Congress, however, to decide the exact meaning of "just" and "equitable". Finally, the Constitution also requires the executive branch to form "regional development councils" to facilitate administrative decentralization and strengthen regional autonomy.

The Aquino government continued its cautious approach to decentralization in late 1987 and 1988. In late 1987 Aquino signed an executive order reorganizing the Regional Development Councils (RDCs) that Marcos had formed but largely ignored. The new RDCs brought the provincial governors, mayors, and the regional heads of national departments together in an effort to better co-ordinate, plan, and monitor the implementation of regional development programmes. In reality, however, few if any RDCs had the autonomy, authority, staff, or budget to play a significant role in establishing or carrying out regional development priorities.

In February 1988, in an effort to improve the implementation of government programmes, members of the Aquino Cabinet were assigned regions for which they would be responsible as Cabinet Officers for Regional Development. In May, a Cabinet Action Committee on Decentralization was established, but it focused primarily on administrative decentralization, particularly with regard to pilot decentralization efforts in the provinces of Laguna, Tarlac, Negros Occidental, and Davao del Norte. Finally, in June a Joint Legislative-Executive Committee on Decentralization and Local Autonomy was formed to study decentralization.

Congressional opposition to meaningful decentralization became clear in 1988 with the drafting of the general appropriations bill for 1989. In the bill the House undermined the autonomy and authority of the RDCs by refusing to appropriate funding for their operation. It also allocated to each congressman P10 million (about US$475,000) in discretionary "pork-barrel" funds, and it allowed already approved capital outlays and public works projects to be "realigned" by the representative of the district concerned.[34] Finally, the bill also left it to each representative to decide which *barangay* roads would be paved under a P1.5 billion (about US$70 million) public works programme.

The House appropriations bill effectively gave the representatives executive as well as legislative powers. According to Luis Villafuerte, the governor of Camarines Sur and the president of the National Governors' League, the House bill:

> consigns to the dustbin the work of the Cabinet Coordinators for Regional Development in strengthening decision-making at the local levels. More importantly, it will erode government's claim to founding decisions on rational and objective grounds. The provision smells of pork barrel through and through.[35]

The influential Philippine Chamber of Commerce and Industry (PCCI) agreed. According to the PCCI, in 1987 local government units received only P3.5 billion (US$175 million) in direct financial assistance out of a national budget of P170 billion (US$8.5 billion). This led the PCCI to conclude that "As long as funds are controlled by the central government, all talk about decentralization and local autonomy will be academic".[36]

Combatting Government Corruption and Ineffectiveness

Corruption, nepotism, and ineffectiveness are longstanding problems of the Philippine government. Not surprisingly, they are seized on by whomever is out of power to criticize those who are in power. Excessive and sustained corruption and nepotism at high levels (as occurred under Marcos) have distorted policy-making, with adverse consequences for the economy. A widespread perception that a government is corrupt or ineffective can result in a serious loss of legitimacy.

How Much Corruption Is Too Much?

Although there are varying definitions of what constitutes corruption and nepotism, most Filipinos would acknowledge that high levels of both exist in the Philippines. The causes of corruption and nepotism are numerous and complex, ranging from cultural factors (such as the importance of family and interpersonal relations) to inadequate standards and controls to low government salary levels. The types of corruption most common in the Philippines range from paying small bribes to officials, "fixers", and policemen to requiring large pay-offs to secure contracts or favourable treatment from the government. The prevalence of nepotism is seen in the tendency at all levels of society to look to family members (both direct and extended) for employment opportunities. While decrying corruption and nepotism, however, most Filipinos accept them as unavoidable facts of life. Others rely on corruption to supplement their incomes by large or small amounts.

The Philippines, like most other developing countries, has a long history of corruption that pre-dates the "kleptocracy" of the Marcos era. Claro Recto's speeches in the early 1950s harped upon the problem of political corruption. Real and alleged corruption has been an important campaign issue in virtually every presidential campaign, and every president since independence has established at least one presidential body to investigate and eradicate corruption.[37] Marcos exploited the perception of a morally bankrupt political system to justify his declaration of martial law. As the scope of the government's control expanded under martial law, so did the opportunities for corruption. The growth of corruption increasingly distorted economic policy-making and eventually undermined the legitimacy of the Marcos government.

Corruption can be divided into two types: bureaucratic and political. Bureaucratic corruption, as the name suggests, is corruption that occurs in the administering of government laws and regulations and in the provision of government services. This can include requiring bribes to "facilitate" needed government approvals; using one's office to secure preferential treatment for oneself or one's family; or accepting understated tax liabilities or overpriced contracts. It also includes the corrupt practices of military officers, such as protecting (or running) illegal gambling, prostitution, or logging operations.[38]

Bureaucratic corruption, though pervasive and problematic, is not as damaging as political corruption.[39] Political corruption can be defined as the illegal use of elected office for the personal gain of oneself or one's friends, family, or followers. It is a more serious form of corruption because it undermines government legitimacy, distorts policy-making, and contributes to the ethical environment that encourages bureaucratic corruption.

The problem of political corruption took on special significance under President Aquino for three reasons. First, the extreme corruption of the Marcos era had increased both the pervasiveness of corruption and the public's revulsion to it. Secondly, much of Aquino's appeal was based on her reputation for honesty. Consequently, there were high expectations for the conduct of her administration − expectations that could not possibly be met given the wheeling and dealing nature of Philippine government and politics. Finally, the RAM group within the military and other opponents of the Aquino government seized upon the corruption issue in an effort to discredit and weaken the Aquino government (at the same time that they tried to deflect inquiries into military corruption).

Charges of corruption in the Aquino government first arose in connection with the military's desire for a Cabinet revamp in November 1986. As a result, two Cabinet members accused of corruption − Ernesto Maceda of the Ministry of Environment and Natural Resources, and Rogaciano Mercado of the Ministry of Highways and Public Works − were forced to resign in connection with the resignation of Juan Ponce Enrile. In the May 1987 congressional elections the anti-Aquino opposition criticized the large number of her relatives running for office and charged members of her family with corruption and the abuse of power. The Presidential Commission on Good Government also became the target of charges of corruption, favouritism, and incompetence. By mid-1988 five PCGG agents faced graft charges and thirteen more were under investigation.[40] In May 1987, in response to mounting public criticism, Aquino created a Presidential Committee on Public Ethics and Accountability.[41] The Committee, however, focused mostly on bureaucratic corruption, and was hampered by a shortage of funds and staff. In late 1987 and 1988 more rumours of corrupt practices by several of Aquino's relatives surfaced. It was accurately reported that one family member, Richard Lopa, had paid a pittance for a controlling interest in thirty-six companies owned by Marcos's brother-in-law five days after Marcos fled.[42] Other family members were accused of being involved in activities from gambling to influence peddling.

Charges of political corruption are rarely substantiated, often exaggerated, and quickly forgotten in favour of the next juicy scandal. Overlooked in the exchange of accusations was the fact that by 1988 the fight against bureaucratic corruption was being waged with some success in several departments. Improvements of varying degrees were made in the Department of Health, the corruption-ridden Department of Public Works and Highways, the Bureau of Internal Revenue, and the Customs and Immigration Commissions. In response to persistent rumours of high-level political corruption in mid-1988 some of Aquino's earliest supporters formed a citizen's movement against corruption and called for the president to establish a "new moral order".

Despite these positive developments bureaucratic corruption will continue to be pervasive because of powerful cultural factors and the low pay of government officials.[43] Political corruption, on the other hand, can be combatted somewhat more effectively. The rivalries between the Congress and the executive branch, and between political leaders, will ensure that real and contrived charges of corruption will continue to be brought to the public's attention. Perhaps the sensationalist and biased press might one day mature into a credible "watchdog". Failing this, Church groups and other non-governmental organizations, which played an important role in monitoring the use of Community Employment and Development Programme (CEDP) funds, can also monitor and publicize political corruption. Finally, the ethics and political will of the present and future political leadership can have an important symbolic effect. Unfortunately, however, as one

Filipino specialist on corruption has pointed out, President Aquino's "honesty has not been matched by the political will to punish the corrupt".[44]

Government Ineffectiveness

Ineffectiveness, like corruption, has been frequently cited as a long-standing defect of the Philippine Government. There is a long history of the government announcing policies and programmes that never seem to get implemented, and there are countless stories of debilitating bureaucratic indifference, incompetence, and red tape. It has been estimated that bureaucratic corruption and inefficiency took up about P50 billion (about US$2.5 billion) or one-third of the government budget.

A large part of the problem is the size of the government bur-eaucracy relative to its meagre resources. In 1986 the bureaucracy numbered 1.3 million people (including teachers and the military). Its ranks doubled in size during the martial law period. Its profession-alism has been undermined by poor management and patronage. Its civil servants have become demoralized and susceptible to corruption because of their low salary levels. Its effectiveness is limited by over-centralization, excessive red tape, and a chronic shortage of funds and equipment.

In an effort to address these problems Aquino established a Presi-dential Commission on Government Reorganization (PCGR) two weeks after she became president and ordered it to draw up a plan for the reorganization of the bureaucracy. The PCGR drafted a plan that identified five major objectives of government reorganization: to "de-Marcosify" the bureaucracy, reduce its size, increase administrative decentralization, reduce the government's role in the economy, and increase accountability, efficiency, and cost-effectiveness. Unfortunately, most of these objectives have not been met. Attempts to de-Marcosify the bureaucracy were unevenly pursued and eventually abandoned. Efforts to significantly reduce the size of the bureaucracy made little progress and were indefinitely postponed following the 1987 coup attempt.[45] Administrative decentralization, as we have seen, has proceeded slowly and unevenly. Privatization of the economy, as we will see in Chapter 10, has also proceeded very slowly. Only in the areas of government accountability and efficiency have there been some small successes.

In 1987 political commentator Alex Magno wrote that "It is one thing to promise to have an honest government and another thing to see that it is an effective one".[46] He was echoing widespread frustrations that the Aquino government was slow in formulating its policies and ineffective in implementing them. These concerns were particularly important for two reasons. First, given Aquino's lack of experience, real questions existed about her ability to run the government. For many observers, these questions evolved into serious doubts as disputes and indecision within the Cabinet at times seemed to paralyse the government. Thus, as with the corruption issue, the perception as much as the reality of government ineffectiveness gradually eroded the support of the middle class, the business community, the media, and the Catholic Church.

Secondly, elements of the military, and in particular the members of RAM, were highly critical of the civilian government's effectiveness, implying that a military-dominated government could do a better job. Indeed, the August 1987 coup attempt was prompted in part by the appearance of disarray caused by the government's poor handling of its decision to raise fuel prices. The December 1989 coup attempt capitalized on the mounting frustration in Metro Manila over the government's inability to deal with energy shortages and transportation problems.

The Aquino government was increasingly criticized for being slow to formulate a variety of important policies, including a new investment code, an agrarian reform programme, and a new local government code. It was also criticized for poorly implementing policies and programmes, such as the Community Employment and Development Programme, the rebel returnee programme, and the introduction of a value added tax.[47] Furthermore, the government's slowness in reviewing and approving development projects resulted in missed opportunities for much-needed additional foreign assistance.[48] Finally, the government was also blamed for not making sufficient progress in improving many of the long-standing inefficiencies in Philippine society, from the poor quality of the domestic telephone service (operated by a regulated monopoly) to inadequate garbage collection in Metro Manila.[49]

There is considerable validity in most of these criticisms. The government's ability to make and implement policies has been, and continues to be, slow and erratic. Initially, this could be explained by the inexperience of Aquino and many of her advisors; the absence of a transition period; personality and policy differences among the members of the Cabinet; and considerable turn-over within the Cabinet.[50] The passage of time has seen only a slight improvement in the government's performance, suggesting that other, more fundamental factors are also responsible. To begin with, the government bureaucracy has never been particularly professional or effective. Even under Marcos's firm rule the bureaucracy was often unresponsive and ineffective. With the restoration of democracy, the government has been further constrained by the separation of powers and public opinion. In addition to this, recurring military coup attempts have forced the government to take an *ad hoc*, reactive, and highly political approach to policy-making, often at the expense of developing coherent longer-term goals and strategies. Finally, the government's ability to implement programmes and projects has been significantly reduced by the payments it must make to service its huge domestic and foreign debt obligations.

Looking to the future, for the Philippine Government to become more effective salaries of civil servants must be increased, the senior government officials must become more professional, the government's infrastructure (computers and other equipment) must be improved, and administrative decentralization must be increased. These improvements, however, will not come quickly, if at all. The influence of personalism and patronage remains strong. The government's debt burden will continue to limit the resources available to improve the bureaucracy. And finally, the political leadership remains ambivalent (at best) to the idea of an independent and professional bureaucracy.

Conclusion: Aquino and the Mixed Record of Redemocratization

The preceding discussion suggests that the Aquino government's restoration of democracy deserves mixed marks. The government deserves good marks for assembling a relatively thoughtful and responsible group of constitutional commissioners and for energetically campaigning for the Constitution. Aquino also selected a respectable senatorial slate for the 1987 elections and conducted the elections freely and fairly. She deserves lower marks for aligning with a number of unsavoury traditional politicians in the 1988 local elections. Her record on restoring judicial independence is good, but her record on protecting human rights is disappointing. She has made little progress with decentralization. Lastly, although the magnitude of corruption has declined from the unprecedented level of the Marcos era, only slight progress has been made in reducing the traditional problems of government corruption and inefficiency.

Why the mixed record? A large part of the responsibility lies with Corazon Aquino, although circumstances and the underlying conservatism of Philippine politics and society also contributed. To begin with, President Aquino had a relatively simplistic and limited vision of what democracy is. She single-mindedly sought to restore traditional democratic institutions and processes, but she seemed to care little about how effectively and equitably they functioned. For example, what mattered to Aquino was the holding of congressional and local elections – not that the elections resulted in a reversion to traditional élite politics.

The Aquino government's mixed record is also the outgrowth of a serious miscalculation Aquino made concerning the need for a political base. Although she remained immensely popular – and perhaps because of her popularity – she was slow to build a base of organized political support. During 1986 she rejected the two options open to her: institutionalizing "people power", or forming her own political party. Initially, it seemed that Aquino believed that "people power" could be institutionalized. At a victory mass on 2 March 1986 she suggested the formation of "people's councils", presumably to substitute for the *barangay* governments created by Marcos. In the weeks following the EDSA revolution cause-oriented and sectoral groups endorsed the establishment of people's councils to fill the void created by the change in government. However, the idea was eventually vetoed by the new government. According to Francisco Nemenzo: "Had the government . . . encouraged people to meet regularly to discuss their community problems and, through the people's councils, transmit to the appropriate government agencies their demands and grievances, people's power could have become a living reality, not just a memory to be recollected once a year".[51]

Aquino was equally averse to developing her own political party. She viewed parties merely as discredited vehicles for generating votes at election time, not as important institutions for building consensus, encouraging participation, and facilitating legislation. In an interview in October 1987, Aquino reiterated her opposition to forming a party, saying that, "the image of a politician is still not very attractive".[52] As a result of her decision not to build an organized base of support, when Aquino was challenged first by Juan Ponce Enrile and then RAM, she did not have a power base to rely on. Lacking this, she had to rely first on General Ramos and other constitutionalists within the military, and then on traditional politicians. In the process of securing this support, the Aquino government adopted more traditional and conservative policies.

Finally, there was a high degree of wishful thinking in many of Aquino's approaches to major problems, particularly the insurgency, corruption, and human rights violations. She seemed to believe that the restoration of traditional democracy would automatically improve things. According to William Chapman, "For months after Aquino's accession, prominent leaders in her government still clung to the belief that the renegades would at any moment come down from the hills to seek amnesty and that their peasant army would exchange their weapons for a few hectares of government supplied land".[53] In addressing the problems of corruption and human rights abuses, Aquino seemed to think that her numerous statements of commitment to the principles of clean government and human rights were an adequate substitute for active enforcement.

Despite the mixed record of redemocratization, the resuscitation of the democratic tradition — even if much of it was élitist and ritualistic — restored an important if somewhat mythical element of Philippine political culture. Filipinos were once again able to take pride in their political freedom, regardless of the abuses and inequities that remained. The restoration of democracy reinvigorated people's expectations of greater freedom, justice, and equitable economic development. Equally important, the restoration of democratic institutions gave the struggling Aquino government legitimacy and credibility.

The restoration of elected congressional and local offices brought a greater degree of direct representation and decentralization, at least compared to the Marcos era. But most of those elected were members of the traditional élite, and the structure of government remained heavily and excessively centralized.

There were, however, a number of serious problems associated with the restoration of democracy. One of the biggest was that the government would not be able to meet the nation's heightened expectations about democracy. If, as many Filipinos thought, many of the nation's problems were caused by the Marcos dictatorship, then it followed that the return to democracy would somehow provide the solutions to these problems. Democracy, it was thought by many, would bring an end to the insurgency, result in better government, produce a more just society, and make economic growth and development more equitable. When gains in these areas were slow to materialize disenchantment and frustration rose.

A second problem was that the increase in government legitimacy and stability bred complacency. With the worst abuses of the Marcos era undone and the communist insurgency on the defensive, there were some leaders who were content to return to the pre-martial law system of politics and government. Once they assumed power, many of the political leaders who had called for changes in the structure of Philippine politics and society while Marcos was still in power became content to pay lip service to reform, while, in reality, they were content to return to "politics-as-usual".

A third problem was that the democratic process, while increasing regime legitimacy, reduced government effectiveness, at least initially. Aquino was hesitant to use the power of decree while she had it. She valued consensus decision-making, but her Cabinet was often divided. Consequently, the executive branch was often unable to act quickly and effectively. The process of restoring democratic institutions, involving as it did a plebiscite and two elections, disrupted policymaking and implementation. Once elected, it took the Congress most of the first year to become genuinely operational.

Finally, the return of élite democracy, almost by definition, promised the continued domination of the élite. But would the post-Marcos élite be any different from the pre-martial law élite? Were élite and the national interests inherently in conflict, or could they be reconciled?

Did other competing groups have significant influence on the democratic process? Would the varied political forces operating within the democratic system allow the attainment of Aquino's goal of "true democracy"? We will address these questions in the following chapters.

NOTES

1. The disdain President Aquino and Joker Arroyo, her Executive Secretary, felt for the Marcos dictatorship made them reluctant to use the decree-making power she held under the provisional "Freedom Constitution". This hesitancy was overcome in the days immediately before the convening of the new Congress, when more than 40 executive orders were decreed. Aquino ended up issuing 302 executive orders in 478 days of unlimited power.
2. Edicio de la Torre, "On the Post Marcos Transition and Popular Democracy", *World Policy Review* 4, no.2 (Spring 1987):343.
3. Institute for Popular Democracy, *Political Clans and Electoral Politics: A Preliminary Research* (Quezon City: IPD, 1987), p.61.
4. Ibid., p.72.
5. *Far Eastern Economic Review*, 18 June 1986, p.42.
6. *Manila Chronicle*, 10 May 1987, p.2.
7. *Asiaweek*, 24 May 1987, p.12.
8. See Carl Lande and Allan Cigler, "Recent Philippine Elections: A Quantitative Analysis" (interim report, April 1988), pp.10–11.
9. *Business Day*, 18 May 1987, p.16.
10. Institute for Popular Democracy, op. cit., p.99.
11. *Far Eastern Economic Review*, 6 June 1987, p.41.
12. *Manila Chronicle*, 17 January 1988, p.11.
13. Ibid., p.11.
14. *Philippine Daily Globe*, 18 February 1988, p.2.
15. *Manila Chronicle*, 4 January 1988, p.1.
16. *Manila Chronicle*, 17 January 1988, p.14.
17. Ibid., p.6.
18. A new element in election violence emerged in some areas: the contest between the NPA and anti-communist vigilante groups. The Philippine military claimed that about half of the election-related killings were by the NPA.
19. *Philippine Daily Globe*, 19 January 1988, p.4.
20. A study of the local elections in two suburbs of Metro Manila, Malabon

and Navotas, suggests some change in urban areas. According to this study:

> In both towns, political factionalism continues to be defined by clan alliances but electoral victory is decided by the migrant, urban poor vote...The middle class vote, while it has begun to articulate in the electoral process, remains insufficient to overcome the traditional mode of electoral politics. On this aspect, at least, the case studies illustrate the transitional configuration of the Philippine political system: a configuration of modified intra-elite competition, less dependent on the former basis of land ownership but still resistant to the development of party-based voting constituencies. Filipino electoral politics remains mired in personalism although less dependent on patronage networks.

See Third World Studies Center Research Team, *Class, Clan and Coalition: The Transformation of Local Political Elites in Two Municipalities* (Quezon City: University of the Philippines Third World Studies Center, 1988), pp.2–3.

21. Amnesty International, *Philippines: Unlawful Killings by Military and Paramilitary Forces* (New York: Amnesty International, 1988), p.11.
22. *Bulletin Today*, 10 February 1987, p.1.
23. Margo Cohen, "Reconciliation or Revenge", *The American Lawyer*, October 1986, p.137.
24. Amnesty International, op. cit., p.16.
25. Task Force Detainees, *Philippine Human Rights Update* 3, no.3 (November–December 1987):21.
26. Amnesty International claimed that seven of them were closed through court action, but in some cases the court action preceded the formation of the PCHR. See Amnesty International, op. cit., p.12.
27. Ibid., p.44.
28. Ibid., p.44.
29. Metro Manila produces about one-third of the Philippines' total gross domestic product and almost one-half of the country's manufacturing output.
30. Alex B. Brillantes, "Decentralization and Local Autonomy: The Source of Frustration of Local Officials" (Quezon City: University of the Philippines, College of Public Administration, November 1988), p.3.
31. *New Day*, 20 February 1987, p.4.
32. Constitution of the Republic of the Philippines, Article X, Section 3.
33. Constitution of the Republic of the Philippines, Article X, Sections 6 and 7.

34. Luis Villafuerte, "How to Subvert Local Autonomy", undated speech, p.2.
35. Ibid., p.5.
36. *Manila Chronicle*, 8 July 1988, p.16.
37. See Ledivina Carino, ed., *Bureaucratic Corruption in Asia: Causes, Consequences and Controls* (Quezon City: University of the Philippines College of Public Administration, 1986), pp.129–31.
38. The numerous possibilities for bureaucratic corruption are illustrated by a complaint filed against a senior official in November 1987. This man was accused of:
   - personally acquiring from the customs bureau a Mercedes Benz for P178,000 (about US$8,700), a fraction of the car's retail value.
   - reserving the use of a car for his executive assistant, who was reported to be a relative of his wife.
   - authorizing the purchase of office equipment without public bidding, resulting in its overpricing.
   - appointing a town-mate without civil service eligibility to a position instead of other, more qualified employees.

   See *Malaya*, 10 November 1987, p.1.
39. See Carino, op. cit.
40. *Newsweek* (Asia edition), 22 August 1988, p.9.
41. According to the Committee's Chairman, Jose de Jesus, there already are enough anti-graft laws on the books, making corruption more of a "management problem" than a legal one. Consequently, he pledged to reduce the opportunities for bureaucratic corruption, increase the risks of engaging in corrupt practices, and decrease the benefits. To accomplish this he pledged to make transactions simpler and more "transparent" and to do away with unnecessary regulations and licences. See *Bulletin Today*, 19 October 1987, p.1.
42. *Newsweek* (Asia edition), op. cit., p.9.
43. An excellent example of the inescapable need to recognize and adjust to powerful cultural influences was a ruling made by Customs Commissioner Mison concerning the acceptance of "gifts" (some would say bribes) by customs officers. The respected commissioner told his customs officials that it was permissable to accept "tokens of appreciation" from importers, provided they are given "without any ulterior motive". See *Bulletin Today*, 5 November 1987, p.19.
44. Ledivina Carino, *Bureaucracy for a Democracy: The Struggle of the Philippine Political Leadership and the Civil Service in the Post Marcos Period*, Occasional Paper No.88-1 (Quezon City: University of the Philippines College of Public Administration, August 1988), p.34.
45. Ibid., pp. 14–19.

46. *New Day*, 20 February 1987, p.4.
47. Under the CEDP P3.9 billion (US$195 million) was allocated in 1986 to fund 20,569 rural-based projects. Only 4,330 (21 per cent) were completed in 1986, and 8,494 (41 per cent) were in various stages of implementation, prompting Japanese officials to voice concern. See *Business Day*, 13 January 1987, p.2.
48. According to NEDA, in late 1987 delays in implementing foreign assisted development projects averaged about 2½ years and were worth some P4.5 billion (US$225 million). See the *Manila Chronicle*, 13 November 1987, p.15.
49. A "get tough" speech Aquino made to business leaders on 20 October 1987, in response to the August coup attempt, was widely applauded. In effect, however, she conceded the failure of her "hands off" approach to policy-making when she pledged, "Henceforth, I shall rule directly as President". She also acknowledged the inability of the national and local bureaucracies to address the country's basic problems when she observed that: "A president is supposed to be above details, but it seems I must do everything myself".
50. In contrast to the high turnover among the civilian leadership, the military hierarchy remained relatively intact, strengthening its position *vis-à-vis* the civilian government.
51. Francisco Nemenzo, "Military Intervention in Philippine Politics", *Diliman Review* 34, nos.5&6 (1986):25.
52. Interview with Amando Doronila in the *Manila Chronicle*, 18 October 1987, p.19.
53. William Chapman, *Inside the Philippine Revolution* (New York: W.W. Norton, 1987), p.260.

chapter 8

The Military and Other Political Actors

I think we have become irrelevant.

— Senator Rene Saguisag (describing
the role of the Senate in the wake of
the 28 August 1987 coup attempt)

The restoration of democracy described in the preceding chapter did not happen in a vacuum. The process was also influenced by a number of other political actors, many of which were not under the control of President Aquino and the executive branch. These actors had an important, and in some cases determining, impact on the shape of politics and policy-making during the first years of the Aquino government.

The single most important of these actors was the military. Other important influences on the democratic process covered in this chapter are the convening of the new Congress, the role of the Catholic Church, the realignment of political parties, and on the local level, the rise of vigilante groups. The role of the communist and non-communist left is examined separately in Chapter 9.

Civilian-Military Relations and National Security

The abrupt fall of Marcos produced a situation for which neither the military nor the new civilian government was adequately prepared.

The military leadership, which had comfortably done Marcos's bidding for fourteen years, was faced with a new president and commander-in-chief, a new form of government, and new internal divisions of its own. The new civilian leadership, which until 23 February 1986 had viewed the armed forces as Marcos's loyal henchmen, now had to deal with the military as an independent actor. Consequently, the first two years of the Aquino administration were strongly influenced by an on-going redefinition of civilian–military relations and by a closely related debate over the government's response to the communist insurgency. In particular, as Gareth Porter has noted, "The issue of negotiating a cease-fire with the communist insurgents or taking the offensive against them militarily became an integral part of the manoeuvering for power in a transitional phase of Philippine politics."[1]

The size and national reach of the Armed Forces of the Philippines (AFP) as an institution, the large role it played under Marcos, and the continued threat of the communist and Muslim insurgencies combined to give the military an unavoidable role in politics after the February revolution. To a degree unprecedented in Philippine history, the stability and eventually even the survival of the civilian government became dependent on its relationship with particular factions within the AFP. Ironically, this resulted in the military having more influence and independence under Aquino's democracy than it had under Marcos's dictatorship.

The expansion of military influence is attributable to a number of factors. The AFP is one of only a few institutions in the Philippines that is genuinely national in scope. In contrast to the civilian government, the military survived the transition from Marcos to Aquino relatively intact. In the months following the EDSA revolt its two senior leaders, Defence Minister Juan Ponce Enrile and Chief of Staff Fidel Ramos were immensely popular, giving them (and the military in general) considerably more prestige and influence than they had enjoyed during the last years of the Marcos era. More ominously, RAM's unsuccessful plot to overthrow Marcos demonstrated the desire of certain elements within the AFP to play a major role in national affairs. As a result, the ever-present possibility that elements of the military – either Marcos loyalists or reformists – would attempt to depose Aquino further strengthened the position of Ramos and other "constitutionalists" in the AFP *vis-à-vis* the civilian government.

The Legacy of a Politicized Military

Corazon Aquino inherited a bloated and seriously decayed military led by an officer corps that, under Marcos, was accustomed to playing an influential role in national affairs. According to General Rafael Ileto, who succeeded Juan Ponce Enrile as Minister of Defence in November 1986:

> We inherited a rotten military. . . . There is poor leadership in the field. Commanders are lazy and unprofessional . . . . It is easy to buy boots and trucks. It's a lot harder to change how the soldiers think.[2]

The first step of the new government, therefore, was to make significant personnel changes. Twenty-four of thirty-six "overstaying generals" (generals retained by Marcos after their mandatory retirement age) were immediately retired; fourteen other generals who had held key posts under Marcos were replaced, demoted, or reassigned; and lower ranking officers thought to be loyal to Marcos underwent "reorientation" courses.[3] Major organizational changes were also made. The National Intelligence and Security Authority (NISA), which General Ver had used to spy on and control opponents of the regime, was abolished. It was replaced with a smaller National Intelligence Co-ordinating Agency (NICA), which concentrated more on covert operations against the insurgency. The Presidential Security Command (PSC), which under Marcos had grown to a strength of about 15,000 soldiers, was reduced to a single battalion of about 600 men. Chief of Staff Ramos also sent into the field a number of battalions that had been stationed in Metro Manila and announced plans to dismantle the Regional Unified Command (RUC) in order to make the military command structure more efficient and responsive.[4]

The Aquino government faced the larger challenge, however, of "getting the military back into the barracks" — that is, of reducing the military's role in policy-making, governance, and the economy. "The military", General Ileto admitted, "is used to lording it over civilians, and they are reluctant to give up that power."

A large part of the problem was generational. Officers and soldiers who had joined the AFP during the 1970s and early 1980s never served under a system of civilian primacy. Furthermore, many of these officers and soldiers had participated in the various socio-economic development schemes initiated by Marcos and his wife. As a result, many of them came to see the military as playing an important role in national development. It was not surprising, then, that many of them also came to see the military as being more dedicated and effective than traditional politicians and bureaucrats. Consequently, it was difficult for many younger officers to cast themselves in a subordinate role, especially after they had risked their lives helping to topple Marcos.[5]

Many younger officers were also politically influenced by either of the two experiences they were likely to have had during the first half of the 1980s. If they were stationed in Metro Manila, they would have been exposed to the intense factional politics within the military caused by a system of promotions based on loyalty to Marcos. If they were in Metro Manila they might also have participated in Marcos's and Ver's often brutal efforts to use the AFP to counter political opposition to the regime. If, instead, they had drawn combat duty, they would have been exposed to two other powerful influences. First, they would have seen the government's failure to address the problems and poverty of the average *tao*. Secondly, they also would have been exposed to the ideology and successes of their opponents, the communists.

Given these experiences it was easy and perhaps inevitable for the young officers to assume that the military had an important role to play in politics and policy-making. A leading member of the RAM reform group, interviewed in late 1986, described the military as "right in the center, balancing the right and the left". He also likened the Philippine political system to a see-saw: "When the right is down the left is up. If the left is up too far, the military has to come down on the left to maintain the balance".[6] Implicit in this statement is the belief that the military has both the right and the responsibility to intervene in politics and policy-making. For officers and soldiers who accepted this as a premise, it was a small step to conclude that they also had the right to determine the very nature and composition of the national government. This is exactly what they attempted to do in August 1987 and December 1989.

Intra-Military Factionalism

The redefinition of civilian–military relations was made considerably more complicated by factional divisions within the military. The AFP was divided into numerous, overlapping, and sometimes competing factions, groups, and associations. Some were legitimate professional associations; some were loosely based on regional and service loyalties; some were factions based primarily on patron–client relationships between senior and junior officers; and a few had political or ideological underpinnings. Some had their own by-laws and constitutions; official headquarters; insignias; sets of officers and boards of directors; elaborate initiation and investiture rites; and, in some cases, even corporate logos.[7] Others were far more informal and secretive. Their objectives ranged from enhancing the professional welfare of their members, to safeguarding the integrity and professionalism of the AFP, to fighting communism. But the net effect was to fuel factionalism, create a complex and uncertain chain of command, and, ultimately, undermine the military's professionalism.

The best known of these groups was the Reform the Armed Forces Movement (RAM). RAM was started secretly in late 1982 by a small group of junior officers who had become frustrated by the deterioration of the military's professionalism and fighting capabilities. Most of RAM's founders and leaders were graduates of the élite Philippine Military Academy (PMA), and many were from the class of 1971. By 1985 RAM had grown large and confident enough to go public during the 1985 PMA commencement when, in front of Marcos and senior military leaders, its members wore T- shirts saying "We Belong", and unveiled placards calling for military reform. During the last two years of the Marcos regime RAM developed with the knowledge and support of Defence Minister Enrile. Although RAM was scrupulously apolitical in public, calling only for reform of the AFP, secretly its leaders were planning to overthrow Marcos. General Ver's discovery of the RAM plot triggered Enrile's break with Marcos and the EDSA uprising. Following the change in government RAM supported Enrile's challenge to Aquino and, after this failed, they organized and led the August 1987 and December 1989 coup attempts.[8]

A second important group was the Guardians Brotherhood. The Guardians included in their membership commissioned, non-commissioned and enlisted personnel, which gave them a broader following than the more elitist RAM. The Guardians had their own organizational hierarchy which was said to supersede the AFP chain of command, making them "an army within an army". Many of the soldiers involved in the July 1986 "Manila Hotel incident" and the January 1987 "Channel 7 revolt" were Guardian members.[9]

The differences that existed among these and other groups within the military were sharpened by the February revolt and its aftermath. The choices made during the four-day uprising resulted in a "complicated web of loyalties and betrayals".[10] As a result, the factionalism that had existed under Marcos was further fuelled by intense new resentments, suspicions, and ambitions.

The first and most obvious new division was between those officers and troops who had remained loyal to Marcos and those who threw their support behind the rebels or remained neutral. As noted, Aquino and Ramos moved quickly to reduce the influence of Marcos loyalists in the military by retiring or reassigning many of them. However, despite these efforts, two loyalist generals, Edgardo Abenina and Antonio Zumel, were able to enlist the support of significant numbers of soldiers in two later coup attempts.

Factional differences also grew between officers who supported Defence Minister Enrile and those who sided with Chief of Staff Ramos. After the revolution many of the leaders of RAM followed Enrile to the Ministry of National Defence, where they assumed influential positions in planning and intelligence. Members of RAM and the Guardians began to criticize Ramos for not representing the military's interests aggressively enough and for being too supportive of Aquino. Ramos, out of a combination of genuine military professionalism and political savvy, refused to join Enrile and RAM in their public criticisms of the civilian government – even though he shared many of their views.

The division between Ramos and Enrile and their followers came to a head in late November 1986, when Ramos moved decisively to quash an anticipated coup attempt by RAM, and by doing so threw his support squarely behind Aquino in her struggle with Enrile. It is unlikely that Ramos had widespread support for his move against Enrile and RAM, but his success suggests that he was able to command the loyalty of a sufficiently large minority of senior officers to dissuade those who supported Enrile.[11] Ramos's success, however, added to the dissatisfaction of Enrile's many supporters in the Army. The depth of their dissatisfaction was revealed in the January 1987 Channel 7 revolt and the August 1987 coup attempt, both of which sought, among other things, to oust Ramos.

A third major source of factionalism was the inter-service rivalry between the Army and the Philippine Constabulary (PC). Inter-service rivalry is not unusual, but the rivalry between the Army and the PC had grown over the years because of the ambiguity of their respective missions, particularly with regard to counter-insurgency operations. In addition to this, many in the Army viewed the PC as being even more corrupt and less professional. After the February revolution this long-standing animosity re-emerged in the debate over the qualifications of General Ramos, who had risen through the ranks of the PC, to be Chief of Staff. Members of RAM and others in the Army believed Ramos was incapable of leading a successful counter-insurgency effort and felt that the PC's role in the effort should be made secondary to that of the Army. The dissolution of the "incompetent" PC was another stated objective of the August 1987 coup attempt.[12]

The failure of the August 1987 coup attempt and the vanquishing of many of RAM's leaders from the ranks of the AFP appeared to diminish the military's internal divisions during 1988 and much of 1989. Factionalism continued to exist within the AFP, although in a more muted form. The government's difficulty in capturing (and then holding) Gregorio "Gringo" Honasan, the leader of the August coup attempt, demonstrated the continued sympathy, and perhaps active support, for RAM within the military. When Secretary of National Defence Ileto resigned in January 1988 he warned of the continued existence of serious divisions within the AFP.[13]

With the passage of time Aquino became responsible for the promotion of more of the senior officer corps. In early 1988 twenty-one colonels were promoted to brigadier general and in May 1988 almost a third of the AFP's generals reached the mandatory retirement age. It was hoped that these changes would increase the loyalty of the senior officer corps to Aquino and Ramos. It appears, however, that instead they may have brought a more politicized group of officers into the upper echelons of the military hierarchy.

The Military's Role in Policy-Making

It did not take long for disagreements to emerge between the civilian government and the military. As early as April 1986 there were

reports of growing military dissatisfaction with the Aquino government
for the following reasons:

1. The release of communist political prisoners detained by Marcos;
2. The appointment to senior positions in the government of human
   rights lawyers such as Joker Arroyo and "Bobbit" Sanchez, whom
   the military viewed as "left leaning";
3. The civilian government's initially conciliatory approach to the
   communist insurgency;
4. The formation of the Presidential Commission on Human Rights
   (PCHR) to probe human rights violations committed by the
   military (but not by the insurgents) under the prominent human
   rights lawyer, Jose Diokno;
5. The wholesale dismissal of local officials, and their replacement with officers-in-charge (OICs), many of whom the military
   thought were left-leaning or inept; and
6. The initiation of inquiries into military graft and corruption.

To this list was soon added another important complaint: dissatisfaction with the nature of the government's counter-insurgency plan.
Shortly after Aquino came to office Ramos and Enrile pressed her to
adopt an "integrated" counter-insurgency plan involving co-ordinated
civilian and military programmes. This would have resulted in an increased AFP budget and greater military influence on the local level.[14]
Aquino refused to accept the integrated plan because she did not want
to jeopardize the possibility of a cease-fire with the communists by
appearing to escalate the military dimension of the insurgency. The
military also pressed Aquino (unsuccessfully at first) to form and
convene a meeting of the National Security Council (NSC), which
would have ensured greater military participation in the formulation
of the government's national security policy.

The Aquino government's commitment to negotiate a cease-fire with
the communists increasingly became the focal point of civilian–military
tensions. The dispute over the negotiations, however, was driven as
much by the struggle for power between the civilian government and
the military as it was by concerns over the effect of the negotiations
on the insurgency. According to Gareth Porter:

The stakes in this political controversy were far-reaching: were Aquino to succeed in negotiating even a temporary *modus vivendi* with the CPP, it would open up the possibility of a gradual re-integration of the armed left into the legitimate political process. It would also mean that the Aquino government had overcome a challenge from Enrile, the military, and the old Marcos political network, with its ability to set policy on a crucial issue. If, however, Aquino were forced to abandon the strategy of negotiations, either because of military pressures or because military officials preempted her strategy by their own initiative, it could mark a transition to a military-dominated regime.[15]

The depth of the military's dissatisfaction was first revealed by the Manila Hotel incident of July 1986. Following the incident Enrile and RAM stepped up their public criticism of Aquino's attempts to seek a negotiated cease-fire with the communist rebels. The military also blocked the negotiation of regional cease-fires in Misamis Oriental and Davao del Norte in Mindanao. It also rejected any future cease-fire agreement that did not require the rebels to lay down their arms or that restricted AFP operations in NPA-controlled areas.[16]

In late September Aquino succumbed to pressure from Ramos and other generals to convene a meeting of the National Security Council. At the meeting she was again presented with the military's integrated counter-insurgency plan, but she made no decision on it, again apparently so as not to jeopardize the ongoing cease-fire talks. Shortly afterwards, however, in an act that threatened to scuttle the negotiations, the military arrested Rodolfo Salas, chairman of the CPP military commission. At the same time Enrile sharpened his attack on Aquino's policy of negotiation and the legitimacy of her government. He claimed that Aquino held power only because he and the military had handed it over to her in February, and claimed further that Aquino had betrayed the military's trust.[17]

In early October, in response to mounting military pressure, the Aquino government made several key concessions. The Cabinet unanimously approved several recommendations by Ramos, including an increase in the military budget, a more comprehensive plan for rebel amnesty and rehabilitation, and the adoption of a "national strategy" to defeat the insurgency.[18] Despite these concessions, military discontent (and the political ambitions of Enrile and RAM) remained high. In late October, on the eve of a visit by Aquino to Tokyo, a new military coup plot, RAM's "God Save the Queen" plan, was exposed. The objective of the plan was to force the removal of "leftist" members of the Aquino Cabinet, make Aquino a figure-head president, and elevate Enrile to Prime Minister. The exposure of the plot meant that Aquino was "no longer fighting for a policy but for the survival of her government".[19]

The challenge posed by Enrile and RAM made Aquino increasingly dependent upon the support of Chief of Staff Ramos. Ramos shared Enrile's views concerning the pursuit of the insurgency, but he did not support Enrile's ambition or RAM's adventurism. Following the exposure of the coup plan, Ramos and six other top commanders wrote to Aquino on 15 November urging her to:

1. replace "left-leaning" Cabinet members and OICs not performing well;
2. increase the AFP budget;
3. strengthen the National Security Council;
4. establish an amnesty and rebel rehabilitation programme;
5. investigate human rights violations by the insurgents; and
6. involve the military in the cease-fire talks.[20]

Ramos also met with the members of RAM and elicited a pledge that they would postpone any further action against the civilian government until Aquino responded to the military's "suggestions". He was also reported to have convinced most of the senior AFP commanders to support the ouster of Enrile as part of a broader reorganization of the civilian government.[21]

What happened next is less certain. According to some accounts, Enrile and RAM, who stood to lose the most, decided to put their coup plan into motion. According to other accounts, Ramos decided to stage a pre-emptive strike against Enrile and RAM.[22] Whatever the case, on 22 November Ramos reported to Aquino that members of RAM were planning to collaborate with Marcos loyalists to seize the Batasang Pambansa building and convene a session of the old National Assembly. Aquino and Ramos acted swiftly: Ramos ordered all members of the AFP to disregard any commands coming from Enrile and RAM. Aquino called an emergency Cabinet meeting at which Enrile was sacked. In the days and weeks that followed, many of the RAM members suspected of plotting against the government were reassigned to less influential posts.

By moving against Enrile and RAM Ramos firmly cast his lot with Aquino, and in doing so he significantly increased his influence in the government. He also demonstrated his opposition to the use of extra-constitutional means to change a popular government. In this sense, he and his followers can be considered military "constitutionalists". This does not mean, however, that they were averse to playing an assertive and sometimes dominant role in policy-making. This was exactly the role that Ramos would increasingly play.

One example of Ramos's increased influence was the decision concerning the future of the 55,000-man Civilian Home Defence Force (CHDF). Under Marcos, the paramilitary CHDF was poorly paid, trained, and led. As a result, most of the units were little more than gangs of armed thugs beholden to local war-lords or politicians. They were responsible for numerous human rights abuses, including illegal arrests, murder, and torture. More than half of all the human rights complaints filed with the Presidential Commission on Human Rights (PCHR) in 1986 concerned alleged abuses by members of the CHDF.

In early 1986 the League of Governors and Mayors passed a resolution urging that the CHDF be disbanded, saying that the units had become "a law unto themselves". The 1987 Constitution also called for its dissolution, stating, "All paramilitary forces, including the CHDF, not consistent with the citizen armed force established in this Constitution, shall be dissolved or, where appropriate, converted into the regular force". Consequently, in mid-March 1987 Malacañang Palace announced that the CHDF would be disbanded. Shortly thereafter, however, Aquino reversed her decision, apparently under pressure from Ramos. In July 1987 Aquino signed an executive decree providing for the creation of a one-million-person "citizen's army" to be trained by the military. This paved the way in 1988 for the transformation of the CHDF into Civilian Armed Forces Geographical Units (CAFGUs). The AFP claimed that the CAFGUs would be more carefully selected, better paid and trained, and more closely supervised than the CHDF. Human rights monitors, however, were much less optimistic and expected that the change from the CHDF to the CAFGUs would be little more than a cosmetic one.

The unsuccessful 25–27 January 1987 mutiny and the relatively

high percentage of soldiers who voted against the new constitution
in February prompted the civilian government to make further concessions to the military.[23] A week after the plebiscite Aquino met
with twenty disgruntled officers, including "Gringo" Honasan and Efren
Arayata, founder of the Guardians. In mid-February Aquino acceded to
the long-standing wish of the military that the Presidential Commission
on Human Rights (PCHR) investigate violations by the communist insurgents and other civilians as well as those by the military.[24] Finally,
in her State of the Nation address in July Aquino placed significant
emphasis on the need for a better equipped and funded AFP.

These concessions, however, were not enough to satisfy the "messi-
anic military idealism" of "Gringo" Honasan and other members of
RAM. Honasan mounted a major coup attempt on 28 August 1987.
The early morning attacks on Malacañang Palace, Camp Aguinaldo,
and the Channel 4 television station involved more than 1,000 mutin-
ous soldiers. Fifty-three people were killed and some three hundred
were wounded. Malacañang Palace was almost taken, units in at
least six provinces participated in the rebellion, and a disconcerting
number of military commanders and soldiers "sat on the fence" to
see which side would prevail.

The August 1987 coup attempt came at a time when most observers
thought that civilian–military relations had begun to stabilize, in large
part because of the numerous concessions made by the Aquino government. What then did the mutineers want? Honasan claimed (after
the coup failed) that the rebels did not seek to overthrow Aquino, but
instead sought the inclusion of the right opposition (including Enrile)
and the military in the government in order to form a "multi-sectoral
unification body". However, the rebels' plans for a change of leadership
apparently did not include returning Marcos to Malacañang Palace.
According to Honasan, "Marcos is history. He had his chance and he
blew it".[25]

Why was there the coup attempt after the civilian government had
made so many concessions to the military? Honasan claimed that the
Aquino government was guilty of "the corruption, . . . the same disunity,
the same over-indulgence in politics, the same nepotism, the same
cronyism, the same polarization of the armed forces" as had existed
under Marcos.[26] He asked rhetorically, "Why was it okay when we
went against Marcos's constitutional authority? . . . Why has it suddenly

become wrong for us to be against a dispensation that is perceived to be one-sided?"[27] To Honasan the coup attempt was a "continuation of the February '86 Revolution, because all we ever wanted then was good government. . . . The military is not prepared to assume the role of a military dictatorship. It is prepared at most to be a guardian".[28]

The significance of the failed coup has been summed up by Carolina Hernandez, a specialist on the Philippine military. According to Hernandez:

> What made it dramatic is its leadership by officers who were acclaimed as "heroes" of EDSA; what made it credible to some quarters is the leadership's identification with the Reform the AFP Movement (RAM) which is widely perceived as a genuine movement to restore professionalism in the military; what made it dangerous is that it vied for the support from the apparently widely-spaced commands in the archipelago, as well as the future officer corps of our military currently undergoing their initiation and training into officership at the Philippine Military Academy; what made it tradition-breaking is the breach it inflicted on the time-honored practice of obedience to legitimate authority and the preservation of military fraternal unity where brother does not fight against brother.[29]

Coup fears continued throughout September and October and into early November. The ease with which Honasan and other wanted rebels continued to hold press conferences and interviews showed that their brethren in the AFP were not enthusiastic about carrying out the repeated orders of Aquino and Ramos to find and capture them. During this period Aquino and the Congress scrambled to curry favour with the AFP. Pay hikes of up to 60 per cent were given to the military and more emphasis was placed on pursuing a policy of "total war" against the communists. The government's rejection of new peace talks with the NDF and its support of vigilante groups were additional steps taken to placate the military.

The government slowly regained its poise and by November Honasan and RAM had clearly lost the initiative. On 9 December, just a week before the ASEAN summit meeting in Manila, Honasan was caught. Following his capture, renegade soldiers claiming loyalty to Honasan issued a statement circulated in military camps which said: "Gringo will remain our rallying point, our symbol. Our enemies will tell you we are finished. Do not believe that".[30] This turned out to be prescient, for in April 1988 the charismatic Honasan used bribery and persuasion to enlist the help of his guards to escape from the navy ship on which he was incarcerated. Honasan went underground and for the next year and a half it appeared that Honasan and RAM were unable or unwilling to attempt another coup.

The tension between the military and the civilian government existed not just on the national level; it was also played out on the provincial and local levels. In many locations across the country military officers, not civilian officials, were effectively in charge. Assertive colonels such as Franco Calida in Davao City, Rudolfo Abedina in Cebu City and Rodolfo Aguinaldo in Cagayan province almost single-handedly determined counter-insurgency strategy and made policies affecting people's civil and political rights. They often had veto power over decisions made by the civilian government. According to Aguinaldo, a staunch anti-communist who openly supported the 28 August coup attempt:

> If the government is only serving its high officials, the military has the divine right to intervene. . . . We are the ones sent out to bleed and die, and they do not even listen to us. We must have a hand in this government.[31]

The military's political influence on the local and provincial levels was also felt during the January 1988 local elections. In some areas military officers overtly or covertly played a role in selecting or promoting particular candidates. In several provinces, active military officers, including Rodolfo Aguinaldo, ran for office and won. In many other areas, military units were deployed to *barangay* suspected of being left-leaning, ostensibly to safeguard the casting and counting of votes. To the supporters of leftist candidates, however, the presence of troops was seen as blatant military intimidation.

Military Prerogatives and Civilian–Military Relations

Alfred Stepan, a specialist on the role of the military in Latin America, has identified three key areas in which the military is likely to challenge civilian supremacy in democratizing nations. These are: the handling of previous human rights violations; the definition of the military's organizational mission; and the determination and control of the military's budget.[32] These three areas of potential "contestation" provide a useful framework for assessing civilian–military relations during the first years of the Aquino government.

How have these three issues been resolved in the Philippines? In the case of the first – the handling of previous human rights abuses – the military, as we have seen, successfully blocked the investigation and prosecution of past (and continuing) human rights abuses by the military. In the case of the second and third issues – the military's mission and budget – there was little serious disagreement between the military and the civilian government. Both agreed that the organizational mission of the military was to protect and enhance national security, and specifically to meet the threats posed by the communist and Muslim insurgencies. The disagreements that occurred between them, therefore, were not over the definition of the AFP's mission so much as over the policies and tactics needed to accomplish this mission. Thus, the disagreements were over negotiating with the communists, the scope of an integrated counter-insurgency strategy, and the need for paramilitary and vigilante groups.

There was also no serious disagreement between General Ramos and the civilian government that the mission of the military did *not* include having a *de jure* institutional role in the political process. Ramos, however, did seek to institutionalize the military's influence over the counter-insurgency effort when he pressed for the convening of the National Security Council. He also successfully blocked efforts to alter the AFP's structure and capabilities when he opposed the dismantling of the CHDF. Finally, there was little serious dispute over the size of the military budget. The Aquino government recognized the need to increase this budget and improve the AFP's capabilities even before the 28 August coup attempt added a greater sense of urgency.

How large a political role did the Philippine military carve out for itself under Aquino? Clearly, its role has expanded, but has its influence become comparable to that of the army in Thailand or Indonesia? In order to answer this question it is helpful to return to Stepan's analysis of civilian–military relations. Stepan identified a number of "prerogatives" that are worth considering when trying to determine the relative influence of the military in the Philippines. According to Stepan, prerogatives are "those areas where, whether challenged or not, the military as an institution assumes they have an acquired right or privilege, formal or informal, to exercise effective control over its internal governance, to play a role within extra-military areas within the state apparatus, or even to structure relationships between the state and political or civil society".[33]

Stepan also noted that countries in which the military enjoyed a high degree of prerogatives had the following characteristics:

1. The constitution sanctions the independent role of the military in the maintenance of internal law and order;
2. *De facto* control and co-ordination of the armed forces is in the hands of the uniformed active-duty service commanders;
3. The military's presence and participation in the Cabinet is high;
4. The legislature's participation in determining the military budget, defining national security, and controlling military promotions is low;
5. National security laws and a military court system cover large areas of political and civil society;
6. Intelligence agencies are controlled by the military with no independent review boards;
7. Police are under military control; and
8. Military officers control key state enterprises.[34]

Using these criteria as a guide it is clear that, as of 1988, the AFP's prerogatives were mixed. The 1987 Constitution established clear-cut civilian supremacy; there was minimal military participation in the Cabinet and in state enterprises; and the Marcos military intelligence apparatus was emasculated. However, there was also *de facto* military control over the operations of the armed forces and limited participation by the Congress in shaping national security policy and controlling military affairs. Military laws and courts had a minor role in civilian affairs, but the military controlled the local police and exerted *de facto* influence over the law and order situation on the local level. In other words, the military's *de jure* prerogatives were low, but its *de facto* prerogatives were significantly greater.

Finally, an assessment of the Philippine military's influence also depends on *which* of the two major elements of the military — the constitutionalists and the interventionists — is being considered. As we have seen, both groups have sought a larger role for the military;

but the constitutionalists who head the AFP have been relatively less power hungry than the interventionists. The constitutionalists accept the legitimacy of the civilian government and reject any extra-constitutional means of replacing the government. However, this has not kept them from extending the influence of the military into those areas they feel affect the AFP and national security. These have included the formulation of counter-insurgency strategies; shaping policies concerning paramilitary forces, the police, and vigilante groups; limiting the prosecution of human rights abuses; and influencing certain political appointments. The constitutionalists, however, have not sought to remove elected officials, alter the constitutionally-mandated functions of government institutions, or dominate policies not affecting their broad definition of national security.

By comparison, the interventionists reject the legitimacy of the existing government and constitution and envision the AFP as playing a role similar to that of the army in Thailand or Indonesia. If their dreams are realized, the AFP will play a dominant role in shaping both the composition of future governments and their policies. Although it is likely that this would result in a right-leaning quasi-authoritarian government, there is the remote possibility that the military, out of disgust with traditional politics and politicians, would adopt more nationalistic and populist policies previously associated with the left.

The Congress in Action

At the inaugural session of the Senate in July 1987 Senate President Jovito Salonga stated, "Sound laws and ethical behavior are the minimum expected of us". Across the capital, in the House of Representatives, Speaker Ramon Mitra proclaimed, "We must make government more responsive to popular grievances and persuade our privileged classes to share". In view of the chequered history of the pre-martial law Congress, these two statements in effect called for the new Congress to behave significantly differently from its predecessor. Many people wondered if it would. Many also wondered if the new Congress would rise to the challenge of effectively addressing the country's numerous political, social, and economic problems.

The 1987 Constitution returned to the legislature all of the powers that Marcos had expropriated, and made the new Congress co-equal to the executive branch. All appropriations and tax bills originate in the House and Congress must approve the president's policies concerning national debt. The joint Commission on Appointments reviews Cabinet and ambassadorial appointments as well as the promotions of all senior military officers. Only Congress can declare war and it can revoke a presidential suspension of habeas corpus or declaration of martial law. The Congress also has the authority to impeach the president and amend the Constitution. The Senate must ratify all foreign treaties.

Who were the people who would wield these powers and determine the nation's laws? The twenty-four member Senate was comprised of nationally known political figures such as Jovito Salonga, Raul Manglapus, and Juan Ponce Enrile, as well as relatively less well-known figures such as Victor Ziga and Santanina Rasul (one of two women in the Senate). More than half of the senators had prior experience in politics or government and four had been in the pre-martial law Senate. Fourteen senators were lawyers, the preferred training of most politicians, although three of them had been active human rights lawyers. Twenty-two were members of the pro-Aquino Lakas ng Bansa coalition.

The composition of the House of Representatives was more uniform, but also more complex. The large majority of new representatives were members of the traditionally conservative families that had dominated local politics. There were 167 representatives, or 84 per cent of those elected, from a traditional political "clan", that is, from a family that had contested or won a local or national election since 1971. Of these, 101 representatives had opposed Marcos prior to 1986 while 66 had supported him. Only 31 representatives, or 16 per cent, had no electoral history or were not related to a traditional political clan.[35] Although some 75 per cent of the new representatives were nominally aligned with the Aquino coalition, about 30 per cent leaned more to the right of the Aquino "centre" and about 15 per cent were more to the left. About 35 representatives were associated with a small progressive bloc within the House, referred to as the "Solidarity Caucus".

To many Filipino observers the composition of the Congress, and particularly of the House, did not bode well for the future of law-making. This concern was voiced by journalist Sheila Coronel who wrote, "To the cynical eye, it looks as if we had slept through the last 15 years and woken up to find the same people, the same names, still debating, still holding court, still charting the course of our lives".[36] However, political scientist Alex Magno identified at least one change in the composition of the Congress. According to him, "Although prominent names representing the landed elites still figure in the new Congress, the urban entrepreneurial and professional sectors enjoy a commanding presence".[37] At the outset the significance of this new dimension was unclear, but as time passed it became increasingly clear that the political behaviour and values of the new generation of representatives were not significantly different from those of previous generations.

One thing that was fairly certain was that the multiplicity of party affiliations, and the traditional weakness of these affiliations, promised to make the new Congress even more unruly than the old one. Although both houses of the Congress were nominally controlled by the pro-Aquino coalition, under this thin veneer of unity existed numerous divisions caused by differing and often multiple party affiliations, genuine ideological differences, and countless political rivalries. Among the 24 senators, 22 were annointed by Aquino's Lakas coalition, but most also remained members of PDP-Laban, UNIDO, or the Liberal Party. Of the 200 members elected to the House, 95 were registered under one party, 22 ran as independents and 83 had multiple endorsements.[38] With half of the representatives having dual or even triple party affiliations, it was likely that they would swing with the most powerful individual or bloc. Representative Francisco Sumulong warned: "We may have serious problems. There will be no party discipline to speak of".[39] This absence of discipline became obvious in the weeks before the Congress convened by the drawn out and sometimes bitter battles for the leadership of the House and key committee assignments in both houses.

Despite the large majority of Aquino supporters in the Senate and House, it quickly became clear that the Congress would not be a rubber stamp for the president's policies and appointments. As in pre-martial law days, both houses sought to establish their independence from the executive branch and individual members of the Congress sought to build their political reputations. Senator Edgardo Angara, a supporter of Aquino, warned: "This is a more powerful Congress than the president. If Cory is not aggressive, Congress will paralyse or swamp her".[40] Wasting no time to assert the authority of the House, Ramon Mitra declared in early August that Congress had the right to review all presidential appointments made since the passage of the new constitution in February. Senator Salonga, who was chairman of the joint Committee on Appointments, agreed, thus beginning a long dispute between the Congress and the executive branch over presidential appointments.

Shortly after the convening of the Congress, Speaker Mitra claimed that the House would pass a land reform bill within ninety days. Initially, three major agrarian reform bills were introduced into Congress. In the House, Representative Bonifacio Gillego introduced a sweeping bill, and in the Senate, Agapito Aquino and Heherson Alvarez each introduced somewhat less dramatic, but still promising, bills. In response to the Gillego bill, landowners in the House later introduced a more limited bill. However, after the initial flurry of activity, the members of both houses shied away from the controversial issue, and six months later these bills were still far from being reconciled or passed. (The process culminating in the passage of agrarian reform legislation in June 1988 is discussed in Chapter 10.)

The House and Senate also set up committees to review a debt restructuring agreement concluded by Finance Secretary Jaime Ongpin earlier in the year and explore other solutions to the problem of the nation's US$28 billion in external debt. In September a Senate "blue ribbon" committee (on which sat 18 of 24 senators) began hearings on the foreign debt problem. Some senators called for the debt agreement to be renegotiated while others advocated limiting debt payments to 15 per cent of foreign exchange earnings. In the end the Senate committee called for debt relief without repudiation and for the creation of a joint executive-legislative commission to shape a new debt-relief policy.

The political instability caused by the 28 August coup attempt threatened the authority of the Congress almost as much as it threatened President Aquino. In response to the crisis, the Congress tried to buy stability during September and October. Legislation raising military pay by an average of 54 to 61 per cent was approved. The Congress also passed bills providing a P10 increase in the daily minimum wage for the private sector and an increase in the cost of living adjustment for 900,000 national government civilian employees (including teachers). In mid-October Sheila Coronel observed that, "to a significant extent the agenda and pace of our national politics are being set not in the halls of Congress but in the streets and also, in the clandestine meetings of conspirators of various political stripes".[41]

The first ninety-day session of the Congress ended in late October. How well had the new Congress performed? The House created 43 committees and more than 100 subcommittees. The proliferation of committees made the House, in the words of one reporter, a "House of Investigation" that sought to hold hearings on everything from the foreign debt problem to the reasons why a leading Filipino boxer was knocked out by his Korean opponent.[42] The House approved 10 bills and 18 resolutions, out of more than 2,000 bills and 450 resolutions filed during the first session. In keeping with pre-martial law tradition, the large majority of bills sought special appropriations for local projects.[43] In the Senate 178 bills were filed but only 12 were passed; while 64 resolutions were filed, of which 15 were passed. The Senate's 34 permanent and 6 *ad hoc* committees produced 55 reports.[44]

Only one bill, however, was passed by both houses – an act renaming Metro Manila's international airport in honour of Ninoy Aquino. Agrarian reform legislation, the greatest and most complex challenge facing the Congress, remained mired in indifference and disagreement. Congressional inaction prompted the influential *Manila Chronicle* to warn: "We are repeating the cycle of Congress trying its best to discredit itself, and in the process paving the way for the people's loss of faith in it at a time when the legislature is expected to be an agent of change and reform".[45]

When the Congress reconvened in early November, House Speaker Ramon Mitra vowed there would be "less talk, more work". During the second session military, government, and minimum wage raises were approved by both houses, as was the national budget for 1988. The House deferred until the year-end (and probably indefinitely) a significant reorganization (and reduction in the size) of the civil service. The House also debated the need to limit the influence of family-based "political dynasties". A bill was introduced that would have excluded family members of politicians or government officials from running for elected office. The proposed legislation was debated until after the January 1988 local elections, at which time a diluted version was passed.

The first annual session of the Congress ended in June 1988. In its first year the House filed more than 14,400 bills and resolutions.

In the Senate 846 bills and resolutions were filed. Only 40 bills were approved by both houses of Congress, and of these only 20 were signed into law by President Aquino. Among the most important bills passed by both houses were the Comprehensive Agrarian Reform Law; pay raises for the military; increases in the minimum wage and most government salaries; and free high school education.

What can be concluded about the Congress based on its first year? The task of starting up a legislative process from scratch after almost fifteen years of rule by decree was huge, complex, and time consuming. Consequently, confusion, delays, and mistakes had to be expected. However, it is still possible to make some preliminary observations concerning the new Congress and its performance relative to its predecessors.

First, the composition and behaviour of the new House was not markedly different from those of its pre-martial law predecessor. The majority of representatives (though perhaps a smaller majority than in the past) were members of the local élite and were concerned primarily with protecting their own economic and political positions. This made the House as conservative, particularistic, and unwieldy as before. The composition and behaviour of the Senate, on the other hand, differed somewhat from its antecedent. This is largely attributable to the important role President Aquino played in the selection and election of most senators in May 1987. Her slate of candidates included a number of non-traditional political figures. Furthermore, the electoral success of the pro-Aquino slate gave the Senate relatively more unity than its predecessor, at least initially. As a result, the new Senate was somewhat more liberal, unified, and effective. Future elections, however, are likely to result in a more conservative and divided Senate.

As expected, the new Congress quickly asserted its independence vis-à-vis President Aquino and the executive branch by challenging appointments and reviewing many presidential decrees she made before the opening of Congress. This natural tendency was exacerbated somewhat by the failure of Malacañang Palace to take the initiative by energetically pushing its own legislative agenda. At the same time, however, the Congress was much more deferential to the military than it had ever been in the past. It was quick to grant the AFP's request for a larger budget and was hesitant to challenge the military on national security policy.

Fortunately, the new Congress did not immediately demonstrate some of the worst traits of its predecessor. The legislative process was not completely dominated by powerful economic blocs. There were few signs of massive influence-peddling and corruption. The drafting and passage of legislation was not quite as sloppy and haphazard as in the past. Still, some of the bad habits of the old Congress had returned. According to the *Manila Chronicle*:

> Names of some congressmen cropped up in a number of embarrassing incidents such as the importation of high-powered guns, a P10 million "pork barrel" allocation for each of them in 1989, and the use of casino money to finance development projects.[46]

Finally, by early 1988 the Congress once again had become an arena for national political rivalries, and in particular the rivalry between the leaders of the PDP-Laban/Lakas combine (such as representatives Jose Cojuangco and Ramon Mitra) and the increasingly independent and assertive Liberal Party led by Senator Jovito Salonga. This rivalry resulted in numerous changes in party affiliations and corresponding shifts in committee chairmanships in both houses. The Congress, and the Senate in particular, once again also became the centre stage for the many members aspiring to become president or vice-president in 1992.

The Revival and Reconfiguration of Political Parties

The organizational weaknesses, lack of ideology, and essential similarity of Philippine political parties have been described in the first part of this book. These weaknesses help to explain why martial law was imposed as easily as it was and why authoritarianism lasted as long as it did. Indeed, one of the most notable characteristics of the opposition parties that emerged in the late 1970s and early 1980s was their unwillingness or inability to unite in common cause against Marcos until late 1985.

The weaknesses and shortcomings of the Philippine political parties have led some observers to conclude incorrectly that their role in politics is relatively insignificant. In reality, however, political parties are still a widely accepted, though not necessarily respected, feature of Philippine politics. Parties remain an important means of building national political coalitions, although this may change in the future. While not known for their ideological differentiation, the parties are the vehicles for the clash of rival political leaders, and sometimes they do represent different and competing social and economic interests. Consequently, parties can be criticized for their many limitations, but they cannot simply be dismissed as meaningless.

During the first two years of the Aquino era, political parties were in considerable flux. The pro-Marcos KBL crumbled, fluid coalitions of pro- and anti-Aquino parties went through several mutations, and the left flirted with and then rejected party politics. These developments occurred in, and were influenced by, a political environment characterized by unprecedented fluidity and uncertainty. Unlike all previous presidents, Aquino was disdainful of political parties and did not make an effort to establish her own. Unlike previous administrations, the Aquino government was a patchwork coalition of four major parties and several other minor ones, all of which were rivals to varying degrees. In addition to this, as we have seen, the military emerged as an important political actor and constituency. Finally, for at least the first year of the Aquino era leftist political organizations had a degree of strength and freedom not seen since the late 1940s.

The revival and reconfiguration of political parties can be divided into three, sometimes overlapping, phases. The first phase saw the dissolution of the pro-Marcos KBL and the growth of divisions within the anti-Marcos coalition. The second phase was marked by the creation of anti-Aquino, pro-Aquino, and leftist coalitions of parties to participate in the 1987 constitutional plebiscite and congressional elections. The third phase revealed new divisions within the pro-Aquino coalition (brought about by the convening of Congress and local elections) as well as the relative weakening of rightist and leftist parties.

The first phase extended until the end of 1986 and was distinquished by the disintegration of the once-powerful KBL and the split between President Aquino's PDP-Laban and Vice-President Laurel's UNIDO. In short, this phase marked the demise of the Marcos-era configuration of parties. In the weeks following Marcos's ouster, his supporters continued to stage noisy and sometimes violent demonstrations in Metro Manila, calling for his return.[47] Behind the scenes, however, the more pragmatic members of the KBL were already adjusting to the realities of post-Marcos politics. The first of these realities was that with Marcos gone, there was no longer a single dominant leader of the KBL. The second was that in the wake of the fraudulent election and subsequent revolt, the KBL simply was no longer politically viable. As a result, the KBL began to break up into its factional components.

The first new party to emerge from the ruins of the KBL was Blas Ople's Philippine Nationalist Party (PNP), which accepted the legitimacy of the new government and opted for "critical co-operation" as a "loyal opposition". A second was the non-Laurel wing of the moribund Nacionalista Party (NP), which was revived by Renato Cayetano, a former KBL member of the Batasang Pambansa and a close associate of Juan Ponce Enrile. The revival of the NP by Cayetano fuelled speculation that the NP would become Enrile's political vehicle. Only Arturo Tolentino, Rafael Recto, and other die-hard loyalists remained the champions of the largely discredited and rapidly declining KBL.

The ouster of Marcos also removed the main source of unity within the now-triumphant anti-Marcos coalition. Aquino, it will be remembered, ran for president under the UNIDO banner, as part of a deal with UNIDO head Salvador Laurel to get him to team up with her rather than running separately. Laurel and UNIDO campaigned tirelessly for the Aquino–Laurel ticket, and clearly the success of the ticket was in no small part due to UNIDO's national organization – the most extensive of any party other than the KBL. Many of Aquino's closest advisors, however, were members of PDP-Laban, and when she formed her first Cabinet more positions went to PDP-Laban than to UNIDO. Laurel and other UNIDO leaders also began to feel they were being short-changed in the appointment of local OICs and other government positions. By August there were persistent reports of an imminent split between UNIDO and PDP-Laban. Although a formal break did not occur, UNIDO further distanced itself from PDP-Laban by refusing to join a new pro-Aquino coalition formed in October and by initially withholding support for the draft constitution (UNIDO subsequently gave its qualified support). By late 1986 UNIDO and PDP-Laban were largely estranged. However, the effect on the pro-Aquino coalition was minimal because defections from UNIDO had caused Laurel to become a leader without a significant following.

The second phase began in late 1986 and continued through mid-1987. This phase was notable for the development of new factional and ideological groupings in response to the February constitutional plebiscite and the May congressional elections. In October 1986 three members of Aquino's Cabinet, Neptali Gonzales, Ernesto Maceda, and Luis Villafuerte, formed the Lakas ng Bansa or Lakas umbrella grouping, to unify all "pro-Cory" parties. PDP-Laban and the Liberal Party (LP) joined, but as noted above, Laurel and the remnants of UNIDO refused to join. Juan Ponce Enrile, following his ejection from the Aquino Cabinet in November, led an informal coalition of groups, including both Marcos loyalists and non-loyalists, in a campaign against the Constitution. On the left, Bayan created the Partido ng Bayan (PnB) in late August 1986 in order to contest the congressional elections, and Bayan-led cause-oriented and mass-based groups also opposed the draft charter. By the end of 1986 there were more than fifty registered political parties with more in the works. The first women's party was also formed.

The overwhelming vote in favour of the new constitution strengthened the pro-Aquino Lakas coalition at the expense of parties on both the right and left. However, the plebiscite was viewed by many as just a dry run for the congressional elections. In preparation for these, Aquino's brother (Jose Cojuangco) and brother-in-law (Paul Aquino) took firm control of PDP-Laban and Lakas, respectively. The pro-Aquino coalition was challenged on the right by the Grand Alliance for Democracy (GAD) and the Union for Peace and Progress-KBL (UPP-KBL). On the left, Partido ng Bayan and the Volunteers for Popular Democracy joined to form the Alliance for New Politics (ANP). The results of the congressional elections, as we have seen, strongly favoured the Lakas coalition and gave minority positions in the Congress to the GAD and, to a lesser degree, the UPP-KBL and ANP. The relatively poor showing of the opposition parties did not encourage further unity, and after the congressional elections, the GAD and KBL-UPP coalitions became inactive while the ANP eschewed electoral politics.

The third phase began with the functioning of Congress in July 1987, included the January 1988 contest for local offices, and continued into 1990. This phase was characterized by the partial splintering of the pro-Aquino coalition and the search for unity within the right opposition (and particularly between Salvador Laurel and Juan Ponce Enrile). The strong showing of the pro-Aquino coalition in the congressional elections did not guarantee its unity. Liberal Party president Jovito Salonga challenged the supremacy of PDP-Laban in both houses of the Congress by enticing a number of newly-elected members to join the LP. By the end of 1987 at least seven senators were members of the LP, including Orlando Mercado and Teofisto Guingona, the majority leader and president *pro tempore*, respectively. In the House, LP members more than doubled, growing from eighteen to about forty representatives. Salonga's efforts to establish the LP as an independent and national party were further helped by the LP's credible showing in the January local elections.

In response in part to the LP challenge, Lakas and PDP-Laban formally merged in June 1988, to become the Laban ng Demokratikong Pilipino (LDP). Ramon Mitra became president of the LDP. Some 150 representatives, 6 senators, and 53 of the 75 governors were reported to have joined the party. The merger was opposed by Senator Aquilino Pimentel, a co-founder of PDP-Laban, who increasingly disagreed with many of the administration's policies and with the Aquino–Cojuangco clan's domination of the party. As a result, Pimentel maintained an independent "progressive" wing of PDP-Laban.

In the anti-Aquino camp, Enrile and Joseph Estrada were the lone opposition voices in the Senate. Laurel distanced himself further from the Aquino administration when he resigned as Secretary of Foreign Affairs following the August 1987 coup attempt. In August 1988 he formally announced his break with the Aquino government, although he did not resign his position of vice-president. Enrile and Laurel flirted with a union, but it took until the beginning of 1988 for them to agree to write under the banner of the Nacionalista Party (NP). As Amando Doronila explained, "After contemplating their marginalization in politics . . . Mr. Enrile and Mr. Laurel have decided that their salvation from political extinction lies in reviving the Nacionalista Party".[48]

During the first three years of the Aquino government political parties played three fairly familiar roles. First and foremost, as in the past, parties remained the vehicles for furthering the interests of leading politicians. PDP-Laban, Lakas, and the LDP all reflected and supported the political ascendancy of the Aquino–Cojuangco clan. Conversely, the demise of UNIDO reflected the decline in the political fortunes of Salvador Laurel. Secondly, parties were also the building blocks for larger political coalitions assembled almost exclusively for the purpose of contesting elections. The transitory nature of these election coalitions contributed to the fragmentation and instability of the party system. Finally, the creation of the LDP in 1988 represented a belated effort to fashion a relatively new kind of party, namely, a genuine ruling party. The LDP sought to work closely with the president to formulate and carry out a legislative agenda and to maintain a modicum of party discipline in the Congress and on the provincial level.

Does the future promise a return to the pre-martial law party system of two identical parties? Carl Lande and Allan Cigler, writing in 1988, have concluded:

> The pre-martial law system of indistinguishable parties cannot be restored. Ferdinand Marcos destroyed a system that was weak to begin with and was becoming increasingly disfunctional. A new, more meaningful party system has not yet appeared. . . . The Philippine political elite, bubbling with both new and returning entrants into electoral politics, has yet to form itself into a stable system of political alliances. In the absence of a latter day Sergio Osmena, Manuel Quezon or Manuel Roxas, it may take some time before it does so.[49]

While it may be futile at this point to speculate if the Philippines is moving to a one-, two-, or multi-party system, it is possible to identify some of the forces that will shape the evolution of the party system. In the short term, that is, until the 1992 elections, the most important influence on party formation will be the ambitions and relative fortunes of the leading political figures with presidential aspirations. A critical aspect of this, of course, will be whether or not President Aquino seeks re-election, and if not, how the Aquino coalition will fragment and regroup.

Looking further into the future, it is unlikely that political parties in the Philippines will shed their personalized and factional nature. Assuming this is the case, certain things will follow. First, parties will continue to be fluid coalitions of factions shaped by the changing political fortunes of leading politicians. Secondly, the personalized nature of traditional parties will make the incorporation of interest groups and sectoral organizations into them highly unlikely. Finally, the nature and number of political parties will depend on how well they perform relative to their competition. If non-traditional parties and organizations become more effective at representing the interests of constituencies not served by traditional parties then the traditional parties will eventually have to change in order to compete.

Increased Role of the Catholic Church

The Catholic Church has had a widespread but uneven influence on Philippine society. In the light of the scope and complexity of its influence, and given the important role it played in replacing Marcos with Aquino, it must be asked if the Church assumed a new and significantly more influential role in government and politics under the Aquino government. If it did, what were the implications for democratic government and politics?

The Catholic Church, together with the AFP, is another of the few truly national institutions in the Philippines. It has more than 2,000 parishes with about 10,300 churches and chapels across the country. In 1986 the Church's work was done by 5,425 priests, 212 monks, 8,625 nuns, and 6,724 seminarians. In addition to this, Opus Dei, a "personal prelature" of the Pope, has some 3,000 members.[50] The Church has the ability to speak powerfully on the national level through the pronouncements of the Catholic Bishops Conference of the Philippines (CBCP) and it can reach the most remote *barangay* through its priests and the broadcasts of its Radio Veritas.

The Catholic Church has been intimately involved in many aspects of Philippine society. It has had a powerful influence on family law, particularly the long-standing prohibition of divorce and abortion. It has influenced, with varying degrees of success over time, the government's commitment to family planning. It has also had an important influence on education. There are 17 Catholic universities, 151 Church-run colleges, and almost 400 Catholic secondary schools with a total enrolment of more than 670,000 students. Many of the Philippines' brightest students are educated at Church-affiliated colleges and universities such as the Ateneo de Manila University, St. Scholastica's College, and De La Salle University. On the local level, the Church has had a more widespread (and benevolent) presence in many remote areas compared to either the civilian government or the military. In some areas it has been the only countervailing influence to the communists.

The Philippine Church became increasingly active in socio-economic development following the Second Vatican Council of 1962–65 (Vatican II). The Church directly or indirectly has supported numerous foundations and other organizations addressing a wide variety of social problems. These have included urban squatters' and farmers' co-operatives, health clinics, counselling centres, and human rights organizations such as Task Force Detainees. It is also estimated that more than 500 of the country's parishes (25 per cent of the total) have Basic Christian Communities (BCCs), many of which are involved in grass-roots socio-economic development projects.

The Catholic Church, however, is no more monolithic than any other group or institution in the Philippines. The more than two decades that have passed since Vatican II have not resolved the disagreements within the Church concerning the extent to which it should be actively involved in fighting existing socio-economic and political injustices. The conservative old guard insists that the Church should restrict itself to strictly spiritual matters. The moderates believe that the Church has a responsibility to respond to the socio-economic problems of the poor, but they have shied away from advocating radical social change. The progressive arm of the Church believes that the Church's energies should be focused on the problems of the poor and that the Church should take the lead in pressing for fundamental social changes.

Marcos's hostility to the Church, particularly during the last five years of his rule, provided all but the most conservative members of the Church with a common problem that helped to minimize internal divisions. The success of the moderates in peacefully unseating Marcos weakened the influence of the conservatives, who had argued that the Church should not get involved in the struggle between Aquino and Marcos. With Marcos gone, the triumphant moderates, led by Jaime Cardinal Sin, the savvy Archbishop of Manila, focused on another concern – leftist infiltration of the Church's social action arms. In January 1987 the CBCP issued a statement saying that it is "inconsistent with the gospel values for lay faithful, priests, religious brothers and sisters, seminarians and church workers to support or join organizations or movements that espouse violence as the road to social transformation".[51] A year later the National Secretariat for Social Action (NASSA) was reorganized because of fears that it was "highly infiltrated" by leftists who allegedly channelled money to the communists.

What influence did the Church have on the Aquino government? To begin with, President Aquino is a deeply religious person who has maintained close personal relations with Cardinal Sin and other Church leaders. As we have seen, her presidential candidacy received critical support from Church-affiliated groups, such as NAMFREL,

Radio Veritas, the CBCP, and the Bishops-Businessmen's Conference of the Philippines (BBCP). During the first, especially uncertain year of her administration she received fairly constant support from Cardinal Sin and other leaders of the Church. Does this mean that the Church has had significantly greater influence on government and politics? The answer is a qualified "yes", for while the Church has had greater influence on the Aquino government than it had on Marcos, its role in politics has diminished somewhat from the extraordinary days of 1984, 1985, and early 1986.

The close relationship between President Aquino and Cardinal Sin was an important influence on church–state relations. Sin has compared the relationship between the Church and the government to the two rails that make up railroad tracks. According to him, the relationship between Church and the state in the Philippines "can't be too close, neither can it be too distant".[52]

It is sometimes difficult, however, to see where Cardinal Sin drew the line to avoid becoming "too close" to the Aquino government. He played a role in mediating the Aquino–Enrile rift in October and November 1986 and pushed for a reconciliation (ultimately unsuccessful) between President Aquino and Vice-President Laurel in November 1987. He also strongly supported the new Constitution in January 1987. Prior to the May congressional elections he urged Catholics not to vote for candidates professing "godless ideology or known to advocate violence and class struggle as the means of changing society" (which meant candidates of the PnB) and told voters to "scrutinize the past performance of the candidate" to see if he "collaborated actively in cheating, oppressing, or robbing our people" (which meant candidates closely associated with the Marcos regime).

Cardinal Sin was not the only religious voice Aquino listened to upon becoming president. She also sought the advice and support of other moderates within the Church in shaping her new government. She appointed four people with close Church affiliations to the Constitutional Commission. Initially, she received guidance on governmental issues from Father Joaquin Bernas, the president of the Jesuit Ateneo de Manila University and other Jesuit-trained advisers who became known as the "Council of Trent". On economic matters she was advised by Bernardo Villegas and Jesus Estanislao of the Centre for Research and Communication, an Opus Dei-backed economic think-tank.

As a result of these numerous close ties, the Church's influence was reflected in many of the new government's policies. Its influence was evident, for example, in the 1987 Constitution's provisions concerning the family, which declare the primacy of the family and outlaw divorce and abortion, and concerning education, which permit religious education in public schools. It also played an important role in the attempt to resolve the communist insurgency. Bishop Antonio Fortich of Negros Occidental and other Church leaders became deeply involved in national and regional cease-fire negotiations in late 1986 and early 1987. Finally, the Church actively and successfully lobbied against the continuation of the relatively active government family planning programme begun by Marcos.

Beginning in late 1986 the Church also began to voice its dissatisfaction with various aspects of the Aquino government. In December, Cardinal Sin criticized bickering and corruption within the government. In January and July 1987, the CBCP issued statements calling for comprehensive land reform. In September 1987 Sin again spoke out against continuing graft and corruption in the government.[53] And in early 1988 the head of the Jesuits in the Philippines, Father Bienvenido Nebres, stated that the Aquino government "is now stable and needs prodding if it is not to degenerate into another graft ridden and corrupt oligarchy".[54]

There were limits, however, on the amount of public pressure the Church was prepared to put on the Aquino government. Cardinal Sin and other Church leaders recognized that they had to approach their role in politics cautiously. Their caution reflected both the Vatican's concern that the Philippine Church was excessively involved in secular affairs and the possibility of a domestic backlash. Felix Bautista, the editor of *Veritas* and Cardinal Sin's spokesman, warned in mid-1986: "The history of the last 50 years shows that Filipinos take a dim view of Church interference in politics. No priest or bishop of any denomination has won national office".[55] Reflecting this, a May 1986 public opinion poll showed a clear-cut sentiment against the Church supporting candidates in elections. The poll also suggested that Filipinos were split (40 to 40 per cent) on whether "any church should get involved in the struggle of the oppressed".[56]

This caution frustrated the more activist members of the Church. One of them, Sister Christine Tan, offered this description of the Church's position:

The Church now is less of a social critic. This is probably because many of us thought that Edsa was the end of our woes. And then Cory comes out so much of a Catholic and she is a woman, so it is hard for the Church to be critical.[57]

Looking to the future, there are a number of areas of possible dis-agreement between the Church and the government. These include the continuing problems of corruption, human rights abuses (although under Aquino the military has been careful not to repeat Marcos's mistake of attacking priests), inadequate social services, and environ-mental degradation. The Church may also clash with the government over changes in family law, and particularly over the issue of divorce, which is still illegal in the Philippines.

Perhaps the most important test of the Church's relationship with the government will be over the issue of family planning. The Cat-holic Church's opposition to the promotion of modern family planning methods is only one of a number of socio-economic, cultural, and bureaucratic factors responsible for the country's rapid population growth, but it is one of the most important. With an annual population growth rate of between 2.5 and 2.8 per cent, the government simply cannot continue to ignore or dismiss the negative socio-economic con-sequences of rapid population growth. It will have to play a more active role in providing both information on family planning methods and other family planning services. Assuming that the government does recognize the need for a more effective national family planning pro-gramme, the Church will have to choose between silently accepting the programme or actively opposing it. The Church's response will affect its relations with the government. More importantly, it will also affect the prospects of the poor majority of Filipinos who suffer the most from unchecked population growth.

The future also presents the Church with a number of significant questions and challenges. Can it continue to walk the fine (or perhaps blurry) line separating Church and state in the Philippines? Can it play a leading role in improving socio-economic conditions without becoming too deeply involved in policy-making and politics? In dealing with its priests, sisters, and lay workers, where will it draw the line between acceptable social activism and unacceptable political action, and between progressivism and extremism? How will it reconcile its stated concern for the poor majority of Filipinos with its conservatism on key social issues such as the role of women and family planning?

Finally, given the disagreements within the Church over these and other questions, can it keep itself together?

The Rise of Vigilante Groups

In late 1986 and early 1987 groups of armed civilians began to spring up in many localities in reaction to the expanded influence of the New People's Army. Many of these groups were directly or indirectly supported by local military commanders – sometimes over the objections of the civilian government. Because these groups took it upon themselves to identify and punish suspected communists they quickly became known as "vigilante" groups. They organized security patrols, set up networks of "spotters" to report the presence of strangers, manned check-points on roads leading into and out of the community, and set up identification systems for community residences. They were armed with rifles and pistols or carried *bolos* (a kind of machete) and knives.[58] Many groups did not hesitate to use intimidation and coercion, and in some cases, extreme violence, to combat the communist menace they perceived.

According to a report by the Lawyers Committee for Human Rights, the victims of vigilante groups

> range from NPA suspects – the standard of suspicion is left to the vigilantes' discretion – to children caught in the crossfire of vigilante violence. Summary executions by vigilante forces frequently take place in the wake of killings by NPA assassination units, but the victims of such retaliatory killings are often surrogates for the rebels who got away. Sometimes relatives of suspected rebels are killed; other times the victims are members of "cause-oriented" groups labelled as NPA sympathizers – labor or peasant activists, church lay leaders and human rights monitors.[59]

The Lawyers Committee report cited numerous examples of "flagrant violations of human rights, including numerous acts of summary execution". The following case was typical:

> On April 5 1987, Lucia Madayan, a member of the United Farmers' Organization (UFO), was abducted by a local vigilante leader in Cebu City. Her partially decomposed body was found 11 days later; her head and one leg had been hacked off. The next day, Cebu

vigilantes killed Lolito Ubod, an official of the UFO, crushing his skull and cutting off his ears.[60]

Some 200 vigilante groups sprouted up in parts of Mindanao, Cebu, Negros, Bicol, Leyte, and Samar between the collapse of the cease-fire in February 1987 and early 1988. The best known of these were the Alsa Masa (Masses Arise) which spread from Davao City to form "chapters" in several provinces; Nakasaka (an acronym for United People for Peace) in Davao del Sur; and the fanatical Tadtad (for "chop-chop", because of its members use of bolo knives to attack their victims) in Mindanao, Cebu, and Leyte. Many other smaller groups also sprang up, including groups of religious fanatics similar to the Tadtad, private armies, and politically-oriented groups like the Movement for an Independent Negros, a group in Negros Occidental that vowed armed uprising and secession if the Aquino government adopted a comprehensive land reform programme. The total size of membership in these groups is not known, but in 1988 Alsa Masa alone claimed to have 10,000 members, and Nakasaka claimed 20,000.

The rapid growth of vigilante groups was attributable to a combination of factors. The first was the near total breakdown of law and order in many parts of the country. The second was the excessive violence used by the NPA in Davao City and other parts of Mindanao in 1986, which was caused in part by the internal purge of suspected informants. The third was the reduction in the size of the CHDF under Chief of Staff Ramos, which created a pool of men ready and willing to join vigilante groups. The fourth factor was the success of the Alsa Masa in Davao City, which encouraged duplication elsewhere. Fifthly, the military embraced vigilantes as an effective counter-insurgency tool. Finally, vigilante groups, and the anti-communist crusade, were seen as a potential new power base for local politicians dispossessed in 1986 by the change in government.

The growth of vigilante groups sparked a heated debate in Manila in early 1987. Supporters of vigilantes, including many military officers and some government officials, saw the growth of these groups as a commendable and needed local response to the inroads of the communists. Some government officials, including President Aquino, called them a new form of "people power". Indeed, some groups, particularly those in the larger cities, were genuine homegrown responses to deteriorating conditions, sincere in their desire to fight communism, and relatively responsible and restrained in their actions.

Other Filipinos, however, strongly opposed the spread of vigilante groups. To them, even the best behaved vigilante groups made a mockery of the legal system and were as coercive as the communists they claimed to be fighting against. Opponents of vigilante groups also charged that they were difficult to control and prone to violence. According to one human rights group in the Philippines, more than fifty people were summarily killed by right-wing vigilante groups between February 1986 and June 1987. Eleven of these deaths were attributed to the Alsa Masa alone.[61] Some vigilante groups were also nothing more than thinly disguised private armies of local élites. In Negros Occidental, for example, the private armies of some sugar planters (some of which comprised as many as 200 men) formed the core of the province's vigilante groups. Still other groups, such as the Tadtad, were fanatical religious cults.

The Aquino government's response to the rise of vigilantism reflected its limited control of events outside Metro Manila. In mid-March 1987 President Aquino ordered the disbanding of all paramilitary groups, apparently including vigilante groups and the CHDF. However, she quickly issued a "clarification" stating that vigilantes and the CHDF were not included. In April Chief of Staff Ramos publicly supported the creation of vigilante groups, as long as they adhered to the following government guidelines: membership in the groups had to be voluntary; the groups' activities had to be "defensive"; carrying arms was restricted to people legally authorized to do so; and groups had to be under police and military supervision.[62] Soon thereafter, Aquino referred to the "unarmed" Nakasaka in Davao del Sur as an extension of "people power". In an October visit to Davao City, she told members of the Alsa Masa, "We look up to you as an example . . . . While other regions are experiencing problems in fighting the insurgency, you here . . . have set the example".[63]

In late October the government formalized the guidelines for vigilante groups, but without giving them the force of law. According to the Lawyers Committee, these guidelines were often "flagrantly disregarded and inadequately enforced".[64] Even if the guidelines had been enforced, there were few other disincentives to abusive behaviour by vigilantes. According to the Lawyers Committee:

> Vigilantes who commit abuses are rarely arrested — victims and their relatives are often too afraid of reprisals to file complaints — and investigations are not vigorously pursued. When arrest warrants are issued, they are often not served, and the vigilantes charged with murder remain at large — armed, and free to intimidate complaintants and witnesses.[65]

In sum, vigilante groups were a successful counter-force to communist encroachment — at least in the short run. While groups were successful in some areas — most notably in Davao City — they relied on force and intimidation, and the potential for extreme abuse was always present. It appeared possible to minimize this potential in the urban areas, where they were subject to the scrutiny of the media, the Church, and the government. But these checks did not exist in most rural areas, creating a situation ripe for violence and fanaticism.

The Aquino government's acceptance and encouragement of vigilante groups was another indication of the increased influence of the military in policy-making. Moreover, the support that most of these groups received from local military commanders undermined the authority of the local civilian government. Indeed, the loyalty of some vigilantes to the civilian government was often uncertain. According to an Alsa Masa member interviewed in Davao City:

> our loyalty is not to Respicio [the OIC mayor in 1987] nor the *barangay* officials. Where were they when we risked our lives coming out into the open against the NPA? . . .Our loyalty is to the Metrodiscom commander [the local military commander].[66]

Finally, the rise of vigilantes was an indication of the national government's inability to project its presence on the local level. Amando Doronila, writing in late 1987, concluded:

> the government is facilitating, wittingly or unwittingly, the erosion of its authority by promoting the vigilante movement as one of the important weapons to fight the insurgency. Essentially the government is ceding its authority to armed groups which, according to evidence, are ill-disciplined, abusive and do not have a notion of public accountability and responsibility.[67]

Once the government ceded this authority, it would find it very difficut to re-establish it.

Conclusion

Despite the Philippines' democratic tradition, the re-establishment of democracy by Aquino was neither simple nor guaranteed. In 1986 the nation had experienced almost fourteen years of dictatorship and was still reeling from three years of political instability and economic crisis. Corazon Aquino, the leader tasked with restoring democracy, was an inexperienced politician and statesman. She presided over a shaky and fractious coalition, was commander-in-chief of a military of questionable loyalty, and was leader of a divided body politic.

In facing these challenges Aquino had to contend with several important political actors, the most powerful of which was the military. After EDSA, the military leadership asserted what it believed was its right to play an influential role in determining a wide range of policy issues. It soon became clear that if the military was denied this role, certain elements within it would not hesitate to exercise an additional right they claimed, namely, to overthrow the civilian government. Additionally, the military's hostility towards political and social forces it considered "leftist" narrowed the boundaries of permissible political activity on the national and local levels. Finally, the ingrained conservatism of the military created a natural affinity between its more hardline elements and the rightist civilian opposition to the Aquino government. Taken together, these developments caused a significant reordering of traditional civilian–military relations and represent a critical new dimension of Philippine politics.

The Catholic Church was a second influential political actor. The Church had played a role in bringing the Aquino government to power, and initially it was an important source of support for the shaky new government. In contrast to the military, the Church also supported the Aquino government's initial efforts at reconciliation with the communist insurgents. It is not surprising then, that the Church had significant influence on the framing of the new Constitution and on other social issues. Gradually, however, the Church began to balance its support for President Aquino with criticisms of her government's failure to protect human rights, fight corruption, implement agrarian reform, and deliver basic social services. The general futility of the Church's calls for reform is evidence of the limits of its influence on government and politics. The causes of the Church's limited influence include the power of the military, restraints imposed by the Vatican, the Church's awareness of the risks of excessive involvement in politics, and divisions within the Church.

In comparison to the important political roles played by the military and the Church, the role of the new bicameral Congress initially was somewhat less significant. Although the Congress was quick to assert its independence from the executive branch, it was too pre-occupied with becoming operational during most of its first year to be very influential. The influence of the Congress (relative to the executive branch) gradually increased, however, because of the absence of strong leadership from Aquino and the accumulation of legislative experience. The first significant test of the Congress came in early 1988, when it finally confronted the controversial issue of agrarian reform. The disappointing performance of the Congress and President Aquino on this issue will be examined in greater detail in Chapter 10.

The changing configuration of political parties reflected factional and political realignments caused by the rapid transition from the Marcos to the Aquino era. Unfortunately, these changes contributed little to the strengthening of democracy. With the exception of the leftist Partido ng Bayan and other cause-oriented groups, none of the major parties were built on anything other than often unreliable factional loyalties. They made little or no effort to develop rank and file memberships or build permanent party organizations. Consequently, none could claim to represent stable and differentiated constituencies.[68] The weakness of the party system was aggravated by President Aquino's disdain for and disinterest in party politics. The 1987 congressional elections forced a degree of party unity and coalition building, but most of this disappeared once the elections were over. Within the Congress, the absence of party discipline and co-operation weakened the legislative process. In an effort to reassert the dominance and unity of parties and factions affiliated with the Aquino administration, the LDP was formed in mid-1988. Although the LDP appears to have met with some initial success, its unity is likely to be seriously eroded as the 1992 elections approach.

Finally, the emergence of vigilante groups in 1987, and their endorsement by the Aquino government, illustrated the influence of the military and the weakness of the national government on the local level. It also represented an important further erosion of the rule of law – a key ingredient of democracy.

The mixed record of democracy under Aquino reflects the insecurity her government felt in the face of serious challenges from the right and left. In order to ensure the survival of her regime, Aquino garnered the support of the military and the traditional élite by adopting conservative policies that reflected a fundamentally traditional approach to government and politics. In the following chapter we examine the largely unsuccessful role played by the communist and non-communist left in opposing this return to traditional politics.

NOTES

1. Gareth Porter, *The Politics of Counterinsurgency in the Philippines: Military and Political Options*, Occasional Paper no.9 (Honolulu: University of Hawaii Center for Philippine Studies, 1987), p.56.
2. *Dallas Morning News*, 22 March 1987, p.18A.
3. Porter, op. cit., p.83.
4. Ibid., p.83.
5. Carolina Hernandez, "Toward Understanding Coups and Civilian-Military Relations", *Kasarinlan* 3, no.2 (4th qtr. 1987), p.22.
6. Porter, op. cit., p.68.
7. Benjamin Muego, "Fraternal Organizations and Factionalism within the AFP", *Asian Affairs 14* (1987), p.154.
8. During the December 1989 coup attempt RAM was joined by a shadowy new group of military rebels, known as the Young Officers Union (YOU). YOU is thought to be an off-shoot of RAM, comprised mainly of junior level intelligence officers. YOU is also considered to be more revolutionary and nationalistic than RAM, as the following statement made by an unidentified leader of YOU indicates:

    > Our political line is the nationalist revolution which, under current conditions takes the form of a coup-cum-revolution. We believe that a military uprising supported by the majority of the Filipino people is the correct vehicle for the complete overhaul of the current socio-economic-political system that will bring about genuine national and social liberation in the country.

    See the *Far Eastern Economic Review*, 7 June 1990, p.26.
9. Muego, op. cit., p.152.

10. Linn Neumann writing in the *International Herald Tribune*, 21 September 1987, p.6.
11. Rafael Ileto estimated in 1986 that Fidel Ramos had the loyalty of 35 per cent of the AFP, Enrile had 25 per cent and that the remaining 40 per cent were not committed or loyal to either leader. See Porter, op. cit., p.71.
12. *Far Eastern Economic Review*, 24 September 1987, p.14.
13. General Ramos replaced General Ileto as Secretary of Defence, and Renato de Villa, another PC general, became Chief of Staff.
14. Porter, op. cit., p.59.
15. Ibid., p.56.
16. Ibid., p.66.
17. Ibid., p.69.
18. Ibid., p.70.
19. Ibid., p.71.
20. *International Herald Tribune*, 28 February 1987, p.2.
21. Porter, op. cit. p.72.
22. See Sandra Burton, *Impossible Dream: The Marcoses, the Aquinos, and the Unfinished Revolution* (New York: Warner Books, 1989), pp.419–20.
23. The overall percentage of "no" votes in the military installations was about 40 per cent; but in some military installations such as Camp Aguinaldo and Villamor Air Base in Metro Manila, the "no" vote was as high as 85 per cent. See Muego, op. cit., p.161.
24. Four PCHR members resigned following the January 1987 Mendiola shootings and PCHR Chairman Diokno died in February 1987. By the time the emasculated PCHR was superceded by a constitutionally-mandated Commission on Human Rights in early 1987 it had not been able to bring any alleged military offenders to trial.
25. *Bulletin Today*, 3 October 1987, p.13.
26. Ibid., p.13.
27. Ibid., p.13.
28. *Newsweek* (Asia Edition), 21 September 1987, pp.12–13.
29. Hernandez, op. cit., p.22.
30. *Straits Times* (Singapore), 13 December 1987, p.15.
31. *Washington Post*, 12 September 1987, p.1.
32. Alfred Stepan, *Rethinking Military Politics: Brazil and the Southern Cone* (Princeton: Princeton University Press, 1988), pp.68–69.
33. Ibid., p.93.
34. Ibid., pp.94–97.
35. Institute for Popular Democracy, *Political Clans and Electoral Politics: A Preliminary Research* (Quezon City: IPD, 1987), pp.97–98.

36. *Manila Chronicle* ("Focus" magazine), 31 May 1987, p.2.
37. Alex Magno, "The New Congress: A Shift in the Power Alignment", *Diliman Review* 35, no.3 (1987):10.
38. Institute for Popular Democracy, op. cit., p.103.
39. *Asiaweek*, 2 August 1987, p.19.
40. Ibid., p.17.
41. *Manila Chronicle*, 18 October 1987, p.16.
42. *Manila Chronicle*, 25 October 1987, p.13.
43. *Bulletin Today*, 23 October 1987, p.1.
44. *Manila Chronicle*, 25 October 1987, p.13.
45. *Manila Chronicle*, 21 October 1987, p.4.
46. *Manila Chronicle*, 11 June 1988, p.9.
47. For months after the revolution, Marcos still claimed he would return. There was also ongoing speculation that Marcos's running mate in the 1986 elections, Arturo Tolentino, would take an oath as vice-president and declare himself to be acting president. He finally did this at the Manila Hotel in July 1986.
48. *Manila Chronicle*, 14 January 1989, p.1.
49. Carl Lande and Allan Cigler, "Recent Philippine Elections: A Quantitative Analysis" (interim report, April 1988), p.29.
50. *Far Eastern Economic Review*, 18 June 1987, p.47.
51. *International Herald Tribune*, 11 February 1988, p.6.
52. *Manila Chronicle*, 13 December 1987, p.18.
53. Robert Youngblood, "The Corazon Aquino 'Miracle' and the Philippine Churches", *Asian Survey* 27, no.12 (December 1987):1255.
54. *Manila Chronicle*, 3 January 1988, p.10.
55. *International Herald Tribune*, 18 June 1986, p.4.
56. See Ateneo-Social Weather Stations, *Public Opinion Report, June 1986* (Quezon City: Ateneo de Manila-Social Weather Stations, 1986).
57. Sister Christine Tan, quoted in the *Manila Chronicle*, 13 November 1987, p.18.
58. Amnesty International, *Philippines: Alleged Human Rights Violations by Vigilante Groups* (New York: Amnesty International, July 1987), p.2.
59. Lawyers Committee for Human Rights, *Vigilantes in the Philippines: A Threat to Democratic Rule* (New York: Lawyers Committee for Human Rights, 1988), p.x.
60. Ibid., p.ix.
61. According to the Philippine Alliance of Human Rights Advocates. See the *Manila Chronicle*, 25 October 1987, p.1.
62. Amnesty International, op. cit., p.3.
63. Lawyers Committee, op. cit., p.xi.

64. Ibid., p.xii.
65. Ibid., p.xiii.
66. *Manila Chronicle*, 22 November 1987, p.11.
67. *Manila Chronicle*, 3 November 1987, p.1.
68. The two partial exceptions to this were the Pimentel wing of PDP-Laban and GAD. Pimentel's wing of PDP-Laban consistently espoused a progressive and nationalist platform. GAD could claim a strong base of support in the provinces in the far north (Ilocos Norte, Ilocos Sur, and Cagayan) because of continued voter loyalty to their native sons, Ferdinand Marcos and Juan Ponce Enrile.

chapter 9

The Communist
and Non-Communist Left

> Philippine society under the U.S.-Aquino regime remains essentially
> the same as it was during the rule of the deposed Marcos fascist
> puppet dictatorship. It is semi-colonial and semi-feudal, and with
> the broad masses of the people exploited and oppressed by U.S.
> imperialism and the local ruling classes of big compradors and
> big landlords.
>
> — The Communist Party of
> the Philippines, March 1987[1]

The communist and non-communist left, as we have seen, grew rapidly
during the first half of the 1980s. The numerous abuses and failures
of the Marcos regime provided the left with ample issues, recruits,
and public sympathy. Consequently, prior to the February 1986 uprising, the left appeared to be one of the most likely beneficiaries
of a change of government. The left blundered, however, by failing
to ally with the more progressive elements in the Aquino camp and
decided instead to boycott the 1986 presidential election. In doing
so, it missed a unique opportunity to influence subsequent political
developments, lost much of its considerable momentum (and a large
portion of its middle-class support), and forfeited whatever claim it
might have had to representation in the Aquino coalition. Moreover,
the boycott decision demonstrated that the leadership of the Communist Party of the Philippines (CPP) was fallible and created strong

288

disagreements on tactics and strategies both within the CPP and between the Party and the non-communist left.

The abrupt change from a dictatorship to a democracy was a mixed blessing for the communist and non-communist left. On the one hand, the CPP could look forward to dealing with an inexperienced and divided new government. On the other hand, the communists faced an unexpected, dramatically different, and more complex political environment – notwithstanding their claims that the Aquino government was little different from the Marcos regime. For the non-communist left, the return of political freedom and democracy provided an unprecedented opportunity to participate in politics and influence policy-making. However, it failed in its brief foray into electoral politics and it had difficulty exerting significant influence on the policy-making process. As a result, the considerable potential of the legal left appeared to be spent by 1988.

This chapter examines the experience of the communist and non-communist left from 1986 to 1988. It describes the complex and changing situation confronting the left, identifies the left's strengths and weaknesses, and explores some of the reasons for its lack of success.

Challenges To and From the Left

In the period immediately preceding the 1986 presidential election the communist and non-communist left could not help but feel optimistic and self-confident – and with good reason. The communist movement had developed a dedicated and experienced group of leaders who, according to one account, were seasoned veterans whose "initial squeamishness at executing the enemy" had long since been overcome.[2] Equally important, the communists had learned how to skilfully exploit the underlying poverty and inequality of Philippine society and the pervasive corruption and ineptitude of the Marcos government. As a result, the communists' numbers were increasing, their underground and above-ground organizations were expanding and becoming more influential, and their guerrillas were out-smarting and out-fighting the government forces. By late 1985, about 20 per cent of the nation's 42,000 *barangay* were either controlled or influenced by the CPP/NPA, and 15,000–20,000 NPA (New People's Army) regulars were operating in 59 of the 73 provinces. The CPP seemed poised to take advantage of the Philippines' political and economic crises.

The growth of the communist movement was directly related to the communists' willingness and ability to respond to the needs of poor and exploited Filipinos, particularly in the rural areas. The *tao* (common man or peasant) was often the victim of crimes, exploited by his landlord, and ignored by the local government. In the areas under its control, the NPA protected peasants against exploitative landlords, corrupt officials, and abusive soldiers. The communists also administered justice by apprehending and punishing livestock poachers, land-grabbers and other criminals. As "Ka (comrade) Joy", a CPP member in Quezon province explained, "Justice is very expensive and very slow in the Philippines. Justice belongs to those who have money to hire the best lawyer. . . .Our revolutionary justice is fast and inexpensive. And it is very democratic".[3] In the areas under its control, the NPA also forced reductions in rents and interest rates for tenant farmers, and in some areas provided rudimentary health care and education and set up co-operatives and income generating projects.

The politicization of the Philippines' major cities following the Aquino assassination provided the CPP and the communist-controlled National Democratic Front (NDF) with an equally fertile urban landscape. In the cities, the CPP and the NDF championed causes such as higher wages and better conditions for workers; the rights of squatters, women, and other disadvantaged groups; and the removal of the U.S. military bases. The CPP worked through the NDF's nominally independent member organizations at the same time that it sought to increase its influence in independent non-communist organizations such as labour unions, human rights groups, the media, student and teachers' organizations, and other cause-oriented and sectoral groups. As we have seen, the Aquino assassination and the subsequent economic crisis also stimulated the growth and development of numerous non-communist cause-oriented and sectoral groups in most major cities.

The seemingly strong position of the left in 1986 should not obscure the fact that the change of government presented it with three new and unexpected challenges: a new and immensely popular president; a fractious and unstable coalition government; and a new, more open, and considerably more complex political environment. Aquino's great popularity, her commitment to democracy, and her ambiguity on many social issues made her a difficult political target to hit. The disparate composition of the Aquino coalition and the civilian leadership's changing relationship with the military made it hard for the left's ideologues to agree on the basic nature and future prospects of the new government. The restoration of democracy created a political environment with which the left had relatively little experience. All of these factors brought out divisions within the left that had for the most part been muted as long as Marcos remained in power.

Initially, the left was in a quandary concerning the character of the new government. Was Aquino's coalition fundamentally progressive or conservative? Was the government controlled by civilians or the military? Was it more or less dependent upon the United States than the Marcos government? These questions provoked considerable debate and disagreement within the left. The communists doubted that the progressive or centrist forces in the new government would be able to survive a challenge from the right and predicted that the new government inevitably would become more reactionary and militaristic. Most non-communist groups, however, felt that there was a significant progressive element within the new government and that an effort had to be made to defend and strengthen the government's progressive tendencies. Moreover, they saw that the challenge from the military and the right threatened not only the Aquino government, but also their own participation in politics – their "democratic space". Therefore, they limited their criticisms of the Aquino administration so as to avoid destabilizing the civilian government and jeopardizing the nascent democracy.

In addition to adjusting to the post-Marcos political environment, the left also had to contend with longstanding challenges posed by Philippine society and culture. Despite the rapid growth of the communist movement during the 1980s, the left was not immune to, nor could it ignore, some of the elements of the country's political culture, described in Chapter 2. The communist and non-communist movements were not able to entirely escape the factionalism or particularism that characterized Philippine politics. Indeed, the communists sensibly bowed to particularism by addressing specific local concerns rather than emphasizing abstract ideology. Most importantly, the left was faced with the deeply-rooted conservatism of many Filipinos.

This conservatism is the product of traditional values and social relationships, as well as economic conditions, particularly the prevalence of subsistence agriculture. When combined with the country's democratic and Catholic traditions, this conservatism produces an unsophisticated but strong strain of anti-communism. Communism is viewed by many Filipinos as being godless, undemocratic, ruthless, and impersonal. The February 1986 "revolution" and restoration of democracy appeared to increase many Filipinos' disdain for communism. A public opinion survey taken in May 1986 revealed that 54 per cent of Filipinos polled did not think the CPP should be legalized – an increase from 44 per cent in June 1985.[4]

Despite these challenges, the communist and non-communist left had a number of important strengths. Unlike traditional political parties, the left possessed an ideology offering a convincing explanation of the causes of the nation's problems, and concrete programmes of action that they claimed would benefit the poor and exploited masses. Unlike many traditional politicians, the leaders of the left had not fled to the United States during the Marcos era, nor were they discredited by collaboration with Marcos. Moreover, the members of the left who had not been caught and jailed by Marcos had acquired years of experience in the underground movement. Finally, staunchly anti-American, members of the left could claim to be true nationalists.

The Communist Party and the Revolutionary Struggle

At the forefront of the left was, of course, the Communist Party of the Philippines. Although national in scope, the CPP's emphasis on decentralized leadership made it relatively less vulnerable to the capture or death of senior leaders. The CPP had developed a wide variety of sectoral organizations that reached down to the grass-roots level in many parts of the nation. In some areas leftist groups were the only organized presence that could provide basic services such as security, justice, basic health care, and education. The CPP also benefited from the growing emphasis on social activism within the Catholic Church. Many of the Church's social action programmes provided financial or moral support for leftist causes. Finally, the communists' political and social programmes were supported by an experienced, battle-hardened, and dedicated fighting force of some 20,000 guerrillas.

Revolutionary Politics

The organizational strengths of the CPP, however, could not undo the mistake it made when it decided not to participate in the events of February 1986. In order to learn from its mistake (and assign blame), the 29-member CPP Central Committee became locked in a major rectification debate for three months after the February revolution. The pro-boycott decision of the five-member Executive Committee of the Central Committee was publicly criticized in May 1986, as was its heavy-handed policy-making and mechanical analysis. According to *Ang Bayan*,

> when the aroused and militant people moved spontaneously but resolutely to oust the hated regime last February 22–25, the Party and its forces were on the sidelines, unable to lead or influence the hundreds of thousands of people who moved with amazing speed and decisiveness to overthrow the regime.[5]

Chairman Rodolfo Salas and General Secretary Rafael Baylosis, both of whom had advocated the boycott, were criticized for incorrectly reading the political situation and were demoted. Benito Tiamzon became acting chairman and NDF head Satur Ocampo appeared to gain influence.[6]

At the same time that the CPP was struggling to get its own house in order, it was also trying to make sense of the Aquino government. To doctrinaire communists the Aquino government was composed of a perplexing mixture of classes that defied easy labelling using conventional Marxist-Leninist-Maoist analysis. While recognizing the presence of some bourgeois "progressive" elements in the new government, the CPP viewed the new government as still representing the "semi-feudal, semi-colonial ruling classes". The CPP believed that the class interests of the government would prohibit it from making meaningful socio-economic changes and that the coalition of disparate forces would not survive for long. It, therefore, expected that the Aquino government would sink into economic and political crisis and the right would consolidate its control.[7] Moreover, the Party recognized that Marcos's repressive "state apparatus" (meaning, primarily, the military) had survived the transition intact, and it believed, with considerable justification, that the apparatus was controlled by Enrile and Ramos rather than by Aquino.[8]

Despite the contradictions the communists saw within the Aquino government, the CPP leadership was wise enough to see also that President Aquino's unparalleled popularity presented them with a major political problem. Confronted with this, as well as with their own internal divisions and a fluid and rapidly changing political environment, the CPP assumed a defensive, "wait and see" position during the early months of Aquino's rule. The NPA was instructed to avoid major encounters with the AFP and the NDF's plans for new *welgang bayan* (people's strikes) were put on hold.

The first political challenge that the CPP faced was the issue of whether or not to enter into negotiations for a cease-fire. In late April 1986, President Aquino on one of her campaign pledges announced her intention to call for a cease-fire with a set and unextendable duration. The possibility of negotiations raised a number of potential problems and opportunities for the CPP. Some members worried that a cease-fire would weaken the momentum of the armed struggle and tempt the Party to place greater emphasis on political struggle. There was also a concern that a cease-fire would give the AFP a much-needed opportunity to regroup.

The leadership realized, however, that while the cease-fire might diminish the momentum of the NPA's military struggle, the CPP could not afford to appear war-like in the face of Aquino's offer of reconciliation. While the Party leadership was sceptical of the government's commitment to a cease-fire — especially given the hostile statements of General Ramos and Minister of Defence Enrile — the talks could be used to show that the Aquino government was militaristic and unwilling or unable to make fundamental political changes. Moreover, the CPP hoped to take advantage of the additional "democratic space" that a cease-fire offered to organize itself. Finally, the talks were an unprecedented opportunity to legitimize the CPP and publicize and explain to the Filipino people the communist movement's ideology and goals.

In mid-May 1986 secret talks on a cease-fire began between the government and the communists. In June, following its internal rectification, the CPP designated Satur Ocampo as negotiator for the cease-fire (he was later joined by Antonio Zumel and Carolina Malay-Ocampo). In July, official talks began between the government and the communists. On 29 September Rodolfo Salas, the CPP chairman from 1977 until he was demoted as a result of the rectification, was arrested in Metro Manila, in what might have been a set-up by rival members of the Central Committee. Despite his capture the communists decided to continue to participate in the negotiations and on 1 November they proposed a hundred-day cease-fire. Less than two weeks later, on 13 November, another attempt was made to sabotage the talks with the brutal murder of Rolando Olalia, head of the leftist KMU labour federation. The talks continued, however, and Aquino's negotiators, at the urging of the military (which feared that the NPA would use a longer cease-fire to expand the areas under its influence), suggested a shorter cease-fire. Eventually, a sixty-day cease-fire was agreed to. The pact was signed on 27 November, five days after the resignation of Enrile from the Cabinet, and the cease-fire began on 10 December.

The safe conduct passes provided to the communist negotiators enabled them to participate in numerous interviews with the curious and generally sympathetic national media. Soft-spoken and smiling as they calmly explained the CPP and NDF's ideology and objectives, they were able to counteract the military's shrill warnings that the communists were ruthless and godless murderers bent on seizing power by force. The NDF printed T-shirts with a caption saying that "NPA" stood for "Nice People Around" and "I love cease-fire". The CPP took advantage of the cease-fire by sending political organizers to areas that had been too dangerous before and expanded its influence in other areas which had been only lightly infiltrated.[9] Priests took five of the twenty NDF seats on regional cease-fire committees, giving the left greater legitimacy by identifying it with Christianity.[10]

The substantive talks between the government and the communists went nowhere, however. This was partially because the ideological gap between the two sides was far too great, and partially because neither side was prepared to make any compromises that might weaken its military position. The government insisted that any discussion of future political changes should occur in the context of the newly drafted Constitution. The communists rejected this, and insisted that an end to the armed struggle could only happen as part of a comprehensive settlement that required political and economic changes outside the constitutional framework. Former Senator Jose Diokno tried to bridge the gap by proposing that common ground could be found by addressing the issues of "food and freedom, jobs and justice". But the two sides were unable to agree on anything more than the importance of these issues, and on 23 January, following the death of some nineteen demonstrators at the Mendiola Bridge, the talks were suspended by the communists. The talks were never reconvened, and the cease-fire expired following the 2 February constitutional plebiscite.

With the breakdown of the talks and the overwhelming ratification of the new Constitution the CPP resumed its hardline criticism of the Aquino government. In late March 1987 *Ang Bayan* branded the Aquino government "a puppet of U.S. imperialism" and "the main instrument of reaction and counterrevolution in the country".[11] From Europe, Jose Maria Sison, the CPP founder, criticized the Aquino government for "keeping itself within the parameters of foreign and feudal domination" and for being "pro-U.S. and reactionary, despite its wish to restore the pre-1972 liberal democratic [government] and its actual efforts to undo some of the worst features of the previous regime. . . . " Sison predicted a swing to the right: "It is utterly impossible for the Aquino regime to build a liberal democratic state or even to retain the liberal-democratic embellishments on the comprador-landlord state for a long time".[12] He also predicted the collapse of the Aquino government at the hands of a military coup within three years, a prediction that came close to being fulfilled in August 1987 and again in December 1989.

As the May 1987 congressional elections approached, the CPP faced another major decision: determining the Party's position with regard to the importance of the "electoral struggle". Some Party leaders saw the elections as an opportunity to expand the political struggle by educating, propagandizing, organizing, and maybe even getting a few leftist candidates elected. Consequently, they favoured devoting the CPP's energies and resources to supporting "progressive" candidates. But the more hardline Party leaders feared that if the left won a number of congressional seats, it would foster a mistaken and dangerous belief within the Party that the electoral struggle could be more effective than the armed struggle. The more orthodox position ultimately prevailed and the Party officially dismissed the elections as being a meaningless sham. On 17 May the CPP reaffirmed that, "armed struggle is still the main form of struggle for the people to achieve fundamental change in Philippine society".[13]

As if to demonstrate the primacy of the armed struggle, in early 1987 the NPA increased its attacks in Metro Manila. In April, the Alex Boncayao Brigade (ABB), a 200-member NPA "sparrow" or assassination unit based in Metro Manila, claimed credit for the murder of eighteen policemen, soldiers, and local officials since February. The ABB warned that they planned to step up their attacks on abusive members of the military and police, and by June there was a notable rise in the number of sparrow attacks in the capital and other major cities.[14] The communists claimed that they were meting out "revolutionary justice" and paying back "blood debts" for crimes and abuses that had not been redressed. But the seemingly random murder of low-level personnel provoked a backlash of public anger in Metro Manila. In response to the adverse public reaction the ABB decided to scale back its operations in the capital. By the end of 1987, however, close to a hundred lawmen had been killed in Metro Manila alone.[15]

The CPP's extremely limited involvement in the January 1988 local elections underscored its complete rejection of the electoral struggle. Its involvement was limited to two types of activity. First, in municipalities where the communists were influential, the CPP supported leftist candidates in the hope that, if elected, they would be able to use their offices to block the national government's counter-insurgency campaign. Secondly, the CPP used the elections to raise money. Sotero Llamas, a leading rebel in Southern Luzon, said that the NPA taxed candidates from P25,000 to P100,000 (about US$1,200 to US$4,800) and that 80 per cent of the candidates met their "requests". He also said that the rebels expected to collect not less than P3 million (more than US$142,000) in cash and arms in the Bicol region, one of their strongholds.[16]

Communism in the Countryside

The communist insurgency has its roots in the Philippines' tradition of sporadic peasant uprisings. But the current, essentially Maoist, rebellion is unlike past peasant uprisings in several important ways.

First, it provides an ideological framework for the reordering of government, the economy, and society. Secondly, it offers a cohesive and comprehensive package of specific remedies for peasants' grievances. Thirdly, it is national in scope. Finally, it has developed a tested revolutionary methodology that has been sustained for more than twenty years.

The communist insurgency has been fuelled less by ideological abstractions than by a host of very tangible social, economic, and political problems in the countryside. These have included:

- a slow and unfair system of justice;
- pervasive rural violence and insecurity;
- unequal land distribution;
- widespread agricultural tenancy that often has involved onerous terms and insecure tenure;
- extensive rural landlessness and unemployment;
- illegal land grabbing;
- national and local governments that have been unable or unwilling to provide basic social services; and
- military abuses.

The slowness and unfairness of the Philippine judicial system in the countryside has been easily and fully exploited by the CPP. According to human rights lawyer Abelardo Aportadera, the CPP-NPA:

> does not wait for the people to bring their cases before it, but seeks out the people, asks them their legal problems, and offers them swift solutions the NPA way. It therefore is not uncommon to hear rural folks talk about the NPAs settling property and personal disputes, and the NPAs effectively combatting criminality in their *barrios*.[17]

The political and psychological importance of the communists' willingness to provide justice and order in the countryside, even in a brutal and error-prone way, can hardly be over-emphasized. The dispensing of revolutionary justice demonstrates to previously powerless peasants that direct action is possible by supporting the communists. It also eliminates possible opponents to the communists and shows the dire consequences of opposing the movement. Although self-serving, *Ang Bayan*'s description of the NPA's role in conflict resolution and justice jibes with those of other observers:

Aside from facing the AFP in combat, units of the NPA now help [the people] resolve conflicts among their ranks. A common assertion among the masses [is]: "Since the arrival of the people's army, cattle-rustling has been eradicated, and so has robbery, rape, gambling, trouble-making, and similar social problems". Contradictions among the people are being resolved, and with head held high, they now confront the landlords and negotiating [*sic*] for their demands.[18]

How has "revolutionary justice" been administered by the communists? In early 1987 Professor Rosario Lucero described the different types of justice administered in the countryside:

There are at present two types of courts that try criminal cases, depending upon the degree of political maturity possessed by the people in the "liberated zone". In a fully organized area, there is the People's Court, which uses the participatory method. There is a public trial, with the whole community actively taking part in the trial as judge, jury, witness and defendant. In less advanced areas, there is a collective judge, consisting of the party branch, the mass organizations, and the sympathetic middle class, with one-third representation from each. There are, of course, no lawyers; the accused defends himself.

This contrasts with our conventional image of the judge, whose integrity is questionable, and whose decisions are usually on the side of power and wealth. Moreover, legitimate court processes are complicated by technicalities of law, which are frequently merely procedural problems; such problems, in turn, become the lawyer's ground for delaying court processes. In the "liberated zone", the people are concerned less with form than with substance.[19]

An NPA trial rarely took more than a week to reach a verdict. The forms of punishment included *barrio* arrest, exile, payment for damages, and in the case of grave crimes ("blood debts") like rape, arson, banditry, and murder, the death penalty. According to Lucero:

A person proven to be guilty of blood debts is first sent a note requesting an appointment with him. If he accepts the invitation, an education process takes place, in which the discussion is meant to convince him of the "folly of his ways" and to warn him to

desist from them. If the guilty party ignores the first encounter,
he is given a series of warnings. Repeated acts of oppression
will finally bring upon him the death penalty.[20]

Is "revolutionary justice" just, or is it thinly disguised intimidation?
Ross Munro, in a controversial article that likened the NPA to the
Khmer Rouge, wrote that: "Where the NPA prevails, a fearful silence
prevails: even if the NPA kills your brother or your best friend, you do
not report it".[21] His assessment is supported by numerous examples
of NPA abuses, particularly the often brutal handling of suspected
informants and "deep penetration agents" (DPAs). Furthermore, in
areas where their presence has reached an advanced stage, their
policies have tended to become increasingly repressive. In some of
these areas the CPP-NPA have imposed taxes and instituted progressively tougher controls over social behaviour.[22] It can also be argued,
however, that the NPA's "revolutionary justice" was the better of the
two options in most rural areas: a judicial system that favours the
rich and powerful or the complete absence of a judicial system. As
William Chapman has pointed out, revolutionary justice "flourished
and became popular only because it replaced something worse,
utter lawlessness".[23]

Another way that the communists have generated support in the
countryside has been by championing the peasantry in land issues.
It is no coincidence that the insurgency is strongest in areas where
there are high levels of tenancy (Central Luzon), large numbers
of landless labourers (Negros Occidental and other sugar growing
areas), and illegal land grabbing (Mindanao). Like the problem of
justice, disputes over land ownership and use are fundamental, long-
standing, and deeply-felt in the Philippines. These disputes are rooted
in the unequal distribution of land, differing understandings of what
constitutes ownership, past and continuing efforts to illegally grab
land, and the often unfair or exploitative terms of agricultural tenancy.
Today, these problems are compounded by the absence of new agricultural land to absorb the country's rapidly growing population. Of
the more than thirty million Filipinos living in the rural areas, some
five million are landless labourers.

The problem of land ownership and usage has been a constant
theme running through Philippine politics since independence. The

national government's unwillingness or inability to implement meaningful land reform has been equally constant. Consequently, the CPP has been able to seize upon the land issue to generate support in the countryside. However, the CPP has actually been quite cautious in its approach to land redistribution in the areas it controls. Instead of confiscating and redistributing large tracts of land, the Party has called for rent reductions, higher agricultural wages, higher prices for crops, and lower interest rates. By limiting the confiscatory aspect of reform the CPP has sought to avoid alienating the many owners of relatively small plots of land who rent out all or part of their land and, therefore, are technically "landlords". According to the NDF's magazine, *Liberation*,

> Only in certain areas are despotic landlords and landgrabbers divested of their land in favor of poor peasants and settlers. Eventually, however, the general land reform policy as stated in the NDF program shall be to "distribute land to the landless tillers equitably and at no cost".[24]

Finally, the communists have received support in the rural areas because they have provided basic social services that the government has been unable or unwilling to provide. It is no coincidence that some of the areas with the highest levels of NPA influence (such as the island of Samar and the Cagayan Valley) are those with the least developed infrastructures and the poorest delivery of government services. In addition to providing its own version of law and order, the communists have provided rudimentary health care and education. In almost all of the areas under communist control uneducated peasants are taught reading, writing and arithmetic – at the same time that they learn about Marxism, Leninism, and Maoism.[25]

For the last twenty years the CPP has learned through a process of trial and error how to exploit these agrarian problems. As a result, unlike previous radical agrarian movements in the Philippines, the CPP has developed a sophisticated, carefully thought out, and time-tested strategy and set of tactics. The CPP strategy is based on the Maoist model for revolution which emphatically establishes the primacy of the revolution in the countryside. Urban areas are to be conquered only after the communists gain control of large portions of the countryside through a protracted guerrilla war.

The communist strategy for guerrilla war combines military and political elements. For example, while raids by the NPA have specific military objectives, such as weakening the AFP or collecting arms, their cumulative effect is intended to be political in nature. As Francisco Nemenzo has pointed out, the NPA's raids:

> . . . back up the farmers in their confrontations with the landlords. The landlords are afraid now. People confront them on wages and benefits and then the landlords assume they are backed up by the NPA, even though sometimes they really aren't. And so then the farmers are in a strong position, they know they need the NPA. Without the NPA they are nothing.[26]

The close relationship between the military and the political dimensions of the insurgency is also seen in the process of communist infiltration and organization of the rural areas. First, a small Armed Propaganda Team (APT) made up of communists from an adjoining area undertakes an investigation to determine the key problems and grievances in the target barrio, and identifies individuals who would make effective and credible activists. The APTs preach "the evils of feudalism and imperialism, but in practical terms a farmer could comprehend: his high interest rates were the inevitable product of an immoral system imposed on millions of farmers".[27]

Next, the APT establishes an Organizing Committee (OC) of ten to fifteen people representing all sectors of the barrio, or in some areas, committees for each sector, such as women, youth, and fishermen. The OC then calls mass meetings to discuss the main problems of the community and suggest solutions to them. At the same time, a CPP branch is organized in the barrio, and the OC becomes a Barrio Revolutionary Committee (BRC) and takes on government functions, with subcommittees for such problems as health and production.[28]

It is only after the BRC is established and a mass base of support is organized that a local NPA unit is formed. At this point the barrio is essentially under the control of the communist shadow government. The communists staff and control the local armed militia, assume all police duties, settle domestic disputes, and mete out "revolutionary" justice. "Revolutionary taxes" are collected and rudimentary health care and education are provided. Land rents might be reduced and small income generating projects might be started.

By using these tactics the CPP was estimated to have built a "mass base" of between four and five million supporters in 1987, or almost 10 per cent of the population.[29] In 1987 the CPP-NPA influenced or infiltrated about 20 per cent of the Philippines' 41,600 *barangay*. In some provinces, however, the percentage of communist influenced or infiltrated *barangay* was as high as 35 per cent. In late November 1987 the then Secretary of Defence Rafael Ileto acknowledged that there were sixty communist guerrilla fronts throughout the country, almost half of which were in Mindanao.[30]

During the early 1980s the rapid growth of the communist movement occurred with very little foreign support. However, without an external supply of weapons, the NPA's expansion was limited by the relatively low-powered arms it could purchase domestically or capture during encounters with the AFP. Consequently, in 1986 the CPP leadership began to seek foreign funds more actively. In November 1987 General Ramos claimed that the CPP and NPA had raised some US$2.5 million from external sources in 1986 and predicted that the amount would increase to US$8 million in 1987. Ramos also claimed that the NPA had collected "revolutionary taxes" of about US$7.5 million in 1986 and 1987.[31] In late 1987 Satur Ocampo admitted that the NDF had "support networks" in more than twenty-five foreign countries.[32]

Communism in the Cities: The Battle for Davao City

Beginning in 1982 the NPA quietly began to infiltrate some of the poorer sections of Davao City, the Philippines' third largest city. The NPA sought to establish communist strongholds there in order to make it a testing ground for the Party's urban revolutionary tactics. The Davao experiment worked remarkably well at first, and for a while it looked as if the communists were on the verge of winning the battle for control of the city. By early 1985 several sections of this sprawling city had been taken over by the NPA. The communists began to entertain the idea that a massive urban uprising or insurrection might be possible − a dramatic departure from the Maoist strategy of protracted guerrilla warfare in the countryside. But within two years − by early 1987 − the NPA had been driven out of most of the city by the government with the critical support of Davao's vigilante groups. For the communists, the Davao City experiment went from success to failure. Their experience highlighted many of the strengths and weaknesses of the communists' urban tactics.

Davao City, with about 800,000 people, is located on the south-western coast of the island of Mindanao. Although Davao is classified as a city, its borders are so expansive that it actually includes considerable amounts of rural area. Consequently, although Davao is the Philippines' third largest city in terms of population, it does not rank among the top twenty cities in terms of population density.

The city has a well-deserved reputation for being an unruly, "frontier town" where "guns, goons, and gold" continue to dominate many aspects of life, including politics. Like the rest of Mindanao, Davao City has received relatively little attention and assistance from the national government in faraway Metro Manila. Consequently, most Davaoeños feel distant from the central government, politically as well as geographically. In the 1986 presidential election, for example, Davao City voted overwhelmingly against Marcos.

In 1982 small groups of NPA guerrillas, called Armed City Partisans (ACPs), first moved into the Agdao section of Davao City, a slum where some 120,000 people (about a sixth of the city's population) live as illegal squatters without adequate water or sanitation. As is the communist practice in the rural areas, the ACPs began by identifying and redressing local grievances, imposing much needed order, and enlisting new recruits. They also did not hesitate to "liquidate" more than thirty members of the local CHDF in Agdao. By using this combination of responsiveness, organization, and intimidation the ACPs, by 1984, had gained effective control of Agdao. Government officials, the police, and even the military did not dare to enter the area, which became known to Filipinos as "Nicaragdao".

From their base in Agdao the NPA mounted attacks on government officials, soldiers, and policemen throughout the city, and began to move into other slum areas such as Punta Dumalag. Davao City became known as the murder capital of the Philippines. In 1986 an estimated 900 people were killed in combat between the government and the communists. NPA "sparrows" killed policemen and CHDF members to demonstrate their power and to acquire weapons. Government security forces and the private armies of leading politicians and businessmen retaliated by attacking almost anyone suspected of being a communist. Check-points dotted the city and the military regularly mounted "zoning" operations in which they sealed off and conducted house-to-house search-and-arrest operations in areas suspected to harbour rebels. The military's ham-handed tactics netted few, if any, communists and it was often innocent residents who were arrested or caught in the cross-fire. According to William Chapman, "selective killings [by the NPA] triggered elephantine responses from the government and brought more and more sympathizers to the rebel side".[33] For most of the city's apolitical and law-abiding residents, however, the primary sentiment was fear.

In late 1985 and early 1986 a combination of factors caused the tide to begin to flow against the communists. First, there was growing popular dissatisfaction with the NPA's tactics. The NPA had become increasingly ruthless in the areas they controlled, exacting high taxes from individuals and businesses and meting out harsh revolutionary justice, including arbitrary executions for minor offences.

The second key factor contributing to the demise of the NPA in Davao City was the rise of the anti-communist vigilante movement aided by the military. At the forefront of the movement was Alsa Masa (Masses Arise), a group initially comprised of CHDF members, former members of the NPA, and the followers (and body-guards) of local political leaders. With the encouragement and support of the local military commander, the Alsa Masa challenged the NPA at their own game – namely, the armed occupation, organization, control and surveillance of barrios in Davao City.

A third important factor, though one not known at the time, was a spreading paralysis of the NPA in Mindanao caused by an extensive internal purge of suspected Deep Penetration Agents (DPAs). DPAs were government informers who had joined the ranks of the NPA in Mindanao during its rapid growth in the early 1980s. In late 1985 the NPA leadership realized that its ranks had been seriously infiltrated and thus began a purge of the suspected DPAs. The purge released a wave of deadly paranoia that resulted in a bloodbath. Although no one knows exactly how many rebels died, estimates vary from a few hundred to as many as six hundred. The purge decimated the local NPA leadership and left many guerrilla units demoralized and confused.

Later, senior Party members acknowledged that the purge had gone out of control and that a number of innocent and dedicated members of the NPA had been unjustly criticized, demoted, or killed.[34]

By the end of 1986 the communists were on the defensive, and in early 1987, thanks to the rapid growth of the Alsa Masa and a wave of anti-communist hysteria, the NPA was driven out of the city, though they were still free to operate in the nearby rural areas. Most residents of Davao City seemed to prefer the presence of the Alsa Masa to that of the NPA. However, some also feared the potential for intimidation and abuse by the vigilantes. As one reporter observed: "The guerilla red-painted warnings to Agdao residents – 'Military informants will be shot' – have been replaced by new Alsa Masa threats, scrawled on crude wooden signs: 'NPA informers will have their heads blown off'."[35] It appeared that the Alsa Masa was as heavy-handed as the NPA in certain respects. Any kind of social or political activism was suspected to be communist inspired and opposition to the Alsa Masa's ideology and methods was not tolerated. When one Alsa Masa leader in Punta Dumalag was asked how many Alsa Masa members there were, he replied simply: "Everyone".

What were the lessons learned from the Davao City experiment? First, both the AFP and the NPA learned that public opinion mattered – that they could not afford to alienate the public by the indiscriminate use of violence. Secondly, both sides learned that vigilante groups were an effective counter-insurgency tool, although with many potential problems. Thirdly, the NPA probably learned that public support was fickle and could change quickly, based at least in part on the public's impression of which side was winning and was able to assert control. Finally, the communists probably also learned that an urban uprising required a better organized, more committed, and better armed mass base than the one they had developed in Davao City.

The AFP Versus the NPA

The years of neglect of the AFP under Marcos and its further politicization under Aquino combined to seriously undermine the AFP's ability to counter the guerrilla war being waged by the NPA. Besides being divided, the AFP was weakened by numerous problems that could not be solved overnight. Few officers had a sophisticated understanding of guerrilla warfare and how to defeat it; troops were demoralized by poor pay, benefits, and equipment; supplies of essential material were inadequate or non-existent; and logistical support was slow and unreliable. Equally important, the years of military abuses had caused many Filipinos, particularly those in the countryside, to view the military with fear and hostility. As a result, even though the AFP leadership claimed during 1986 that the Aquino government was keeping it from fighting the insurgents, it is extremely unlikely that the AFP could have mounted a successful counter-insurgency effort. One U.S. Government official, summing up the situation in 1987, said: "the military is so ineffective it uses the civilian government as a scapegoat for its own inadequacies and inefficiencies".[36]

Part of the problem facing the AFP was that it simply was not large enough to easily defeat the expanded insurgency. In 1986 it was estimated that the NPA had at least 22,500 regular and 15,000 part-time guerrillas with a total of 11,200 to 11,900 firearms. (The size of the MNLF was estimated to be 5,300 to 6,000 armed regulars.) The government, with 146,000 regular soldiers, 42,000 men in the Philippine Constabulary, and about 50,000 members in the Civilian Home Defence Force, appeared on paper to have an overwhelming advantage in troop strength. However, in addition to fighting the insurgency, the mission of the AFP included protecting government leaders and guarding government property, enforcing law and order, guarding ballot boxes, and disciplining belligerent provincial warlords.[37] Consequently, as Gareth Porter noted in 1987, "the actual balance of combat superiority is far less advantageous to the AFP. According to a Defence Ministry official, the AFP has between 40,000 and 50,000 troops in actual combat with the NPA at one time or another, thus giving it a superiority of 2 or 3 to 1, depending on which figure for NPA full-time guerrillas is used".[38] Given the many other problems of the AFP, its slight numerical superiority was clearly inadequate to contain the communist insurgency, let alone eliminate it.

The AFP had other important shortcomings. Only a small percentage of government forces was capable of conducting sophisticated counter-insurgency operations. More than 90 per cent of all officers in the field were from the reserve officers training programme, and lacked the more rigorous training provided at the élite Philippine Military Academy.[39] Poor logistical support was another major problem.

Inadequate transportation and communications equipment made offensive operations difficult, and defensive positions precarious. For example, in a rebel attack on government forces in Kalinga Apayao in early January 1988 it took about eight hours for the attack to be reported to the provincial command and four more hours for government forces to be reinforced by helicopter, during which time they were reportedly pounded by rebel mortar fire.[40] Often equipment, when available, was ill-suited for counter-insurgency efforts. Sixteen Sikorsky helicopters purchased in 1983 were reported to be so expensive and difficult to operate that they were rarely used in military operations.

Another problem concerned strategy and tactics. Whereas the NPA had clear-cut military and political objectives, the AFP continued to have a reactive, "body count" mentality reminiscent of the U.S. Army during the Vietnam War.[41] As Gareth Porter has noted:

> . . . the military's counterinsurgency has long since taken a life of its own that has little or nothing to do with objective measures of reducing insurgency. The generals and colonels who plan and implement counterinsurgency fall back on programs and operations not so much because they have been successful in the past, but because they are familiar and because the officers know no alternative except inaction.[42]

One potentially important element of the counter-insurgency effort, the government's rebel returnee programme, was little more than a programme in name and on paper only. Beginning in late 1986, the Aquino government promised amnesty, land, and jobs for surrendering rebels. It was only able to make good on the first of these promises with any consistency. The government claimed that some 7,000 rebels surrendered between late 1986 and early 1988. However, Task Force Detainees and international human rights monitoring groups have claimed that many people were forced by local military and vigilantes to make fake surrenders. A returnee centre in Davao del Norte visited by the author in early 1988 was barely functioning. Most of the shrinking number of former rebels still in residence there had minimal education and few marketable skills, and were unable to find employment. Said one: "If I had known there wouldn't be work I wouldn't have left [the communist movement]."

Finally, recurring human rights abuses by the military and the paramilitary CHDF also undermined the government's counter-insurgency effort. The military's recognition of the importance of avoiding human rights abuses increased under General Ramos. But distinguishing between combatants and non-combatants is difficult in a guerrilla war, and as noted in Chapter 7, there continued to be intentional as well as accidental abuses by military and paramilitary forces.

By 1988, however, there were some signs of improvements within the AFP. Regional commanders were given greater autonomy and some units were reassigned from larger towns, where they had been garrisoned, to smaller towns and villages so that they could better patrol the countryside. The increases in military pay in 1987 boosted morale, and reduced the soldiers' need to steal from civilians or to sell their weapons and ammunition to the NPA. Military intelligence gathering also improved, leading to the capture of a number of communist leaders. Civic action and propaganda were also more effectively utilized. Small units called Special Operations Teams (SOTs) were used with some success to "counter-organize" villages surrounding NPA base areas. Finally, some military commanders did a better job of avoiding the excesses and mistakes of the Marcos era and became more adept at working with religious and civilian groups and the media.

Because of these improvements President Aquino confidently claimed that 1988 would be the year the government "broke the back" of the communist insurgency. At the time it seemed that there was some basis for her optimism. The CPP clearly had been set back by its own internal divisions, the capture of some of its leaders, improvements in the AFP, the spread of vigilante groups, and economic growth. However, AFP reports of NPA losses and surrenders, encounters, and numbers of captured arms were of questionable reliability. Indeed, a leaked AFP internal report indicated that despite the AFP's public assertions, the communist rebels continued to initiate the majority of encounters with the AFP throughout 1988. Moreover, while there were some parts of the country (such as parts of Mindanao and Luzon) where the military was successful, there were other regions where the communists were holding their own or expanding.

In sum, at the end of 1988 it was still too early to tell if, in fact, the tide had turned against the insurgency. Under the best of circumstances it would take several years of constant socio-economic

improvements combined with an effective counter-insurgency strategy
to seriously weaken the insurgency. If this was not forthcoming, it
seemed likely that the communist insurgency would persevere, losing
strength in some places and gaining it in others, but remaining capable of defying the government and growing rapidly if socio-economic
conditions took a serious turn for the worse.

Rise and Decline of the Legal Left

The advent of Aquino brought an immediate and dramatic increase
in political freedom — what the left called "democratic space". The
growth of democratic space presented the legal (non-communist)
left with challenges as well as opportunities. It provided them with
unprecedented visibility and freedom. However, it also introduced the
new and unfamiliar phenomenon of electoral politics, and pitted them
against a highly popular president. Furthermore, the left's decision
to take advantage of the democratic space eventually exposed many
of its members to attacks by right-wing extremists. By early 1988
attacks on the left by members of the military and vigilante groups
had driven many members underground or out of the country. For
those whose lives were threatened because of their political beliefs,
the political freedoms enshrined in the 1987 Constitution became
a hollow promise.

The return to democracy resulted in the expansion, multiplication,
and increased differentiation of the many groups that made up the left.
The differences among them increased as new ideologies emerged,
new priorities arose, and new political tactics were developed. Consequently, the label "the left" referred to a broad and varied spectrum of
groups ranging from progressive pro-Aquino groups to the communist
National Democratic Front. In between these two ends of the spectrum
were groups such as the Christian Democrats, Popular Democrats,
Socialists, Social Democrats, independent Marxists, and other cause-
oriented and sectoral groups.

The distinction between the two ends of the spectrum — the progressive reformers on the centre-left and the revolutionary communists
on the extreme left — was clear enough. But as one travelled along
this continuum the distinctions between groups became blurred. The
simplest distinction, of course, was whether or not the leftist groups

advocated armed revolution. The groups advocating "armed struggle" included most of the twelve organizations that were members of the NDF, and several small socialist groups. This distinction lost some of its meaning, however, because some leftist groups (such as Bayan and some members of the NDF) did not openly advocate armed struggle, but were sympathetic towards those groups that felt it was necessary.

A second way to differentiate among groups on the left is by identifying those influenced or controlled by the CPP. This category clearly included most of the members of the NDF (such as the Nationalist Youth, the Association of Nationalist Teachers, and Christians for National Liberation). However, this was also not an entirely accurate indicator, because CPP influence extended in varying degrees to groups not belonging to the NDF. For example, it was difficult to determine exactly how much influence the CPP had over Bayan, the KMU, and the KMP. The CPP also exerted a measure of direct or indirect influence over some human rights and cause-oriented groups and social action organizations. It is therefore impossible to generalize about the extent of communist infiltration and the influence of these groups. In some cases the CPP actually established and closely controlled "front" organizations; in others, it exerted great but not total influence; and in still others it was influential on some but not on all issues.

A third way to differentiate groups is by their political ideologies, platforms, and strategies. The range of leftist ideologies includes "popular democracy", "national democracy", "social democracy", and Marxist and Christian socialism. All of these ideologies advocate mass mobilization and political organization, redistributing economic and political power, reducing "militarism", conducting an "independent and nationalist" foreign policy, and controlling or reducing foreign economic and cultural influence in the Philippines. They differed in varying degrees on issues such as the desired form of government, the scope of land reform, and the level of private and foreign participation in the economy. They were further differentiated from 1986 to 1988 by the relative size and composition of their membership, the level of militancy they advocated, and their willingness to enter into a "united front" alliance with the NDF.

Despite the multiplicity of groups and the sometimes murky differences between them, it is possible to group them into three major blocs based on their ideology and tactics. The three are: the National Democrats (Natdems), the Popular Democrats (Popdems), and the Social and Liberal Democrats (Socdems and Libdems). Straddling the line between the Natdems and the Socdems was "Bisig", a small but influential group of militant socialists or "independent Marxists".

The Natdems were militantly opposed to a return to traditional élite democracy, capitalistic and export-oriented economic development, and continuing close ties with the United States. The Natdems coalesced to form Bayan in 1985 and then Partido ng Bayan (PnB) in July 1986. PnB claimed to be "the political party of patriotic and progressive workers, peasants and students, professionals, businessmen and other sectors of the middle class". It is noteworthy that this description reflected PnB's recognition, in the wake of the February revolution, of the importance of the middle class as a political force and source of support.

The Popdems were represented by the Volunteers for Popular Democracy (VPD) led by Edicio de la Torre, a former priest and founder of the Christians for National Liberation, and Horacio "Boy" Morales, the former head of the NDF. The Popdems advocated the replacement of traditional élite democracy with "popular democracy". According to de la Torre, "The idea is simply that the people must have means of direct participation in government so that they retain a certain amount of power".[43] He advocated a system that included both representative and popular democracy, involving a pluralistic, multi-party system with institutions and mechanisms that allow for "direct democracy" based on cause-oriented groups, "people's councils", and mechanisms for recall, initiative, and referendum.[44]

The most centrist groups were the Social and Liberal Democrats, whose members came from the ranks of cause-oriented and sectoral groups, human rights groups, and other non-traditional political organizations. They advocated liberal democracy, socio-economic reform that emphasized a more equitable distribution of wealth, and the removal of the U.S. military bases. Many prominent Socdems and Libdems had supported Aquino's bid for the presidency. As a result, a number of Socdem and Libdem leaders such as Raul Manglapus, Jose Diokno, Joker Arroyo, Butz Aquino, Teofisto Guingona, and Emmanuel Soriano joined the new government. They became the liberal or progressive wing of the Aquino coalition.

The issue of these three groupings' relations with the Aquino government brought their differing ideologies and approaches into sharp relief. The centrist Social and Liberal Democrats enthusiastically supported Aquino in the hope that she would make progressive and populist reforms. The Popular Democrats were less sanguine about the progressive nature of the new government. They opted for "critical collaboration" – supporting the government on certain issues and criticizing it on others. Still further to the left were the National Democrats who had few illusions about the government's progressivism and supported Aquino largely because she was seen as the lesser evil compared to a military government.

The National Democrats saw the Aquino government as a curious, contradictory, and inherently unstable coalition of "liberals" and "fascists". Bayan initially adopted a policy of "vigilant and principled support" of the new government, but there was general skepticism that the liberal forces would be able to consolidate a position of political dominance over the rightists. Moreover, they expected that the new government would not attempt any genuine and significant reforms in the socio-economic area, and that the dynamics of social and political polarization would gradually reassert themselves.[45]

The independent Marxists of Bisig also welcomed the replacement of Marcos by Aquino. They were quick to note, however, that the change in government was merely from a "bourgeois dictatorship" to a "bourgeois democracy". They also believed that the Aquino government would be unstable because of the indecisiveness and timidity they felt were inherent in bourgeois democratic regimes. According to Francisco Nemenzo, a Marxist scholar and the leader of Bisig:

> the new government is excessively cautious because it wants to avoid confrontation with powerful forces in the neocolonial establishment. Instead of taking the fullest advantage of the revolutionary circumstances that brought it to power and capitalizing on the tremendous popularity it still enjoys, it hesitates to tamper with socio-economic and political structures other than those directly linked to Marcos.[46]

All of these groups initially staged rallies, sometimes together and sometimes separately, to press for political reforms, labour rights, land reform, debt repudiation, a cease-fire, and closure of the U.S.

bases. They then shifted their efforts to lobby for progressive and nationalistic provisions in the Constitution. During late 1986 and early 1987 Bayan, for example, focused on lobbying the public hearings held by the Standing Committees of the Constitutional Commission as they travelled around the nation. When these nationalist provisions were not included, Bayan campaigned for a "no" vote against the Constitution while the VPD, Bisig, and the Social Democrats campaigned for a "critical yes".[47]

After the Constitution was ratified in February 1987 the left's focus shifted to the May 1987 congressional elections. Here a major split occurred between the communist and non-communist left. The communist left, as represented by the NDF, rejected the value of the elections. According to the NDF's newspaper, *Liberation*:

> Beneath the veneer of political pluralism which the new system of electoral politics offers, is the process of political consolidation, where the dominant Aquino faction establishes its political preeminence over other sections of the ruling elite. . . . Meanwhile, the basic issues of national sovereignty, of land, of poverty, disease and miseducation are set aside.[48]

The non-communist left, however, decided to participate in the elections for the first time since 1946, when six victorious leftists were barred from taking their seats in the old Congress. With this history in mind Edicio de la Torre of VPD identified some of the challenges facing the left in the May elections. According to him, "the popular movement must learn to handle both traditional and new methods of electoral struggle. Candidates will have to do the same: in addition to dodging bullets and death squads, they will have to avoid being unseated on charges of fraud and terrorism, as happened in the late 1940s".[49] He might also have added that the left faced the additional challenges of Aquino's popularity and the continuing appeal of traditional, personality-based politics.

To meet these challenges, the left formed the Alliance for New Politics (ANP) as an umbrella for the Partido ng Bayan, Bayan, and the VPD. The ANP's seven-member slate of senatorial candidates included Bernabe "Kumander Dante" Buscayno, founder of the NPA; Horacio "Boy" Morales, a former leader of the NDF; Jose Burgos, publisher of *Malaya*; Crispin Beltran, Chairman of the leftist KMU labour federation; and Jaime Tadeo, head of the KMP peasant federation. The ANP also fielded 104 candidates for the House, including Leandro Alejandro, the Bayan Secretary-General.

The ANP campaign called for, among other things, genuine land reform, "national industrialization" based on greater control of foreign investment, removal of the U.S. bases, strengthening of labour rights, a new foreign debt policy, and improvement of conditions for women. The ANP hoped it would win a few senate seats based on what it claimed to be a "mass base" of 3.5 to 3.9 million voters. They expected to do well in the Western and Eastern Visayas, Bicol, Mindanao, Central Luzon and Cordilleras.

However, on 11 May none of the ANP's senatorial candidates came close to being elected. The two most popular ANP candidates, "Boy" Morales and Bernabe Buscayno, each received just over 1.3 million votes, placing them fifty-fifth and fifty-sixth respectively (out of a total field of eighty-four). In the House races, only two ANP candidates were elected (from Samar and South Cotabato), and about twenty other non-ANP candidates who had been endorsed by the ANP won House seats. Overall, the ANP's share of the national vote was much smaller than was expected by many, but it also demonstrated that the ANP had pockets of support in almost all parts of the Philippines.

The poor showing of the left in the elections was caused by a variety of factors. To begin with, the left, like the right, was a victim of Aquino's popularity. In addition to this, the left's call for more change was not appealing to most voters, many of whom felt that they had experienced enough upheaval and change for a while. Recognizing this, Bernabe Buscayno observed during the campaign that, "People are in no mood to support armed struggle. . . . The people want peace. They want to give Cory and democracy a chance".[50] The ANP also had no experience with election campaigns and was hampered by a lack of funds. Finally, it also faced harrassment, intimidation, and vote buying. The ANP claimed that fifty of its volunteers were arrested and detained during the course of the campaign and eighteen were killed.[51]

It has also been suggested that the left's defeat was due more to a flawed electoral strategy than to an absence of a large pool of progressive voters. According to this view, there was a strong tendency on the part of the left to approach the campaign simply as an opportunity for raising issues and doing educational work among the masses. Consequently, the ANP failed to make the logistical arrangements necessary to actually turn out the vote on election day and to combat cheating during the vote count.[52] According to the leftist Institute for Popular Democracy, "Ironically, for cause-oriented organizations that are considered to be good at organizing, one of the key shortcomings was in organization . . . . The main failing was at the stage of actual voting, counting and transmission of the count".[53]

The May 1987 elections proved to be the high point of the legal left. The period following the elections was marked by increasing political polarization, resurgent extremism, and the erosion of the left's democratic space. Following the election, Bayan and the PnB shifted from "vigilant and principled support" of the Aquino government to "principled opposition". They returned to organizing demonstrations, particularly in support of land reform, and in August mounted a successful *welgang bayan* (national strike) against the Aquino administration to protest oil price increases. The threat of the *welgang bayan* forced the Aquino government to roll back most of the price increases, and thus contributed significantly to a prevalent perception at the time that the government was weak and adrift. This situation encouraged extremists in the military to launch the nearly successful coup attempt on 28 August.

Political violence also increased. In early June, Bernabe Buscayno was ambushed and wounded. Three weeks after the August coup attempt Bayan Secretary General Leandro Alejandro was murdered; and in November a university president sympathetic to the left was ambushed and wounded. The assailants were never arrested, but were suspected to be members of the military, the police, or a vigilante group. During the latter half of 1987 the tally of policemen, soldiers, and officials in Metro Manila assassinated by the Alex Boncayao Brigade, the NPA "sparrow" unit, grew rapidly. Increasingly, the members of the legal left became the targets of extremists on both the far left and the far right.

By the end of 1987 the increasing influence of the military, the sacking of Executive Secretary Joker Arroyo, and the crack-down on "illegal" strikes had led many in the legal left to dismiss any remaining hopes for progressive policies under Aquino. The murder of Leandro Alejandro and other acts of intimidation prompted many in the legal left to go underground. By 1988 some of the more prominent members, such as Edicio de la Torre, had gone abroad or were in hiding. De la Torre, who had been a detainee during martial law, once noted, "Those who are committed to legal struggle get thrown into jail first". He might have added they also run the risk of being the first ones to be shot.

Conclusion: The Left's Problems and Prospects

The advent of the Aquino coalition put the legal left in a delicate position. It was compelled to support the Aquino government against the extreme right, for if the government was too unstable it would have invited a military take-over that would have been detrimental to its democratic space. The left also had to find a way to support the government without abandoning its own ideology and constituencies. However, if the Aquino government became too secure and popular it would not need the support of the left, which would then lose its already limited influence. Consequently, the legal left found itself in a largely reactive role.

The May 1987 congressional elections revealed both the continuing strength of traditional politics and the inexperience and weaknesses of the ANP as a political party. After the ANP's poor showing in the congressional elections the left essentially abandoned the electoral struggle. By early 1988 the democratic space of the legal left had been seriously eroded. The result was increased political polarization and the strengthening of extremists both within the CPP and on the far right.

The communist movement also faced a number of new challenges and problems during the first two years of the Aquino government. Unlike the Marcos government, the Aquino government was popular and legitimate in the eyes of most Filipinos. Moreover, Aquino was successful, at least at first, at making the communists engage in a primarily political contest with the government, rather than a military one. This was favourable for the government, given Aquino's popularity and the AFP's weaknesses.

The CPP was also weakened by its own internal disputes between hardliners, who emphasized the primacy of armed struggle (many of them were active in Mindanao, and were therefore known as the

Mindanao faction), and moderates or "rectificationists", who felt greater emphasis should be placed on political struggle. Disagreement over this fundamental issue caused divisions in the Party over the cease-fire, its activities in the cities, and the congressional and local elections. By late 1987, however, a degree of unity had been restored (or enforced) within the CPP following the triumph of the Mindanao faction. The triumph of the hardliners was due in large part to the fact that they could claim that the electoral struggle had been discredited by the left's poor showing in the elections and by the growing power of the military and the vigilantes. Their victory represented the continuation of the historical, essentially Maoist, approach to the insurgency.

By mid-1988 the military strength of the NPA appeared to have diminished in some parts of the country and it had lost some of its aura of invincibility. This was due to the DPA purge in Mindanao, NPA abuses in Davao City, the defection and/or capture of a number of its leaders, and the committing of tactical military mistakes in provinces such as Negros Occidental. These mistakes, combined with some improvement in the combat and intelligence capabilities of the AFP and the reassertion of local authority (whether by the civilian government, the military, local war-lords or vigilante groups) challenged the NPA's ability to hold on to some of the areas they controlled and made expansion more difficult and time consuming.

In sum, the communists have suffered political and military setbacks; but many, if not all, of the underlying social and economic problems that gave rise to the insurgency remain. If the past history of the communist movement is an indication of the future, the CPP and the NPA will continue to be flexible and pragmatic and will learn to adjust to present and future circumstances. This suggests that they will continue to have a strong, if not expanding base of support. In the coming years the movement may benefit from frustration caused by unfulfilled expectations and from continued poverty and inequity in the countryside.

NOTES

1. *Ang Bayan*, 29 March 1987, p.2.
2. William Chapman, *Inside the Philippine Revolution* (New York: W.W. Norton, 1987), p.83.

3. *St. Petersburg Times*, 26 November 1987, p.44A.

4. Ateneo-Social Weather Stations, *Public Opinion Report, June 1986* (Quezon City: Ateneo de Manila University and Social Weather Stations, 1986).

5. Reprinted in *Kasarinlan* 2, no.1 (3rd qtr. 1986):65.

6. The 1986 rectification campaign was the continuation of a recurring debate within the CPP over the relative importance of armed and political struggles. This issue first caused a sharp split in the Party in 1978, when the leadership of the Manila-Rizal regional committee, against the wishes of the Politburo of the Central Committee, decided to engage in the "electoral struggle" and forged an alliance with the Laban Party candidates contesting the Batasang Pambansa elections in Metro Manila. The CPP's decision to boycott the May 1984 Batasan elections met with somewhat less internal disagreement, but the decision to boycott the 1986 presidential election reignited the debate. According to Gareth Porter: "While no one in the party has denied the importance of a strong NPA, critics of the existing line have argued that an overemphasis on protracted armed struggle has obscured the possibilities for much earlier victory through political struggle, both legal and illegal, in urban areas, particularly Metro Manila." See Gareth Porter, *The Politics of Counterinsurgency in the Philippines: Military and Political Options*, Occasional Paper No.9 (Honolulu: University of Hawaii Center for Philippine Studies, 1987), p.32; and Gregg Jones, *Red Revolution: Inside the Philippine Guerrilla Movement* (Boulder: Westview Press, 1989), pp.156–63.

7. Porter, op. cit., p. 41.

8. Ibid., p.41.

9. Chapman, op. cit., p.251.

10. *Far Eastern Economic Review*, 18 June 1987, p.42.

11. *Ang Bayan*, 29 March 1987, p.2.

12. *Philippine Daily Inquirer*, 15 February 1987, p.10.

13. *Washington Post*, 18 May 1987, p.1.

14. According to the AFP, 88 policemen, soldiers, and civilians in Metro Manila were killed by urban guerrillas from January through October 1987. See the *Manila Chronicle*, 13 December 1987, p.1.

15. *Manila Chronicle*, 27 December 1987, p.12. Additionally, in late October three American servicemen were killed outside Clark Air Base – the first assassinations of Americans since April 1974. Although the attacks had all the markings of "sparrow" operations, the communists did not claim responsibility for the murders until late November, a month later. Apparently, the communists hesitated because the assassinations were a mistake and there were concerns that the acts would hurt the public image of the NPA.

16. *Manila Chronicle*, 18 January 1988, p.6.

17. Abelardo Aportadera, Jr., "Justice in the Philippines: A Case of Access to Two Parallel Judicial Systems", *Solidarity*, no.112 (May–June 1987), p.73.

18. *Ang Bayan*, January 1986, p.13.

19. Rosario Cruz Lucero, "Revolutionary Justice and Jurisprudence", *Solidarity*, no.112 (May–June 1987), p.77.

20. Ibid., p.77.

21. Ross Munro, "The New Khmer Rouge", *Commentary*, December 1985, p.21.

22. Larry Niksch, *Insurgency and Counterinsurgency in the Philippines* (Washington, D.C.: Library of Congress, Congressional Research Service, 1985), pp.30–32.

23. Chapman, op. cit. p.179.

24. *Liberation*, May–June 1985, p.13.

25. *Far Eastern Economic Review*, 15 January 1987, pp.14–17.

26. Francisco Nemenzo, quoted in Chapman, op. cit., p.115.

27. Chapman, op. cit., pp.108–9.

28. Porter, op. cit., p.8.

29. Ibid., pp. 8–9.

30. *Manila Chronicle*, 23 November 1987, p.1.

31. *Straits Times* (Singapore), 18 November 1987, p.5.

32. See the *Far Eastern Economic Review*, 28 July 1988, pp.13–14.

33. Chapman, op. cit., p.163.

34. See Jones, op. cit., pp. 265–68.

35. *Washington Post*, 2 February 1987, p. A24.

36. *Straits Times* (Singapore), 26 September 1987, p.10.

37. *Far Eastern Economic Review*, 26 November 1987, p.36.

38. Porter, op. cit., p.5.

39. *Far Eastern Economic Review*, 26 November 1987, p.37.

40. *Manila Chronicle*, 11 January 1988, p.1.

41. The specificity of the AFP's reports on the size of the insurgency suggests that the AFP can precisely measure the growth or decline of the CPP-NPA. In reality, the military's reports are considered less than reliable by most journalists because they are almost always based on unconfirmed or unconfirmable estimates.

42. Porter, op. cit., p.98.

43. Edicio de la Torre, "On the Post Marcos Transition and Popular Democracy", *World Policy Review* 4, no.2 (Spring 1987):345–46.

44. Ibid., pp.345–46.

45. See Max Lane, "The Urban Mass Movement in the Philippines" (unpublished manuscript, 1988), pp.46–50.

46. Francisco Nemenzo, "Beyond February: The Tasks of Socialists", *Kasar-inlan* 2, no.1 (3rd qtr. 1986):32.
47. See Lane, op. cit., p.66–77.
48. *Liberation*, April–May 1987, p.2.
49. de la Torre, op. cit., p.344.
50. *Washington Post*, 18 May 1987, p.A4.
51. *Manila Chronicle*, 10 May 1987, p.3.
52. Lane, op. cit., p.96.
53. Institute of Popular Democracy, "Between Honesty and Hope", *Diliman Review* 35, no.2 (1987):9.

chapter 10

The Politics of Economic Recovery and Reform

> As an agenda for action, our government has set three broad economic goals for the short and the long term. The first and most urgent is immediate provision for the least of our brothers, or the alleviation of mass poverty. The second goal is actually a means of reaching the first, and that is by the generation of employment. The third goal is to provide a just and equitable sharing of the fruits of development and the structuring of an economy where the benefits reach quickly and regularly to those on the lowest socio-economic levels.
>
> — Corazon Aquino
> 30 April 1986

When Corazon Aquino became president she assumed the leadership of a nation with an economy in its third consecutive year of serious decline. Many large and small businesses had failed, more than a quarter of the work-force was unemployed or underemployed, real per capita income had fallen more than 16 per cent from its high in 1982, and about 60 per cent of all families were living below the poverty line. Moreover, capital flight had drained the economy of a large amount of its lifeblood since 1981, and the country was saddled for years to come with the burden of repaying foreign debt totalling more than

322

US$26 billion. On top of all of this, the government Aquino inherited was virtually bankrupt and was being bled by the losses and debts of some 300 government-owned corporations.

Reversing this economic decline was a key objective of the Aquino government. A quick improvement in the economy was needed to demonstrate that the new government had the managerial ability which Marcos claimed he alone possessed. A turn-around was necessary to retain the support of Manila's business and middle classes, and to reduce the appeal of the communist movement in the cities, where it influenced the labour movement, and in the countryside where most of the rebels were recruited. It was also necessary to show international creditors, donors, and investors that the economic and political situation had stabilized and was improving. In short, economic recovery was crucial to the survival of the new government.

In the face of numerous intimidating economic problems, and with only relatively meagre resources available to it, the Aquino government achieved significant success in stopping and reversing the country's economic decline. Beginning in the second half of 1986 economic growth returned, buoyed by government spending and an explosion of pent-up consumer demand. Gross national product (GNP) grew 1.9 per cent in 1986, 5.9 per cent in 1987, and 6.7 per cent in 1988. Inflation was kept under control and unemployment declined. The result of this growth was an increase in real per capita GNP of almost 10 per cent by the end of 1988. But even with this gain, per capita income was still only 90 per cent of its 1982 level.

The economic recovery was caused in part by a timely improvement in the international economy in 1986 and 1987. Oil prices were relatively low, sugar and copra prices were strong, interest rates were moderate, and significant amounts of bilateral and multilateral loans and grants were made available. Moreover, the Aquino government had the added advantage of coming to power *after* the harsh economic stabilization policies required by the 1984 IMF (International Monetary Fund) programme had been, for the most part, successfully carried out by the Marcos government. "The costs of stabilization", economist Robert Dohner has noted, "had already been paid by, and were attributable to, the previous government".[1] Finally, the recovery was in no small part attributable to the generally sound policy decisions made by the Aquino government in the areas of employment generation (and wage increases for officials, teachers and the military), debt restructuring, and dismantling of Marcos-era monopolies.

A second objective of the Aquino government was to correct a variety of long-standing distortions and inequities in the economy. Although the government's commitment to economic reform appeared genuine, it was unclear how far reform would go. There was a broad consensus inside and outside the government that certain reforms were critical preconditions for short-term economic stabilization and recovery. There was somewhat less, but still considerable, agreement that other reforms were necessary to ensure long-term economic growth. Beyond this point, however, there was less agreement. Would the reforms merely undo the worst aspects of the Marcos-era economy and restore an updated version of the pre-martial law economy? Or would the reforms address fundamental economic problems that predated Marcos, such as the unequal distribution of economic assets and income, the collusion of the economic and political élite, an over-emphasis on import substitution manufacturing, and the relative neglect of the agricultural sector? The evidence provided in this chapter suggests that the government's commitment to far-reaching economic reform was limited, particularly when it held the potential for a significant redistribution of economic and political power.

This chapter assesses the Aquino government's and the Congress' approach to economic recovery and reform. It will not attempt a complete analysis of the government's economic policies or the Philippine economy.[2] Instead, it will be confined to examining: 1) the political debates and influences on major economic policy issues during the first two years of the Aquino government; and 2) the critical and controversial issues of agricultural development and agrarian reform.

Reversing the Economic Decline

During her presidential campaign, Corazon Aquino spelled out the broad outline of the economic programme she would implement if elected. Her programme was essentially market-oriented, reformist, and internationalist, reflecting the views of business leaders such as Jaime Ongpin and Jose Concepcion, and prominent economists such as Solita Monsod and Bernardo Villegas. She promised that her government would do the following:

1. Increase agricultural productivity and incomes;
2. Implement land reform;
3. Promote labour- rather than capital-intensive industry;
4. Reduce the government's role in the economy;
5. Dismantle the complex network of monopolies and favoured businesses controlled by Marcos's "cronies";
6. Seek but not rely on foreign investment; and
7. Renegotiate rather than repudiate the country's heavy foreign debt burden.

However, it was not until early June 1986 that President Aquino formally transformed her campaign promises into official policy with the publication of the government's *Policy Agenda for People-Powered Development*. In this document the government stated that "social justice will be the primary consideration in the pursuit of development objectives". It committed the government to breaking the "vicious cycle of real income declines, sluggish investment and poor trade performance and to steadily steer the economy towards sustainable growth". Over the medium-term, the government plan envisioned "an employment oriented, rural based development process which will lead to better export performance".[3] In December 1986 the government "policy agenda" was succeeded by a much more detailed five-year (1987–92) Medium-Term Philippine Development Plan prepared by the National Economic Development Authority (NEDA).

The Politics of Economic Policy-Making

Economic policy-making in the Philippines, as elsewhere, is shaped as much by political considerations as by purely economic ones. In the Philippines, however, many economic issues are somewhat more politicized than in other countries. The economic élite's historical manipulation of the government in order to defend and further its interests has created an inherent distrust among many Filipinos of the equitableness of the economic policy-making process. This traditional suspicion about who benefits from the government's economic policies was reinforced by the abuses of the Marcos regime. Because of this legacy, and the exceedingly unequal distribution of assets and income in the Philippines, many Filipinos view economic policy issues in terms of their impact on equity rather than their contribution to the overall growth or efficiency of the economy. The existence of a strong strain of economic nationalism has also caused many issues involving international economic relations to be seen as tests of the Philippines' sovereignty and independence.

Given the politicized nature of economic issues it was not surprising that the formulation of the Aquino government's economic programme and policies generated considerable controversy, both within the government and outside it. Within the Cabinet, the process of translating Aquino's very general campaign promises into specific economic policies triggered a series of major disagreements. Disputes occurred among Cabinet members over the new government's labour policies, the scope and speed of import liberalization, the handling of the country's foreign debt, and agrarian reform. These debates reflected the lack of consensus over economic issues that existed not just within the Cabinet, but throughout Philippine society.

The Constitutional Commission (Con Com) was another important forum for debate over the future of the nation's economy. The debate in the Con Com revolved around basic economic issues that Filipinos have argued over for more than forty years. One of the most fundamental of these is the question of the primacy of agricultural or industrial development. One school of thought, subscribed to by an unlikely coalition of wealthy import-substitution manufacturers and economic nationalists, has viewed rapid industrial development as the benchmark for, and ultimate goal of, economic development. The supporters of this school have sought (quite successfully over the years) protection for Filipino industries, exchange rate and credit policies favourable to import-substitution manufacturing, government subsidization of large industrial projects, and limits on foreign participation in the economy.

A differing school of thought has argued that there can be no short cuts to industrial development, and that industry can only be built on the foundation of a productive and affluent agricultural sector. This school has called for government resources to be concentrated on the agricultural sector; the promotion of labour-intensive rather than capital-intensive, and small-scale rather than large-scale industry; and for exchange rate policies that are neutral or beneficial to the agricultural sector. Ultimately, the commissioners opted for a compromise. The result was a constitutional provision that called for the state to "promote industrialization and full employment based on sound agricultural development and land reform".

Another area of debate in the Con Com was between the economic nationalists, who were in the minority, and the economic internationalists. There is, as we have seen, a powerful tradition of economic nationalism in the Philippines dating back to the 1950s. Coexisting within this tradition are two schools, one leftist and the other élitist. The leftist school is influenced by theories on imperialism and dependency dating from the 1950s and 1960s and by the country's unpleasant experiences in the 1980s with the World Bank, the International Monetary Fund, and commercial creditors. It views foreign (and particularly U.S.) economic interests as exerting neo-colonial control over the Philippine economy, and sees most international economic relations as being inherently exploitative.

The élitist school is decidedly non-leftist; but it is equally "nationalistic", although for entirely different reasons. This school consists of members of the economic (and political) élite who have prospered because of tariffs and quotas, exchange rate policies, cheap credit, government subsidies and other measures that have protected Filipino manufacturers from foreign competition in the Philippine market. Consequently, they see foreign competition as a threat to their own domination of the Philippine economy.

Arrayed against both the leftist and the élitist nationalists are economic internationalists who see foreign trade and investment as being beneficial to Filipino consumers, and to the Philippines' economic growth and international competitiveness. According to the internationalists, misdirected economic nationalism has been responsible for "a pervasive attitude that we need protection to prevent ourselves from being devoured by alien behemoths". They have opposed the nationalists' calls for protection, arguing that "to insist that the Filipino producer be shielded from competition is to say that he cannot fight". They have also criticized the nationalists for "numbing our self-confidence, belittling our self-image, devouring our sense of self-worth".[4]

The battle in the Con Com between these two schools was fought over two major issues. The first was the use of tariffs and quotas to protect domestic manufacturers. A compromise of sorts was reached and the Constitution proclaims that, "the State shall protect Filipino enterprises against *unfair* (emphasis added) foreign competition and trade practices". The second issue was the maximum level of foreign ownership to be permitted. The constitutional limit was set, in most cases, at 40 per cent, which was higher than what the nationalists preferred, but lower than the limits set by several other ASEAN countries that were more eager to attract foreign investment.

Economic Goals and Challenges

In this environment of crisis and controversy, the Aquino coalition attempted to formulate and implement the government's economic policies. It focused on five key economic objectives in 1986 and 1987:

1. Securing much needed new foreign aid;
2. Stimulating domestic consumption by increasing government spending on employment generating projects;
3. Freeing the economy from the numerous distortions caused by Marcos's policies and monopolies;
4. Restructuring and reducing the burden of the country's more than US$26 billion in foreign debt; and
5. Encouraging new domestic and foreign investment.

The results of the government's efforts were mixed, but in general successful.

The most immediate economic challenge the Aquino government faced was how to pay for itself. Because of Marcos's unchecked use of government funds for his re-election campaign, the Aquino team discovered that the government deficit in the first quarter of 1986 was already 40 per cent more than the US$330 million deficit originally planned for the entire year.[5] The additional financial drain caused by more than 300 government-owned corporations and financial institutions and domestic and foreign debt repayments caused the new government to project a deficit of about US$1.5 billion by year end. In response, the government immediately sought additional foreign assistance and increased its borrowing from domestic financial markets. Over the course of 1986 (and 1987 as well) it received more than US$1 billion in new foreign loans and grants to help keep it afloat.

The second challenge Aquino faced was having her economic programme accepted by the international financial community. Marcos's election-related spending had violated the government's 1984 agreement with the IMF. Rather than requesting for a waiver, the Aquino government decided to seek a new credit agreement with the Fund. In late July 1986 the IMF agreed to provide more than US$500 million in new credit facilities. In return, the government agreed to a package of structural reforms and performance targets.[6] In contrast to the terms of the 1984 agreement, the performance targets of the new agreement allowed the government to resort to moderate monetary growth and deficit spending to stimulate economic growth. However, the agreement also called on the government to implement a variety of economic reforms, some of which were politically difficult. These included import liberalization, tax reform, and the restructuring (and reduction in size) of government financial institutions such as the Philippine National Bank and the Development Bank of the Philippines.[7]

The Philippines needed the IMF loans to help finance the country's serious balance of payments shortfall. Consequently, the agreement, which was finalized in August 1986, was an essential prerequisite to short-term economic stabilization and medium-term recovery. It also served as a "seal of approval" for later negotiations on commercial debt restructuring and for securing new loans and grants from international donors.

Employment Generation

Another critical task facing the government was generating employment. In 1986 unemployment was more than 12 per cent, and more than 30 per cent of the work-force was underemployed. This meant that some 2.6 million employable Filipinos had no work and another 6.6 million had less work than they wanted. In Metro Manila the unemployment rate was more than 20 per cent and in the rural areas the underemployment rate was more than 40 per cent.[8] At the same time, the labour force continued to grow by at least 3.3 per cent annually, requiring that some 730,000 new jobs be created just to keep the unemployment rate from rising.[9]

The tragedy of a rapidly growing labour force in a declining (or even slowly growing) economy was and is readily apparent in the Philippines. It is personified in the men and women, young and old, who sit around with little or nothing to do. It is revealed by the growth of prostitution and theft. It is reflected in the low wages or salaries most Filipinos — including those with college degrees — receive for their work. It is also seen in the large number of Filipinos who seek work abroad. Sadly, one of the Philippines' most valuable exports is its own people, including construction workers and maids, nurses and entertainers, computer programmers and business executives. Between 1976 and 1987 the number of Filipinos working abroad increased almost tenfold from about 48,000 to almost 450,000.[10]

In an attempt to give a quick boost to employment (and therefore incomes) the Aquino government created the P3.9 billion (US$195 million) Community Employment and Development Programme (CEDP). The CEDP was intended to generate over 600,000 temporary jobs during the second half of 1986 and throughout 1987. The focus was primarily on employment generation in the rural areas, through the construction or improvement of roads and irrigation systems. The implementation of the project progressed slowly, however, in part because the disbursement of funds was often delayed by bureaucratic red-tape and wrangling. Consequently, by the end of 1986 only about half of the projects were under way or completed. In 1987 funding for the CEDP was increased to P8.6 billion (about US$410 million). The National Economic Development Authority estimated that some 405,000 temporary jobs were created in 1987 − 63 per cent of the number planned. Despite the delays in implementing the CEDP, and reports that some funds were misused or wasted, in general it was successful as a stop-gap measure.

In 1987 and 1988 the overall increase in economic activity generated about 1.1 million new jobs each year, resulting in a decline in the unemployment rate to about 10 per cent. As long as the economic recovery continues the prospects for job creation appear reasonably good. In the longer run, however, increases in employment large enough to absorb the pool of unemployed and underemployed Filipinos will have to come from the development of many small-scale and labour-intensive industries across the country, and particularly in the rural areas. Equally important, the rapid growth of the labour force will have to be slowed.

Labour Relations

In addition to being hurt by the high level of unemployment, the Philippine labour force had been the victim of a long-term decline in real wages caused by the excess labour supply, high inflation, and the

Marcos government's control of labour unions. Marcos sought to keep organized labour weak and labour costs low in order to maintain his own political power and to attract investment into manufacturing. He skilfully controlled the relatively small and fragmented labour movement through a combination of intimidation, co-optation, and manipulation of union rivalries.[11]

Following the ouster of Marcos, organized labour sought from the Aquino government the increases in wages, improvements in working conditions and rights denied it by Marcos. During 1986 unions took advantage of their new-found democratic space to organize and press for higher wages and other concessions. The result was a dramatic rise in labour militancy and strikes. In the first seven months of 1986 there were more strikes than in all of 1985.

The Aquino government, in contrast to its predecessor, initially was sympathetic towards labour. Labour Minister Augusto "Bobbit" Sanchez, a human rights lawyer, was a vocal proponent of increased labour rights. During the first months of the new government Sanchez criticized local and multinational management and advocated profit-sharing. His statements prompted business leaders – many of whom had supported Aquino in her presidential bid – to brand him as radical and anti-management. On Labour Day 1986 Aquino announced the revision of the labour code in ways seen as favourable to labour, and in succeeding months the government remained tolerant towards the mounting number of legal and illegal strikes. In an effort to reduce the growing hostility between labour and management, the government sought the creation of a voluntary "tripartite accord" on industrial relations among labour, management, and the government. But neither labour nor management was prepared to make significant concessions and little progress was made.

The government's embrace of labour was short-lived, however, and was ended by pressure from the business community and the military. In November 1986, following the resignation of Enrile as Defence Minister, Labour Minister Sanchez was removed from the Cabinet to placate members of the business community and the military who viewed him as "leftist". On Labour Day 1987 Aquino offered to provide an increase in the cost-of-living-allowance (COLA), but rejected labour's call for an increase in the minimum wage, prompting labour leaders to walk out of a Labour Day reception.

The August 1987 *welgang bayan* and coup attempt, however, forced

Aquino to heed labour's demands for an increase in the minimum wage. The *Far Eastern Economic Review* observed,

> For more than a year, President Aquino held extraordinary law-making powers (whicʰ ceased with the opening of the new Congress in July), but she avoided making any decree to increase the minimum wage, despite widespread pressure from labour, which had backed her rise to power. But on 3 October, she asked Congress to do what she had failed to do.[12]

In December the Congress passed, and Aquino signed into law, a bill increasing the statutory minimum wage earned by most workers by P10 to P11 per day (about US$.50). With this increase the minimum wage now ranged from a high of P64 (US$3) per day for industrial workers to P43 (about US$2) for non-plantation agricultural workers. The effect of the increase on real wages, however, was unclear, for in practice most small employers do not obey the law. Nevertheless, by 1988 the increase in the statutory minimum wage, the improvement in the economy and the defensiveness of the left all combined to produce a significant reduction in labour militancy.[13]

Reducing Government Intervention in the Economy

The Aquino government, to its credit, was quick to begin the complicated and politically sensitive process of reducing the government's excessive role in the economy. The Medium-Term Philippine Development Plan stated that "the government is determined to move away from the system of granting privilege to selected groups to a system which emphasizes equity, efficiency and social justice. Cronyism shall be eliminated, and monopolies shall be fully dismantled".[14]

The first step was the decontrol of key sectors of the economy, particularly the termination of the sugar and coconut monopolies created by Marcos. The dismantling of these two monopolies was done quickly and successfully. The dismantling of the coconut monopoly and the lifting of the ban on copra export in April, combined with a rise in international copra prices, benefited some 15 million coconut farmers. In June the sugar monopoly was abolished and sugar trading was decontrolled. This was followed by decontrol of wheat, soy bean, and meat imports.

The second step was the privatization of government-owned businesses, which was a major test of the government's commitment to reducing its role in the economy. The task of privatization was as essential as it was daunting. At the end of 1985 the government owned almost 300 corporations. The 14 largest government-owned non-financial corporations, which included the National Development Corporation, the Philippine National Oil Company, and the National Irrigation Authority, was responsible for a combined deficit of P11.6 billion (about US$580 million) in 1987. The deficit was projected to increase to P13.7 billion in 1988 (over US$650 million).[15] According to one analysis, "The hemorrhage of the state financial institutions, and dealing with their rapidly growing inventory of non-performing assets and acquired corporations, demanded immediate attention".[16]

In response to this problem, President Aquino quickly created the Presidential Commission on Good Government (PCGG) and appointed former Senator Jovito Salonga as its chairman. The PCGG became best known for its efforts to identify and sequester or take temporary control of companies and assets owned by Marcos and his cronies. However, it was also tasked with developing procedures for rehabilitating the government financial institutions and disposing of public corporations. Based on the recommendations of the PCGG, 130 government-owned and controlled corporations and 390 "non-performing assets" (NPAs) held by the Development Bank of the Philippines and the Philippine National Bank were transferred to a newly created Asset Privatization Trust (APT). In early May 1987, 117 government firms were approved for privatization, including National Steel, Philippine Airlines, the Manila Hotel, 5 commercial banks, 19 subsidiaries of the Philippine National Oil Company, 17 sugar mills, 11 cement companies, and several mining companies. The number was later reduced to 86, in part because of valid economic and legal considerations, but also in part because of the opposition of some officials within the new government to parting with the assets under their control.

Not surprisingly, the government's privatization programme became a source of controversy because of its potential impact on the (re)distribution of political and economic power. To some Filipinos it raised the spectre of the traditional "oligarchs" reviving their grip on the Philippine economy by buying up key government-owned firms (including firms that Marcos had divested them of a decade before). To others, privatization was viewed with suspicion because of fears that it would result in greater foreign control of the economy.

Political as well as financial and legal reasons caused the sale of government-owned corporations to proceed slowly. According to one study, there was "confusion about which corporations . . . received final approval for sale, and persistent delays and equivocation in offering major assets such as Philippine Airlines and the Manila Hotel despite the high degree of investor interest".[17] By mid-1988 only 9 government corporations had been sold and another 5 partially sold for a total of just over P2 billion (under US$100 million). By early 1989, 19 corporations had been fully or partially sold, generating P4.35 billion (about US$207 million).[18] Despite repeated statements by President Aquino of her commitment to privatization, little progress was made in the corporate sector.[19]

The sale of the NPAs, estimated to be worth P110 billion (about US$5.35 billion), also proceeded slowly. As of June 1987 only 4 NPAs had been sold and about three-quarters of the assets were still unsaleable because of unsettled legal claims. But by the end of 1987, the APT had sold assets worth P3.47 billion (about US$169 million), close to its target of P3.82 billion. By early 1989 more than 150 had been fully or partially sold for gross proceeds of P7.7 billion.[20]

There are many reasons why the privatization programme was bogged down, and why it is unlikely to make much progress in the future. These are:

1. The resistance within government departments to part with the companies under their control, for to do so meant the loss of income, influence, and patronage;
2. The pervasive suspicion that officials and well-connected business executives would illegally benefit from the disposition of government assets;
3. The concern among some government officials and politicians that they would be accused of "giving away the store" when assets were sold at a discount;
4. The fear of further concentration of economic (and therefore political) power in the hands of the existing élite and the Filipino-Chinese community;

5. The concern that, to the extent that the privatization of some government-owned corporations resulted in a reduction in their size, it would contribute to unemployment; and

6. The influence of economic nationalism, which created resistance to foreign ownership.

Collectively, these impediments to privatization amounted to the triumph of the adherents of the traditional approach to the political economy (in which the government maintains sizeable, if inefficient, corporate assets) over the supporters of a diminished government role in the economy.

Debt Restructuring and Relief

The Philippines was burdened with a foreign debt of more than US$28 billion at the end of 1986. More than half of it was owed to foreign, mainly American, commercial banks (about 15 per cent was yen denominated). A relatively high percentage of it — about 20 per cent — was short-term, maturing in one year or less. Three quarters of the debt was held by the Philippine government or government-owned corporations. In 1986 the Philippines paid its creditors about US$2.9 billion in principal and interest payments, an amount equal to 34 per cent of its total earnings from the export of goods and services.[21]

The economic consequences of the debt burden are numerous and profound. Like many other developing countries saddled with debt, since the mid-1980s the Philippines has been a net exporter of capital — that is, each year the Philippines has paid more in principal and interest payments than it has received in new foreign loans and grants. In the absence of new loans from commercial banks the Philippine economy has become increasingly dependent on a smaller pool of official loans and grants and foreign investment. This has created an acute shortage of foreign exchange for investment, trade, and exchange rate management, and slowed down economic growth.

The political consequences of the debt burden are equally serious. To begin with, the government is vulnerable to charges that it is protecting the interests of foreign creditors at the expense of the Filipino people's welfare. Secondly, the large debt payments the government has had to make (on both its domestic and foreign debts) have left it with inadequate revenues for expenditures on much needed salary

increases, social services, and investment in infrastructure. The destabilizing strikes in response to government attempts to raise oil
prices in August 1987 and the military's discontent over poor pay and
equipment are at least in part attributable to the government's debt
burden. According to Economic Planning Secretary Solita Monsod,

> It is ironic that the Philippine government could not afford the
> [US]$250 million reduction in revenues that would have resulted
> from the inclusion of crude oil and petroleum products in our tax
> and tariff reforms; could not afford the [US]$125 million increase
> in expenditures needed for the improvements in the military
> budget; because it had to pay in 1987 [US]$700 million more to
> its creditors than it was receiving in aid or official development
> assistance.[22]

The question of how to handle the country's heavy debt burden
caused sharp divisions within the Aquino Cabinet. Solita Monsod
argued that the government should consider the "selective repudiation"
of "unjust and illegal" foreign loans. Her position conflicted with that
of Finance Minister Jaime Ongpin and Central Bank Governor Jose
Fernandez, both of whom ultimately prevailed upon Aquino to uphold
her campaign pledge to rely on negotiated restructuring rather than
unilateral repudiation.

In November 1986 the Philippines began the long and complex
process of lightening the burden of its foreign debt payments by beginning negotiations aimed at restructuring its commercial bank debt.
Finance Minister Ongpin and Central Bank Governor Fernandez sought
a significantly reduced interest spread and an extended maturity of
twenty years for about US$12 billion in existing loans maturing from
October 1983 to December 1992. The twelve-bank Advisory Committee representing the Philippines' 483 commercial creditors offered
a slightly smaller reduction in the interest spread and a sixteen-year
maturity for only US$3 billion in existing loans maturing between 1987
and 1992. The two sides were unable to bridge the considerable gap,
and consequently an agreement on the commercial bank debt was
reached during 1986.[23] In March 1987 Ongpin met again with the
commercial banks and in late March the banks agreed to a spread
of 7/8 per cent over the London Interbank Offering Rate (LIBOR) on
a total of US$13.2 billion (including a US$2.9 billion short-term trade

facility) for seventeen years with a seven and a half-year grace period on principal repayments.

The debt agreement reduced interest payments by about US$82 million in 1987 and promised a total savings of some US$900 million.[24] The restructuring caused the country's external debt service burden as a percentage of exports to decline from 48 per cent in 1986 to 35 per cent in 1987.[25] Despite the restructuring, the net transfer of resources to creditors was estimated to be some US$1.7 billion in 1987.[26]

The economic benefit of the restructuring, such as it was, did not bring an end to the political controversy surrounding the foreign debt issue. Many Filipinos were resentful of the heavy-handedness and intransigence of the foreign banks during the negotiations. Resentment turned to outrage shortly after the agreement was concluded, when Argentina was given slightly better terms in its commercial debt agreement. President Aquino fuelled the flames further when she accused the commercial banks of strong-arm tactics and greed during her State of the Nation address at the opening of the Congress in July 1987. Following her address, several congressional committees began reviews of the debt situation and the debt agreement. Finance Secretary Ongpin, viewed as the chief architect of the commercial debt agreement, was attacked from all sides and removed from office in the Cabinet shuffle following the August 1987 coup attempt. In December he committed suicide. Congressional and popular resentment continued to simmer during 1988 and the Congress considered legislation limiting the country's foreign debt payments to a fixed percentage (from 10 to 20 per cent) of export earnings.

Import Liberalization and Foreign Investment

Signs of foreign penetration of the Philippine economy are almost everywhere. American and Japanese brands compete in and dominate many sectors of the economy. Filipinos drive Japanese cars and trucks, ride in Japanese buses, use Japanese electronic products, eat American fast food, drink Coca-Cola and Pepsi, and brush their teeth with Colgate and Pepsodent toothpaste. Many Filipinos instinctively view foreign brands — even if they are locally produced — as superior to their local counterparts.

Many Filipinos, however, also resent the extensive presence, and in many cases domination, of foreign products and corporations. (In 1987, for example, Caltex Oil was the Philippines' fourth largest corporation and Citibank was the third largest private bank.) With varying degrees of justification, economic "nationalists" blame multinational corporations in the Philippines for a multitude of sins including supporting martial law; producing inappropriate products (such as a plethora of expensive and unnecessary pharmaceuticals); "exploiting" low-paid Filipino labour; absorbing local capital that would otherwise be available for the expansion of Filipino businesses; and using transfer pricing to covertly export profits rather than reinvesting them in the Philippines. Consequently, the role of foreign trade and investment has been and continues to be a sensitive political and economic issue in the Philippines.

The issue of import liberalization — the reduction of tariffs and the elimination of quotas on imports — pitted domestic producers for the Philippine market, who had profited from years of protection, against consumers and manufacturers of exports. It also pitted economic nationalists, who feared increased foreign penetration of the Philippine market, against economic internationalists, who believed that Philippine manufacturers must become internationally competitive. Finally, it pitted members of the government who felt that they should continue to enjoy the political and economic power of allocating import licences (a favourite activity of all governments since the 1950s) against those in the government who wanted to reduce the government's role in the economy.

Under the terms of the 1984 agreement with the IMF the government was committed to end quotas and licences for more than 1,200 categories of imported goods. However, little progress had been made prior to the February 1986 elections. Upon taking power the Aquino government had to decide what to do with the IMF agreement. Minister Monsod and other free market economists argued that rapid and widespread import liberalization was necessary to increase the efficiency of manufacturing, improve international competitiveness, and lower costs to consumers. But protected domestic producers, backed by Minister of Trade and Industry Jose Concepcion, countered that rapid liberalization would deal a dangerous blow to the manufacturing sector after several years of being battered, and would result in additional plant closings and higher unemployment.

A compromise of sorts was reached when Aquino approved a plan to proceed with the liberalization of about two-thirds of the 1,200 items during 1986. Included in the 400 items not liberalized, however, were key intermediate goods such as wheat and soya bean flour; fertilizers and other chemicals; synthetic fibres; textile yarns and threads; and iron and steel products. Although this decision began the process of liberalization, it also meant that domestic manufacturers of finished goods (such as textiles) continued to be dependent upon higher priced domestically produced inputs (such as synthetic fibres), which increased their production costs and decreased their international competitiveness.

Jose Concepcion and the import substitution manufacturers continued to push for the further postponement of the liberalization of the remaining 400 items and successfully delayed the process throughout 1987. In April 1988, however, import restrictions on the remaining 400 items were finally lifted. In place of the quantitative restrictions tariffs of 10 to 50 per cent were imposed on imports. Consequently, the Philippines, which once had one of the highest levels of import protection of any ASEAN country, now has protective levels in the lower range of that grouping.[27]

The appropriate role of foreign investment was also a controversial issue. Heavily in debt, the Philippines had to rely on attracting new investment to finance its economic recovery, generate foreign exchange, and create new jobs. Most members of the Aquino government recognized the need for foreign investment. It was hoped that wealthy Filipinos, who were thought to have sent up to US$15 billion out of the country during the last years of the Marcos regime, would begin to reinvest in their country along with foreign investors. There was disagreement within the government, however, over how much foreign control to allow and in which sectors of the economy. The debate intensified once the government began to privatize government-owned corporations and banks.

The debate over the appropriate role of foreign investment was academic throughout 1986 because the uncertain political climate reduced the interest of many potential foreign investors. The instability of the government coalition, the uncertain future of the Constitution and investment regulations, the increase in labour militancy and strikes, and the PCGG's seemingly unlimited power of sequestration combined to keep foreign investors on the sidelines. By 1988, however, many of these concerns had diminished and foreign investment inflows particularly from Taiwan, the United States, and Japan, more than doubled.

Assessing the Consequences of Aquino's Economic Policies

After the restoration of democracy, the reform and recovery of the economy is perhaps the most significant accomplishment of the Aquino government. Despite considerable domestic disagreement over economic policies, the government fairly consistently pursued policies that generally were market-oriented, private-sector driven, and internationalist. The government implemented a number of important economic reforms including dismantling most of the Marcos-era monopolies, liberalizing imports, restructuring the financial and tax systems, and beginning the process of privatization. It also managed its international economic relations relatively well. It secured a new agreement with the IMF, received new grants and loans from bilateral and multilateral donors, and restructured its foreign commercial debt.

These policies, combined with an explosion of pent-up consumer demand and a generally favourable international economic environment, resulted in a steady improvement in the economy beginning in late 1986. After posting negative growth in 1984, 1985, and the first half of 1986, the economy began to grow again during the second half of 1986. GNP grew at an average of almost 6 per cent per annum from 1987 to 1989. Initially, the growth was consumer-led, but by late 1988 it was becoming increasingly investment-driven. The recovery was led by growth in the industrial sector, and particularly in manufacturing, construction, and exports. This growth created an estimated 2.3 million new jobs by early 1989, causing the unemployment rate to drop from almost 13 per cent in mid-1986 to under 10 per cent in 1988. Rising employment and income levels caused the incidence of poverty to decline from almost 60 per cent in 1985 to about 50 per cent in 1988. At the same time, inflation, which had risen to more than 50 per cent in 1984, remained between 10 and 15 per cent. This performance made the Philippines one of the best performing of the world's heavily indebted economies.

These significant improvements were offset somewhat by a number of problems and failures, some of which were long-standing and structural in nature, such as the country's chronic balance of payments problem. Some, such as the foreign debt burden, were the legacy of the Marcos era. Others, however, were new. The government ran sizeable budget deficits in order to stimulate the economy, service its debts, and give pay raises to disgruntled soldiers, teachers, and civil servants. Although the government's deficits were relatively moderate in size, they had to be financed by additional domestic and foreign borrowing, which had the effect of "crowding out" private-sector borrowers and raising interest rates.

A second problem was inadequate external financing. Although exports grew considerably in 1987-89, imports grew at an even faster rate, causing persistent trade and current account deficits. The growing trade deficit, combined with annual debt service payments of more than US$2 billion caused an increasingly serious balance of payments problem. The need to finance its deficit position aggravated the Philippines' dependency on foreign financing (in the form of new loans, aid, and investment) and reduced its ability to manage its exchange rate.

Finally, the recovery itself caused a number of problems. The growth of the current account deficit is one. The overburdening of the country's decrepit infrastructure is another. Equitable distribution of the benefits of growth is a third. Clearly, the urban areas in general and the traditional business community had benefited from the economic recovery, but the benefits in the rural areas and for the poor were less certain. Indeed, in 1989 government statistics revealed that the poorest 30 per cent of all Filipinos had not benefited from the economic recovery.

Agricultural Development and Agrarian Reform

A visitor to the Philippines who visits only Metro Manila will miss one of the most basic facts of life about the Philippines: it is a predominantly rural and agricultural society. About 35 million Filipinos, or roughly 60 per cent of the population live in the rural areas and more than 10 million Filipinos, or just less than half of the total work-force, are engaged in agriculture (including fishing and forestry). Agriculture produces slightly less than a third of the gross domestic product (GDP) and a third of total merchandise exports.

Covered with coconut trees and rice and corn fields, the Philippine countryside appears to be a generous and reliable provider of food and income. Unfortunately, this is not the case. For the majority of Filipinos living in the rural areas and engaged in agriculture, life is marked by poverty, uncertainty, hardship, and often violence. The majority of peasants farm small plots of land in rugged and relatively unproductive upland areas without the benefit of irrigation. Many are in debt to money-lenders, and about one-quarter are tenants who do not own the land they work on. Moreover, some four to five million Filipinos in the countryside have no access to any land at all and work as agricultural labourers or fishermen. Rural underemployment (which stood at 41 per cent in 1987) is more than twice the rate in the urban areas, and rural family incomes, on average, are about half that of urban families. Government social services, such as education and health care, tend to be concentrated in the urban areas. Consequently, illiteracy and infant mortality rates are significantly higher in the rural areas, and school enrolment and life expectancy are lower.[28] Finally, law, order, and justice are often absent in the countryside. Peasants are frequently victimized by bandits and land-grabbers, unscrupulous landlords and officials, communist rebels, vigilantes, and undisciplined troops.

The Aquino government's response to the many problems facing the agricultural sector was critical to the country's economic and political development. Policies concerning the agricultural economy had an important impact on the country's economic growth and directly affected the standard of living of tens of millions of Filipinos. These same policies also had important political significance, for they revealed the extent of the government's commitment to improving the welfare, rights, and status of the poor majority of the population. Finally, these policies also had an important potential impact on national security, affecting as they did the conditions that contributed to the communist insurgency in the countryside. The following provides a brief description of the agricultural sector and examines the government's handling of the single most significant issue affecting that sector — agrarian reform.

Key Features of Philippine Agriculture
The typical peasant farmer in the Philippines ekes out a living with

his family of six on a small plot of marginal, often unirrigated, land. The majority of farmers nation-wide own their land, but in some provinces as many as half are tenant farmers who pay either a fixed rent in cash or a set share of their crop. Almost 40 per cent of all Filipino farmers grow rice, roughly 30 per cent grow coconuts, and 20 per cent grow corn. The rest grow sugar or other crops.

Farming is a complex and high-risk endeavour, with the success of the peasant farmer dependent upon a frightening number of variables. These include the quality of the soil; the amount of rainfall; access to irrigation; the price of seeds, fertilizer, and pesticides; the availability and cost of credit; the accessibility of transportation and storage facilities; and commodity prices. In addition to these variables, the viability of the peasant farmer is also affected by the government's changing policies concerning agricultural prices and credit, exchange rates, agricultural exports and the importation of food and agricultural inputs. Finally, a significant portion of many farm families' income (sometimes as much as 40 per cent) is derived not from farming *per se*, but from working as paid labour, fishing, or producing handicrafts. Thus, the peasant farmer must also contend with the uncertainty of the availability of off-farm employment.

Other key characteristics of Philippine agriculture are described below.[29]

Land Shortages and Depletion. The absence of productive virgin land is a fundamental aspect of Philippine agriculture. The land frontier was reached some time in the late 1960s or early 1970s. Since then, increases in the area of land under cultivation have come from upland and forested regions, which are considerably less productive than lowland areas. The increase in upland farming has been a major cause of deforestation, which, in turn, causes soil erosion, flooding, and siltation. Because of upland farming and commercial logging, the total area of productive forest land has declined by more than a third between 1970 and 1984. If the current rate of deforestation persists, all primary forests will be gone within twenty years. Consequently, the opening of virgin areas to homesteading, as was done in Mindanao in the early 1950s and 1960s, is simply not an option in the 1990s.

Small Size of Landholdings. Although the political left's rhetoric often gives the impression that a vast portion of land in the Philippines is owned by a handful of large landowners (as in Latin America), the reality is that landholdings in the Philippines, on average, are quite small. Rapid population growth, the practice of dividing landholdings among multiple heirs, and the absence of new land have combined over time to create relatively small-sized farms. The average farm size in 1980 was 2.8 hectares (a hectare is equal to about 2.5 acres), although this varied considerably among regions and crops. Rice farms, for example, averaged 2.3 hectares, coconut farms 4 hectares, and sugar farms 9 hectares.[30] There are relatively few huge estates remaining in the Philippines, with the notable exception of some sugar haciendas exempted from Marcos's 1972 land reform decree (including the Cojuangco's sprawling Hacienda Luisita) and large pineapple and banana plantations in Mindanao leased from the government. Consequently, a "large" landowner in the Philippines is someone with more than 10 hectares.

High Tenancy Rates. Nationally, in 1980, about one-quarter of all farms were rented or leased, although this varied greatly from province to province. In Bukidnon province, a corn-growing area, only about 15 per cent of corn and rice lands were worked by tenants. In Quezon province, however, a coconut growing area, about 52 per cent of corn lands and 45 per cent of rice lands were tenanted. The majority of tenant farmers worked not on large estates, but on land owned by medium or small landowners.[31]

There are two types of tenancy: share and leasehold. Under share tenancy the landlord and tenant split the cost of seeds and other inputs. In return, the cultivator typically pays the landlord between 40 and 50 per cent of his crop — even though the Agrarian Reform Act of 1953 limited the landlord's share to only 30 per cent. Under leasehold tenancy, the peasant leases land from the owner for a set period of time and makes fixed cash payments rather than share a percentage of his crop.

In the Philippines, share tenancy is most prevalent for several important social and economic reasons. Share tenancy traditionally involves the establishment of a patron–client relationship between the landlord and the tenant in which the landlord is a source of food and loans in the event of an emergency or a failed crop. Consequently, though share tenancy provides the peasant with less security of tenure than leaseholding, the patron–client relationship provides the tenant with more security against economic disaster. Secondly, leasehold tenancy, because it involves cash payments, has been less attractive to many tenants because it exposes them to the market risk associated with selling their crops. Thirdly, although the fixed rent of a leaseholder allows him to keep more of his crop in good years, it also requires him to pay the same amount in bad years – something he might not be able to do in a particularly bad year. Share tenancy, on the other hand, increases the amount the tenant must pay to the landlord in good years, but more importantly (to the poor peasant), it reduces the amount he must pay in bad years. As subsistence level farmers tend to be risk averse, many consequently prefer share tenancy to leaseholding.[32]

A Large Landless Rural Labour Force. The absence of new land has created a large and growing number of landless agricultural workers. The percentage of landless agricultural workers grew from under 10 per cent of the rural labour force in 1950 to 30 to 35 per cent in 1987.[33] In 1987 it was estimated that there were some five million landless agricultural workers. This means that even under the most comprehensive land reform programme imaginable, it will be impossible to provide the landless workers with enough land to make a living. As the *Far Eastern Economic Review* observed, "Today, all arable land divided equally among all land claimants would place families of five or six on less than a fifth of a hectare – an equality of misery." [34]

Over-reliance on Less Profitable and More Volatile Export Crops. The Philippines' two most important traditional agricultural exports have been sugar and copra. With the rise of vegetable oil and sugar substitutes, however, both coconut and sugar have become relatively less lucrative and their prices considerably more volatile. In the 1970s the Philippines began to diversify agricultural exports to include bananas and pineapples, and during the 1980s there was further diversification into prawns and fish. However, some 15 to 18 million Filipinos still depend on the coconut industry for some portion of their income.

Relatively Low Agricultural Productivity. Successive Philippine governments have taken agriculture and the peasant farmer for granted, preferring instead to focus on developing urban-based manufacturing. Gains in production, to the extent that they occurred during the 1950s and early 1960s, came primarily from the expansion of the area under cultivation, not from gains in productivity (that is, not from higher crop yields per hectare). The rural infrastructure development and "Masagana 99" programmes undertaken by Marcos increased agricultural productivity but the gains were not sustained. Moreover, they did not offset the larger problems of inequitable land distribution and government policies that benefited urban manufacturing at the expense of agriculture. As a result, while productivity growth in agriculture has occurred, it has lagged behind countries like Thailand and Indonesia (see Table 4.1). Because of the absence of new land, future gains in agriculture must come from productivity increases.

Inequitable Land Ownership. Even the best intentioned and designed plan for agricultural development in the Philippines faces a fundamental problem – the inequity of land distribution. Table 10.1 shows the skewed nature of the country's landholdings. In 1980 half of all farms (50.9 per cent) were very small – under 2 hectares in size – and more than 85 per cent were under 5 hectares. About half of farmers eke out their living on less than a fifth of the total farm area. Conversely, the small group of relatively large farms (those of 10 hectares or more), which account for 3.4 per cent of all farms, take up more than one-quarter of all the farmland in the Philippines.

These national figures disguise significant regional variations. Landholdings are very small and equitably distributed in Batangas province, a rice and sugar growing area, where more than two-thirds (68.4 per cent) of all farms are under 2 hectares in size, and 95.7 per cent are under 5 hectares. In Bukidnon province, a corn and rice growing province, landholdings tend to be larger and more than half (57.9 per cent) of all farms are between 2 and 7 hectares in size. In the predominantly sugar growing province of Negros Occidental, land distribution is the worst, with less than one tenth (8.7 per cent) of all farms occupying almost 60 per cent of the farmland in the province.[35]

These figures also do not convey the complex and evolving nature of land ownership. As already noted, the type of crops cultivated and the size of landholdings vary from province to province. The history

Table 10.1
**Land Distribution in the Philippines
by Farm Size, 1980**

Farm size (in hectares)	Percentage of Total Number of Farms	Percentage of Total Farm Area
Under 2	50.9	16.0
2–4.9	35.2	35.0
5–7	8.3	16.6
7.1–9.9	2.2	6.5
10–24.9	3.0	14.5
25 and over	0.4	11.5
Total	100.0	100.0

SOURCE: NEDA, *Statistical Yearbook*, 1987, pp. 280–81.

of land settlement has left small rice holdings in the oldest areas (such as Luzon), and larger homesteads and plantations in areas more recently cultivated (particularly Negros Occidental and Mindanao). Many family holdings have, over time, been divided and redivided among the succeeding generations of children. In addition to this, Marcos's land reform programme resulted in the breakup and redistribution of most remaining large corn and rice holdings. Meanwhile, during the 1960s and 1970s many middle-class professionals and government employees bought small plots of land as investments. More recently some of the younger members of traditional landowning families have sold off their land, preferring urban life to rural, and business to farming. Finally, the spread of the NPA in many rural areas since the late 1970s have further persuaded some landowners to divest and move to the cities.

Overall, however, the Philippines' traditional landowning élite and a sizeable portion of the small rural middle class remain firmly attached to the land. The reasons for this are complex, involving economic, political, and psychological factors. The ownership of land has been and continues to be an important determinant of economic and political power. For large and small landowners alike land continues to be a relatively safe form of investment with potentially high rates of return.

But several less tangible reasons are perhaps equally important: land ownership is a factor in determining social standing, it contributes to many Filipinos' sense of identity, and it provides emotional security.

For many poor Filipinos who do not own land, however, it remains a much sought after dream. The inequitable distribution of land, income, and political power in the countryside has contributed to the sporadic peasant revolts that began during the Spanish period. These have continued into the twentieth century in the form of the Sakdalista, Huk, Muslim, and communist revolts. The peasantry's "endemic rebellious tendencies" are in response to a long list of injustices involving land. According to agrarian reform specialist Mahar Mangahas, these have included:

> the injustice of land acquired merely by conquest or by physical dispensation; the injustice of land maintained, in the face of community resistance, only by repression; the injustice of patently illegal landgrabbing; the injustice of inequitable access to land tilling privileges, discriminating against the poor and the unschooled in favor of the wealthy and those knowledgeable of the legal system.[36]

Importance of Agricultural Development

There are four compelling reasons for promoting agricultural development in the Philippines. The first is simply statistical: a majority of Filipinos live in the rural areas and they are mainly engaged in agriculture. Therefore, programmes that seek to improve the quality of life of the average Filipino should focus on the development of the rural areas and of the agricultural sector.

The second reason is humanitarian: Filipinos engaged in agriculture – and particularly upland farmers and landless rural labourers – are among the very poorest of the poor in the Philippines. Although the slums of Metro Manila are often singled out as vivid examples of Philippine poverty, the reality is that there are many more people living in equally bad or far worse conditions in the rural areas. As we have seen, most of the Philippines' 35 million rural inhabitants are poorer, less educated, and less healthy than the inhabitants of the cities and towns. Life is harder, opportunities fewer, and prospects dimmer in the countryside. Therefore, any programme that seeks to address mass poverty in the Philippines must focus on rural poverty.

A third reason springs from the fact that not all of the rural poor in the Philippines are prepared to suffer silently and passively. Consequently, there is a close correlation between high levels of tenancy and rural poverty and the success of the communist insurgency. It is not a coincidence that the insurgency is strongest in several regions where incomes are among the lowest in the Philippines: the Eastern Visayas, Cagayan Valley, Bicol, and Western and Central Mindanao. Agricultural development is, therefore, essential if the communist insurgency is to be contained and eventually defeated.

Finally, there is also a powerful economic reason: agricultural development is a prerequisite to industrial development. According to economist Harry Oshima:

> In predominantly agricultural economies it is the increase in agricultural incomes and output which triggers the growth in demand for food, textiles, footwear, and other consumer products . . . and which supplies the main inputs to the main manufacturing sectors. It is the commercialization and modernization of agriculture which expand the demand not only for chemicals and equipment, but also for construction, transport, storage and public utilities. One important function of industries in supporting the rise of agricultural family incomes is as a source of industrial employment to farm families, as the experience of Japan in the late 1950s and 1960s and of Taiwan in the 1960s and 1970s clearly demonstrates.[37]

The 1987 Constitution, to its credit, recognizes the importance of agricultural development. One of its provisions calls for the state to promote "industrialization and full employment based on sound agricultural development and agrarian reform". NEDA's Medium Term Philippine Development Plan also recognizes the primacy of an "employment-oriented, rural-based development strategy". To accomplish this, it calls for an increase in basic infrastructure support, particularly in the rural areas, and the development of small- and medium-scale, labour-intensive rural industries.[38] According to the NEDA plan: "With a public investment program supportive of employment in rural areas, agricultural productivity would rise and, with it, incomes, generating in turn, an increased demand not only for food and other agricultural products but for industrial goods and services as well".[39] The NEDA plan projected that the real annual growth in agriculture (including fishery and forestry) would average 5 per cent a year between 1987 and 1992. Consequently, the incidence of rural poverty was targeted to decline from 64 per cent in 1985 to 48 per cent in 1992.

Need for Agrarian Reform

Given the characteristics of Philippine agriculture already described, it is impossible to imagine significant and sustained agricultural development without a major reform of the agrarian sector. According to agricultural economist Christina David:

> With increasing population pressure on limited land resources, the current agrarian structure has become a major constraint to efficient growth and development. Structural adjustments in farm size and farming systems are required for more intensive use of scarce land. Small family farm operations, in contrast to plantation-type agriculture, tend to use relatively more labor, have higher yields, and have more flexible and diversified farming systems.[40]

The "structural adjustments" referred to by David include land reform in particular, and agrarian reform more broadly. Land reform, simply put, involves the redistribution of a productive asset, land, in order to make the ownership of that asset more equitable. However, while land reform may achieve a more equitable distribution of land, it does not guarantee that the peasants who receive land will be successful farmers. In order to assure that the agricultural sector will be stable and productive, comprehensive agrarian reform is required. Agrarian reform in non-communist countries, at its simplest, seeks to improve the agricultural sector by making the small farmer a viable and productive economic unit. Thus, in addition to the redistribution of land, comprehensive agrarian reform requires the following:

1. Increasing the supply of capital (both investment and credit) to the rural areas, and making its distribution more equitable;
2. Introducing new, more profitable crops and farming systems;
3. Creating or strengthening farmers' co-operatives and associations;
4. Improving the delivery of government services to farmers (such as training and information); and
5. Building rural infrastructure such as irrigation systems, electric lines, farm-to-market roads, storage facilities, and markets.

Agrarian reform, in addition to increasing economic efficiency and equity, can also redress the unequal and unjust social and political relationships that have arisen from the maldistribution of land. Indeed, the provisions in the 1987 Constitution dealing with agrarian reform are contained in the article on social justice, rather than in the section on the economy. According to Section 1 of this article:

> The Congress shall give highest priority to the enactment of measures that protect and enhance the right of all the people to human dignity, reduce social, economic, and political inequalities, and remove cultural inequities by equitably diffusing wealth and political power for the common good. . . . To this end, the State shall regulate the acquisition, ownership, use, and disposition of property and its increments.[41]

In sum, agrarian reform, by improving the distribution of land and increasing the productivity (and, therefore, usually the wealth) of small farmers, seeks a redistribution of economic and political power in the countryside. In a predominantly traditional and agricultural society like the Philippines this is tantamount to a fundamental reordering of society and politics. Consequently, there is no other issue as complex, politically charged, and potentially significant as agrarian reform. Nor are there many issues as difficult or potentially traumatic.

Aquino and Agrarian Reform: 1986–87

Marcos's second martial law decree, issued just two days after he imposed martial law, declared all of the Philippines subject to land reform. In contrast, it took President Aquino almost a year to unveil a preliminary proposal for agrarian reform, and then another five months – until July 1987 – to sign an Executive Order that left most of the important aspects (such as retention limits, compensation, and timing) to the Congress to decide. It then took the Congress almost another year – until June 1988 – to draft and finally pass a limited and loophole-filled agrarian reform law.

During this period of more than two years the debate over agrarian reform, and the Aquino government's participation in it, proceeded in fits and starts. It included periods of crisis and complacency, action and inaction, high expectations and bitter disappointments. It was also filled with rhetoric, ideology, and emotion. In an article in early 1987 the *Far Eastern Economic Review* captured the posturing that was occurring:

> Sure of its ground, the revolutionary left offers a mantra-like refrain of "land to the tillers" using class-based reasoning. The influential Roman Catholic Church speaks of a "genuine" land reform prompted by moral dictates of social justice. Not to be outdone, politicians and parties of a more traditional cast urge "meaningful" land reform, often for purely opportunistic reasons. Even those with the most to lose, such as sugar plantation owners, embrace "responsible land reform" — on the understanding that the change may turn out to be no change at all.[42]

The battle over agrarian reform mobilized groups across the political spectrum. On the left, the Kilusang Magbubukid ng Pilipinas (KMP) peasant federation and the Congress for a People's Agrarian Reform (CPAR), which together claimed to represent more than 2.5 million farmers and fishermen, demanded the immediate and extensive redistribution of land with minimal compensation to landlords. On the centre-right were landlord groups which called for a gradual, phased programme providing for a high retention limit and large up-front payments based on market value. On the far right were radical groups such as the Movement for an Independent Negros which threatened to secede if a comprehensive reform programme was enacted. In the centre, struggling to find a compromise that would be accepted by peasants and landlords alike, were the Church, urban-based reform groups, and most government technocrats.

The Constitutional Commission was the forum of the first battle over agrarian reform. Fearing that any future legislature would be dominated by representatives of landowners, pro-agrarian reform groups pressed the Commission to include an explicit, rather than a general, commitment to agrarian reform in the new Constitution. They succeeded, to a limited degree. The 1987 Constitution stipulates that "the State shall encourage and undertake the just distribution of all agricultural lands" (that is, regardless of the type of crop being cultivated, the tenurial arrangement, and the legal status of the land).[43] It also calls for the State to recognize the right of "farmers, farmworkers and landlords" to participate in the "planning, organization and management" of the programme, and requires the state to provide the physical, financial, and marketing infrastructures essential to effective agricultural production.

The 1987 Constitution, however, left it to the Congress to determine the "priorities and reasonable retention limits" of the programme. It also states that land reform must involve "the payment of just compensation" to landowners — which was interpreted to mean the market value. Although the Constitution also expands the coverage of reform to non-tenants, it refers only to "regular farm workers", thereby excluding seasonal workers like the *sacadas* (migrant sugar-cane workers) in Negros Occidental.

At about the same time that the constitutional commissioners were debating agrarian reform, members of the Aquino administration were struggling to formulate the government's own programme. In May, Heherson "Sonny" Alvarez, the newly appointed Minister of Agrarian Reform announced that the expansion of land reform to include sugar and coconut lands was being "seriously studied" by his ministry. He was quickly opposed, and ultimately overruled, by Ramon Mitra, the influential Minister of Agriculture, who himself was a large coconut planter.[44] The Medium-Term Philippine Development Plan, released in December 1986 stated:

> The concern for equity and distributive justice shall be at par
> with the concern for economic productivity. Agrarian reform shall
> be at the centerpiece of the effort towards distributive justice to
> ensure that the gains from agricultural growth are fully transmitted
> to small farmers.[45]

Once faced with the reality of having to turn her government's rhetoric into reality, President Aquino became increasingly ambivalent about agrarian reform and appeared to avoid the complex and controversial issue as much as possible. Consequently, she took no action during 1986, which prompted the Philippine Institute for Development Studies to conclude in a study in early 1987 that the government "appeared to have vacillated and was overtaken by events".[46] One of these events was the completion of the draft constitution in late 1986. Another was the Mendiola Bridge incident in January 1987 in which some nineteen demonstrators calling for land reform were killed by government forces. In response to the Mendiola incident Aquino renewed her pledge to implement land reform and appointed a Cabinet Action Committee (CAC) to prepare a programme. In February the government announced its plans for an Accelerated Land Reform Programme (ALRP), timed in part, sceptics thought, to make the government appear progressive in the wake of the collapse of the cease-fire with the communists.

If implemented, the ALRP would have been a five-year programme (1987–92) affecting over 3 million landless Filipinos and 11.1 million hectares of agricultural land. The cost was estimated to be P63 billion (US$3 billion), which would have been funded by domestic resources, the recovery of the "ill-gotten wealth" of Marcos and his cronies, and foreign loans and assistance. The first phase (1987–89) would have completed the reform of 1.3 million hectares of tenanted rice and corn lands begun under the Marcos land reform programme. The second phase (1987–89) would have expanded the reform to about 900,000 hectares of lands that were idle and abandoned, foreclosed and sequested, voluntarily offered, and expropriated. The third phase (1989–92) promised to be the most controversial, for it would have extended agrarian reform to about 3.5 million hectares of privately owned plantations, haciendas, and other tenanted non-rice and corn lands. The fourth phase (1987–92) would have distributed 5 million hectares of public alienable and disposable land suitable for agriculture.

Some members of the Aquino Cabinet were critical of the scope, expense, and potential political fall-out of the ALRP, and whatever support there might have been for the programme in the Cabinet was reduced in March 1987, when Heherson Alvarez, the Minister of Agrarian Reform, resigned from his position to run for the Senate. His office remained vacant until July. In the absence of a strong commitment to the ALRP by Aquino, the Cabinet ultimately approved a more limited version of the plan in late April 1987, shortly before the congressional elections. The scope was reduced from 11.1 to 3.8 million hectares and the number of landless farmers affected declined from 3 to 2.1 million. The budget was cut to about P43.5 billion (US$2.3 billion) to be funded through loans, the recovery of "ill-gotten wealth", and the sale of non-performing assets.

The diminution of the ALRP was watched with concern by agricultural economists in the Philippines. According to one group at the University of the Philippines:

> While the reduction in scope may be due to initial overestimation and/or the desire of the government to set more realistic targets, we contend that the disproportionate reduction . . . may weaken significantly the distributive impact of the program . . . . [The government's] hesitation to impose a progressive land tax may serve as a deterrent to reforming the land ownership structure as well as to rationalizing the tax structure of the Philippines.[47]

In May the World Bank concluded a study that was even more critical of the government plan. According to the Bank, the phased nature of the programme was expensive, difficult to administer and encouraged evasion by landlords. The Bank also feared that the programme did not provide for ample peasant participation and left too much control arbitrarily in the hands of landlords. Finally, the Bank also warned that the administrative expenses of the programme would be so high that they would be comparable to the cost of land payments.[48]

Over the course of several months the Aquino administration went through sixteen drafts of a proposed presidential decree on agrarian reform. All the while there was considerable speculation about whether or not Aquino would sign an Executive Order for agrarian reform before the new Congress convened in July. Landowners called on Aquino to leave the matter to the Congress, knowing that the House would be dominated by representatives sympathetic to their interests. Some sugar growers in Negros Occidental went even further, threatening war and secession if the President declared a sweeping reform programme. Farmers' groups like the KMP and CPAR called on Aquino to use her executive powers before the Congress convened, fearing that the House would emasculate any land reform legislation it considered.

Finally, in late June Malacañang Palace ended the speculation by announcing that an Executive Order would be issued before the Congress convened. However, it added that many of the details for the implementation of the order had not been decided and might be left to the Congress. On 14 July the Catholic Bishops' Conference issued a pastoral letter, entitled "Thirsting for Justice", which urged the adoption of a comprehensive and effective land reform programme.[49]

On 22 July, just five days before the opening of the Congress and the loss of her legislative powers, Aquino issued Proclamation No. 131 and Executive Order No. 229 which provided the mechanism for the

implementation of the Comprehensive Agrarian Reform Programme
(CARP). Under the CARP, all public and private agricultural lands were
subject to reform, regardless of tenurial arrangement and crop. Over
a ten-year period plots of 1.5 to 2 hectares were to be sold by the
government on concessional terms to 1.6 million farmers. Recipients
of land titles would make 30 equal annual payments at 6 per cent
annual interest. The CARP included two important concessions to
landowners. First, it did not fix retention limits for sugar or coconut
lands, leaving this to the Congress. Secondly, it allowed compensation
to be based on the landowner's declaration of current fair market
value (as opposed to the lower value declared by landlords for tax
purposes). The landlords would receive a 10 per cent deposit, with
the balance paid over ten years. The CARP also created a P50 billion
(US$2.5 billion) Agrarian Reform Fund to finance the programme
from the proceeds of the sale of government-owned corporations
and the recovery of "ill-gotten wealth".

The KMP denounced the CARP as a sell-out and burned effigies
of Aquino. The NDF called the CARP "fake and hypocritical". On the
right, sugar growers in Negros renewed their threats to secede. Some
of them formed a "blood pact" to defend their rights and land. Another
group of landowners in Mindanao said they would ally with the Muslim
secessionists. To other, more objective observers, the last-minute agrarian reform decree (which could be, in any event, disregarded by the
Congress) demonstrated that Aquino had abandoned her commitment
to genuine agrarian reform. According to one observer, "She left the
impression that she had been delivered of an unwanted baby".[50]
Others, however, supported Aquino's action, pointing out that an issue
as important as agrarian reform should be decided by the people's
elected representatives. Still other, somewhat more cynical, observers
noted that by making the Congress responsible for land reform, Aquino
could shift the blame for the programme to the legislature.

The Congress and Agrarian Reform: 1987–88

After vacillating for more than a year, Aquino left it to the Congress
to work out the legislative details of an agrarian reform programme
within ninety days. If the Congress did not do this, she threatened
hollowly, the executive branch would reclaim the initiative and write

the legislation itself. Some congressional leaders predicted the quick passage of a bill similar to Aquino's executive order. House Speaker Ramon Mitra confidently (but naively) predicted having a bill ready in thirty days. Others, however, were less optimistic. Senator John Osmena, for example, warned: "There will be a lot of tension and class conflicts. Historically, no one work[s] against his class interests and classes do not legislate against their own interests".[51] He accurately predicted it would take at least a year to pass legislation.

On the first working day of the Senate, Heherson Alvarez, now the Chairman of the Senate Agrarian Reform Committee, filed an agrarian reform bill resembling Aquino's CARP. It had variable retention limits from 7 to 15 hectares and provided beneficiaries with 3 hectares of land. In October Aquino's brother-in-law, Senator Agapito "Butz" Aquino, filed a second, more comprehensive, bill providing for a 3 hectare retention limit, which he claimed would give land to 3.1 million farmers. In order to placate landlords, both bills based the value of land on the landowner's declarations. In addition, Senator Aquino's bill offered a 30 per cent cash payment to the landlords.

In the House, Representative Bonifacio Gillego, the progressive Chairman of the House Agrarian Reform Committee, filed a bill giving beneficiaries 3 hectares and providing for a fixed 7 hectare retention plus 7 hectares for one heir. In response, Representatives Romeo Guanzon and Hortencia Starke, sugar planters from Negros Occidental, filed a much weaker bill establishing a 7 hectare retention limit and permitting each heir to retain 3 hectares. Given the large size of most Filipino families this would allow a retention limit per family of more than 20 hectares – which alone would exclude about 85 per cent of private agricultural land.[52] The Guanzon-Starke bill was co-sponsored by 108 congressmen, sending a clear signal that the House had no intention of passing land reform legislation that would result in a significant redistribution of land.

In late October, President Aquino's ninety-day "deadline" passed, with little progress having been made in either the House or the Senate. Aquino, happy to leave the controversy with the Congress, extended her deadline for another ninety days. Thereafter, with legislation still deadlocked, the deadline was conveniently forgotten by everyone.

In the House the majority of representatives sympathetic to the landowners continued to undermine the efforts of the progressive minority to fashion a comprehensive agrarian reform bill. The obstructionism in the House prompted the *Philippine Daily Inquirer* to comment: "Congress has evidently lost sight of why land reform is necessary in the first place, which is to release the landless peasantry from feudal bondage".[53] The Gillego bill was eventually modified beyond recognition, prompting its author to vote against it. According to Gillego: "When it was reported out [of Committee], it went through a period of neglect until it went through a state of delirium tremens during the period of protracted interpellation. During the period of amendment it went into a coma, and finally into a state of *rigor mortis*".[54]

In late March 1988 both the Senate and the House bills reached their final versions. The House passed a bill modelled after the Guanzon-Starke bill that provided 3 hectares to potential beneficiaries and a set retention limit of 7 hectares for the landowner and 3 hectares for each direct heir. It also provided a 50 per cent cash payment to landlords and made the redistribution of private lands contingent upon the successful prior distribution of public, seized, and other lands. The final Senate bill established a ten-year phased programme under which peasant beneficiaries would receive 3 hectares of land. It allowed a 5 hectare retention limit for all types of land, with no provision for heirs, and provided landlords cash payments of 10 to 25 per cent.

In May a 22-member conference committee met to reconcile the House and Senate bills. The two Houses differed on retention limits, the inclusion of heirs when establishing retention limits, the timing of the redistribution of private lands, and the size of cash payments to landlords. The deadlock was finally broken in early June, and a final, compromise version of legislation for a Comprehensive Agrarian Reform Programme, officially Republic Act No. 6657, was unveiled.

The compromise bill set a uniform 5 hectare retention limit, but allowed an additional 3 hectares of land for each child over fifteen years of age who actually tilled or managed the farm. This would allow an average family to retain from 14 to 20 hectares of land. Landlords would receive a 20 to 40 per cent cash down-payment, depending on the size of their landholdings. Peasant beneficiaries would receive 3 hectares and would pay 30 annual amortizations at 6 per cent annual interest. If completely implemented the CARP would redistribute 2.8 million hectares of land, benefiting about 2 million landless farmers.

The CARP legislation established a ten-year phased programme of redistribution. During the first phase (July 1988 to June 1992) rice and corn lands not distributed under the Marcos programme would be distributed, along with sequestered, foreclosed, and seized lands; idle and abandoned lands; public lands; and private lands in excess of 50 hectares. During the second phase, which would not begin until 1992 (the end of the Aquino administration), private lands from 50 to 24 hectares would be redistributed. During the third phase, beginning in 1994, private lands of less than 24 hectares would be redistributed.

The implementation of the CARP was expected to cost at least P170 billion (about US$8 billion) over ten years, or an average of P17 billion (US$800 million) per year.[55] The final bill, however, did not include a specific funding allocation, leaving it to the Congress to appropriate funds. In the past, Congress, it will be remembered, had weakened previous attempts at land reform by not appropriating or releasing adequate funds.

On 8 June 1988 both Houses voted on the agrarian reform bill. The bill was passed by a vote of 154 to 20. Representative Gillego warned that the Congress was "foisting a grand deception on our people".[56] His opponents on the right, including Negros sugar planters Guanzon and Starke, also voted against the measure. In the Senate 18 senators voted for the bill, 1 abstained, and 4 were absent.

Aquino signed the CARP bill into law on 10 June, calling it a "tolerable compromise". Cardinal Sin claimed it was "another miracle" and "a genuine, far reaching, effective land reform program". The KMP labelled it "nothing more than a hoax" and the CPAR criticized the bill as being "fake, pro-landlord, and deceptive". The CPAR rejected the CARP and adopted its own version of agrarian reform that called on farmers to unilaterally claim the lands they tilled.

Was the CARP a "tolerable compromise" or a "grand deception"? Supporters of the bill claimed it was the best legislation that could have been achieved in the existing political environment. They pointed out that the CARP, unlike previous reform efforts, subjected all agricultural land to reform, regardless of crop and tenurial arrangement. They also optimistically predicted that the incremental redistribution of land required by the CARP would result in a significant reform of the agricultural sector. According to one such supporter, economist Bernardo Villegas:

> The final version of CARP was not a concession to landowners.
> It made sure that the ownership of land will no longer be con-
> centrated in the hands of a few after the prudent period of 10
> years. But it also made sure that the small farmers will not be
> abandoned to fend for themselves by a government that is patently
> incapable of delivering some vital farm support services. It made
> it sufficiently attractive for the moneyed landowners to continue
> investing in agriculture by graduating to the upstream activities
> of post-harvest facilities, finance, technical, processing, and mar-
> keting services.[57]

This optimistic assessment was not shared by many Filipinos, jaded
as they were by the long history of false and failed land reform efforts.
The critics of the CARP estimated that the large retention limit permitted by the law would exempt perhaps three-quarters of all private
land from redistribution, and reduce the number of potential beneficiaries to less than one million (as opposed to up to three million
for a five-hectare retention limit).[58] They noted that the provision for
compensation based on market value was a step backwards from the
Marcos programme and that it would reduce the redistributive effect
of the programme. Moreover, the programme's high cost would make
it much less likely that it would be adequately funded by the Congress.
They also charged that the law's land registration provisions were
weak, and that many opportunities existed for exemption, evasion,
and deferment. Finally, it was pointed out that "the main losers in
this agrarian reform law are landless rural workers who have neither
a farm to rent for their own cultivation nor permanent employment
in plantations".[59]

The evidence suggests that the CARP, while not quite a "grand
deception", is even farther from being a "tolerable compromise". First,
the potential redistributive impact of land reform was greatly diminished by the constitutional requirement that landlords be paid "just
compensation" for their land. This eliminated from the outset one
route to greater equity: the partial expropriation and redistribution
of land. Secondly, it is regrettable that the CARP is limited in its
potential impact on land distribution because of the high retention
limit it sets. Thirdly, given the past history of agrarian reform, it is
very likely that the CARP will be emasculated or evaded over its ten-
year life. Fourthly, President Aquino made almost no effort to promote

a strongly pro-reform policy or to build a national constituency for agrarian reform, so we are left wondering how much more could have been achieved if she had taken the lead? In sum, the compromise may have been "tolerable" to the Aquino government because it preserved the president's position *vis-à-vis* the more conservative elements of society. But it remains to be seen how many peasants will actually benefit from the CARP and, thus, how many will find it tolerable.

Whatever one's assessment is of the CARP, it is difficult to dispute that agrarian reform was the most significant social issue addressed by the Aquino government and the Congress up to 1988. As such, the way they dealt with the issue says a great deal about President Aquino's leadership, her government's priorities, the emerging political process, and the interests of the political élite in the post-Marcos era. In particular, the handling of agrarian reform highlighted a number of problems that plague Philippine politics. These are described below.

Élite Conservatism and Complacency. The prospects for genuine agrarian reform in the Philippines were undermined, in large part, by the conservatism and complacency of the élite. As we have seen, the Congress did not begin to seriously focus on agrarian reform until early 1988. By that time the sense of crisis that had infused the country during 1986 and most of 1987 had diminished and had begun to be replaced by complacency. By early 1988 the economy had improved, the growth of the insurgency had slowed, and in response to the threat of military intervention, the Aquino government had shored up its political base by supporting the traditional élite in the local elections. Consequently there was no longer a sense of urgency about redressing social problems. David Wurfel has observed, "The ruling elite felt no lack of legitimacy or popular support, and the lack of any scheduled national election until 1992 reduced the urgency for aspiring elites to seek mass support".[60] Under these circumstances, it was more important to Aquino to have an agrarian reform bill that was acceptable within the landowner-dominated House than one that would have significant redistributive impact.

President Aquino's Limited Commitment to Reform. During her campaign for the presidency, Corazon Aquino had pledged to undertake genuine agrarian reform. After becoming president, however, she sought to avoid the complex and controversial issue, seemed uncertain of what she wanted, and was unwilling to take a strong stand — either politically or personally (for example, concerning the disposition of her family's Hacienda Luisita). She waited almost two months to appoint a Minister of Agrarian Reform and then appointed Heherson Alvarez, a bright leader of the anti-Marcos opposition in the United States, but someone with relatively little political influence and even less experience with agricultural issues. She then left it to the Congress to decide the major features of the programme. As another sign of her temerity, under the CARP the most controversial phase of land redistribution — the redistribution of private lands from 24 to 50 hectares in size — will not begin until 1992, that is, at the end of her term.

Aquino claimed that her unwillingness to issue an executive order strongly in favour of comprehensive agrarian reform was because of her deference to the democratic process. While this explanation probably is genuine and commendable up to a point, she also hid behind her commitment to democracy in order to avoid taking a position on a critical social issue. For without undermining the democratic process she could have taken a stronger pro-reform position, used her popularity and the power of her office to campaign for it, and dared the Congress not to thwart the popular will. She did not do this, partly because of her own social background, partly because of the fragile nature of her government in 1986 and 1987, and partly because of her understandable concerns about the cost of a more comprehensive reform programme, its possible effects on productivity, and its political repercussions.

Divisions between the House and the Senate. The differences in the agrarian reform bills passed by the House and Senate prior to their reconciliation reveal important disagreements between them. First and foremost, it quickly became obvious that the majority of the members of the House were intent on defending the property of landowners. The majority of these landowners, however, were not owners of large plantations. Instead, they were the landed rural middle class consisting of teachers, small businessmen, officials, and military officers who owned small- and medium-sized plots of land less than 24 hectares in size.[61] In contrast, the large majority of senators were more urban- and industry-oriented, and had national constituencies which made them less beholden to local landed élites. As a result, the members of the House saw agrarian reform as an issue directly affecting the political and economic fortunes of their families and their supporters. The Senate, by comparison, saw agrarian reform as being necessary for political stability and national economic development. Finally, the members of the House were also more concerned with protecting their own political interests, even if it meant ignoring Aquino's requests. The majority of senators, however, owed their position to Aquino to a considerable degree and were less inclined to go against her wishes.

Limited Influence of Peasant Groups. The two major peasant-based groups advocating comprehensive agrarian reform suffered a serious defeat with the passage of the CARP. The militant KMP under Jaime Tadeo demanded that a policy of "land to the tiller" be adopted immediately and at no cost to the peasants. The Congress for a People's Agrarian Reform (CPAR), a slightly less militant federation of thirteen major peasant and fishermen's organizations, called for a zero retention limit, progressive compensation (with reduced compensation for larger holdings), and the creation of village-level councils of cultivators to have a voice in the formulation and implementation of agrarian reform.[62]

Although the KMP's demands were radical, its demonstrations during 1986 were peaceful, and its campaign for land occupation was limited to idle, abandoned, and sequestered lands. However, the murder of nineteen demonstrators at the Mendiola Bridge in January ended whatever slight chance there might have been for the KMP and the Aquino government to work together. The CPAR was formed in early 1987, in part to try to bridge this gap; but the failure of the left in the May congressional elections gave it minimal influence in the new Congress, and the increasing conservatism of the Aquino government made the differences unbridgable. Consequently, according to David Wurfel, an "effective mechanism for peasant pressure on the policy process" was missing and pressure tactics were less effective than in 1971.[63]

Prospects for Agrarian Reform

The challenges to the successful implementation of even a limited agrarian reform programme such as the CARP are formidable. The

World Bank has observed that "Undertaking an agrarian reform program involves taking difficult decisions which affect the interests of
vast numbers of people, and calls for a strong and unwavering political
commitment on the part of government".[64] Unfortunately, however, the
history of agrarian reform in the Philippines is littered with legislation
(and presidential decrees) that failed because of intentional subver-
sion by the Congress and landowners, a lack of interest or political
will on the part of the president, and other shortcomings in design
and implementation. While it is too soon to say with complete certainty
that the 1988 CARP will fail for these same reasons, the history of
agrarian reform suggests that the probability of failure is high.

The 1988 CARP significantly limited the potential scope and impact of agrarian reform in the Philippines. However, it could still
produce some positive results if it is effectively and fully implemented.
For this reason, the success of the CARP will depend on the many
skirmishes that take place over its interpretation, funding, and implementation. The outcome of these battles, in turn, will depend on the
following factors.

The Government's Commitment to Rural Development. Land redistribution is the beginning, not the end, of agrarian reform. Redistribution
has to be accompanied by improvements in rural infrastructure, support
services, credit, marketing, and a host of other policies. For agricultural
development to succeed there must be adequate funding, intelligent
planning, effective implementation, and good fortune. More importantly, however, it requires a genuine and sustained commitment on
the part of the leaders and policy-makers to the larger economic and
social goals of rural development. It cannot be viewed, as it often
has been in the past, as something to be temporarily emphasized in
reaction to sporadic outbursts of agrarian unrest.

For agricultural development to be successful, it must also occur
in conjunction with the development of rural-based, labour-intensive
industries. With some five million landless labourers in the countryside,
the challenge of providing them with non-agricultural employment
has become as great or greater than the challenge of creating more
equitable land ownership. Moreover, the problem of rural landlessness
is closely linked to deforestation, soil erosion, the decline of fisheries,
and other serious environmental problems.

Institutional and Individual Capabilities. Agrarian reform, as we have seen, is a complex and expensive undertaking even under the best of circumstances. It involves extensive cadestral surveys, widespread distribution of information, creation of voluminous records and documents, provision of legal and financial services, and effective administration of justice and law enforcement. Past governments in the Philippines have not demonstrated a genuine and sustained commitment to agrarian reform, and as a result, the bureaucracy, for the most part, has not been very successful in mounting and sustaining nation-wide programmes. For the CARP to succeed, the bureaucracy will have to become better staffed, equipped, co-ordinated, and funded.

Certain long-standing agricultural relationships must also be changed. In Negros Occidental, for example, Governor Daniel Lacson, a relatively progressive landowner, has argued that, "We are not culturally ready to accept sweeping land reform. The workers can not make decisions about running the land".[65] Although the case of the sugar workers in Negros is more extreme than most, it is true that tenant farmers in many parts of the country remain dependent on landlords for credit, other inputs, and a market for their crops. In order for these farmers to become more productive and independent they must have access to alternate, and equally secure, credit and support services. In addition to this, agricultural labourers, such as the *sacada* in Negros, must be taught how to become farmers. This requires that the government and non-governmental organizations provide innovative and effective training programmes, and develop credit and marketing co-operatives and new arrangements for contract growing.

Peasant Expectations and Organization. In 1988, in the wake of the passage of the CARP, the CPAR announced that it would seek to replace the CARP with a People's Agrarian Reform Code (PAR Code). To accomplish this, the CPAR said it would begin a campaign to invoke a people's legislative initiative, as provided for in the 1987 Constitution. It also announced its support for peasant efforts to occupy abandoned or sequestered lands, force rent reductions, and form co-operatives.

It is unclear how successful these initiatives will be, and how the government will respond. Will the shortcomings of the CARP lead to greater frustration and militancy on the part of peasants? It is difficult to tell at this juncture. The answer will depend in part on the condition of the agricultural economy, including the prices of crops (particularly coconut) and the growth of rural employment opportunities. It will also depend on the law and order situation in the countryside, and in particular on the protection of peasants' economic, political, and human rights.

Leadership and Political Will. The process of interpreting, funding, and implementing the CARP will involve making many important, difficult, and controversial decisions in the coming years. If the modest potential of the CARP is to be achieved, the political leadership will have to demonstrate a genuine and consistent commitment to the reform programme. Will this commitment exist in the future? Or will the programme be overtly and covertly undermined as in the past? The answers to these questions will depend in part on the vigilance and effectiveness of pro-reform groups and in part on the level of foreign support the programme receives. Unfortunately, it is difficult to be optimistic, for as Bruce Koppel has written:

> Where agrarian reform programs have worked in fundamentally reformist settings – as they did in South Korea, Japan and Taiwan – they did so with an effective combination of political support from peasants and the urban middle class; secure financing and incentives through taxes, budget commitments, and foreign assistance; and effective and comprehensive activities to support both new farmer-operators as well as former farmer-operators and landlords. The Philippines simply does not present these forms of coalition and convergence.[66]

In the absence of the "forms of coalition and convergence" described by Koppel, the prospects for agrarian reform will remain dependent in large part on the interests of the élite and the political will of the leadership. This does not bode well for reform, for as development economist Michael Lipton maintains, successful land reform requires either outside implementation or a very frightened élite. Neither condition exists in the Philippines.

In sum, the enactment of the CARP in 1988 temporarily defused agrarian reform as a pressing political and social issue. But the CARP's positive impact on the agricultural sector is likely to be limited, and the shortcomings of the CARP ensure that agrarian reform will resurface as an important and perhaps explosive issue.

Conclusion: Prospects for
Sustained Economic Recovery and Reform

The Philippines underwent a significant and impressive economic recovery from 1986 to 1988, and the prospects appear good for continued moderate growth.[67] The country has the benefits of a decent resource endowment, a relatively large (but poor) domestic market, an educated and low-cost labour force, and a medium-sized corps of entrepreneurs and managers. The Aquino government has reduced (though by no means eliminated) government-induced distortions in the economy and has taken steps that will push domestic manufacturers to become more efficient and internationally competitive. Surrounded by the rapidly industrializing economies of East and Southeast Asia, the Philippines should benefit from these countries' increasing investments in places with lower labour costs.

The economic recovery, however, remains vulnerable to a variety of domestic and international factors including the triple threat of declining international commodity prices (particularly for coconut oil, sugar, copper, and gold), increasing interest rates, and rising petroleum prices. While it is impossible to predict the movements of these factors, it is reasonable to assume that during the 1990s they will continue to fluctuate as much as they did during the 1980s.

The Philippines is also very dependent upon continued (and increased) access to foreign markets (particularly in Japan and the United States) in order to earn foreign exchange with which to service its debt and to generate jobs in the manufacturing sector. Consequently, it is a potential victim of any increase in global protectionism. Market access is not the only problem the Philippines faces, however. The demand abroad for its products is also dependent on improvements in the quality and price competitiveness of the country's manufactured goods. These improvements are by no means assured, for according to the *Far Eastern Economic Review*, "The notion that the country is or could be competitive in areas such as electronics and textiles is now being questioned, as superficially low labor costs disguise poor productivity in the manufacturing sector".[68]

Thirdly, the country's economic prospects will be constrained by its heavy foreign (and domestic) debt burden, and the difficulty of securing foreign capital. Yearly foreign debt repayments, which are projected to reach US$3.6 billion by 1992, will continue to be a significant drag on government expenditures and on the growth of the entire economy. (Domestic debt repayments are even larger.) Moreover, the large size of the country's debt servicing could be used by the conservative élite as an excuse for not devoting government resources to important social programmes such as agrarian reform.

Because of its foreign debt payments, the Philippines is expected to suffer a total shortfall of some US$7.7 billion in the funds it needs to generate economic growth between 1988 and 1992. The economy, therefore, will remain extremely dependent on the continued (and increased) flow of foreign loans, investments, and grants, thus reinforcing a historical over-reliance on foreign assistance. The availability of these financial resources, however, has become more and more limited and competitive. The difficulty of securing adequate foreign capital was suggested by the slow pace of two international financial negotiations in 1989. The first was to establish a US$5 billion multi-year and multilateral economic assistance programme (called the Multilateral Assistance Initiative, or MAI, in the United States and the Philippine Assistance Plan, or PAP, in the Philippines). The second was to secure more than US$1 billion new commercial bank loans. Moreover, the growth in foreign investment may be threatened by the Philippines' strong strain of economic nationalism and an increase in labour militancy. The country also faces stiff competition for foreign investment from Thailand, Malaysia, and Indonesia.

A variety of domestic factors will also shape the country's economic prospects. Domestic demand for manufactures will remain dependent on increases in rural, predominantly agricultural, incomes and consumption. In turn, the healthy growth of the manufacturing sector should, over time, begin to absorb the large pool of excess rural labour. A booming manufacturing sector may entice larger landowners to leave agriculture and invest in industry. Domestic investment must continue to grow, but this will require appropriate and consistent government policies and improvements in infrastructure outside Metro Manila. However, the economic recovery, and the country's long-term economic development, could be seriously damaged by political instability and the more insidious problems of corruption and favouritism.

Finally, and perhaps most fundamentally, long-term economic growth and income distribution will be undermined if the country's rapid population growth is not slowed. The Philippines' population growth rate is at least 2.4 per cent (it may be as high as 2.8 per cent), making it one of the highest in Southeast Asia. At this rate there will be more than 75 million Filipinos by the year 2000. The future size of the population is cause for concern, but it is not as daunting as the immediate economic challenges posed by rapid population growth. This rapid growth rate puts a great deal of pressure on both the Philippines' fragile economy to keep pace with the growing population and the heavily indebted government to provide additional social services. Today, almost half of the population is under the age of twenty, creating a huge demand for primary health care, education, and jobs (more than 730,000 new jobs must be created each year). The perpetual surplus of labour drives wages down, which in turn limits the growth of domestic consumption and government tax revenues. On top of this, rapid population growth is causing serious resource depletion and environmental damage, much of which may be irreparable.

What are the prospects for further economic reform in the Philippines? Will the government demonstrate a commitment to the more equitable distribution of economic benefits and opportunities? Or will it be content with restoring the traditional system of "trickle down" capitalism? There is a danger that the economic recovery will create complacency that will diminish the government's commitment to more fundamental economic reforms. There is also a danger of backsliding in the privatization programme, and to a lesser degree, the import liberalization programme. The Congress, which is influenced by powerful domestic economic interests, could once again legislate special tariff preferences and import quotas or determine the "desired" number of entrants into the domestic markets (such as the automotive market). Finally, the existence of corruption and favouritism among policy-makers and the bureaucracy will continue to threaten the wise formulation and effective implementation of economic policies.

NOTES

1. Robert Dohner, "Aquino and the Economy: An Assessment of the First Three Years", *Pilipinas*, no.11 (Fall 1988), p.5.
2. For detailed examinations of macro-economic performance from 1986–88, see ibid.; Hal Hill, "The Philippine Economy Under Aquino: New Hopes,

Old Problems", *Asian Survey* 28, no.3 (March 1988):261–85; Merrill Lynch, *The Philippines* (September 1989); and National Economic and Development Authority (hereafter referred to as NEDA), *Philippine Development Report* (Manila:NEDA, annual).

3. See NEDA, *Philippine Development* 13, no.4 (July–August 1986).
4. *Malaya*, 19 October 1987, p.1.
5. *Far Eastern Economic Review*, 1 May 1986, p.60.
6. Dohner, op. cit., pp.17–18.
7. By 1985 more than half of the assets of the PNB and almost 90 per cent of the assets of the DBP were non-performing.
8. NEDA, *Philippine Statistical Yearbook 1987* (Manila: NEDA, 1987), p.25.
9. *Business Day*, 26 January 1987, p.3.
10. In 1987, Filipinos working abroad remitted more than US$800 million to the Philippines.
11. Only about 4.9 million, or 22 per cent, of the total labour force of about 22 million is unionized. Unions are formed along company, not industry lines, and therefore are small (they average only 1,750 members each) and are relatively disunified. However, most unions are members of one of several rival labour federations, the biggest being the leftist KMU and the Trade Union Congress of the Philippines (TUCP), originally formed under Marcos. The KMU claims a membership of 650,000 and the TUCP claims more than 2 million members. The labour movement was so fractious that the TUCP and KMU could not agree on a common date for an October 1987 strike to demand an increase in the minimum wage.
12. *Far Eastern Economic Review*, 15 October 1987, p.77.
13. In early 1988 there were reports that rank-and-file KMU members had become resentful of the leadership's emphasis on politically-motivated strikes at the expense of bread-and-butter issues.
14. NEDA, *Medium-Term Philippine Development Plan: 1987–1992* (Manila: NEDA, 1986), p.3; hereafter referred to as the *Medium-Term Plan*.
15. *Bulletin Today*, 12 March 1987, p.1.
16. Louis Berger International, "Assessment of the Philippine Economic Reform Program, Evaluation of Past USAID Program Assistances, and Future Recommendations" (Draft version of a report prepared by Louis Berger International, Inc., dated 10 October 1988), chapter 6, p.1.
17. Ibid., chapter 6, p.5.
18. Government of the Philippines/Philippine Assistance Programme, *The Philippine Agenda for Sustained Growth and Development* (Manila: Government of the Philippines, 30 May 1989), p.9.
19. Louis Berger International, op. cit., chapter 6, p.5.

20. Government of the Philippines/Philippine Assistance Programme, op. cit., p.9.
21. Robert Dohner, *Philippine External Debt: Burdens, Possibilities, and Prospects* (New York: The Asia Society, October 1989), Table 5, p.15.
22. From a speech at a conference on developing country debts held on 21–23 September 1987. Reproduced in the *Manila Chronicle*, 27 September 1987, p.19.
23. According to Ongpin, the difference between the two proposals resulted in about US$60 million more in interest payments annually; see *Asiaweek*, 25 January 1987, p.59. In January 1987, the Philippine Government successfully negotiated a restructuring agreement covering US$933 million in official debt from the fourteen governments that make up the "Paris Club" group of creditors.
24. NEDA, *Philippine Statistical Yearbook 1987*, p.345.
25. Dohner, *Philippine External Debt*, p.12.
26. NEDA, *Philippine Statistical Yearbook 1987*, p.345.
27. Dohner, *Aquino and the Economy*, p.33.
28. See NEDA, *Philippine Development Report* (annual); and Ruth Callanta, *Poverty: The Philippine Scenario* (Manila: Bookmark, 1988), pp.41–65 and 90–97.
29. As the last national census in the Philippines was done in 1980 most of the figures used in this section will have changed over the years but they remain valid as indicators of relative orders of magnitude.
30. According to the 1980 Census of Agriculture. From Yujiro Hayami, Agnes Quisumbing, and Lourdes Adriano, *In Search of a Land Reform Design for the Philippines*, Monograph Series no.1 (Los Banos: University of the Philippines Agricultural Policy Research Programme, June 1987), p.69.
31. According to David Wurfel, in 1960 57 per cent of all tenants farmed land owned by people whose total land ownership was under 7 hectares. See David Wurfel, "The Development of Post-War Philippine Land Reform: Political and Sociological Explanations", in *Second View from the Paddy*, edited by Antonio Ledesma, Perla Makil, and Virginia Miralao (Manila: Institute of Philippine Culture, 1983), p.8.
32. See James Scott, *The Moral Economy of the Peasant: Rebellion and Subsistence in Southeast Asia* (New Haven: Yale University Press, 1976), chapters 1 and 2.
33. *Far Eastern Economic Review*, 5 March 1987, p.33.
34. Ibid., p.33.
35. The retention limit of seven hectares has been used for rice and corn lands under both the Marcos land reform programme and the 1988 CARP. In 1987 the World Bank concluded that the seven-hectare retention limit

was viable, given that Japan and South Korea successfully adopted three-hectare limits. If all farms larger than seven hectares were redistributed, it would affect just under 6 per cent of all farms nationally, but almost one-third (32.5 per cent) of the nation's total farm area. If applied to Negros Occidental, this would affect only about one out of every ten farms, but it would mean redistributing almost two-thirds (64.3 per cent) of the province's total farmland because of the large size of these farms.

36. Mahar Mangahas, "Land and Natural Resources Reform", *Kasarinlan* 2, no.1 (3rd qtr. 1986):20.

37. Harry Oshima, "Postwar Philippine Economic Growth in Comparative Perspective: An Overview" (Makati: Philippine Society for International Development, November 1982), p.21.

38. NEDA, *Medium-Term Plan*, p.16.

39. Ibid., p.36.

40. Hayami et al., op. cit., p. 2.

41. *Constitution of the Republic of the Philippines*, Article XIII, Section 1.

42. *Far Eastern Economic Review*, 5 March 1987, p.32.

43. Based on this, the potential total coverage of the reform programme was estimated at some 16 to 17 million hectares of land, affecting about half of the nation's population.

44. David Wurfel, "Land Reform: Contexts, Accomplishments and Prospects Under Marcos and Aquino" (Paper presented at the annual meeting of the Association of Asian Studies, San Francisco, March 1988), p.18.

45. NEDA, *Medium-Term Plan*, p.43.

46. Philippine Institute for Development Studies, "Economic Recovery and Long-Run Growth: A Review of the First Eleven Months of the Aquino Government" (Manila: PIDS, February 1987), p.iv.

47. Hayami et al., op. cit., p.59.

48. See William Thiesenhusen, *Land Reform in the Philippines*, Occasional Papers on Southeast Asia, No.14 (Madison: University of Wisconsin, 1988), pp.13–15; and the *Far Eastern Economic Review*, 2 July 1987, p.22.

49. Wurfel, "Land Reform: Contexts, Accomplishments and Prospects Under Marcos and Aquino", p.15.

50. *Manila Chronicle*, 23 July 1987, p.1.

51. *Manila Chronicle*, 24 July 1987, p.2.

52. Wurfel, "Land Reform: Contexts, Accomplishments and Prospects Under Marcos and Aquino", p.26.

53. *Philippine Daily Inquirer*, 4 September 1987, p.4.

54. *Manila Chronicle*, 24 April 1988, p.11.

55. Yujiro Hayami, Agnes Quisumbing, and Lourdes Adriano, "In Search of

a New Land Reform Paradigm: A Perspective from the Philippines" (unpublished manuscript, 1988), chapter 3, p.39.

56. *Manila Chronicle*, 8 June 1988, p.1.
57. *Manila Chronicle*, 16 June 1988, p.14.
58. *Philippine Daily Inquirer*, 3 April 1988, p.9.
59. Hayami et. al, "In Search of a New Land Reform Paradigm: A Perspective from the Philippines", chapter 3, p.43.
60. Wurfel, "Land Reform: Contexts, Accomplishments and Prospects Under Marcos and Aquino", p.16.
61. Hayami et al., "In Search of a New Land Reform Paradigm: A Perspective from the Philippines", chapter 3, p.43.
62. Wurfel, "Land Reform: Contexts, Accomplishments and Prospects Under Marcos and Aquino", p.25.
63. Ibid., p.11.
64. *Asia Magazine*, 24 January 1988, p.290.
65. May 1987 World Bank report on the Accelerated Land Reform Programme, reproduced in the *Manila Chronicle*, 23 June 1987, p.11.
66. Bruce Koppel, "Land Reform in the Philippines — A Bumpy Road", in *The World and I* (October 1988), p.139.
67. Real GDP was projected to grow between 5.5 and 6.0 per cent in 1989 and 1990.
68. *Far Eastern Economic Review*, 24 September 1987, p.87.

chapter 11

The Prospects for Change in a "Changeless Land"

I had taken the oath to be President of a country that had lost everything, everything but honor. But with honor came a renewed faith in national leadership and in the ability of our race to change things for the better given the will and the courage to do it.

— Corazon Aquino
State of the Nation Address
27 July 1987

We conclude by returning to some of the questions asked at the outset of this book. What aspects of Philippine politics and government have changed and what have stayed the same? What are the consequences of the mix of continuity and change for democracy in the Philippines? How stable is the democratic system? How effective will it be in meeting the challenges of the 1990s? What are the prospects and mechanisms for change in the future?

To answer these questions we begin by assessing Aquino's legacy. We then summarize the key elements of continuity and change in politics and government. Finally, we identify a number of future challenges for Philippine politics and government, and suggest some of the factors that will determine the stability, responsiveness, and effectiveness of democracy in the future.

The Aquino Legacy: The Restoration of Traditional Politics

A balanced assessment of the Aquino legacy must begin with an appreciation of the extremely difficult situation she inherited on 25 February 1986. On that day Corazon Aquino became president of a divided and traumatized nation. She had relatively little experience, almost no time to prepare, and her original Cabinet was a fractious coalition of anti-Marcos figures. The national government she inherited was comatose and bankrupt; foreign debt payments sapped the government's extremely limited resources; and local government had ceased to function in many parts of the country. The communist insurgents, although set back by the peaceful ouster of Marcos, still possessed a formidable capability to challenge the new government politically and militarily.

Compounding these problems was the questionable loyalty of many politicians, officials, officers, and soldiers. Particularly menacing was the Armed Forces of the Philippines (AFP), which was ridden with factions, some of which challenged the authority and legitimacy of the civilian government. Finally, the EDSA "revolution" had caused most Filipinos' expectations to rise to extremely high levels − but it had not produced a clear-cut mandate for action.

Although Aquino was immensely popular, many of her initial policies antagonized or alienated key groups. Her conciliatory approach to the communists aggravated the military. Her decision to replace all local officials angered many members of the traditional political élite. Her toleration of labour unrest upset big business. Her failure to advocate rapid and genuine socio-economic reforms disappointed progressives in her government and on the left. Finally, the apparent confusion and indecision of her government frustrated the middle class.

At the same time, Marcos loyalists, supporters of Juan Ponce Enrile, and other threatened or ambitious groups attempted to destabilize or dominate the young government. In the face of these challenges, Aquino slowly began to realize that her popularity did not translate into a tangible, reliable, and usable source of support. Faced, at least in theory, with the choice of seeking the support of the left or the right, the government quite naturally (given its composition) opted to move right. The rhetoric of institutionalizing "people power" quickly gave way to the restoration of more traditional democratic institutions. In November 1986 Aquino sought and received the support of the Ramos faction of the military in order to counter the challenge posed by Enrile. After initially repudiating them, the Aquino coalition also began to court former Marcos supporters during the May 1987 congressional elections, and continued to do so during the January 1988 local elections. By mid-1987, following the collapse of the cease-fire with the communists and the left's poor showing in the May congressional elections, the government had adopted an essentially adversarial relationship with the left.

In addition to self-preservation, the Aquino government had three broad objectives during its first three years: national reconciliation, reconstructing democratic institutions, and economic recovery and reform. How successful was the government in achieving these goals? What are the consequences of its success or failure?

The government, or more specifically President Aquino, succeeded in reconciling and unifying the nation on one, very important level. Aquino was the only leader who had the popularity, stature, and personality to hold the nation together, both politically and emotionally, in the crisis-ridden months following the fall of Marcos. Despite all the shortcomings of her government, Aquino remained the legitimate and preferred leader in the eyes of most Filipinos. During the first two critical years of her government she preserved much of her saint-like stature by keeping clear of the political in-fighting and bickering that took place within her Cabinet and the Congress. The fundamental goodness of Aquino as a person and a leader was one of the few things most Filipinos could agree on.

In other important ways, however, the task of reconciliation and unification was not completed. The reconciliation that occurred was mostly between the warring factions of the traditional élite − that is, between the anti- and pro-Marcos groups. A degree of élite *rapprochement* was necessary to reduce the extreme polarization that had characterized Philippine politics since the assassination of Benigno Aquino; and it probably was inevitable, given Philippine culture and the fluidity of political affiliations. Unfortunately, however, this form of reconciliation took precedence over that between the government and the more progressive groups in society. Beginning in mid-1987 the legal left was increasingly harrassed by the military and vigilantes, and subsequently driven underground. Their democratic space began to disappear, and as it did, so did many people's hopes for genuinely pluralistic politics.

As for President Aquino's second objective, that of reconstructing democratic institutions, we have seen that she stubbornly carried out her commitment to restore democratic institutions and processes. By doing so, she deserves credit for successfully resuscitating the Philippines' democratic tradition and defending it in the face of considerable threats. But we have also seen that Aquino's vision of democracy was extremely limited. She chose the comfort and security of traditional élite government and politics and abandoned whatever populist and progressive leanings she might have had. She saw the restoration of democratic institutions as an end in itself; or as F. Sionil Jose has observed, she was more concerned with "the form rather than the substance of democracy".[1]

With the notable exception of her firm commitment to restoring democratic institutions and political freedoms, Aquino was ambivalent and tentative about many of the policy issues that affected the *quality* of Philippine democracy. She took more than a year to propose a faint-hearted agrarian reform programme. Although she spoke out against human rights abuses, corruption, and nepotism, she did little to deter their occurrence. She failed to address in a timely or effective manner the challenge of decentralization, the failure of law and justice at the grass-roots level, the need for family planning, and the problem of environmental degradation. Although she remained popular, Aquino's ambivalence on many of these issues resulted in the gradual erosion of her once-unmatched moral authority.

President Aquino presided over a significant economic recovery and freed the economy from the worst abuses of the Marcos era. Her government carried out important economic reforms needed to make the economy more efficient and increase the influence of domestic and international market forces. But the government's commitment to another kind of economic reform – the more equal distribution of economic assets and opportunities – was limited. Consequently, while the economy was freed from many government-imposed distortions, the control of economic assets and access to economic opportunities remained so skewed that the restoration of a more market-driven economy is likely to reinforce existing inequalities, not reduce them. While a reduction in the government's role in the economy is generally commendable, there is a risk that the traditional economic élite will use privatization as a way to increase its control over the government's economic development programme for its own benefit.

The frustrations some Filipinos have felt with the Aquino government have caused them to claim that "nothing has changed". By saying this, some mean to suggest, inaccurately and unfairly, that the Aquino government is no different from that of Marcos. Others say this as a way of suggesting, with considerably more validity, that there has been a revival of traditional élite democracy. Implicit in these criticisms is the notion that the Aquino government either betrayed a commitment to be more innovative and progressive, or that it missed opportunities to effect change.

Could President Aquino have done more? It was unrealistic, of course, to expect that one person could single-handedly cause a dramatic remaking of Philippine politics and society – especially given the country's numerous problems and divisions. It was equally unrealistic to expect that Aquino would somehow be a different kind of person than her background and personality suggested; or that she would demonstrate a high degree of expertise in governing when she did not have any prior experience. In addition to her own inexperience, conservatism, and cautiousness, Aquino was also constrained by the military, the strength of the traditional élite, the poor condition of the government bureaucracy, the government's debt burden, and the communist insurgency.

It was also unrealistic, in retrospect, to expect a widespread receptivity to major change in the months and years following the February 1986 revolution. By 1986 Filipinos had been buffetted by almost three years of political and economic crises. As the February 1987 constitutional plebiscite and May 1987 congressional elections showed, most Filipinos wanted stability and a return to normalcy, not more change and uncertainty. Moreover, many problems simply could not be solved by presidential decrees or legislation. Many issues, like corruption and nepotism, were deep-rooted and long-standing and were, therefore, not susceptible to quick change.

Finally, it was also unrealistic to expect that the Aquino government would not do whatever was necessary to protect and strengthen its own position, given the array of real and perceived challenges it faced. It was also naive to think that the Philippine élite would voluntarily make changes that it perceived would threaten its own power and position. For all these reasons, the Aquino government's move to a more traditional and conservative stance was probably inevitable.

Despite these constraints, President Aquino could have used the power of her office and her person more actively and effectively. For example, she could have done more to limit her family's influence in government and politics. This would have set an important example for other political families and protected her government from charges of corruption and nepotism. She could have brought to trial (in civilian courts) some of the soldiers accused of major human rights violations in order to underscore her government's commitment to human rights and demonstrate its control of the military. She could have experimented with the creation of a mass-based political party or organization. This would have made her less dependent on the military and the traditional élite. She could have made more principled choices concerning which Marcos-era politicians and local "war-lords" she was prepared to have associated with her government. Finally, she could have been more outspoken in support of agrarian reform, and set an example for landowners by voluntarily subjecting her family's 6,000-hectare Hacienda Luisita to land reform, rather than going along with the minimum requirements under the 1988 legislation.

All of these options were available to Aquino, and all would have been beneficial to the nation. They would have required a willingness to take some risks, and some of them would also have involved sacrifices on the part of her family. But all of them could have been pursued by Aquino without seriously jeopardizing her government. Instead, she opted for an excessively conservative and cautious stance. She accepted the pre-martial law status quo, and she (and her advisors) became overly protective of her office and her family.

The Aquino legacy, then, is a mixed one. She held the country together, restored political freedoms and democracy, and resuscitated the economy. These are all major accomplishments, given the challenges and constraints her government faced. They were critical to national recovery and are essential prerequisites for future progress.

At the same time, however, a variety of factors combined to make the Aquino government's approach to government, politics, and socio-economic issues an essentially conservative one. As a result of this and other cultural and political factors beyond the government's direct control, the Philippines now has a system of government and politics that combines elements of change with powerful traditional influences and structures. The following two sections summarize these elements of change and continuity.

What has Changed?

No society is completely changeless. The period since 1986 has produced a number of significant changes in the Philippines. These include many dramatic departures from the Marcos era as well as several important changes from the pre-martial law era.

The single most significant change is the increased role of the military in politics. There are two distinct, but related, dimensions to this change: 1) the increased influence of the military in governance and policy-making; and 2) the emergence of groups of military extremists intent on overthrowing the Aquino government and creating a new political order. As we have seen, Chief of Staff and then Secretary of Defence Fidel Ramos, by allying with Aquino against Enrile and then defending the president against extra-constitutional attempts to unseat her, became perhaps the second most powerful member of the Aquino government. As a result of the influence of Ramos and other "constitutionalists" in the AFP, by the end of 1986 the military had claimed the right to determine or heavily influence a wide range of government policies. It also played a part in deciding the extent and character of permissable political participation and played a sometimes dominant role in local politics and governance.

Although they were unsuccessful, the recurring attempts by military extremists to overthrow the Aquino government had a number of important consequences for government and politics. First, the coup attempts undermined the civilian government's efforts to establish its stability and authority. Secondly, as noted, the coup attempts increased the influence of the military "constitutionalists" within the civilian government, although they also further aggravated divisions within the military. Thirdly, they emboldened the otherwise ineffective rightist opposition to the Aquino government at the same time that they bolstered the sagging fortunes of the communists. Fourthly, they damaged the prospects for a sustained economic recovery by reducing the country's attractiveness to investors, bankers, and tourists. Finally, they required the Aquino government to repeatedly focus on the problem of maintaining (or restoring) political stability, often to the neglect of other pressing issues, such as agricultural underdevelopment, rapid population growth, and environmental degradation.

Despite the increased influence of the military in the Philippines, it is important to emphasize that its role is not comparable to that of the military in Thailand or Indonesia — at least, not yet. In these two countries the military remains the single most powerful influence on government and politics (although this appears to be changing in Thailand). In contrast, in the Philippines the military is one of a number of groups competing for political power and influence. In some issue areas it is clearly the single most powerful actor. But there are limits on its influence, including public opinion (which is heavily influenced by the Church, the Congress, the media, and other groups wary of the military), the military's unsavoury past performance under Marcos, its own internal divisions, and its reliance on American military assistance.

A second significant change from the pre-martial law era is the entrenchment of the revolutionary left. The communist presence throughout much of the country is the result of years of organizing by the CPP, the NPA, and other sympathetic groups; the abuses of the Marcos era; the weakness of the government in the countryside; and the fundamental inequality of Philippine society. Since 1986, however, the revolutionary left has been weakened by Aquino's popularity; by improvements in the economy and in the military's counter-insurgency capabilities; and by the spread of anti-communist vigilante groups. The movement has also been divided by internal rivalries and by long-standing and recurring disagreements over tactics and strategies. Finally, it must also continually contend with the underlying conservatism of peasant society.

For all of these reasons the prospects for the communist movement are uncertain, and its fortunes will fluctuate over time and vary from province to province. Nevertheless, the revolutionary infrastructure is sufficiently entrenched so that it will not be easily or quickly dismantled. For the foreseeable future the communists will continue to have the capability to attack the government militarily and undermine it politically. They will encourage extremism on both the left and the right in order to destabilize the democratic system, and will oppose the efforts of reformists on the non-communist left. Finally, they will provide an alternative to traditional politics and society and will remain a nucleus for a larger movement in the event of a return to authoritarianism, a dramatic economic downturn, or some other national crisis.

The increased role of the Catholic Church in politics and society is another notable change from the pre-martial law period. Looked at in the context of the last century of Philippine history, the increased role of the Church during the 1980s can be considered to be in the tradition of religious-cum-political activism begun by Fathers Burgos, Gomez, and Zamora in the late 1880s. But the role of the Church in shaping political events, particularly in late 1985 and early 1986, went well beyond that tradition. The influence of the Church on events and on the Aquino government was unprecedented. However, despite the Church's considerable influence, its power to affect policy-making is limited, as shown by the disregard most congressmen demonstrated towards the Church's call for genuine agrarian reform.

The peaceful unseating of Marcos resulted in the triumph of centrist activists within the Church. Consequently, the Church appears to be firmly committed to encouraging moderate socio-economic progress. But it remains to be seen how it will reconcile its conservative dogma (concerning, for example, its views on the role of women and its prohibition on artificial birth control) with its concern with socio-economic progress.

Another notable break with the past is the increased role that non-governmental organizations (NGOs) and the private sector are now playing in public affairs, on both the local and national levels. NGOs involved in socio-economic development were consulted in the drawing up of the Medium-Term Philippine Economic Development Plan. They helped to plan and monitor the Community Employment and Development Programme and they will also play a role in the planning and implementation of the Philippine Assistance Plan (PAP). Cause-oriented and sectoral groups such as women's rights and legal aid organizations, peasant groups, anti-U.S. bases and anti-nuclear groups, anti-foreign debt groups, and environmental groups are involved in public education, organizing, and lobbying. NGOs encourage local initiatives and strengthen local capabilities; they produce new leaders and build new constituencies; and they make government officials and politicians more responsive and accountable.

Members of the business community have also become more socially and politically active. Business executives who were apolitical in the early 1980s are now involved in socio-economic development organizations such as the Bishops'and Businessmen's Conference on Human Development, the Makati Business Club, and Philippine Business for Social Progress. A number of prominent business leaders, such as Jaime Ongpin, Jose Concepcion, and Daniel Lacson ended up serving in government. There is a risk that the increased role of the private sector in government will result in an over-emphasis on the privatization of government services and result in a "trickle-down" approach to economic development. Nevertheless, on balance the increase in private sector activism is a very positive development.

There have also been other significant, but less dramatic, structural changes in government and politics since 1986. The 1987 Constitution reduces the power of the president somewhat, makes the judiciary more independent, and provides some mechanisms for increased participation by the people. The return to an American-style system of checks and balances reduces the risk that power will be abused or misused. However, it also runs the risk of dispersing power and responsibility even more. The absence of a strong leadership, unified political parties, and a national consensus, has made the government even less able to act.

There have also been two subtle but important developments in the Philippines' political culture. First, the Filipino view of democracy has been affected by two historical experiences: the abuses of the Marcos dictatorship and the triumph of "people power" during the EDSA revolt. The failure of the Marcos dictatorship may have reduced the appeal that authoritarianism has for some Filipinos. The EDSA "revolution" created a myth of popular participation that had not previously existed, except perhaps during Ramon Magsaysay's presidential campaign. These two experiences are now a part of the collective national psyche. Taken together, they may strengthen the national commitment to democratic government and political freedom.

Secondly, the restoration of democracy has also contributed to an increase in Philippine nationalism. This is due to the pride most Filipinos felt in evicting Marcos, the manipulation of nationalism for domestic political purposes, and the increased activism of nationalist groups. Not surprisingly, much of this nationalism is focused on the

Philippines' relationship with the United States. There is a lingering resentment of American support for Marcos; frustration with the niggardly way foreign (predominantly American) banks have responded to the government's calls for debt relief; dissatisfaction with the social and security consequences of the U.S. military bases in the Philippines; and opposition to the nuclear weapons presumed to be stored in the bases and the nuclear-powered naval vessels that dock at Subic Naval Base.

Philippine nationalism, and its strong current of anti-Americanism, are not new, of course. What is notable, however, is the increased scope of its appeal. This is primarily attributable to generational change. Filipinos under the age of forty (who now comprise a large majority of the population) have no recollection of, and little appreciation for, the once mythical "special relationship" with the United States. Instead, during their lifetimes, these younger Filipinos have seen the United States as a sometimes bullying superpower that has pursued its own military and economic interests — even if it meant supporting dictators such as Ferdinand Marcos.

As a result of this experience, more Filipinos are questioning the benefits of the Philippines' historically close ties with the United States. Criticisms of the United States, and particularly of the U.S. military bases, used to be voiced primarily by students, leftist academics, and other nationalists. Increasingly, however, the urban middle-class and "mainstream" political leaders have also become more critical. Consequently, there is a growing consensus among politically active Filipinos that the U.S. bases should be phased out, although there is less agreement about how quickly this should happen.

The end of the American military presence in the Philippines will go a long way in eliminating the remaining vestiges of the "special relationship" with the United States. This will undoubtedly be beneficial to Filipinos' sense of independence, self-determination, and national identity. But it will also require that Filipinos be prepared to accept a more distant and perhaps less cordial relationship with the U.S. Government. The challenge for both the Philippines and the United States will be to successfully manage the transition to a new relationship.

Finally, with the passage of time the global environment has changed significantly. The world of the 1990s is very different from the world of the 1960s or 1970s. In Asia, the interests and capabilities of the United States, the Soviet Union, and Japan have changed dramatically. Most notable are the ascendancy of Japan as a regional (and global) power and the end of the cold war rivalry between the United States and the Soviet Union. With the end of the cold war, the Philippines will become less important to the United States, both militarily and politically. If Filipinos want the attention of Washington they are going to have to compete for it; and if they want economic or other types of assistance, they are going to have to show that it is both appreciated and effectively used.

The situation in Southeast Asia has also become far more complex and competitive. The most notable change from the 1970s is the rapid economic development of the region's non-communist countries. As a result, Singapore, Thailand, Malaysia, and Indonesia have become more active, sophisticated, and effective players in regional and international affairs. In contrast, the Philippines has been preoccupied with its internal affairs for most of the last fifteen years. Too few Filipinos have focused their attention on their nation's diminishing position in the world, and particularly in the international economy. If Filipinos do not recognize their country's non-competitiveness and take steps to reverse it, they run the risk of falling even further behind in the fierce contest for international investment, loans, and technology.

What Remains the Same?

The restoration of traditional élite democracy reflects the fact that many aspects of Philippine politics and society remain largely unchanged. The absence of change is rooted in the continuing influence of traditional political culture, the concentration of economic and political power in a conservative élite, and in the face of these conditions, the inability of radical or reformist groups to significantly alter the *status quo*.

Philippine political culture continues to be extremely personalistic. Political parties are vehicles for promoting leading political figures rather than policies. Personal ties rather than ideology or issues determine most elections, especially on the local level. When it comes to getting things done, personal relationships are often far more important than institutions, laws, and procedures. This tradition of personalism was manifest in Aquino's initial cult-like popularity, and it was reinforced by her advisors' willingness to exploit her popularity. The 1987 Constitution became known as the "Cory Constitution", the pro-administration candidates for Congress became "Cory's candidates", and "Cory" was both the restorer and the defender of democracy. As a result, most Filipinos have looked to Aquino – rather than to laws and institutions – to somehow provide all the solutions to their problems. Consequently, the legitimacy of democracy in the Philippines has become too closely linked to the popularity and effectiveness of President Aquino.

The primacy of family ties also continues to exert a powerful influence on politics – despite the prohibition against family-based "political dynasties" contained in the 1987 Constitution. For an example of a powerful political dynasty one needs to look no further than President Aquino's own family. The Aquino-Cojuangco clan has replaced the Marcos-Romualdez family as the country's dominant political clan. At least six of President Aquino's relatives hold elected office, and for part of the first two years of her administration, her brother and brother-in-law headed the two leading political parties in her coalition. Even the left, which so vociferously criticized traditional politics, recognized the importance of family ties. When the ANP challenged the results of the May 1987 congressional elections it cited, among other things, the improbability that candidate Horacio "Boy" Morales could lose in his own town, where he is related to about 40 per cent of the residents.[2]

The strength of family ties, combined with the economic power of a number of families, have given the traditional élite remarkable resilience. Filipinos have exchanged Marcos's "dictatorship with a smiling face" for Aquino's élitism with a smiling face. Many of the leading names in national politics today are the same as they were in 1970: Aquino, Laurel, Salonga, Sumulong, Manglapus, Pimentel, and Osmeña, to name just a few. After being denied a role in government and politics for over a decade, these families are intent on reclaiming their power and prestige. On the provincial and local levels the members of long-standing political families are once again vying among themselves for pre-eminence. At the same time, however, the emergence of a small group of more technocratic local and provincial leaders (such as Governors Lacson, Pagdanganan, and O'Campo) suggests that personalistic and family-based politics may be in decline in some areas.

The lack of fundamental change in socio-economic conditions has meant that the culture of poverty has more or less remained the same. The Aquino government's poverty alleviation programme has been dependent on sustained economic growth — essentially a "trickle down" approach to poverty alleviation. It does not appear that the recovery has significantly improved the economic well-being of the poor in the Philippines. Moreover, there is little evidence of improvement in the delivery of most government services to the countryside, where the majority of the poor live. The government's heavy debt burden will continue to limit its expenditures on poverty alleviation. At the same time, the effect of agrarian reform on poverty alleviation is likely to be minimal and slow in coming. Finally, rapid population growth will undermine any gains made by either the economy or the government. Improvements take time, of course, but as of 1989 the prospects for a rapid or significant reduction in absolute and relative poverty did not appear bright. As a result, poverty, inequity, and dependence are likely to continue to characterize the countryside. This makes for a very shaky foundation upon which to build a democracy.

There is also considerable continuity in key aspects of the government. As Alex Magno noted in 1987, "Many see the present political situation not as a lively experiment with new and dynamic democratic forms but as an intellectually timid return to the past".[3] A unitary state was restored with a highly centralized, but resource-starved, bureaucracy. The re-creation of a presidential system with a bicameral legislature restored traditional checks and balances as well as the potential for debilitating rivalry between the executive branch and the legislature. The House of Representatives once again is dominated by conservative landowning interests, while the current relative liberalness of the Senate is not likely to last. Finally, the government continues to play an influential, though reduced, role in the economy.

Traditional patterns of political behaviour have changed little. The major political parties remain non-ideological groupings of factions that are personality-based and election-driven. Regular party switching continues, particularly within the nominally pro-Aquino coalition; and it is likely to continue until the 1992 elections compel the formation of temporary alliances. Meanwhile, sectoral, cause-oriented, and other interest groups continue to play a relatively limited role because of their own institutional weaknesses, divisions among themselves, and their inability to deliver (or withhold) the vote of their constituencies.

There is also continuity in the fierce — and often illegal and violent — competition for elected office. Once in office, staying there still depends on the office-holder's ability to dispense favours, patronage, and money. This, in turn, generates a never-ending litany of charges of election fraud, corruption, nepotism, favouritism, and incompetence. This behaviour undermines the credibility of the electoral process and the legitimacy of laws and institutions.

Finally, the behaviour of the media is another constant. The extremely competitive market for newspapers in Metro Manila (where the majority of the nation's papers are sold) encourages sensationalism as well as superficial and inaccurate reporting. Furthermore, the print and broadcast media often reflect the political interests and biases of their owners. Consequently, it is extremely difficult to distinquish between fact, opinion, and "disinformation". This lack of accuracy and credibility is more than just a regrettable idiosyncracy of the press. The shortage of accurate and credible reporting weakens the public's understanding of public affairs and reduces the accountability of government officials and politicians.

What accounts for the Philippines' "changelessness"? First, there is the strength of cultural influences, and in particular personalism, *pakikisama*, and traditional Catholicism. When combined with the conservatism engendered by subsistence agriculture, these cultural influences have caused most Filipinos to be remarkably patient and accepting, sometimes bordering on passive and fatalistic. This is reflected in public opinion polls, which, according to Felipe Miranda,

> testify to the inherent reluctance of most Filipinos to press radical
> demands on their political authorities. . . . Filipinos responding
> to survey probes have generally been optimistic as regards their
> living conditions, whether they be poor or not.[4]

A second reason is the large disparity in wealth and incomes, which gives overwhelming advantage to the conservative élite that controls the government and economy. The power of the élite, combined with the conservatism and passivism of many peasants, has made it difficult to organize and mobilize the forces of change. Moreover, regional rivalries and linguistic differences have made it difficult to form national organizations.

Martial law is another contributing factor. A decade of political development and at least half a decade of economic development were lost because of martial law. The relatively strict political control exerted by Marcos from 1972 to 1981 retarded the development of new political leaders, groups, and ideas. The traditional political leadership was emasculated, controls were placed on the creation of new organizations, and independent political thinking was discouraged. As a result, the thinking and behaviour of many of the leaders today are shaped by their memories of the pre-martial law era. The decline and collapse of the economy during the first half of the 1980s have also contributed to the country's changelessness. The country's economic stagnation reduced the expansion of the middle class and entrepreneurs – two groups that could be expected to reject traditional politics.

Finally, there is the appeal of familiarity. Conditions had become so bad under Marcos, and the problems facing the country by 1986 were so intimidating that many Filipinos welcomed the restoration of a political and social system that was known to them.

Challenges for the Future

Does the mixture of continuity and change create a stable and effective political system? Or are the two elements at odds with each other, thus creating an inherently unstable and unworkable system?

Despite the instability caused by successive coup attempts by members of the military, the traditional democracy restored by President Aquino is not *inherently* unstable or unviable. Democracy – even in its élite form – has considerable appeal to most Filipinos. The majority accept and understand personalistic and family-based politics. They enjoy political competition and look to it as a way of advancing their personal interests in large and small ways. Furthermore, the alternatives to democracy are limited. Authoritarianism has been discredited, and socialism and communism are considered alien by many.

There is, however, one major threat to the stability and viability of democracy in the Philippines: a significant decline in its legitimacy.

There are several ways that this might happen. First, the legitimacy of the democratic system might be undermined by the irresponsible and self-interested behaviour of the political élite. Regrettably, there are signs that this is happening. Indeed, many of the most common features of traditional political behaviour — the appearance and reality of political corruption, claims of election fraud, and the manipulation or selective application of laws — can erode the system's legitimacy.

Secondly, the democratic system's legitimacy might be undermined if key political actors do not abide by a set of rules governing their participation in the system. The right opposition's flirtation with military interventionism and other extra-constitutional paths to power is a disturbing example of this problem. Looking to the immediate future, the conduct of the 1992 elections — which are likely to include simultaneous presidential and congressional elections — will play a critical role in either bolstering or eroding the legitimacy of electoral politics.

Finally, the legitimacy of the democratic system will also be affected by the government's effectiveness. Seymour Lipset has warned that "a breakdown of effectiveness, repeatedly or for a long period, will endanger even a legitimate system's stability".[5] In 1989 it appeared that the Aquino government was experiencing a "breakdown of effectiveness". This was most visible in politically critical Metro Manila, which suffered from crime, daily power shortages, poor garbage collection, endless traffic jams, and an acute shortage of public transportation. Growing public frustration with the government's inability to solve these problems was a contributing factor in the decision to launch the December 1989 coup attempt.

Can the Philippines' traditional democratic system deal effectively with the major challenges the country faces during the 1990s? We conclude by outlining the dimensions of these challenges and suggesting some of the factors that might determine their outcomes.

Strengthening National and Local Government

The Philippines faces the paradox of needing to strengthen the effectiveness of its national government at the same time that it begins to correct its over-centralization. Put another way, the national government must do fewer things better and sub-national government units must be given more responsibility and more resources. This will be difficult to accomplish, given the unitary structure of government, the limited capabilities of most local governments, and the persistence of traditional political behaviour. It will require a gradual transfer of fiscal, planning, and administrative authority to the provincial and local levels. For this to happen, however, the quality of local officials must be upgraded (through the electoral process and training) and local groups such as the Church, the media, and NGOs must be sufficiently vigilant to ensure honesty and accountability. While political devolution cannot be done hastily, it also cannot be avoided or postponed.

One of the most important tests of government on both the national and local levels will be the extent to which it demonstrates a sustained commitment to a more equitable distribution of political power and economic opportunity. A government that is highly effective, but that serves only the interests of the political and economic élite, is only slightly more desirable than an ineffective government. Not surprisingly, history suggests that political élites (in the Philippines and elsewhere) rarely are the champions of greater political and economic equity – especially if it results in a diminution of their power and wealth. Therefore, it will be up to a new generation of political parties and non-governmental groups – including interest- and cause-oriented groups, the Church, and the media – to bring pressure to bear on the elected officials.

Finally, given the highly (but selectively) legalistic nature of Philippine society, ways must be found to make the legal system a vehicle for change rather than an impediment to it. Historically, the legal system has been used as a way to protect élite interests, particularly with regard to the ownership of land. Prior to its emasculation under Marcos, the Supreme Court had not used its independence or authority to significantly effect social change. In the future, the legal system must demonstrate that it is responsive to the needs of the poor majority of Filipinos. In most cases new laws are not needed to make the system more responsive. What is needed are more and better-trained prosecutors and judges, more courts outside of Metro Manila, and more legal aid and education. There is also a need for quicker and firmer punishment for corruption and human rights violations, evasion of agrarian reform and taxes, and illegal or wanton exploitation of natural resources.

Reducing the Military's Role in Politics

The military is likely to continue to play a significant role in politics and policy-making for the foreseeable future. Military extremists will continue to pose an armed threat to the government and the constitution. Even if this threat is contained, the "constitutionalists" within the AFP will continue to assert their right to have a major say in shaping government policies, particularly on the wide range of issues related to national security.

The challenge for the civilian government will be to reduce the role of the military in policy-making by gradually establishing civilian credibility and by asserting civilian authority on national security affairs. Put another way, the civilian government must earn the respect of the military. To do this, politicians and officials must govern more effectively, develop greater expertise in national security issues, and work more closely with the military. The long-term goal should be to earn the respect of the younger generation of officers in order to restore their belief in the primacy of civilian rule. For this to happen it must occur on both the national and local levels.

Democracy in the Philippines will continue to face the threat of military intervention as long as the civilian political leadership fails to demonstrate its ability to govern effectively. The democratic system might be undermined in a more subversive way, however, if the military uses intimidation or force to limit the political participation of groups on the non-communist left. This, of course, would benefit the right. But more importantly, barring any group from participating in the democratic process would seriously undermine the legitimacy of the system.[6]

Reducing Poverty and Inequity

The Philippine economy is likely to grow at a rate of 4–6 per cent per year during the early 1990s. If this growth rate is maintained, it should improve the economic well-being of many Filipinos, particularly the relatively more skilled members of the work-force. But respectable macro-economic growth alone is not enough — there must also be a more equitable distribution of the benefits of economic growth. Only in this way can there be a significant reduction in the country's pervasive poverty.

The Aquino government's economic development plan called for a reduction in the incidence of poverty from 59 per cent of all families in 1985 to 45 per cent by 1992.[7] For this to be accomplished, the economy must grow almost 7 per cent each year (agriculture must grow 5 per cent a year, a rate considerably higher than the average for the 1980s). Furthermore, domestic investment must grow almost 20 per cent a year; about 950,000 new jobs must be created annually; and the government must spend relatively more on social services and less on defence.

These are appropriate and ambitious economic development targets. However, past Philippine governments have also drawn up impressive development plans, only to have them be ignored, circumvented, or undermined. The challenge in the coming years will be to sustain a genuine commitment to poverty reduction, and to secure the legislation and funding necessary to achieve it. A second challenge will be to address some of the other fundamental causes of poverty and inequality. These include the inequitable distribution of economic assets and opportunities, rapid population growth, uncontrolled environmental degradation, and the deterioration of the education system.

There are no quick or easy solutions to the inequitable distribution of wealth and economic opportunity in the Philippines. The most significant effort to address the problem, the 1988 Comprehensive Agrarian Reform Programme will have limited redistributive impact. Even if all the country's agricultural lands were distributed more equitably, there still would not be enough to go around. So although land reform is a political necessity, even a far more comprehensive redistribution of land would not be a panacea for socio-economic inequality. It would, however, be an important step in the right direction.

There are other causes of poverty and inequality that will be equally difficult to attack. Perhaps the most important is rapid population growth. Slowing the growth of the population has proven to be a complex and difficult task. Even the Marcos government's relatively active family planning programme during the late 1970s produced limited, though not inconsequential, results. At current rates of growth, the population will double from 60 million to 120 million in about 30 years. Rapid population growth has also contributed to two other vexing causes of poverty: the deterioration of the environment and the decline in the public education system.

The degradation of the Philippine environment and the mismanagement and destruction of its natural resources have reached crisis
proportions. Because of population pressure, poverty, and commercial
logging only about 7 per cent of the country's virgin forest remains.
At present rates of cutting this will disappear by the end of the 1990s.
Deforestation in turn causes soil erosion, flooding, and siltation of
rivers and lakes. The country's coastal zones and coral reefs are also
being rapidly destroyed by commercial development, pollution, and
over-fishing. In major cities, and particularly in Metro Manila, the air
is blackened by auto and bus exhaust, and human and industrial waste
are contaminating water supplies.

Protection of the environment and the careful management of natural
resources are not luxuries that only developed countries can afford. The
destruction of the Philippines' natural resources seriously threatens
the prospects for sustainable economic development over the long-
term. The contamination of air and water is creating huge future
costs for health care and clean-up. Equally important, environmental
degradation perpetuates and deepens existing inequities in society.
The poor are the ones who are victimized the most by environmental
destruction. They are the ones who suffer, for example, when deforestation causes their land to erode, their firewood supplies to dwindle,
and their catch of fish to decline because of siltation. Consequently,
the emerging environmental movement in the Philippines is being
driven by demands for socio-economic equity as much as by a desire
to protect the country's ravaged ecology. The success of this movement
will be critical to sustaining economic growth and improving equity.

The deterioration of public education also contributes to socio-
economic inequity. The Philippines' public education system was
once the pride of the country and gave it an important comparative
advantage because it produced a high literacy rate and a large pool
of English speakers. Equally important, it provided an opportunity for
upward social mobility. Today, however, the public education system is
impoverished and shoddy.[8] Although the country still boasts a high
literacy rate and an extremely large number of college graduates,
literacy is often in a regional dialect or "Taglish", and most colleges
and universities are little more than "diploma mills" or glorified high
schools. Equally important, the system no longer offers the promise
of a good education to those who cannot afford private schooling.

As a result, the system now reinforces the existing social stratification rather than diminishes it.

Finally, the government's domestic and foreign debt burden will reduce the amount it can spend on poverty alleviation. Consequently, the debt burden hurts poor Filipinos the most because they are the ones who rely on the government for basic social services. The debt burden also provides a convenient excuse for conservative congressmen to reduce the amounts budgeted for social programmes, particularly agrarian reform.

Ending the Communist Insurgency

The communist insurgency is largely, though not exclusively, a function of the problems discussed above: the weaknesses of the national and local governments, the role of the military, and pervasive poverty and inequity. The insurgency is, therefore, more a dependent than an independent variable. The solution to the problem will be found in the successful treatment of the challenges described above.

Looking to the future of the insurgency, three points should be kept in mind. First, in order for the communists to successfully control the countryside, they must first remove or otherwise neutralize any competing sources of authority, whether they be the government, landlords, or local "war-lords". This explains why the rise of local vigilante groups has been a problem for the communists. It is also the reason why the presence of a functioning local government apparatus is so critical to any counter-insurgency effort.

Secondly, communist infiltration does not succeed simply because of superior military force. The communists make a point of redressing grievances and providing other services that the government is unable or unwilling to provide. They offer a form of law and justice; reductions in rents paid by tenants; some basic social services; and intangibles such as pride, hope, and a cause. The challenge falls on the local and national governments to offer these as well.

Thirdly, the prospects for the insurgency will be significantly affected by the future of the rural economy. As we have seen, the economic decline of the early 1980s fuelled the insurgency, and the improvement in economic conditions during the first years of the Aquino government contributed to a decline in its strength. It is therefore safe to assume that the insurgency will rebound if coconut and sugar prices drop significantly (which is quite likely, given their volatility) and rural landlessness and unemployment continue to grow.

Building a National Consensus

Contrary to the hopes of many Filipinos, the restoration of traditional democracy has not produced solutions to many of the country's problems. Journalist Sheila Coronel has pointed out the paradox of the Philippines' restored democracy. According to her, "rather than helping build a national consensus, it has only engendered greater fragmentation and encouraged the further cleaving of our society into smaller and more antagonistic political and ideological loyalties".[9] As Coronel points out, a consensus concerning national interests and goals continues to elude Filipinos. There is little agreement about what the future should look like and how to get there.

The absence of consensus is caused in part by the diversity of Philippine society and the ambiguity about what it means to be Filipino. Philippine nationalists, for example, have been more successful at criticizing real and imagined foreign influences than at establishing an alternative vision of Philippine society that has broad appeal. The lack of consensus is also caused by the great disparity in power and wealth. Because the political power of the élite has been based on local and highly particularistic politics, the élite has been disinterested in developing genuinely national organizations or promoting national programmes.

The consequences of a lack of national unity and national purpose are subtle but profound. Journalist James Fallows has written that "When a country with extreme geographic, tribal, and social-class differences, like the Philippines, has only a weak offsetting sense of national unity, its public life . . . become[s] the war of every man against every man".[10] In such a situation, self-interest naturally takes precedence over the national interest. Because of this, as Fallows observed, "Practically everything that is public in the Philippines seems neglected or abused".[11] Taxes are not paid, laws are broken, corruption flourishes, and notions of civic duty are weakened. Finally, the absence of national unity also encourages a no-holds-barred struggle between competing groups within society. Differences, rather than commonalities, are emphasized; polarization increases; and norms governing political competition are discarded.

What will it take to create a stronger sense of national unity and to build a national consensus concerning the country's future? To begin with, existing sources of national unity must be identified and emphasized. This might include emphasizing the aspects of traditional culture that encourage mutual self-help and compassion, the religiousness of most Filipinos, the vitality that springs from ethnic and cultural diversity, and the experience of losing and then reclaiming democracy. Filipinos must also believe that they control their nation's destiny — and accept more responsibility for it. They need to stop viewing the United States as both the source of and the solution to most of their country's problems. Unfortunately, it will probably take a dramatic and possibly wrenching break with the United States to make this happen.

A second requirement for national unity is an unequivocal commitment to democracy. As we have seen, many Filipinos are attracted to the abstraction of democracy more than to its actual practice. William Overholt has pointed out that, "despite all the very real democratic euphoria, [the Aquino government's] social base was a populace that had repudiated democracy once before for not delivering growth, equity, and order, and would quickly do so again if those values still proved lacking".[12] Given the country's decidedly mixed experience with democracy over the last forty years and its difficulty with translating its love for democracy into practice, there must be a strengthening and redefinition of the democratic tradition in the Philippines. A new style of democratic government and politics must emerge that emphasizes greater participation and pluralism. This, in turn, requires a responsible and non-violent opposition, an apolitical military, a strong guarantee of human rights, and the ability of diverse groups to build political coalitions.

Transforming Philippine Politics

Can traditional élite democracy effectively address the challenges described above? Judging from the record of pre-martial law governments and the limited success of the Aquino government, there is no real cause for optimism. If élite democracy is not sufficiently responsive and effective, can it be improved? Will the traditional political and economic élite recognize that reform is in its long-term best interests? Might other sectors of society effectively pressure the élite to reform the system? Or is élite democracy so deeply rooted in traditional political culture and the élite so firmly in control that reform is impossible?

Regrettably, the conservatism and inequality of Philippine society make the prospects for either dramatic reform from above or revolution from below slight. There are, however, a number of ways that the political system might become more effective and more responsive to national needs. One way is through successful economic development. For example, the creation of a large class of self-sufficient peasant farmers might reduce the traditionally clientelistic nature of politics. The growth of the middle-class might create a powerful force for the modernization and liberalization of politics.

A second, less desirable, way to effect change is by experiencing another political or economic crisis. A dramatic increase in the communist insurgency, violent or disputed elections in 1992, or another economic crisis might discredit the existing system (and the élite) enough so that other political alternatives become attractive. These alternatives, however, might include undesirable forms of government such as a military junta or some other form of authoritarianism.

A third and more desirable way is through a gradual improvement in the political leadership. Clearly, there is a great need for better leadership in the Philippines. The sad fact is that there are too many politicians and too few statesmen. The élite's narrow self-interest traditionally has triumphed over larger national interests. Moreover, many of today's ageing political leaders are captives of the politics of the 1960s and 1970s.

The newness and vulnerability of the Philippines' democratic institutions require that Filipino politicians be more responsible than their counterparts in more established democracies. The relative youth of democratic institutions in the Philippines means that they lack well-established precedents, time-tested procedures, and clearly defined norms of conduct. As a result, there are relatively fewer institutional constraints on the political behaviour of politicians. Conversely, the Philippines' political institutions and processes are more vulnerable to damage caused by the irresponsibility or self-interest of politicians.

The political leadership, therefore, must begin to show greater respect for the nation's democratic institutions and processes. Clear standards of political conduct must be established and enforced. The rightist opposition must stop flirting with the military and hinting at taking extra-constitutional roads to power. The losers of elections must refrain from automatically blaming their loss on electoral fraud. Unless these and other types of irresponsible behaviour end, the credibility and legitimacy of the democratic system will be gradually and perhaps irreparably eroded.

There is, however, some cause for hope concerning the future quality of political leadership. The passage of time is gradually causing generational change, which is bringing to the forefront a younger and somewhat less traditional generation of leaders. New sources of leadership are emerging, including the private sector, cause-oriented groups, non-governmental organizations and even the military. The increased scrutiny of these same groups (and of the media) may also provide a greater degree of accountability.

A significant and lasting improvement in political leadership, however, will also require Filipino voters to be more selective about whom they elect and more demanding concerning the conduct of their elected officials. To their credit, most Filipinos are patient and indefatigable optimists. But they also often seem to have low expectations of their leaders and government. The challenge, therefore, is to reduce the widespread acceptance of corruption, favouritism, and inefficiency as norms for politics and government. To accomplish this difficult task the Church, non-governmental organizations, and the media must set higher standards of performance for public officials and encourage the public to do the same.

Perhaps it was inevitable that the Philippines had to take a step backward during the latter half of the 1980s, to the familiar system that existed before the Marcos dictatorship, so that it could take two steps forward into the twenty-first century. Based on the first three years of the Aquino government, however, it appears that the motivation of the leadership to boldly stride into the twenty-first century is not as strong as it should be. This raises the question of whether the Philippine élite will have, as President Aquino put it, "the will and the courage" to "change things for the better". If the élite does not possess the will and the courage, it raises the disturbing question of where the impetus for change will come from.

The most optimistic scenario for the future is one in which political change will be forced upon a reluctant élite by the increased power of emerging groups such as the middle class, sectoral and cause-oriented groups, and other non-governmental and Church-backed organizations. If change occurs in this way, however, it will be in spite of the desires of the traditional political élite rather than because of them. If this is the case, it will be critical that both the traditional élite and the emergent groups have a stronger commitment to peaceful, democratic change than was exhibited in the past.

NOTES

1. *Manila Chronicle*, 29 September 1987, p.5.
2. *Asiaweek*, 24 May 1987, p.14.
3. *Business Day*, 20 February 1987, p.5.
4. Felipe Miranda, *The March 1987 Public Opinion Report: A Political Analysis* (Quezon City: Ateneo de Manila/Social Weather Stations, 1987), p.49.
5. Seymour Martin Lipset, *Political Man: The Social Bases of Politics* (New York: Doubleday, 1963), p.67.
6. Alfred Stepan, *Rethinking Military Politics: Brazil and the Southern Cone* (Princeton: Princeton University Press, 1988), p.137.
7. National Economic Development Authority, *Medium-Term Philippine Development Plan: 1987–1992* (Manila: NEDA, 1986), p.33.
8. See *Far Eastern Economic Review*, 6 July 1989, pp.37–46.
9. *Manila Chronicle*, 22 October 1987, p.4.
10. James Fallows, "A Damaged Culture", *Atlantic Monthly* (November 1987), p.56.
11. Ibid., p.57.
12. William Overholt, "The Rise and Fall of Ferdinand Marcos", *Asian Survey* 26, no.11 (November 1986):1163.

Bibliography

Abinales, P.N. "The Philippine Military and the Marcos Regime". Quezon City: University of the Philippines Third World Studies Center, undated.

Abueva, Jose V. "Ideology and Practice in the 'New Society'". In *Marcos and Martial Law in the Philippines*, edited by David Rosenberg. Ithaca: Cornell University Press, 1979.

Abueva, Jose, and Raul de Guzman, eds. *Foundations and Dynamics of Filipino Government and Politics*. Manila: Bookmark, 1973.

Adversario, Patricia. "New Politics". *Veritas*, 23–29 April 1987, p.8.

Agoncillo, Teodoro. *Filipino Nationalism, 1872–1970*. Quezon City: R.P. Garcia Publishing Co., 1974.

Agpalo, Remigio. "The Philippines: From Communal To Societal Pangulo Regime". *Philippine Law Journal* 56, no.1 (March 1981).

Almond, Gabriel, and G. Bingham Powell. *Comparative Politics: A Developmental Approach*. Boston: Little, Brown, 1966.

Amnesty International. *Report on an Amnesty International Mission to the Republic of the Philippines*. London: Amnesty International, September 1982.

_____. *Philippines: Alleged Human Rights Violations by Vigilante Group*. New York: Amnesty International, July 1987.

_____. *Philippines: Unlawful Killings by Military and Paramilitary Forces*. New York: Amnesty International, March 1988.

Aquino, Belinda A. *Politics of Plunder: The Philipines Under Marcos.* Occasional Paper No.87-1. Quezon City: University of the Philippines, College of Public Administration, January 1987.

_____. "The Philippines in 1987: Beating Back the Challenge of August". In *Southeast Asian Affairs 1988.* Singapore: Institute of Southeast Asian Studies, 1988.

Aquino, Corazon C. Speeches of Corazon C. Aquino. Office of the President, Quezon City, 1986, 1987.

_____. Major campaign speeches:
"Building From the Ruins", 6 January 1986.
"Broken Promises in the Land of Promise", 16 January 1986.
"Tearing Down the Dictatorship, Rebuilding Democracy", 23 January 1986.

Asia Society, The. *The Philippines: Facing the Future.* Asian Agenda Report No.4. New York: The Asia Society, 1986.

Ateneo-Social Weather Stations. *Public Opinion Report.* Quezon City: Ateneo de Manila University and Social Weather Stations, June, October 1986, March 1987, September–October 1987.

Berry, William "The Changing Role of the Philippine Military During Martial Law and the Implications For the Future". In *The Armed Forces in Contemporary Asian Societies,* edited by Edward Olsen and Stephen Jurika. Boulder: Westview Press, 1986.

Bishops-Businessmen's Conference for Human Development, The. *The BBC Nationwide Sociopolitical Opinion Surveys of 1984 and 1985.* Manila: The Bishops-Businessmen's Conference, August 1985.

Boado, Eufresina. "Incentive Policies and Forest Use in the Philippines". In *Public Policies and the Misuse of Forest Resources,* edited by Robert Repetto and Malcom Gillis. New York: University of Cambridge, 1988.

Bonner, Raymond. *Waltzing With a Dictator: The Marcoses and the Making of American Policy.* New York: Times Books, 1987.

Bresnan, John, ed. *Crisis in the Philippines: The Marcos Era and Beyond.* Princeton: Princeton University Press, 1986.

Brillantes, Alex B., Jr. *Dictatorship and Martial Law: Philippine Authoritarianism in 1972.* Manila: Great Books Publishers, 1987.

Brillantes, Alex B., Jr. "Decentralization in the Philippines: An Overview". *Philippine Journal of Public Administration* 31, no.2 (April 1987):131–48

_____. "Decentralization and Local Autonomy: The Source of Frustration of Local Officials". Quezon City: University of the Philippines, College of Public Administration, November 1988.

Broad, Robin. *Unequal Alliance: The World Bank, the IMF and the Philippines*. Berkeley: University of California Press, 1988.

Broad, Robin, and John Cavanagh. "Disintegration of an Economic Model". *Southeast Asia Chronicle*, no.92 (December 1983), pp.14–17.

Burton, Sandra. *Impossible Dream: The Marcoses, the Aquinos, and the Unfinished Revolution*. New York: Warner Books, 1989.

Buruma, Ian. "Who can Redeem Mother Filipinas?" *New York Review of Books*, 16 January 1986, pp.27–33.

_____. "St. Cory and the Evil Rose". *New York Review of Books*, 11 June 1987, pp.14–16.

Callanta, Ruth S. *Poverty: The Philippine Scenario*. Manila: Bookmark, 1988.

Canoy, Reuben R. *The Counterfeit Revolution: Martial Law in the Philippines*. Manila: Philippines Edition Publishing, 1980.

Carino, Ledevina. "Living in the Dark Times: How Ordinary Filipinos Cope With the Crisis in the Philippines". Unpublished and undated.

_____. *Bureaucracy For a Democracy: The Struggle of the Philippine Political Leadership and the Civil Service in the Post Marcos Period*. Occasional Paper No.88–1. Quezon City: University of the Philippines College of Public Administration, August 1988.

Carino, Ledivina, ed. *Bureaucratic Corruption in Asia: Causes, Consequences and Controls*. Quezon City: College of Public Administration, University of the Philippines, 1986.

Carroll, John J. "Sources of Social Unrest". In *The Philippine Economy in the 1970s*. Manila: Institute of Economic Development and Research, University of the Philippines, 1972.

Center for Research and Communication. *Agrarian Reform: Experience and Expectations.* Manila: Center for Research and Communication, 1987.

Center for Strategic and International Studies. *U.S.–Philippines Economic Relations.* Washington, D.C.: Center for Strategic and International Studies, 1971.

Chapman, William. *Inside the Philippine Revolution.* New York: W.W. Norton and Co., 1987.

Christian for National Liberation. *The Militant Church and the Repressive State: A New Twist in Church and State Relations.* Utrecht: Filippijnengroep Nederland, 1982.

Cohen, Margot. "Reconciliation or Revenge?" *The American Lawyer,* October 1986, pp.132–37.

Constantino, Renato. *The Post-Marcos Era: An Appraisal.* Quezon City: Karrel, Inc., undated.

Constantino, Renato, ed. *The Recto Reader.* Manila: Recto Memorial Foundation, 1983.

Constantino, Renato, and Letizia Constantino. *The Philippines: The Continuing Past.* Quezon City: The Foundation for Nationalist Studies, 1978.

Constitutional Commission. *The Constitution of the Republic of the Philippines.* Manila: National Bookstore, 1986.

Corpuz, O.D. "Political Trends in the Philippines". In *Trends in the Philippines,* edited by Lim Yoon Lin and M. Rajaretnam. Singapore: Institute of Southeast Asian Studies, 1972.

Corpuz, Victor. *Silent War.* Manila: VNC Enterprises, 1989.

Coordinating Council for the Philippine Assistance Program. *The Philippine Agenda for Sustained Growth and Development.* Manila: Coordinating Council for the Philippine Assistance Program, 30 May 1989.

Crouch, Harold. *Economic Change, Social Structure and the Political System in Southeast Asia: Philippine Development Compared with the Other ASEAN Countries.* Singapore: Institute of Southeast Asian Studies, 1985.

de Dios, Aurora, Petronilo Daror, and Lorna Kalaw-Tirol, eds. *Dictatorship and Revolution: Roots of People's Power.* Manila: Conspectus Foundation, 1988.

de Dios, Emmanuel, ed. *An Analysis of the Philippine Economic Crisis.* Quezon City: University of the Philippines Press, 1984.

de Guzman, Raul. "Philippine Local Government: Issues, Problems, and Trends". *Philippine Journal of Public Administration* 10, nos.2–3 (April–July 1966)

de Guzman, Raul, and Mila Reforma, eds. *Government and Politics of the Philippines.* New York: Oxford University Press, 1988.

de la Costa, H. *Readings in Philippine History.* Manila: Bookmark, 1965.

de la Torre, Edicio. "On the Post Marcos Transition and Popular Democracy". *World Policy Review 4,* no.2 (Spring 1987):333–51.

de los Angeles, Eduardo. "Misadministration of Justice". *Solidarity,* no.112 (May–June 1987), pp.56–78.

de Parle, Jason. "The Slum Behind the Sheraton". *Washington Monthly,* December 1987, pp.32–44.

Doherty, John F. "Who Controls the Philippine Economy: Some Need Not Try As Hard as Others". In *Cronies and Enemies: The Current Philippine Scene,* Occasional Paper No.5. Honolulu: University of Hawaii Philippine Studies Program, August 1982.

———. *The Philippine Urban Poor.* Occasional Paper No.8. Honolulu: University of Hawaii Philippine Studies Program, June 1985.

Dohner, Robert. "Aquino and the Economy: An Assessment of the First Three Years". *Pilipinas,* no.11 (Fall, 1988), pp.1–33.

———. *Philippine External Debt: Burdens, Possibilities and Prospects.* New York: The Asia Society, October 1989.

Dohner, Robert, and Carter Brandon. "Assessment of the Philippine Economic Reform Program". Louis Berger, Int'l, October 1988.

Dohner, Robert, and Ponciano Intal, Jr. "Debt Crisis and Adjustment in the Philippines". In *Developing Country Debt and the World Economy*, edited by Jeffrey Sachs. Chicago: University of Chicago Press, 1989.

Doronila, Amando. "The Transformation of Patron-Client Relations and its Political Consequences in Postwar Philippines". *Journal of Southeast Asian Studies* 16, no.1 (March 1985):99–116.

――――. "Class Formation and Filipino Nationalism: 1950–1970". *Kasarinlan* 2, no.2 (4th qtr. 1986):4–6.

Dorr, Steven, and Deborah Mitchell, eds. *The Philippines in a Changing Southeast Asia*. Washington: Defence Academic Research Support Program, 1989.

Dresang, Joel. "Authoritarian Controls and News Media in the Philippines". *Contemporary Southeast Asia* 7, no.1 (June 1985):34–47.

Economic Survey Mission to the Philippines (the "Bell Mission"). *Report to the President*. Washington, D.C., 9 October 1950.

The Economist. "The Philippines: A Question of Faith" (special survey), 7 May 1988.

Economist Intelligence Unit. *Country Report: Philippines*. London: Economist Intelligence Unit, quarterly and annually for 1986, 1987, 1988.

Fallows, James. "A Damaged Culture". *Atlantic Monthly*, November 1987, pp.49–58.

Far Eastern Economic Review. *Asia Yearbook*. Hong Kong: Review Publishing Co., various years.

Fernandez, Doreen, "The Culture of Revolution: Tentative Notes". *Diliman Review* 35, no.2 (1987):26–29.

Flora, Joey. "The Senators of the Philippine Republic". *Diliman Review* 35, no.3 (1987):11–18.

Friend, Theodore. *Between Two Empires*. New Haven: Yale University Press, 1965.

――――. "Marcos and the Philippines". *Orbis*, Fall 1988, pp.569–86.

_____. "What Marcos Doesn't Say". *Orbis*, Winter 1989, pp.97–105.

Gleeck, Lewis E., Jr. *President Marcos and the Philippine Political Culture*. Manila: Loyal Printing, 1987.

Golay, Frank H. *The Philippines: Public Policy and National Economic Development*. Ithaca: Cornell University Press, 1968.

Government of the Philippines/Philippine Assistance Programme. *The Philippine Agenda for Sustained Growth and Development*. Manila: Government of the Philippines, 30 May 1989.

Grossholtz, Jean. *Politics in the Philippines*. Boston: Little, Brown and Co., 1964.

Guerrero, Amado (Jose Maria Sison). *Philippine Society and Revolution*. Oakland: International Association of Filipino Patriots, 1979.

Hart, Donn. *Philippine Studies: Political Science, Economics, Linguistics*. Occasional Paper No.8. DeKalb: Northern Illinois Center for Southeast Asian Studies, 1981.

Hawes, Gary. "Aquino and Her Administration: A View from the Countryside". *Pacific Affairs*, Spring 1989, pp.9–28.

Hayami, Yujiro. *Anatomy of a Peasant Economy: A Rice Village in the Philippines*. Los Banos: International Rice Research Institute, 1978.

Hayami, Yujiro, Agnes Quisumbing, and Lourdes Adriano. *In Search of a Land Reform Design for the Philippines*. Los Banos: University of the Philippines (Los Banos) Agricultural Policy Research Program Monograph Series No.1, June 1987.

_____. "In Search of a New Land Reform Paradigm: A Perspective from the Philippines". Unpublished manuscript, 1988.

Hayden, Joseph. *The Philippines: A Study in National Development*. New York: Macmillan, 1947.

Hernandez, Carolina. "Toward Understanding Coups and Civilian-Military Relations". *Kasarinlan* 3, no.2 (4th qtr. 1987):19–22.

_____. "The Philippines in 1987: Challenges of Redemocratization". *Asian Survey* 28, no.2 (February 1988):229–41.

_____. "The Philippines in 1988: Reaching Out to Peace and Economic Recovery". *Asian Survey* 29, no.2 (February 1989): 154–64.

Hickey, Gerald, and John Wilkinson. "Agrarian Reform in the Philippines". Washington, D.C: The Rand Corporation, August 1978.

Hill, Hall. "The Philippine Economy Under Aquino: New Hopes, Old Problems". *Asian Survey* 28, no.3 (March 1988):261–85.

Hollnsteiner, Mary R. *The Dynamics of Power in a Philippine Municipality.* Manila: University of the Philippines Community Development Research Council, 1963.

Hooley, Richard. "Macroeconomic Policy Framework for Employment Generation in the Philippines". Manila: U.S. Agency for International Development, April 1981.

Ileto, Reynaldo. *Pasyon and Revolution: Popular Movements in the Philippines, 1840–1910.* Quezon City: Ateneo de Manila Press, 1989.

Institute For Popular Democracy. *Political Clans and Electoral Politics: A Preliminary Research.* Quezon City: Institute for Popular Democracy, 1987.

International Labour Organization. *Sharing in Development, A Programme of Employment, Equity and Growth for the Philippines.* Geneva and Manila: International Labour Organization, 1974.

Johnson, Bryan. *The Four Days of Courage.* New York: The Free Press, 1987.

Jones, Gregg. *Red Revolution: Inside the Philippine Guerrilla Movement.* Boulder: Westview Press, 1989.

Karnow, Stanley. *In Our Image: America's Empire in the Philippines.* New York: Random House, 1989.

Kerkvliet, Benedict J. *The Huk Rebellion, A Study of Peasant Revolt in the Philippines.* Berkeley: University of California Press, 1977.

Kerkvliet, Benedict J., ed. *Political Change in the Philippines: Studies of Local Politics Preceding Martial Law.* Honolulu: University of Hawaii Press, 1974.

Kessler, Richard. "Marcos and the Americans". *Foreign Policy,* Summer 1986.

_____. "Development and the Military: Role of the Philippine Military in Development". In *Soldiers and Stability in Southeast Asia*, edited by J. Soedjati Djiwandono and Yong Mun Cheong. Singapore: Institute of Southeast Asian Studies, 1988.

Koppel, Bruce. "Land Reform in the Philippines — A Bumpy Road". *The World and I*, October 1988, pp.133–39.

Krinks, Peter, ed. *The Philippines Under Aquino*. Canberra: Australian National University's Australian Development Studies Network, 1987.

Lachica, Eduardo. *Huk: Philippine Agrarian Society in Revolt*. Manila: Solidaridad Publishing, 1971.

Lande, Carl. *Leaders, Factions, and Parties: The Structure of Philippine Politics*. Monograph Series No.6. New Haven: Yale University Southeast Asian Studies Program, 1965.

_____. "Philippine Prospects After Martial Law". *Foreign Affairs* 59, no.5 (Summer 1981):1147–168.

_____. "Authoritarian Rule in the Philippines: Some Critical Views". *Pacific Affairs* 55, no.1 (Spring 1982):80–93.

_____. "The Political Crisis". In *Crisis in the Philippines: The Marcos Era and Beyond*, edited by John Bresnan. Princeton: Princeton University Press, 1986.

Lande, Carl, ed. *Rebuilding A Nation: Philippine Challenges and American Policy*. Washington, D.C.: Washington Institute Press, 1987.

Lande, Carl and Allan Cigler. "Recent Philippine Elections: A Quantitative Analysis (Interim Report)." April 1988.

Lande, Carl, and Richard Hooley. "Aquino Takes Charge". *Foreign Affairs*, Summer 1986, pp.1087–107.

Lane, Max. "The Urban Movement in the Philippines". Unpublished, 1988.

Lawyers Committee for Human Rights. *The Philippines: A Country in Crisis*. New York: Lawyers Committee for Human Rights, December 1983.

Lawyers Committee for Human Rights. *Vigilantes in the Philippines: A Threat to Democratic Rule.* New York: Lawyers Committee for Human Rights, 1988.

Laxalt, Paul. "My Conversations With Ferdinand Marcos". *Policy Review,* Summer 1986, pp.2–5.

Ledesma, Antonio, Perla Makil, and Virginia Miralao, eds. *Second View From the Paddy.* Manila: The Institute of Philippine Culture, Ateneo de Manila University, 1983.

Leichter, Howard. *Political Regime and Public Policy in the Philippines: A Comparison of Bacolod and Iloilo Cities.* Special Report No.11. DeKalb: Northern Illinois University, Center for Southeast Asian Studies, 1975.

Lim, Noel, "Economic Stabilization Policies in the Philippines". In *Economic Stabilization Policies in Asia,* edited by Pradumna Rana and Florian Alburo. Singapore: Institute of Southeast Asian Studies, 1987.

Lindsey, Charles. "Economic Crisis in the Philippines". *Asian Survey* 24, no.12 (December 1984):1185–208.

Linz, Juan. *Crisis, Breakdown and Disequilibrium: The Breakdown of Democratic Regimes.* Baltimore: Johns Hopkins University Press, 1978.

Lipset, Seymour Martin. *Political Man: The Social Bases of Politics.* New York: Doubleday, 1963.

Lopez, Mario A. "The Philippines: Managing Reform in a New Democracy". In *Southeast Asian Affairs 1989.* Singapore: Institute of Southeast Asian Studies, 1989.

Lynch, Frank, ed. "View From the Paddy: Empirical Studies of Philippine Rice Farming and Tenancy". *Philippine Sociological Review* 20, no.1 and 2 (January and April 1972).

Lynch, Frank, and Alfonso de Guzman II, eds. *Four Readings on Philippine Values.* Quezon City: Institute of Philippine Culture, Ateneo de Manila University, 1981.

Lynch, Frank, and Alfonso de Guzman, eds. *Four Readings on Philippine Values*. Paper No.2. Manila: Institute of Philippine Culture, Ateneo de Manila University, 1981.

Machado, Kit. "The Philippines 1978: Authoritarian Consolidation Continues". *Asian Survey* 19, no.2 (February 1979):131–40.

_____. "Philippine Politics: Research 1960–1980: Areas for Future Exploration." In *Philippine Studies: Political Science, Economics and Linguistics*, edited by Don Hart. Occasional Paper No.8. Northern Illinois University Center for Southeast Asian Studies, 1981.

Magno, Alex, "The Anatomy of Political Collapse". In *The February Revolution: Three Views*. Quezon City: Karrel Inc., 1986.

_____. "Meaning of the May Elections". *Diliman Review* 35, no.2 (1987):10–13.

_____. "Imperilled Experiment in Democracy: The Progressive Forces and the Threat of Neo-Fascism". *Kasarinlan* 3, no.2 (4th qtr. 1987): 23–28.

Magno, Jose, and A. James Gregor. "Insurgency and Counterinsurgency in the Philippines". *Asian Survey* 26, no. 5 (May 1986):501–17.

Majul, Cesar. "The Moro Struggle in the Philippines." *Third World Quarterly*, April 1988.

Malin, Herbert. "The Philippines in 1984: Grappling with Crisis". *Asian Survey* 25, no.2 (February 1985):198–205.

Manalang, Priscilla, ed. *A Nation for Our Children: Selected Writings of Jose Diokno*. Quezon City: Jose W. Diokno Foundation, 1987.

Manansala, Aida. "Polarization in Philippine Politics". *Diliman Review*, January–February 1986, pp.3–11.

Mangahas, Mahar. "Land and Natural Resources Reform". *Kasarinlan* 2, no.1 (3rd qtr. 1986):19–26.

_____. "The Political Economy of Land Reform and Land Distribution in the Philippines". Quezon City: Social Weather Stations, Inc., November 1986.

Manila Chronicle. "Countdown for the New Congress". 10 May 1987, pp.1–4 of "This Week's Focus".

Manning, Robert. "The Philippines in Crisis". *Foreign Affairs* 63, no.2 (Winter 1984/85):392–410.

Marcos, Ferdinand. *Today's Revolution: Democracy.* Manila: The Marcos Foundation, 1971.

⸻. *The Democratic Revolution in the Philippines.* Manila: The Marcos Foundation, 1977.

⸻. *An Ideology For Filipinos.* Manila: The Marcos Foundation, 1980.

⸻. *Progress and Martial Law.* Manila: The Marcos Foundation, 1981.

⸻. "A Defense of My Tenure". *Orbis*, Winter 1989, pp.91–97.

May, Glenn. *A Past Recovered.* Quezon City: New Day Publishers, 1987.

May, R.J., and Francisco Nemenzo, eds. *The Philippines After Marcos.* London and Sydney: Croom Helm, 1985.

McCoy, Al, Gwen Robinson, and Marian Wilkinson. "How the February Revolt Was Planned". *The Philippine Daily Inquirer,* 5 and 12 October 1986, p.1.

Mediansky, F.A. "The New People's Army: A Nation-wide Insurgency in the Philippines". *Contemporary Southeast Asia* 8, no.1 (June 1986):1–17.

Mercado, Eliseo R. "Culture, Economics and Revolt in Mindanao: The Origins of the MNLF and the Politics of Moro Separatism". In *Armed Separatism in Southeast Asia*, edited by Lim Joo-Jock and Vani S. Singapore: Institute of Southeast Asian Studies, 1984.

Miller, Stuart Creighton. "Compadre Colonialism". *Wilson Quarterly,* Summer 1986, pp.92–105.

Miranda, Felipe. "The Political System and Nation-building in the Philippines". Quezon City: Social Weather Stations, Inc., January 1987.

⸻. *The March 1987 Public Opinion Report: A Political Analysis.* Quezon City: Ateneo de Manila University and Social Weather Stations, 1987.

Miranda, Felipe, and Ruben Ciron. "The Philippines: Defence Expenditures, Threat Perception and the Role of the United States". In

Defence Spending in Southeast Asia, edited by Chin Kin Wah. Singapore: Institute of Southeast Asian Studies, 1987.

_____. "Development and the Military in the Philippines: Military Perceptions in a Time of Continuing Crisis". In *Soldiers and Stability in Southeast Asia*, edited by J. Soedjati Djiwandono and Yong Mun Cheong. Singapore: Institute of Southeast Asian Studies, 1988.

Mojares, Resil B. *The Man Who Would Be President: Serging Osmena and Philippine Politics*. Cebu: Maria Cacao Publishers, 1986.

Morais, Robert. *Social Relations in a Philippine Town*. Special Report No.19. Dekalb: Northern Illinois University Center for Southeast Asian Studies, 1981.

Muego, Benjamin. "The Executive Committee in the Philippines: Successors, Power Brokers and Dark Horses". *Asian Survey* 23, no.11 (November 1983):1159–170.

_____. "Fraternal Organizations and Factionalism within the AFP". *Asian Affairs* 14 (Fall, 1987):150–62.

Munro, Ross. "The New Khmer Rouge". *Commentary*, December 1985, pp.19–38.

Mutual Security Agency. *Philippine Land Tenure Reform: Analysis and Recommendations* (The "Hardie Report"). Manila: Mutual Security Agency, 1952.

National Movement for Free Elections (NAMFREL). *The NAMFREL Report on the February 7, 1986 Philippine Presidential Elections*. Manila: NAMFREL, undated (1986 or 1987).

National Economic Development Authority (NEDA). *Philippine Statistical Yearbook 1987*. Manila: NEDA, 1987.

_____. *Medium-Term Philippine Development Plan, 1987–92*. Manila: NEDA, 1986.

_____. *Philippine Development Report 1987*. Manila: NEDA, 1988.

Neher, Clark. "The Philippines in 1979: Cracks in the Fortress". *Asian Survey* 20, no.2 (February 1980):155–67.

Nemenzo, Francisco. "Beyond February: The Tasks of Socialists". *Kasarinlan* 2, no.1 (3d qtr. 1986):27–34.

Nemenzo, Francisco. "Military Intervention in Philippine Politics". *Diliman Review* 34, no.5 and 6 (1986):1–25.

Niksch, Larry. "Internal Conditions in the Philippines: Deterioration and its Causes". *Wharton Pacific Basin Economic Review* 2, no.2 (Fall 1982):64–72.

_____. *Insurgency and Counterinsurgency in the Philippines.* Washington, D.C.: Library of Congress, Congressional Research Service, July 1985.

Noble, Lela Garner. "Muslim Separatism in the Philippines, 1972–81: The Making of a Stalemate". *Asian Survey* 21, no.11 (November 1981):1097–114.

_____. "Politics in the Marcos Era". In *Crisis in the Philippines: The Marcos Era and Beyond*, edited by John Bresnan. Princeton: Princeton University Press, 1986.

_____. "The Philippines: Autonomy for the Muslims". In *Islam in Asia: Religion, Politics and Society*, edited by John Esposito. New York: Oxford University Press, 1987.

_____. *Government in the Philippines: The Privatization of Politics.* New York: The Asia Society, September 1989.

Office of Media Affairs. *The Philippines Today: Stability Amid Change.* Manila: Office of Media Affairs, 1984.

Oshima, Harry T. "Postwar Philippine Economic Growth in Comparative Perspective: An Overview". Makati: Philippine Society for International Development, November 1982.

Overholt, William. "The Rise and Fall of Ferdinand Marcos". *Asian Survey* 26, no.11 (November 1986):1137–163.

Peagam, Norman, "The Spectre that Haunts Marcos". *Euromoney*, April 1984, pp.46–63.

Phelan, John Leddy. *The Hispanization of the Philippines.* Manila: Cacho Hermanos, Inc., 1985.

Philippine Economic Society. "Report on a Survey of Opinions of the Membership of the Philippine Economic Society of the Current Economic Crisis". *Philippine Economic Journal* 24, no.1 (1985):64–79.

Philippine Institute for Development Studies. "Economic Recovery and Long-run Growth. A Review of the First Eleven Months of the Aquino Government". Manila: Philippine Institute of Development Studies, 15 February 1987.

Philippine Partnership for the Development of Human Resources in Rural Areas (PHILDHRRA). *Workshop Report of the Tripartite Dialogue on Agrarian Reform*. Manila: PHILDHRRA, 1988.

Po, Blondie, and Christina Montiel. *Rural Organization in the Philippines*. Paper No.13. Manila: Institute for Philippine Culture, Ateneo de Manila University, 1980.

Porter, Gareth. *The Politics of Counterinsurgency in the Philippines: Military and Political Options*. Occasional Paper No.9. Honolulu: University of Hawaii Center for Philippine Studies, 1987.

Porter, Gareth, with Delfin Ganapin, Jr. *Resources, Population, and the Philippines' Future: A Case Study*. WRI Paper No.4. Washington: World Resources Institute, October 1988.

Presidential Commission on Human Rights. *Annual Report for 1986*. Quezon City: Presidential Commission on Human Rights, 1987.

Pye, Lucien. *Asian Power and Politics. The Cultural Dimensions of Authority*. Cambridge: Harvard University Press, 1985.

Rajaretnam, M., ed. *Trends in the Philippines II*. Singapore: Singapore University Press, 1978.

_____. *The Aquino Alternative*. Singapore: Institute of Southeast Asian Studies, 1986.

Rajaretnam, M., and Lim Yoon Lin, eds. *Trends in the Philippines*. Singapore: Institute of Southeast Asian Studies, 1972.

Rand Corporation, The. *A Crisis of Ambiguity: Political and Economic Development in the Philippines*. Santa Monica: The Rand Corporation Report R-473-AID, January 1970.

Richter, Linda. "Public Bureaucracy in the Post Marcos Philippines". *Southeast Asian Journal of Social Science 15*, no.2 (1987):57–76.

Rivera, Temario. *Political Opposition in the Philippines: Contestation and Cooperation*. Wisconsin Papers on Southeast Asia No.9. Madison: University of Wisconsin-Madison, March 1985.

Rocamora, Joel. "Economy in Crisis". *Southeast Asia Chronicle*, no.83 (April 1982), pp.19–23.

_____. "Is Marcos a Lameduck Dictator?"*Southeast Asia Chronicle*, no.92 (December 1983), pp. 2–11.

Rosen, George. *Peasant Society in a Changing Economy: Comparative Development in Southeast Asia and India*. Chicago: University of Illinois Press, 1975.

Rosenberg, David, ed. *Marcos and Martial Law in the Philippines*. Ithaca: Cornell University Press, 1979.

Rush, James. *The Philippine Church, Part I*. UFSI Report No.31. University Field Staff International, 1984.

_____. *The Voice of Veritas in Philippine Politics*. UFSI Report No.27. University Field Staff International, 1985.

_____. *Bringing Down Marcos*:
Part I: The Electoral Tradition. UFSI Report No.3 (1986).
Part II: The Opposition Divided. UFSI Report No.6 (1986).
Part III: Suspending Disbelief. USFI Report No.7 (1986).
Part IV: Conclusion. UFSI Report No.29 (1986).

_____. *The Cory Constitution*. UFSI Report No.4 (1987).

Salamanca, Bonifacio. *The Filipino Reaction to American Rule, 1901–1913*. Quezon City: New Day Publishers, 1984.

Sandoval, Romulo, ed. *Prospects of Agrarian Reform Under the New Order*. Quezon City: Urban Rural Mission, National Council of Churches in the Philippines, 1986.

Schirmer, Daniel, and Stepen Shalom, eds. *The Philippines Reader: A History of Colonialism, Neo-colonialism, Dictatorship and Resistance*. Boston: South End Press, 1987.

Scott, James C. *The Moral Economy of the Peasant: Rebellion and Subsistence in Southeast Asia*. New Haven: Yale University Press, 1976.

Senate of the Philippines. "A Moral Recovery Program: Building a People – Building a Nation". Manila: Senate Committee on Education, Arts and Culture, 9 May 1988.

Shalom, Stephen. *The United States and the Philippines: A Study of Neo-colonialism.* Quezon City: New Day Publishers, 1986.

Shaplen, Robert. "Letter from Manila". *The New Yorker,* 20 December 1969; 14 April 1973; 3 May 1976, and 26 March 1979.

_____. "A Reporter at Large: From Marcos to Aquino". *The New Yorker,* 25 August 1986; and 1 September 1986.

_____. "The Thin Edge, Parts I and II". *The New Yorker,* 14 and 28 September 1987.

Sicat, Gerardo, "A Historical and Current Perspective of Philippine Economic Problems". *Philippine Economic Journal* 24, no.1 (1985): 24–63.

Simons, Lewis. *Worth Dying For.* New York: William Morrow and Co, 1987.

Stanley, Peter W. *A Nation in the Making: The Philippines and the United States, 1899–1921.* Cambridge: Harvard University Press, 1974.

Steinberg, David J. *Philippine Collaboration in World War II.* Manila: Solidarity Publishing House, undated.

_____. *The Philippines: A Singular and a Plural Place.* Boulder: Westview Press, 1982.

Steinberg, David J., ed. *In Search of Southeast Asia.* Honolulu: University of Hawaii Press, 1987.

Stepan, Alfred. *Rethinking Military Politics: Brazil and the Southern Cone.* Princeton: Princeton University Press, 1988.

Tadem, Eduardo C. "The Agrarian Question Confronts the Aquino Government". *Kasarinlan* 2, no.4 (2nd qtr. 1987):33–40.

Task Force Detainees. *Philippine Human Rights Update* 3, no. 3 (November–December 1987):21.

Thiesenhusen, William. *Land Reform in the Philippines.* Papers on Southeast Asia, No.14. Madison, Wisconsin: University of Wisconsin, 1988.

Third World Studies Center. *Marxism in the Philippines.* Quezon City: University of the Philippines, 1984.

_____. *Marxism in the Philippines (Second Series)*. Quezon City: University of the Philippines, 1988.

Third World Studies Research Team. *Class, Clan and Coalition: The Transformation of Local Political Elites in Two Municipalities*. Quezon City: University of the Philippines Third World Studies Center, 1988.

Timberman, David G. "Unfinished Revolution: The Philippines in 1986". In *Southeast Asian Affairs 1987*. Singapore: Institute of Southeast Asian Studies, 1987.

_____. "Leadership Change and National Security in the Philippines: 1983–88". *Contemporary Southeast Asia* 11, no.2 (September 1989):186–212.

Time. "Now For The Hard Part". 10 March 1986, pp. 14–37.

Turner, Mark, ed. *Regime Change in the Philippines: The Legitimation of the Aquino Government*. Political and Social Change Monograph No.7. Canberra: Australian National University, Research School of Pacific Studies, 1987.

U.S. Agency for International Development. "Economic Assessment of the 'New Society' and Key Problems and Issues facing the 'New Republic' of the Philippines". Manila: USAID, 1 October 1981.

_____. "Country Development Strategy Statement for the Philippines, FY 1986–90". Manila: USAID, 29 March 1985.

_____. "1988 Country Development Strategy Statement, The Philippines". Manila. USAID, May 1987.

U.S. House of Representatives. "United States–Philippines Relations and the New Base and Aid Agreement". Washington, D.C.: House Subcommittee on Asian and Pacific Affairs, 17, 23, 28 June 1983.

_____. "The Consequences of the Aquino Assassination". Washington, D.C.: House Subcommittee on Asian and Pacific Affairs, 13 September, and 6, 8 October 1983.

_____. "Recent Events in the Philippines, Fall 1985". Washington, D.C.: House Subcommittee on Asian and Pacific Affairs, 12 and 13 November 1985.

U.S. Senate Committee on Foreign Relations. *The Situation in the Philippines.* Washington, D.C.: US Government Printing Office, October 1984.

van der Kroef, Justus. "The Philippine Vigilantes: Devotion and Disarray". *Contemporary Southeast Asia* 10, no.2 (September 1988):163–81.

Villacorta, Wilfrido. "Contending Political Forces in the Philippines Today: The Political Elite and the Legal Opposition". *Contemporary Southeast Asia* 5, no.2 (September 1983):185–204.

––––––. "The Catholic Church in Contemporary Philippine Politics". Mimeograph, undated.

Villafuerte, Luis. "Local Autonomy: The Safety Valve Against the Implosion of Political Power". Speech given on 8 July 1988.

Wolters, Willem. *Politics, Patronage and Class in Central Luzon.* Quezon City: New Day Publishers, 1984.

World Bank. "Financing Local Government". In *World Development Report 1988.* New York: Oxford University Press, 1988.

––––––. *The Philippines: Country Economic Memorandum.* Report No.1765-PH. Washington, D.C.: World Bank, 26 October 1977.

––––––. *Industrial Development Strategy and Policies in the Philippines, Vol. II.* Report No.2513-PH. Washington D.C.: The World Bank, 29 October 1979.

––––––. *Aspects of Poverty in the Philippines: A Review and Assessment.* Report No.2984-PH. Washington, D.C.: The World Bank, December 1980.

––––––. *Philippines: Environment and Natural Resource Management Study.* Washington, D.C.: The World Bank, 1989.

Wurful, David. "Individuals and Groups in the Philippine Policy Process". In *Foundations and Dynamics of Filipino Government and Politics,* edited by Jose Abueva and Raul de Guzman. Manila: Bookmark, 1973.

––––––. "Martial Law in the Philippines: The Methods of Regime Survival". *Pacific Affairs* 50, no. 1 (Spring 1977):5–30.

_____. "Elites of Wealth and Elites of Power, The Changing Dynamic". In *Southeast Asian Affairs 1979*. Singapore: Institute of Southeast Asian Studies, 1979.

_____. "The Development of Post-War Philippine Land Reform: Political and Sociological Explanations". In *Second View from the Paddy*, edited by Antonio Ledesma, Perla Makil and Virginia Miralao. Manila: Institute of Philippine Culture, 1983.

_____. "The Aquino Legacy and the Emerging Succession Struggle in the Philippines, 1984". In *Southeast Asian Affairs 1985*. Singapore: Institute of Southeast Asian Studies, 1985.

_____. *Filipino Politics: Development and Decay*. Quezon City: Ateneo de Manila University Press, 1988.

_____. "Land Reform: Contexts, Accomplishments and Prospects Under Marcos and Aquino". Paper presented at the Association of Asian Studies annual meeting, 25–27 March 1988.

Youngblood, Robert. "The Philippines in 1981: From 'New Society' to 'New Republic'". *Asian Survey* 22, no.2 (February 1982):226–35.

_____. "The Philippines in 1982: Marcos Gets Tough with Domestic Critics." *Asian Survey* 23, no.2 (February 1983):208–16.

_____. "Church and State in the New Republic of the Philippines." *Contemporary Southeast Asia* 6, no.3 (December 1984):205–20.

_____. "The Philippines in 1985: A Continuing Crisis of Confidence". In *Southeast Asian Affairs 1986*. Singapore: Institute of Southeast Asian Studies, 1986.

_____. "The Corazon Aquino 'Miracle' and the Philippine Church." *Asian Survey* 27, no.12 (December 1987):1240–255.

Newspapers and Philippine Periodicals

Ang Bayan

Asian Wall Street Journal

Asiaweek

Bulletin Today

Businessday

Diliman Review

The Economist

Far Eastern Economic Review

International Herald Tribune

Kasarinlan

Liberation

Manila Chronicle

Newday

Philippine Daily Globe

Philippine Daily Inquirer

Philippine Journal of Public Administration

Solidarity

Straits Times

Veritas

Washington Post

Index

THE AUTHOR

DAVID G. TIMBERMAN is an American specialist on Southeast Asian affairs who lived in or frequently visited the Philippines from 1988 until 1989. He has degrees from Tufts University and Columbia University's School of International Affairs. He has worked for and been a consultant to The Asia Society, New York, and was a Research Fellow at the Institute of Southeast Asian Studies, Singapore, in 1987–88. Since 1990, he has served as Director of Studies of The Asia Foundation's Center for Asian Pacific Affairs.

*For Product Safety Concerns and Information please contact
our EU representative GPSR@taylorandfrancis.com Taylor & Francis
Verlag GmbH, Kaufingerstraße 24, 80331 München, Germany*

T - #0076 - 270225 - C0 - 234/156/24 - PB - 9781563240126 - Gloss Lamination